The Greening of Markets

NEW HORIZONS IN ENVIRONMENTAL ECONOMICS

Series Editors: Wallace E. Oates, *Professor of Economics, University of Maryland, USA* and Henk Folmer, *Professor of General Economics, Wageningen University and Professor of Environmental Economics, Tilburg University, The Netherlands*

This important series is designed to make a significant contribution to the development of the principles and practices of environmental economics. It includes both theoretical and empirical work. International in scope, it addresses issues of current and future concern in both East and West and in developed and developing countries.

The main purpose of the series is to create a forum for the publication of high quality work and to show how economic analysis can make a contribution to understanding and resolving the environmental problems confronting the world in the twenty-first century.

Recent titles in the series include:

Voluntary Approaches in Climate Policy
Edited by Andrea Baranzini and Philippe Thalmann

Welfare Measurement in Imperfect Markets
A Growth Theoretical Approach
Thomas Aronsson, Karl-Gustaf Löfgren and Kenneth Backlund

Econometrics Informing Natural Resources Management
Selected Empirical Analyses
Phoebe Koundouri

The Theory of Environmental Agreements and Taxes
CO_2 Policy Performance in Comparative Perspective
Martin Enevoldsen

Modelling the Costs of Environmental Policy
A Dynamic Applied General Equilibrium Assessment
Rob B. Dellink

Environment, Information and Consumer Behaviour
Edited by Signe Krarup and Clifford S. Russell

The International Yearbook of Environmental and Resource Economics 2005/2006
A Survey of Current Issues
Edited by Henk Folmer and Tom Tietenberg

The Greening of Markets
Product Competition, Pollution and Policy Making in a Duopoly
Michael Kuhn

Managing Wetlands for Private and Social Good
Theory, Policy and Cases from Australia
Stuart M. Whitten and Jeff Bennett

Amenities and Rural Development
Theory, Methods and Public Policy
Edited by Gary Paul Green, Steven C. Deller and David W. Marcouiller

The Evolution of Markets for Water
Theory and Practice in Australia
Edited by Jeff Bennett

The Greening of Markets

Product Competition, Pollution and Policy
Making in a Duopoly

Michael Kuhn

*Max-Planck-Institute for Demographic Research, Rostock, and
Department of Economics, University of Rostock, Germany.*

NEW HORIZONS IN ENVIRONMENTAL ECONOMICS

Edward Elgar
Cheltenham, UK • Northampton, MA, USA

© Michael Kuhn 2005

Published by
Edward Elgar Publishing Limited
Glensanda House
Montpellier Parade
Cheltenham
Glos GL50 1UA
UK

Edward Elgar Publishing, Inc.
136 West Street
Suite 202
Northampton
Massachusetts 01060
USA

A catalogue record for this book
is available from the British Library

ISBN 1 84542 012 8

Printed and bound in Great Britain by MPG Books Ltd, Bodmin, Cornwall

Contents

Figures

Tables

Acknowledgements

This book is based on my PhD thesis written at the University of Rostock. It was completed and edited during my time as lecturer at the Department of Economics and Related Studies and Centre of Health Economics, at the University of York, UK.

I am deeply indebted to my academic teachers Thusnelda Tivig and Michael Rauscher for their friendly and non-abating advice, support, patience and encouragement. Without them I would not have been able to complete this work.

Furthermore, I am grateful for valuable discussions with and encouraging comments from my former colleagues at the University of Rostock Rainer Frey, Nicole Gürtzgen, Pascal Hetze, Erik Lehmann, Stefan Müller and Uta-Maria Niederle. Special thanks to Silke Siebert for co-ordinating communication lines.

I am also indebted for helpful discussion and comments on this work to the participants of the Departmental seminars at the Universities of Rostock and York; and at York, in particular, to Gianni de Fraja.

1. Out of the grey . . . introduction

With the problems of pollution and environmental degradation growing ever more pressing, the last two decades have also witnessed a rise in people's awareness of the anthropogene causes of these problems. To a degree at least, increased environmental consciousness has even brought with it a change towards more sustainable consumption. Arguably, green consumerism is still a very limited phenomenon regarding both the share of green consumers in the overall population and the willingness to pay for environmentally superior products even amongst those concerned about the environment. This notwithstanding, with regard to a number of products green consumerism has had a significant effect up to the point of environmentally friendly products driving their conventional counterparts from the market. The rapid replacement in all industrialised countries and many developing economies of refrigerators relying on ozone-depleting chlorofluorocarbons (CFCs) by methane-based models is one notable example. This is even more remarkable, as the slightly less polluting hydrofluorocarbons (HFCs) that were favoured as alternative cooling agents by producers were exempt from regulation but were still not introduced. The markets for cleaning detergents, paint and other household chemicals, (recycled) paper products, (energy or water saving) household appliances and office equipment provide further examples of environmentally superior variants gaining a substantial market share. In contrast to these success stories of 'greening markets', there are many markets where the introduction and penetration of green product variants is lagging behind or has not even started. These include the environmentally important food and transport industries.

The environmental improvement of consumption goods is high on the agenda of environmentalists, environmental policy makers and even executives. This is because of an increasing realisation that only a cleaning up of products will reconcile high levels of consumption with a healthy environment. Indeed, incorporating low emission levels into the products and their production processes is a far more effective way of dealing with the environmental degradation than any cleaning up measures ex post. Such an integrated form of pollution abatement – or rather prevention – therefore appears not only to be more effective from an environmental point of view but in many cases more efficient as well.

Given the importance attributed to a greening of products, an understanding of the determinants of the successful introduction of environmentally superior products, or the failure thereof, becomes tantamount, in particular if it is a policy objective to foster this development. Policy analysis must seek to clarify the following fundamental questions. First, what is the impact of policy on competition and what are the incentives for firms to improve the environmental features of their products? Second, what are the implications for emission levels at product, firm and industry level? Third, what (side) effects arise concerning profits, consumer surplus and industry surplus? It is the aim of this work to shed light on these issues and thereby contribute towards an understanding of the greening of markets.

The approach we take is focused on an individual and imperfectly competitive industry. One constituent feature of greening – rather than green – markets is the coexistence of clean variants of a product with their more polluting conventional counterparts. This set-up lends itself to a model of a vertically – or rather environmentally – differentiated industry, where some consumers purchase the green variant and others the conventional one. We narrow this down to a duopoly framework in order to enable us to explicitly analyse the strategic interaction within such a market. Our work then focuses on the following questions.

- Given preferences and technology, what is the market outcome in a duopoly, in which firms differentiate their products with regard to the degree of environmental friendliness? How can the market outcome and the resulting level of industry emissions be explained in terms of technology and preferences?
- How do selected environmental policies at product level affect the firms' market conduct and what are the implications for industry surplus and emission levels?
- What are the likely implications of different assumptions with regard to market structure and behaviour, and what determines the developments over time of greening markets?

In the remainder of this chapter we highlight some of the foundations of this work, which we take from the existing literature without elaborating them much further. The next section addresses the motivation for green consumption behaviour. Section 1.2 reviews the explanations offered for voluntary environmental activity on the part of companies. Section 1.3 introduces the notion of environmental product differentiation. The following section introduces a selection of environmental policies that are relevant for the greening of products and feature in this book. Section 1.5 surveys the empirical evidence available on the greening of markets. The chapter concludes with an outline of the subsequent analysis.

1.1 EXPLAINING GREEN CONSUMERISM

From a traditional rationality point of view green consumerism, i.e. the voluntary consumption of environmentally friendly products, is something of a paradox, as it should usually fall prey to a typical social dilemma (e.g. Hanley et al. 1997: section 2.5). Consider a representative consumer. As an individual she can generally not expect to influence the aggregate pollution level by her behaviour. She will, therefore, not take into consideration the impact of her consumption choice on pollution. Suppose that the private surplus (marginal utility less price) derived from consuming one unit of an environmentally friendly product is lower than the surplus derived from consuming one unit of its harmful counterpart. This is justified in a lot of cases, where environmentally friendly variants of products are either more expensive or yield a relatively lower (marginal) utility from consumption.[1] In this case, the individual consumer would not purchase the green variant. While this decision is individually rational, it is socially inefficient whenever the gap between private surplus from green vis-à-vis non-green consumption falls short of the (marginal) disutility from pollution. If green consumption took place as a collective action the aggregate pollution level would fall measurably and everybody would enjoy a benefit exceeding the 'cost' of green consumption.

Individuals' failure to co-operate usually justifies a political solution. For instance, the appropriate subsidisation (taxation) of green (non-green) products would restore a socially efficient consumption pattern. However, green consumerism takes place even in the absence of governmental policies. Recall the assumption that consumption of a green product yields a lower net benefit to the individual than consumption of a conventional product. While this is crucial for the existence of a social dilemma, it is by no means to be taken for granted. If the consumption of an environmentally friendly product generates an extra benefit, then there exists a private incentive to engage in green consumerism and the social dilemma is overcome.

Just what does this extra benefit look like? It has to be unrelated to a reduction in the externality, which consumers do not expect to influence. The benefit therefore needs to be private in kind. As such it may be of a physical, monetary or psychological nature. Examples of physical or monetary benefits are abundant. A lot of goods produced in an environmentally benign manner are also of a higher physical quality. For example, food or textiles originating from organic agriculture are not only characterised by comparatively low externalities in production but also by a low content of harmful substances. Handcrafted as compared to manufactured products are often associated with relatively low degrees of emissions and/or energy intensity as well as with a high quality, in a general sense. The use of energy-efficient commodities allows private savings on the energy bill in addition to the public benefit of conserving energy.

Psychological benefits from green consumption can be seen as intrinsic motivation (e.g. Andreoni 1990, Frey 1992) or social rewards (e.g. Hollander 1990, Rauscher 1997). An intrinsically motivated individual derives the benefit from behaving in what she perceives to be a morally desirable way. Thereby, the individual will exhibit such behaviour independent of her peers' attitudes or actions. Andreoni (1990) points out that voluntary contributions towards a public good are to some extent driven by egoistic rather than by altruistic reasons. Here the individual receives a 'warm glow' from the charitable act itself. A purely altruistic consumer who is directly concerned about the state of the environment but rationally expects her purchasing decision to have no measurable impact will not engage in green consumption. In contrast an individual solely driven by the green glow would purchase environmentally friendly products. Paradoxically, the egoist outperforms the altruist. Intrinsic motivation explains how green consumption can derive from an individual's ethical principles, a feeling of 'at least doing something about it', or her socialisation and education. As Hollander (1990) points out, intrinsic motivation reflects the internalisation of a social norm, where the individual behaves even in the absence of observers as if there were a social reaction to her behaviour.

In the case of social rewards, the benefit from consuming green products depends on whether the individual complies with or deviates from a social norm. Green consumption behaviour will then occur only if it is honoured by society or at least by the individual's peers. Like intrinsic motivation, the social interaction model can explain green purchasing behaviour even in the presence of a social dilemma. Again, it does not rely on altruism but rather on an egoistic desire for social acclaim. In contrast to intrinsic motivation, social interaction features an interaction between the individual's performance and the average, where an improvement of the latter serves to raise the norm. In the presence of (negative) sanctions, an increase in the norm unambiguously raises the incentives to contribute for those who under-perform (Hollander 1990). For those who over-perform, the incentives arising from a higher norm are ambiguous. They are positive and enhance contribution if there is competition to outperform the norm (Hollander 1990, Rauscher 1997). Rauscher (1997) points out, however, that the effect may also be negative if, in the light of everyone else having caught up, social rewards are withdrawn at the margin.

Naylor (1990) demonstrates that there is a further and altogether more dramatic feedback. He assumes that individuals differ in their perceptiveness towards social sanctions. He therefore conditions the participation decision on the size of the population who have adopted the norm. With the group size now being endogenous, three equilibria can arise: a stable equilibrium with high participation, an unstable equilibrium with intermediate participation and a stable equilibrium with zero participation. Becker (1991) applies a similar framework to explain the influence of social interaction on the demand for a product. These models have some appeal in explaining green consumerism as a phenomenon that exhibits inertia. It may take an exogenous shock, such as an environmental catastrophe or a scandal relating to the environmental features of a particular product, to trigger a wave of green consumerism. Recent examples include the boost in the demand for organically produced food in the wake of various food scandals, such as the BSE crisis. Likewise opposition to genetically modified food has grown in many countries after failed public relations attempts on the part of firms such as Monsanto or Nestlé. However, if a critical mass of green consumption is not attained after such a triggering event the demand for green products may collapse in the event and the market may revert to a non-green equilibrium.

1.2 EXPLAINING THE GREENING OF FIRMS

The advent of green consumerism in recent years has been paralleled by the increasing importance of corporate initiatives towards improving firms' environmental record. Voluntary approaches of firms towards environmental protection include participation in public voluntary programmes, initiatives that are bilaterally negotiated between firms and the regulator and pro-active approaches at the firm's own initiative, with information disclosure strategies acting as a facilitator.[2] When explaining voluntary pollution control on behalf of firms, economists face a problem that in many ways parallels that of explaining green consumption. If the introduction of environmentally friendly processes or products increases current costs, a profit maximising firm would undertake such a step only if it expected a long-run advantage from this.[3] This advantage may flow from the relationship of the firm with the regulator or its stakeholders including the company's owners, employees, customers and competitors.

First, firms or groups of firms may strike an explicit or implicit bargain with the regulator.[4] By taking voluntary steps to reduce pollution, they preempt the imposition of regulatory measures that are more costly to the firm because they are stricter or because they leave the firms with less flexibility in compliance.[5] Indeed, both the firm and the regulator should be interested in an agreement as co-operation reduces the transaction costs comprised of compliance, monitoring and enforcement costs.[6] Segerson and Miceli (1998) show within a bargaining framework that if the regulator can threaten to impose a standard, a voluntary agreement is always reached no matter how small the threat.[7] If the bargaining power lies entirely with the regulator the agreement may entail a reduction in emissions in excess of what would be achievable under the best possible regulation. Thus, over-compliance can arise.

Segerson and Miceli (1998) consider an uncontested monopolist. If the industry consists of more than one firm a problem may arise due to free-riding on the part of firms who are not participating in the agreement. Segerson and Miceli (1999) and Millock and Salanié (2000) provide models in which voluntary agreements are reached as self-enforcing contracts even in the presence of free-riding. In this case, however, voluntary agreements may be socially inferior as compared to mandatory regulation. Salop and Scheffmann (1983) argue that dominant firms may have an incentive to lobby for stricter regulation if this raises their rivals' marginal cost to a sufficient extent. In this case the associated price increase may outweigh the increase in the dominant firm's average cost.[8]

Finally, firms may use voluntary agreements if they can, thereby, bias the political process in a way that leads to the legislation of more favourable regulation. By striking a voluntary agreement with a regulatory agency, for instance, firms may circumvent emissions taxes that may otherwise be legislated by a congress who values tax revenue (Hansen 1999). A voluntary agreement may also prevent costly lobbying for legislation on the part of consumer groups (Maxwell et al. 2000). Here, a voluntary agreement is Pareto-optimal, with even consumers being better off. This is because a voluntary agreement that is accepted by consumers implies a level of environmental protection for which the additional gains to consumers from mandatory legislation fall short of the lobbying cost. Baron (2001) examines how firms can assume corporate social – or environmental – responsibility in order to counter the efforts of activists threatening to initiate a boycott of the firm.

Investors are interested in a good environmental performance of the company in as far as they expect it to impact on the value of the firm. Here, a poor environmental performance may erode the market value of a firm for reasons of impending regulation, the greater risk of this company facing litigation after adverse environmental events, and because of a poor image vis-à-vis its customers and employees. Empirical analysis has established a positive correlation between stock value and environmental performance data in the short run (Hamilton 1995) as well as when this data is reported repeatedly (Lanoie et al. 1997, Khanna et al. 1998). Likewise the participation of a firm in a voluntary programme (the US 33/50 programme) has been found to raise its average excess value per unit sales (Khanna and Damon 1999), while the establishment of stringent internal management practices and standards raises the firm's Tobin's q (Dowell et al. 2000). Finally, Anton et al. (2004) find that greater reliance on investors increases the comprehensiveness of the corporate environmental management system.

Employees' concerns about the environment may play a role under the following circumstances. First, in the presence of managerial slack, environmentally conscious managers have the foresight to introduce environmental measures even if they are not (directly) profitable to the firm.[9] Note, however, that if managers are not environmentally motivated they may neglect the environmental goals of their enterprise unless these are explicitly incorporated into incentive contracts (Gabel and Sinclair-Desgagné 1993). Harford (1997) argues that this problem is aggravated if managerial incentive systems are biased towards financial performance because it is easier to measure than environmental performance.[10] Second, a poor environmental performance on the part of the company may destroy the motivation of environmentally concerned employees. This may be due either to an intrinsic feeling of doing something morally deplorable or to the social stigma attached to working for a dirty employer. Firms with a poor environmental reputation may then be unable to hire qualified employees unless they pay a higher compensating wage. This is especially true if environmental consciousness is correlated with education and skills. Dasgupta et al. (2000) found that a more educated workforce is, indeed, correlated with greater environmental management effort. Finally, a firm may take voluntary environmental action in response to its customers.

1.3 ENVIRONMENTAL PRODUCT DIFFERENTIATION

Motta and Thisse (1993, 1999), Cremer and Thisse (1994a, 1999) and Arora and Gangopadhyay (1995) were the first to produce models of firms responding to customer demand and competitive pressure when introducing green products. The last pair of authors motivate their study by pointing out two empirical observations. First, there is considerable variation within industries in the degree of over-compliance with existing standards. Second, participation in the US Environmental Protection Agency's 33/50 programme, which invites voluntary reductions of selected chemicals, was higher in

industries with low degrees of concentration (Arora and Cason 1995). Arora
and Gangopadhyay (1995) draw the conclusion from these observations that
in order to avoid competition individual firms may have an interest in
differentiating their product with respect to its environmental performance.
The feasibility of such a strategy has increased considerably since the
collection and public documentation of environmental performance has been
improved. Product differentiation would then explain the asymmetric pattern
of compliance, while the incentive to differentiate products increases with the
degree of competition and is, thus, negatively related to concentration.

The idea of vertical product differentiation being a driver in the
introduction of environmentally friendly products will provide the backdrop
for most of the analysis in the present work. The model of vertical product
differentiation has been developed by Gabsewicz and Thisse (1979) and
Shaked and Sutton (1982) on the basis of Hotelling's (1929) model of spatial
product differentiation.[11] The hallmark of vertically differentiated markets is
that consumers agree on the ranking of products but that they differ in their
marginal willingness to pay for the product. To fix ideas consider two variants
of a product, where, everything else equal, one variant is of greater quality. If
the two variants were offered at the same price only the high quality would be
bought. However if the high quality variant is offered at a premium price
some consumers with a low willingness to pay will buy the low quality
variant. Consumer heterogeneity with respect to their willingness to pay for
quality therefore allows firms to differentiate their products as a means of
stifling price competition. Note that in contrast to models of horizontal
product differentiation, that allow symmetry between firms, vertical product
differentiation features an intrinsic asymmetry, where quality differences map
into a price gap between the two variants. This asymmetry lies behind a
number of unconventional results with respect to firm strategies and policy
impact. Generally the model is set up as a two-stage game, in which firms
choose quality in stage one and price or quantity in stage two. In either case
of Bertrand or Cournot competition in the market stage it is optimal for firms
to differentiate their products in the first stage. For Cournot competition this
requires the presence of a fixed or variable cost of quality (Bonanno 1986,
Motta 1993).

An interpretation of environmental differentiation as a form of vertical
differentiation relies on the assumption that consumers unanimously rank
products according to their environmental friendliness with the 'cleanest'
product attaining the top rank. This implies that environmental friendliness is
an additive feature of a product when all other attributes are (perceived as)
identical.[12] The model then implies that green variants are sold at a premium
and are purchased by the consumers with the highest willingness to pay for

environmental performance, whereas everybody else purchases more polluting alternatives.

At this point let us pause in order to clarify the concept of 'environmental friendliness' – or 'environmental performance'– we have in mind.[13] In practice it is not an easy task to determine the environmental friendliness of a product due to the many environmental impacts over its life cycle including the stages of production, consumption and disposal as well as transportation.[14] We abstract from these difficulties by assuming that products can be ranked according to their (true) environmental impact per unit of service flowing from the product. The environmental impact can either be measured by the emissions per unit of service or by a technological measure that is correlated to the emissions. For instance, the environmental impact of an automobile can be measured by its emissions per mile or, as a proxy, by its fuel efficiency.

We will defer an extensive review of the literature on environmental product differentiation to the individual chapters of this book, where the various issues are discussed in context.[15] At this point we will therefore provide only a brief outline of some of the more salient aspects of this work. As we have seen already, firms are using environmental differentiation as a vehicle for stifling competition. However this is not the only factor that determines firms' environmental choices. If improvements in the environmental performance drive up variable production costs a clean firm will be placed at a cost disadvantage. This is traded off against the quality/environmental advantage that allows the firm to extract a premium from its consumers. Competitive strategy within such an industry will then be determined in the triangle of cost advantage vs. quality/environmental advantage vs. product differentiation.

In line with the literature we assume a utilitarian policy maker who is concerned about industry surplus and the damage generated from industry emissions. To some extent environmental differentiation proves a double-edged sword both with regard to industry surplus and pollution levels. The anti-competitive effect of product differentiation obviously harms consumers. This is contrasted, however, by a tendency towards the under-provision of environmental performance at least for the clean variant. This is because companies focus their environmental efforts only on attracting the marginal consumer who is indifferent between the clean and a dirtier variant. However, this implies that a number of consumers purchase the clean variant simply for lack of alternatives although they would be willing to pay for an even higher environmental performance. In the absence of price discrimination the firm is unable to extract this surplus and environmental performance is under-provided to these consumers.[16]

Industry emissions are determined as the sum of emissions across the different variants, where total emissions at product level are determined by the unit emissions as applied to the output of this variant. Improved environmental performance on the part of any firm lowers the unit emissions associated with their product and thereby contributes towards a reduction in industry emissions. However these effects are moderated and potentially offset by the changes in market shares and industry output that arise for changes in the degree of product differentiation. While the anti-competitive effect of an increase in the environmental performance of the clean firm exerts further downward pressure on industry emissions, environmental improvements on the part of the dirty firm enhance competition and may lead to an increase in output that offsets the effect of lower unit emissions (Moraga-González and Padrón-Fumero 1997, 2002). It should be clear already that the variety of different effects and trade-offs within a vertically differentiated industry renders policy-making a rather tricky task.

1.4 PUBLIC POLICY TOWARDS THE GREENING OF MARKETS

While there is some scope for optimism with regard to corporate environmental efforts, it is likely that voluntary initiative falls far short of what is required from an environmental point of view. This applies to the limited scope of companies' programmes as well as to the confinement to certain product groups. Hence there is clear scope for policies aimed at enhancing the introduction of environmentally friendly products.[17] The present work will address in detail the following approaches.[18]

Environmental product standards: Standards can relate to emissions released both during the process of consumption and after disposal of the product. Examples include standards on the exhaust gases from automobiles, on the contents of toxic traces in food, household chemicals and other consumer products and on the content of sulphur and lead in fuel. Standards may also require a minimum content of environmentally superior, e.g. recycled, input. The intention of product standards is a reduction in overall emission levels by improving the environmental performance of at least the dirty variants. Although a maximum emission standard targeted at the dirty firm usually implies that green firms are in over-compliance, its introduction may still have knock-on effects through changes in product differentiation and competitive advantage.[19]

Environmental taxes and charges: Direct emission taxes are usually not located at the product level and are levied from producers rather than consumers. Producer based taxes are usually not implemented for the purpose of enhancing green consumption. This notwithstanding, they may have important side-effects on the provision of green product variants by affecting the suppliers' cost structure and changing their competitive position. Examples include carbon taxes, taxes on (hazardous) waste, on wastewater, on air pollutants and on surplus manure. Note that charges on household waste provide a direct stimulus for green consumption to consumers, as a reduction in the expenditure on charges constitutes a direct monetary benefit.

Input-related taxes generally affect producers and consumers alike. The most important group of input taxes are fuel and energy charges. In many instances they are differentiated to allow for different types of inputs (e.g., leaded vs. unleaded fuel or diesel) or sources of energy (tax exemption for 'green' energies). Input-related taxes give rise to an important incentive for green consumption in that they provide a direct monetary benefit associated with the purchase of fuel or energy saving durables.

Environmentally related product taxes and charges include taxes on batteries, on packaging or throwaway products as well as environmentally differentiated vehicle taxes. These taxes are directly aimed at changing consumption patterns by raising the relative price of the dirty as opposed to the clean variant.

While not being an environmentally related tax itself, an ad-valorem tax has an impact on emissions through determining market structure and coverage as well as the choices of product technology. The latter is the case if improvements in a product's environmental performance can only be achieved through investment. By reducing net revenue an ad-valorem tax reduces a firm's incentive to invest in green product design. A number of countries have begun to differentiate ad-valorem taxes in order to provide a stimulus for green purchasing (Opschoor and Vos 1989).[20]

Subsidies: Extensive use is being made of subsidies to improve the environmental performance of products and processes (OECD 1999a: table 3.25). Most of these subsidies take the form of lump-sum grants on investment outlays.[21]

Environmental labels: Environmental labelling is proposed as one tool to overcome the problem of asymmetric information between firms and their consumers regarding the environmental properties of the various products (OECD 1991, 1997). If consumers are willing to pay a premium on environmental friendliness but are unable to observe it as a product attribute, there is an incentive for dirty producers to sell their products as green. Anticipating such cheating, consumers reduce their willingness to pay, which in consequence does not allow true green firms to recover their higher cost of production. Due to this process of adverse selection a market for environmentally friendly products would break down (Akerlof 1970). The informational problem is particularly grave as the environmental attributes of many products cannot be identified by the consumer, neither upon inspection nor during the course of consumption. Two mechanisms remain available. First, a firm can acquire a reputation for being 'green', which is maintained under public scrutiny about the firm's activities. One example of the reliance on reputation is the credibility attached to some of the private trademarks of long-established distributors of organic food. Alternatively a reputable third-party organisation may award a label to products/firms that satisfy a set of published environmental criteria.[22]

1.5 EMPIRICAL EVIDENCE

This section establishes an empirical context for what will otherwise be an entirely theoretical analysis. We begin by stating a few summary statistics in order to provide a feeling for the 'orders of magnitude' involved in the greening of markets. 1993 IPOS survey data on German consumers' willingness to pay an environmental premium, as reported by Brockmann et al. (1996), is presented in Table 1.1.

Table 1.1 Willingness to pay for environmentally labelled products

Premium on environmentally labelled product (%)	Consumers willing to pay premium (%)
None	48.7
<5	36
6–10	12
11–15	2.5
>15	0.8

Source: IPOS 1993 as cited in Brockmann et al. (1996).

The willingness to pay for environmental performance is thus limited even in a high-income country. Moreover, the data show that a firm's market share would drop significantly if it were to charge a substantial premium on an environmentally superior product.

Table 1.2 The European market for organically produced food, 1997

Country	% of total food market	Annual growth rate (%)
Austria	2	10–15
Denmark	2.5	30–40
France	0.5	20
Germany	1.2	5–10
Italy	0.6	20
Netherlands	1	10–15
Sweden	0.6	30–40
Switzerland	2	20–30
United Kingdom	0.4	25–35

Source: ITC, 1999.

The International Trade Centre (ITC 1999) reports information on the market share of organically produced food as depicted in Table 1.2. In most countries the market share of organic food is still very low but growing at considerable rates.[23] The European Environmental Agency (EEA 2001) reports that in some countries and for some products the market share reaches about 5 percent. Notably in Denmark organically produced milk accounts for 15 to 20 percent of the market. Willer and Richter (2004) report that the Swiss market for organic produce has experienced the best development with a recent (2004) market share of 4 percent, with 12 percent for eggs, 11 percent for milk and vegetables, 8 percent for bread and 7 percent for fruit. They argue that large-scale and co-ordinated green purchasing strategies on the part of big retail chains (Migros and Coop) account for rapid development in Switzerland. The growth potential in Germany, in contrast, is more limited, as organic produce is predominantly sold by small specialist retailers, the big food discount stores standing aside.[24]

EEA (2001) provides data on the market share of energy-efficient appliances. The EU Energy Labelling scheme requires manufacturers to display the energy efficiency of a product on a scale from A (best) to G (worst). Here the combined market share for A and B labelled refrigerators has increased from 15 percent in 1994 to 20 percent in 1996. Yet the most energy-efficient class-A refrigerators only hold around 3 percent of the market (as compared to 1 percent in 1994). The market share of energy efficient freezers did not follow this positive development. There is considerable variance between countries. In Sweden, for instance, the market shares of A and B labelled refrigerators and freezers have increased from 2 to 16 percent and from 29 to 63 per cent, respectively. Starting from a zero market share in 1997, class-A washing machines had by 2000 captured a share of 33 percent of the Swedish market

Lorek and Lucas (2003) report case study evidence on the German markets for eco-textiles and green power. For the textile market they report that in 1999 the companies organised in the International Natural Textile Association, a group of small and medium-sized enterprises subscribing to the highest environmental standards, held a combined market share of only 0.5 percent. However, they also find that large mail order companies increasingly include eco-textiles in their product range. Regarding the potential for green energy they report forecasts of 2 to 4 percent for the market share of renewable energy in the short term and between 20 and 30 percent in the long run. Sterner (2003: chapter 10) reports for the Swedish energy market that 'green electricity' was able to capture a price premium of some 5 percent in 2000–1 and held a market share of around 5 percent in 1999 (zero percent in 1996, the time of deregulation).

One market in which environmentally superior product variants have made considerable inroads is the market for household chemicals. Brockmann et al. (1996) consider the award of environmental labels in Germany to paints that contain few or no solvents. They report that the domestic market share of these paints increased from 16.4 percent in 1989 to 20.5 percent in 1993. Their calculations also show that the value per unit produced of environmentally benign emulsion lacquer paints had almost doubled from 4.7 to 8.0 DM per kg. In tandem with the rising market share this hints at a revealed (and increasing) willingness to pay for environmentally friendly paint on the part of consumers. Sterner (2003: chapter 10) reports the following 1996 market shares in the Swedish market for cleaning agents: facial and bathroom tissue 100 percent; laundry detergent 65 percent; other detergents and cleaning products 50 to 70 percent; and soap and shampoo 1 to 10 percent.

This data is illustrative but provides only a patchy view on the development of green markets. A sounder understanding can only be gained on the basis of econometric analysis. Overall there is still surprisingly little analysis devoted to the determinants of green markets. Two major lines of inquiry can be distinguished. One approach is focused on products and seeks to establish whether environmental attributes have an influence on prices, market shares or consumer choice. A second approach is focused on corporate environmental behaviour and examines whether it can be explained by consumer and competitive pressure.

A number of authors estimate the hedonic prices of environmental product attributes (Couton et al. 1996, Nimon and Beghin 1999 and Anstine 2000). Here, it is assumed in the tradition of Lancaster's (1966) theory of consumption that consumers have preferences over a whole range of characteristics $\theta_1, \theta_2, ..., \theta_n$, which are bundled and provided by firms in form of goods. A product's price $p(\theta_1, ..., \theta_n)$ can then be written as a function of the amounts of characteristics included, where the hedonic price of characteristic i is given by the marginal effect $\partial p / \partial \theta_i$ (Rosen 1974). In principle it is then possible to determine the hedonic prices by estimating the $\partial p / \partial \theta_i$'s.[25]

Couton et al. (1996) estimate the hedonic prices of environmental and safety attributes for the French car market. The authors arrive at a hedonic price of 8 percent for a catalytic converter (i.e. an increase in vehicle price of 8 percent in the presence of a catalytic converter) and 25 percent for a diesel engine.[26] In a separate estimation the authors examine how the percentage share of car owners being satisfied with the quality of their own brand depends on a number of characteristics. The presence of a catalytic converter and low fuel consumption turn out to be significant in explaining consumer satisfaction, both bearing the expected sign.

In contrast to this, Berry et al. (1995) find in their study of the US automobile industry that fuel efficiency as measured by miles per gallon (MPG) carries a negative hedonic price. Having imposed a zero-profit condition so that price equals marginal cost they explain their counter-intuitive result by referring to a constant-return-to-scale assumption. Small cars are associated with greater fuel efficiency and are produced in greater quantities. Since output does not enter the estimation separately the authors suspect that the MPG variable picked up scale effects leading to a lower marginal cost and by implication a lower price. In a more complete model, involving a discrete choice specification of demand and oligopolistic interaction on the supply side, the authors find that an index attached to fuel efficiency decreases with a car's ranking in terms of its mark-up (Berry et al. 1995, table 5). This shows that in the US car market environmental performance is not considered to be a dominating quality attribute.[27]

Nimon and Beghin (1999) use apparel catalogue data from the US in order to estimate hedonic price functions depending on environmental attributes as signalled by eco-labels. They identify a significant and robust premium for organic cotton but find little evidence for a premium on environmentally friendly dyes. Nonetheless the average organic mark-up amounts to 33.8 percent. They also investigate the pricing behaviour of organic suppliers and find that significant differences in pricing do not appear to be present. Finally Anstine (2000) uses a hedonic price approach in order to estimate consumers' willingness to pay for recycled content in garbage bags. He finds a significant and negative effect on price of both a 'recycled content' variable and, alternatively, an 'eco-label' dummy. This suggests that US consumers perceive recycled bags to be of inferior quality.

Teisl et al. (2002) use an 'almost ideal demand system' in order to estimate the effect of critical media attention and dolphin-safe labelling on the market share of tuna as opposed to other seafood and meat in the US food market. They identify a significant negative effect on tuna consumption of media reporting suggesting that at least some consumption is motivated by environmental concerns. They also report a significant and positive effect of labelling corresponding to a 1 percent increase in estimated market share over and above the estimate in the absence of the label. Their results also suggest that the label variable follows an S-shaped function, this being well in line with theories of information diffusion. Their model suffers from the limitation that their time series data is aggregated at product level and therefore rules out an analysis of individual labelled and non-labelled brands. There is thus a risk that the label variable may pick up a time trend rather than environmentally motivated changes in demand as stimulated by the label.

Bjoerner et al. (2004) use a repeated mixed logit model of brand choice in order to derive the household willingness to pay for the Nordic Swan label as a summary indicator of environmental friendliness, at least as perceived by consumers. Significant effects of the label on marginal willingness to pay are found for toilet paper, the label allowing for a premium of 13 to 18 percent of the price, and for detergents. There is no significant effect on the marginal willingness to pay for kitchen rolls, where the authors presume that this may be due to environmentally conscious households using cotton dishcloths repeatedly.

In summary these studies confirm the picture obtained from casual observation, namely that there is wide variation in the revealed willingness to pay for environmental product attributes across products and consumers. Green consumption is by no means universal. However, the evidence also suggests that green consumerism is by no means irrelevant as is being suggested by some.

Whereas previous approaches focus on the demand side another line of investigation has followed the determinants of environmentally responsive behaviour on the part of firms. These studies seek to understand if and how factors such as competitive pressure, regulatory pressure, past environmental performance, size, financial health, technical feasibility, shareholder pressure and, indeed, customer pressure tend to affect corporate environmental strategies (Khanna 2001). The focus of these studies being necessarily much wider, they still provide useful information on the extent to which environmental product upgrades are driven by customer demand and/or a desire to differentiate a clean product. In that regard customer pressure and competitive pressure are the groups of variables of interest to us.

Arora and Cason (1995) use a probit model to explain the probability of a company's participation in the US 33/50 programme for voluntary reductions in toxic chemical releases. In one model they include industry fixed effects in the form of the intercepts relating to seven relevant two-digit standard industrial classification codes. These turn out to be significant with chemical firms being the most likely participants and rubber and plastics firms being the least likely. Unfortunately the authors do not elaborate to what extent these results really imply that competition/customer proximity are drivers as opposed to other industry-specific factors. In an alternative specification of the model they replace the industry variables by the advertising and research and development (R&D) intensity as alternative descriptors of activity/customer proximity and by the Herfindahl index as a measure of competition. The advertising and R&D variables turn out to be insignificant, perhaps because the effects are picked up by the highly significant size variable. The Herfindahl is significantly and negatively related to the participation decision. According to the authors this suggests that there is indeed an incentive to avoid strong competition by environmental differentiation.[28]

Henriques and Sadorsky (1996) use data from a survey of Canadian firms in order to estimate the influencing factors on the adoption of an environmental plan. Customer pressure turns out to be significant and positive. Anton et al. (2004) examine the determinants of the comprehensiveness of corporate environmental management systems (EMS) as measured by the number of environmental management practices (EMPs).[29] They use a Poisson regression in order to estimate the expected number of EMPs, with a Negative Binomial model providing an independent estimate of the variance. They complement this analysis with a quantile regression in order to study the effect of the determinants on each of the quantiles of the distribution. They find a significant and positive effect of a 'final goods industry' dummy as a measure of consumer pressure. The quantile regression suggests that customer pressure is stronger for firms at the bottom end of the EMP spectrum. This finding illustrates nicely an observation we have made earlier, namely that firms within an environmentally differentiated industry face a trade-off between differentiating their products and trying to establish a competitive advantage.[30] The findings by Anton et al. (2004) suggest that while environmental product differentiation is clearly present it may not be maximal if dirty firms are facing strong incentives to upgrade their performance.

Anton et al. (2004) also examine the impact on firms' unit emissions of the adoption of EMPs and find this to be negative. As the final goods variable does not have a significant direct impact on emissions, this suggests that customer pressure is transmitted into lower emissions through the adoption of more comprehensive EMS.[31]

Prakash (2000) uses a case-study approach to explain the greening of firms. He studies in detail the environmental practices of Baxter, a US supplier of medical equipment, and Eli-Lilly, a US pharmaceutical company. While both firms have adopted EMS, only Baxter has explicitly introduced 'green' product lines. This difference in strategies illustrates the widely different scope for creating environmentally enhanced products. In principle there is nothing to suggest that consumers of pharmaceuticals may not have a preference for 'green' drugs. However Eli-Lilly's product range consists of either prescription drugs or over-the-counter drugs for which consumers regularly obtain a prescription. As physicians make the purchasing decision on behalf of their patients it is the physician's environmental preferences the company would have to account for. Medical research suggests that physicians are predominantly interested in the drug's medical effectiveness and its price. As environmental aspects are completely overridden there is no incentive for Eli-Lilly to introduce a green drug range. In contrast for the medical equipment supplied by Baxter packaging and waste is of considerable importance, a lot of their products being disposables. Baxter's customers, hospitals and other health-care providers have an interest in reducing waste if they themselves are subject to the cost of disposal. Incentives towards waste reduction targeted at the consumers then translate into a willingness to pay for the recyclable products and intelligent packaging systems offered by Baxter.

Finally there is a literature that seeks to establish the determinants of environmental innovation. Jaffe and Stavins (1995) consider the effects of energy prices and command-and-control regulation on the adoption of thermal insulation technologies in residential construction in the US between 1979 and 1988.[32] They find energy prices to have had a significant positive impact. Surprisingly perhaps, their analysis also shows that an equivalent percentage reduction in adoption cost is three times as effective in enhancing adoption. This is a clear indication that in many instances the presence of transaction costs relating to information deficits or switching may substantially slow down the introduction of green products or technologies. The presence of standards had little effect on the introduction of green technology. The authors propose that this was due to the simple fact that most of the standards were set below the standard of current practice and therefore were simply not binding.

Newell et al. (1999) ask whether changes in energy prices have induced innovations leading to improvements in the energy efficiency of air-conditioners and gas water heaters. Assuming heterogeneous consumers and a homogeneous seller (Sears-Roebuck) they interpret deflated hedonic price regression as supply functions of the product characteristics, amongst them energy efficiency. They distinguish three kinds of technological change. Autonomous technological change captures the movement of the characteristic surface along a ray in characteristic space, and directional technological change captures the movement on the surface. Both types occur at given levels of energy prices. Induced technological change, the third type, embraces movement along the characteristic surface associated with changing energy prices. They show that higher levels of energy prices strengthen directional technological change towards energy efficiency. For central (as opposed to room) air-conditioning as well as for gas water heaters this corrects a bias of autonomous technological change against energy efficiency. The evidence of the effect of energy efficiency standards on directional technological remains mixed. The study finds strong evidence for induced technological change where the impact of price changes on the product mix is significant. This is particularly true in the presence of product labelling requirements, again hinting at the importance of transaction costs relating to incomplete information. Counter-factual simulation (holding relative energy prices at their all time minimum in 1973) suggests that one quarter to one half of the increase in energy-efficiency would not have occurred, were it not for an increase in prices. Finally the authors find a significant effect of energy-efficiency standards on induced technological change

1.6 OUTLINE OF THE BOOK

The book falls roughly into three parts. The first part, comprising chapters 2 and 3, introduces in some detail the model of environmentally differentiated duopoly. The second part, chapters 4 to 7, studies environmental policies and the final part, comprising chapters 8 and 9, provides a summary and outlook.

The following chapter develops a model of environmentally differentiated duopoly and solves for equilibrium prices and environmental performance levels. Price and environmental strategies as well as the resulting distribution of market shares and profits are characterised depending on the structure of preferences and cost. The chapter also introduces environmental orientation of a market as a measure of the intensity of consumers' environmental preferences. We study the model both for the absence and presence of investment costs in environmental improvements.

The third chapter studies the implications for emissions at product and industry level. It contrasts our results against some contrary findings in the literature and relates this back to the different assumptions about preferences and cost. We also discuss some comparative static properties of industry emissions, and in particular the effect of product differentiation.

Chapter 4 studies the effects of an environmental product standard targeted at the dirty firm. The first part analyses the effects of the standard on consumer surplus, profits and gross surplus and shows how the impact depends on the degree of environmental orientation. The chapter then turns to the effect of a standard on industry emissions, again highlighting important differences from the literature. The chapter points out under which circumstances a trade-off exists between environmental and industrial policy objectives and when the standard contributes towards an unambiguous increase in total welfare.

Chapter 5 examines the effects of a third-party environmental label as a device of differentiation for the clean firm. In particular it considers an optimal labelling policy and compares it to the labelling decisions preferred by the firm. Chapter 6 studies the impact of subsidisation of environmental investments on the two firms' environmental performance and analyses the impact of different forms of subsidies on industry surplus and emissions.

Chapter 7 is concerned with environmental taxation. It studies the effects of a specific quality related unit tax or subsidy on the duopolists' environmental product choices. We highlight how a specific tax/subsidy improves the competitive position of the clean firm. The impact of the tax/subsidy on industry surplus and industry emissions is characterised depending on the environmental orientation. The general model of the transfer we use allows us to compare the effects of a tax and a subsidy. Our analysis demonstrates the scope for perverse incentives of environmental taxes but also the scope for unambiguous welfare improvements on both environmental and industrial policy grounds.

Chapter 8 summarises our theoretical findings and draws out some conclusions for policy making. In particular, it shows how the effects of policies can at least to some degree be inferred from easily observable data on market shares, profits and the two firms' technology choices.

The final chapter is devoted to an outlook on a range of issues that are pertinent to the development of green markets but lie beyond the scope of the formal analysis within this work. Drawing on insights from the present work as well as transferring insights from the literature to the context of greening markets, we can make a number of conjectures and point out future research needs. Inter alia the chapter addresses social interaction as a motivation for green consumption and the role of crowding out effects; the implications of alternative assumptions about the technological relationship between environmental performance and other product features; environmental policies in a covered market; the implications of quantity competition; the role of collusion for environmental policies; and more general assumptions regarding the number of firms and products per firm. We also address some dynamic issues in the development of markets, including inter-temporal quality and policy choice, entry, exit and entry deterrence. A final summary concludes the work.

NOTES

1. Fuel-efficient cars have a poorer performance in terms of horsepower and acceleration; environmentally friendly textiles are not so colourful and variable in the style of their fabrics, and reusable food containers have to be collected and carried back to the shop.
2. See Khanna (2001) for a survey of the theoretical and empirical literature on the issue and Prakash (2000) for a case study of the pro-active environmental approaches taken by Baxter and Eli-Lilly.
3. Oates et al. (1989) point out that over-compliance may arise simply as a side-effect of bulky investments in abatement capital.
4. Khanna (2001) discusses, inter alia, the US 33/50 programme for reductions in toxic chemicals releases, the Green Lights as examples of public voluntary schemes, and the Project XL as a bilateral scheme. Boerkey and Levêque (1998) provide a European perspective. They distinguish between unilateral commitments (27 EU centred), public voluntary schemes (e.g. the EU and German eco-labelling initiatives or the Danish scheme on greenhouse gas emission avoidance), and negotiated agreements (312 EU wide, the majority being in Germany and the Netherlands). While only the last group is classified as the outcome of explicit negotiations, one could interpret unilateral commitments as forms of implicit agreements. This is because the parties essentially face the same threats: potential imposition of mandatory regulation by the policy maker and the scaling down of domestic operations by the firm. If the regulator's ability to punish a deviation from an explicit agreement is limited, the agreement has to be self-enforcing and is then similar to a tacit agreement.
5. Firms participating in the US Project XL, for instance, are allowed to disregard existing command and control standards (for specific environmental media) if they can demonstrate that their overall emissions are lower than if they were to meet these standards. See Blackman and Boyd (1999) for an economic analysis.
6. Glachant (1999) compares the transaction costs of voluntary and mandatory approaches in greater detail and concludes that they are not universally lower under voluntary approaches. If informational asymmetries matter and the number of firms is large a voluntary approach may be more costly.
7. See Schmelzer (1999) for a model where the regulator threatens to impose a tax.
8. Maloney and McCormick (1982) provide empirical evidence.
9. The presence of managerial slack requires the firm to wield some market power. Clearly, competitive firms do not provide any scope for the introduction of unprofitable measures.
10. This is, of course, an instance of the notorious multi-tasking problem in agency (Holmstrom and Milgrom 1991).

11. The models in Hotelling's (1929) tradition assume that each consumer has a single peaked preference ordering over a range of (potential) product variants. Hence each consumer can be attributed a definite address relating to his most preferred product specification. Product differentiation then arises from consumer heterogeneity. The advantage of this approach over the representative consumer approach (Spence 1976, Dixit and Stiglitz 1977) is that it allows an explicit modelling of product choice. The more complex discrete choice approach to product differentiation (Anderson et al. 1992) reconciles the different strands of the literature. For an overview on the literature on product differentiation see Tirole (1988: chapter 7), Eaton and Lipsey (1989), Beath and Katsoulacos (1991) and Anderson et al. (1992).

12. Together with the growing literature on environmental product differentiation we accept this assumption as a basis for our work. However, we will discuss alternative scenarios in section 9.2.

13. We will make liberal use of terminology here and for the sake of variety use expressions such as 'environmentally friendly', 'environmentally superior', 'green', 'clean', etc., as synonyms. We will try to avoid the term 'environmental quality', which we believe to refer to the state of the environment rather than to particular features of a product. We will, however, refer to 'environmental performance', 'environmental effort' or 'abatement effort'.

14. See Ayres and Kneese (1969) for a seminal statement of how, in principle, the environmental impacts of goods can be aggregated using a materials flow approach. For practical purposes a life-cycle analysis is usually employed that tries to assess and balance against each other the most relevant environmental impacts of a product (e.g. Kemp 1997). OECD (1991) contains a description of how life-cycle analysis is used in determining the criteria for eco-labels.

15. This literature comprises Motta and Thisse (1993, 1999), Cremer and Thisse (1994a, 1999), Arora and Gangopadhyay (1995), Crampes and Ibanez (1996), Moraga-González and Padrón-Fumero (1997, 2002), Rothfels (2000), Lombardini-Riipinen (2002), Bansal and Gangopadhyay (2003) and Amacher et al. (2004).

16. We address the provision of multiple product lines as a means of environmental price discrimination in section 9.3.

17. For general overviews of environmental policy instruments and their use see Golub (1998), Opschoor and Vos (1989), OECD (1999a) and Sterner (2003).

18. A number of other policies, such as quota and green public procurement, are discussed in the concluding chapter 9.

19. Motta and Thisse (1993, 1999), Arora and Gangopadhyay (1995), Moraga-González and Padrón-Fumero (1997, 2002), Rothfels (2000) and Lombardini-Riipinen (2002) all address standards.

20. Interestingly the literature on environmental product differentiation focuses exclusively on this form of taxation (Cremer and Thisse 1994a, 1999; Arora and Gangopadhyay 1995; Moraga-González and Padrón-Fumero 1997, 2002; Bansal and Gangopadhyay 2003).

21. Subsidies in the context of environmental product differentiation are addressed by Arora and Gangopahdyay (1995), Moraga-González and Padrón-Fumero (1997, 2002) and Rothfels (2000).

22. Crampes and Ibanez (1996) and Amacher et al. (2004) provide models of environmental labelling.

23. Far lower growth rates, between 1.5 and 10 per cent per annum, are expected however for the period 2002 and 2007 (Willer and Richter 2004).

24. See ITC (1999) and Willer and Yussefi (2004) for an international overview on organic agriculture.

25. There are issues arising from supply-demand-simultaneity (Rosen 1974; for a critique, see Bartik 1987) as well as from an endogeneity problem, where both θ and the resulting price of a most-preferred product $p(\theta, u)$ depend on the consumer's preferences (Bartik 1987).

26. The authors point out that the 0.25 elasticity represents a ceteris paribus assumption of equal engine power for diesel and petrol engines. However as the coefficient on engine power only amounts to 0.0075, we would expect a premium on diesel engines even when taking account of lower power. As the study does not include any supply-side data the interpretation of their results remains somewhat unclear.

27. The negative correlation between fuel efficiency and mark-up could be explained with reference to the negative technological trade-off between fuel efficiency and both car size and horsepower/weight (HPW) together with the fact that the latter two characteristics are positively correlated with mark-up. However, the relationships involved may be somewhat more complicated. The estimates of prices and cross-price elasticities (Berry et al. 1995: tables 6 and 8) suggest the presence of about three distinct market segments that can be described in terms of {price, size, HPW, MPG}. They roughly correspond to a luxury segment, a family segment and a small car segment, where cross-price elasticities are high within but not across segments. While comparison of any two cars from different segments will generally produce the same ranking with regard to all characteristics, there is no unambiguous ranking for cars within the segments. In this case fuel efficiency may still be a tie-breaking attribute within each segment.

28. Khanna and Damon (1999) confirm in their study the finding that customer proximity increases the likelihood of pariticipation in the 33/50 programme.

29. See also Khanna and Anton (2002).

30. They also find that the average number of practices adopted within the same industry group has a positive and significant effect on the comprehensiveness of an individual firm's EMS. Such peer pressure also hints at the role of environmental competitive advantage within some industries.

31. Examining panel data from Canada's National Pollutant Release Inventory, Antweiler and Harrison (2003) also find a statistically significant but weak negative effect of green consumerism on a number of emission measures. One shortcoming of their approach is that they use a very indirect measure of customer pressure. Under the assumption that

consumers target companies rather than particular facilities, they argue, green consumerism can be identified through intra-firm inter-plant spillovers in abatement. However it is unclear why these spillovers may not equally well be driven by economies of scope or knowledge spillovers within the company. The results therefore remain open to wide interpretation.

32. See Jaffe et al. (2000) for a survey of recent empirical studies on the innovation and diffusion of green technologies.

2. Environmentally differentiated duopoly

2.1 INTRODUCTION

We have argued in the introduction that some individuals receive a private benefit from consuming environmentally friendly products. Suppose environmental friendliness and other quality attributes are unrelated or positively related. Then a product can be designed and/or produced in an environmentally superior fashion without compromising other quality aspects. Assuming all other quality aspects as given we can then apply the conventional model of vertical differentiation to the environmental context by reinterpreting 'quality' as 'environmental friendliness', 'environmental performance' or 'environmental effort'.[1] The assumption of a given level of performance in all other product dimensions may sound strong in not only ruling out a trade-off between environmental friendliness and other dimensions of performance but in positively imposing equal (average) performance in all non-environmental dimensions. However, it may be justified on empirical grounds at least for some products. A study by the Open University's Design Innovation Group, *The Commercial Impacts of Green Product Development* (1996, cited in OECD 1997), concludes that environmental attributes gain relevance in competition only if competitive levels are attained with regard to all other dimensions of product performance. This suggests a tie-breaking role for environmental friendliness as a product attribute, which corresponds exactly to the notion of product differentiation as a means of breaking up product homogeneity. If 'environmental friendliness' and other quality aspects are complements, the case is even more straightforward. Here we can maintain our general notion about quality, while acknowledging that 'environmental friendliness' is one aspect thereof.

In this chapter we use a model of vertical differentiation to model an environmentally differentiated market. While in recent years green variants have been able to capture considerable market share for many products, they still occupy just a niche in most markets.[2] As we will see, the effects on industry surplus and emissions of environmental policies within such a

25

market are strongly correlated with the market share and (relative) profitability of green products. Indeed, in many cases the effects of policies reverse when moving from a market configuration leading to dominance by the dirty firm to one in which the clean firm dominates. The reason is of course that market share and profitability reveal the underlying structure of preferences and technology, where this same structure also determines the effects of policies. As the impact of policies can therefore be expected to depend critically on the market configuration, this needs to be an aspect of any relevant model of environmental policy making. Specifically the model should allow scope for the dominance in market share and/or profit on the part of the polluting firm that is frequently observed. We shall argue below that, surprisingly enough, the standard model of vertical differentiation and its applications to environmentally differentiated markets do not allow for this. It will be one concern of this chapter, as indeed of the book, to remedy this shortcoming by using a generalised model of vertically differentiated duopoly that allows scope for all possible market configurations including the polar cases of dominance by the dirty or the clean firm. In the remainder of this introduction we first present a more detailed discussion of the issue of market dominance under vertical differentiation and then go on to present a brief overview of the received literature on environmentally differentiated duopoly.

Vertical Differentiation and Market Dominance

Following the seminal work by Gabsewicz and Thisse (1979), the model of vertically differentiated duopoly has been established as a workhorse to analyse firms' quality choices in a framework of strategic competition. However the question of dominance – in terms of market share or profit – has rarely been commented upon. In fact in the majority of the work the high quality firm is the leader both in terms of market share and profit. Within a model in which vertically differentiated firms compete on price and face a zero marginal cost, Shaked and Sutton (1982) demonstrate the case for high quality leadership.[3] If any two qualities are offered at the same price consumers unambiguously favour the higher one. Thus a producer of superior quality can always capture the complete market share of a low quality competitor by matching its price. The high quality firm can then set a price guaranteeing a profit at the least equal to the low quality producer's and usually greater. Lehmann-Grube (1997) extends their argument by showing that, in the presence of a sunk cost of quality, the high quality firm still emerges as the profit leader. For a non-covered market this result holds no matter whether firms choose qualities simultaneously or sequentially. The Shaked and Sutton (1982) argument applies irrespective of the number of firms. Naturally in a triopoly model of vertical differentiation (e.g. Donnenfeld and Weber 1992, 1995 or Scarpa 1998) the firms' ranking in operating profit coincides with their ranking in quality.

The focus on high quality leadership in vertically differentiated markets is at odds with intuition. It should be noted at this point that by the symmetry of these models dominance in profit implies dominance in market share and vice versa. However anecdotal evidence suggests that, for many markets, high quality firms are not always leaders in market share.[4] Frequently quality leaders sell at high prices to a narrow circle of customers. In their empirical study of the automobile industry Berry et al. (1995) estimate price-cost margins and operating profits (their table 8). Although they work with a multi-attribute model of product differentiation, where an unambiguous ranking with regard to quality is not present, their findings show that there exists no correlation between mark-up and operating profit. The reason is that firms selling at a low mark-up may capture a large market share. If in this model we interpret quality as a latent variable determining the distribution of prices, it follows that high quality does not imply dominance in operating profit. Indeed there appears to be an inherent asymmetry in the industry. Some firms rely on quality leadership mainly to generate a high mark-up, whereas other firms rely on a cost advantage in order to capture a large share of the market.

In order to assess the role of preferences and variable cost in determining market dominance we consider a vertically differentiated duopoly in a non-covered market. A consumer's relative evaluation of quality is captured by a gross surplus function consisting of a quality-dependent benefit and a quality-independent baseline benefit. The baseline benefit captures three aspects of vertically differentiated markets that are not included in the standard model.[5] First, it accounts for benefits received from consumption that are independent of quality. If 'quality' relates to a particular attribute of the product, such as its environmental friendliness, the baseline benefit measures the utility stream from all other attributes of the product.[6] We use the baseline benefit as a benchmark, against which we measure the importance consumers attach to quality/environmental performance. Standard models of vertical differentiation do not take the baseline benefit into account and therefore lack this benchmark. This is one of the reasons for the unambiguous finding of high quality dominance. Second, from a firm's point of view, the baseline benefit then represents a source of revenue unrelated to the provision of quality. The relative importance of quality related and unrelated revenue becomes a determinant of a firm's quality choice additional to the cost of quality. Moreover even if the marginal cost of quality exceeds the consumer's willingness to pay, a high quality firm can survive in the market as long as the baseline benefit creates a sufficient amount of revenue. Finally, the baseline benefit captures the relative importance of heterogeneity both with regard to products and consumers. As baseline benefit increases, the relative importance of product differentiation and heterogeneity of consumer tastes decreases. Both effects tend to enhance competition (Wauthy 1996).

Low quality dominance, with respect to both market share and profit, is then realised if and only if the low quality firm has a cost advantage that is leveraged to a sufficient extent by the baseline benefit. A high baseline benefit implies relatively price-sensitive consumers. In this case a minor cost advantage may suffice to generate low quality leadership. The switch from high to low quality dominance is sequential. For intermediate values of willingness to pay a situation can arise in which the low quality firm is leader in market share but not in profit. This is the empirically relevant case of high quality profit leadership under a niche strategy. If willingness to pay for quality is large relative to the baseline benefit our model gives the conventional result of high quality leadership.[7]

An Environmental Interpretation of the Model of Vertical Differentiation

Motta and Thisse (1993), Arora and Gangopadhyay (1995), Cremer and Thisse (1999), Lombardini-Riipinen (2002), Bansal and Gangopadhyay (2003) and Amacher et al. (2004) rigorously interpret the model of vertical product differentiation in an environmental economics context. Although we adopt a similar interpretation let us note that a number of different approaches are possible. The above models interpret 'environmental friendliness' as a characteristic valued by the consumer. Crampes and Ibanez (1996) and Moraga-González and Padrón-Fumero (MGPF) (2002) take the opposite approach by modelling a disutility from the degree of environmental harm caused by the product.[8]

The prediction of market share dominance of the green (= high quality) product in these models is clearly at odds with the empirical facts reported in section 1.5.[9] Hence, in this particular context, a model that does not allow for dominance of the dirty firm in terms of market share is clearly of limited empirical relevance. More seriously, however, we will demonstrate in subsequent chapters that dominance on the part of the dirty firm gives rise to distinct implications for environmental policies, where many results obtained in the conventional model are overturned.

In the following subsection, we introduce the model. Section 2.3 derives the price equilibria and comments on dominance by the dirty/low quality firm. Section 2.4 derives the equilibrium structure of environmental performance/quality and extends the discussion of dominance. In section 2.5 we show that our dominance results carry over to the setting in which environmental performance/quality is associated with initial investment. Section 2.6 contrasts our model with the model in MGPF (2002) that serves as an important benchmark. Section 2.7 concludes. Proofs are relegated to the Appendix A2 at the end of this work.

2.2 THE MODEL

Technology

Let the index θ, $\theta \in \left[\underline{\theta}, \overline{\theta}\right]$ be a measure of the environmental friendliness or environmental performance of a product. As such it will be negatively related to the unit emissions from a product, which for expositional purposes we are not going to introduce however until section 3.1. For the moment let us assume that the lower and upper bounds $\underline{\theta} \geq 0$ and $\overline{\theta}$, respectively, are exogenous and determined by the current vintage of the technology.

The marginal cost of production is given by

$$MC = c\theta + c_0,$$

where $c\theta$ relates to the environmental performance of the product. This could embrace a direct abatement cost or the additional cost of producing a less polluting variant. The latter may entail the use of more expensive 'clean' inputs (e.g. regenerative energy; organic fibres); the production of more sophisticated material (e.g. bio-degradable or recyclable material); the more extensive use of labour in artisan production or organic agriculture; or the use of higher quality labour or capital inputs in the production of more durable or recyclable goods. Furthermore, in the case of end-of-pipe technologies, the capital cost of installing abatement capacity may also be reflected in the variable cost. Finally the firm may have acquired the green technology by way of a licensing agreement. If the contract specifies royalty payments depending on the licensee's sales, then this also implies a marginal cost that increases with quality.

For many products the improvement of their environmental characteristics can only be achieved by changes in design. The required R&D then gives rise to sunk costs of quality. This integrative type of pollution abatement may apply both to the production process or the product itself. There are two additional reasons for sunk costs to play an important role. First, if investment in end-of-pipe technologies is lumpy, this gives rise to a quantity independent cost. Second, there may be a sunk cost if a firm wishes to signal 'environmental friendliness' to uninformed consumers. This cost can either be the cost associated with the acquisition of an eco-label (including the cost of preparing expert reports), or it can be foregone profit if a firm establishes a reputation.[10] Let the investment cost be given by the function

$$F(\theta) = \tfrac{k}{2}(\theta - \underline{\theta})^2, \ F'(\theta) = k(\theta - \underline{\theta}), \ F'' = k > 0.$$

Note that for this cost specification we do not require an upper bound to technology, $\overline{\theta}$. Much of the analysis in this chapter (sections 2.2 and 2.3) applies irrespective of whether we allow for the presence of investment in environmental performance or not. The analysis in section 2.4 is carried out for the case in which investment is absent. Section 2.5 presents some extra results for the set-up with investment costs.

Preferences and Demand

A consumer's gross surplus from one unit of the differentiated good is given by $v\theta + u$. Following Motta and Thisse (1993), Arora and Gangopadhyay (1995) and Cremer and Thisse (1994a, 1999), we interpret v as a consumer's willingness to pay (WTP) for environmental friendliness. This willingness to pay arises from some form of 'green glow', i.e. a strictly private benefit from green consumption unrelated to the consumer's disutility from pollution (see section 1.2 of the introduction). Consumers differ in their WTP, where we assume that v is uniformly distributed on $[\underline{v}, \overline{v}]$. Consumer heterogeneity with regard to WTP may arise for two reasons. Consumers either differ in their 'genuine' preference for environmental friendliness, or they differ in income in the presence of a decreasing marginal rate of substitution (MRS) between income and quality.[11] As will be seen below, only the second interpretation is intuitive. Therefore, we interpret v as a consumer's MRS between quality and income, as suggested by Tirole (1988: section 2.1.1) and Arora and Gangopadhyay (1995). Consumers are homogeneous with respect to the benefit they receive from environmental performance. Differences in their WTP arise from differences in income alone.[12]

The baseline benefit u incorporates the general benefit from consumption of the product. The introduction of a baseline benefit is warranted if environmental friendliness is unrelated to the overall quality of the product. In the absence of a baseline benefit, consumers would purchase the product by virtue of its environmental friendliness alone: clearly not a reasonable presumption. Under most circumstances, we would expect the baseline benefit to be large relative to the benefit from green consumption. The problem is less pronounced in those cases in which environmental friendliness and other quality attributes are positively correlated.[13] As θ becomes a more general measure of quality then, it is plausible that consumers purchase the product even if $u = 0$. Here $u > 0$ merely amounts to assuming an additional homogeneous part to the consumer's benefit.

An individual's net surplus from consumption is given by

$$U = v\theta + u - p(\theta).$$ (2.1)

if she purchases one unit at price $p(\theta)$ and zero otherwise.[14] Suppose two variants with environmental performance θ_G (G: green, clean) and θ_B (B: brown, dirty), where $\bar{\theta} \geq \theta_G \geq \theta_G \geq \underline{\theta}$, are offered at prices p_G and p_B, respectively.

Using (2.1) we find

$$v_1 = \frac{p_G - p_B}{\theta_G - \theta_B}, \qquad v_0 = \frac{p_B - u}{\theta_B}$$

as the indices corresponding to consumers who are indifferent between purchasing the green or brown variant and between purchasing the brown variant and making no purchase, respectively. If both firms face non-negative demand, this implies $v_1 \in [v_0, \bar{v}]$, which will be verified in equilibrium. Furthermore, a non-covered market configuration in which some consumers refrain from purchasing the product arises if and only if $v_0 > \underline{v}$. Here

$$\underline{v} - c < 0; \qquad u - c_0 + (\underline{v} - c)\underline{\theta} \leq 0$$

is sufficient for $v_0 > \underline{v}$. The consumer with WTP for quality amounting to $\underline{v}$ would not even purchase if the variant with the poorest environmental performance were offered at marginal cost.[15] The market is then never covered. This will be the case we focus on throughout this work.[16] Without loss of generality for our purposes we assume $\bar{v} - \underline{v} = 1$, implying a density of the consumer distribution of 1. In a non-covered market the demand functions for the green and brown variants are then given by

$$q_G = \bar{v} - v_1; \qquad q_B = v_1 - v_0$$

The ordering $\bar{v} > v_1 > v_0 > 0$ implies that the consumers with the highest WTP purchase the environmentally friendly variant, the consumers with intermediate WTP purchase the environmentally harmful variant, and the consumers with the lowest WTP do not purchase the product at all.

Note that such a structure of demand is not always intuitive. Motta and Thisse (1993) and Cremer and Thisse (1994a, 1999) assume that consumers vary in their concern about the environment as measured by v. This would imply that in a non-covered market the least concerned consumers do not purchase the product, whereas the most concerned consumers do. This is what happens in Motta and Thisse (1993). Realistically, we would expect the consumers with the greatest concern for the environment to be the ones to abstain from consumption, consumers with some concern to consume the green variant, and consumers without much concern to consume the non-green variant. Hence, the market should be non-covered at the top end of the preference spectrum. The model delivers the counter intuitive result for the following reason. As v constitutes a benefit from consumption, it is implicitly assumed that all consumers rate the purchase of the product higher than abstinence from consumption. Contrary to intuition, the consumers with the highest v are the most eager to buy given their high valuation of the product. Obviously, the (green) consumers' failure to take into account the option of not consuming at all generates the perverse result of the model. This implies that consumers are irrational to a degree. There are three ways around this problem.

First, Cremer and Thisse (1994a, 1999) consider a covered market. In this case, consumers with a high WTP buy the green and those with low WTP buy the non-green variant. However, this rules out an analysis of a non-covered market with a potentially important quality–quantity trade-off. Second, Arora and Gangopadhyay (1995) avoid the pitfall by interpreting v as the MRS between 'environmental friendliness' and income, an interpretation, which we follow in our analysis.[17] In a non-covered market, the consumers with the highest income purchase the green variant, the consumers with some intermediate income purchase the non-green variant, while the poorest consumers do not purchase the differentiated good at all. In this interpretation of the model, all consumers have the same positive benefit from green consumption. Heterogeneity arises from an unequal income distribution. Whereas rich consumers are able to obtain the green benefit by purchasing the more expensive green variant, consumers with a relatively lower income are constrained to buy the non-green variant. The poorest consumers, who for lack of income are not able to purchase the differentiated commodity at all, become, in a perverse way, the environmentally most benevolent consumers. Clearly, this is intuitive. As Arora and Gangopadhyay

(1995) consider only a benefit from quality, they implicitly assume either that quality and environmental friendliness are perfectly correlated or that consumers receive a benefit from environmental friendliness alone. This shortcoming can be avoided by extending Arora and Gangopadhyay's (1995) line of argument by taking into additional account the presence of a baseline benefit. Here, consumers primarily purchase the product to obtain the general benefit from consumption, while taking into additional account a side-benefit from green consumption. It is likely that they only enjoy this side benefit if they can afford to do so. Finally, Crampes and Ibanez (1996) and MGPF (2002) consider a different specification of preferences, where environmentally aware consumers suffer a (moral) disutility from the pollution generated through their personal consumption. We discuss this model in greater detail in section 2.6 below.

Environmental Orientation

At this point let us introduce 'environmental orientation' of a market as a measure of the extent to which environmental performance as opposed to price is an effective tool to stimulate demand. Using the price and 'environmental' elasticity of market demand as given by

$$\varepsilon(q, p) := -\frac{\partial q}{\partial p} \frac{p}{q} ; \qquad \varepsilon(q, \theta) := -\frac{\partial q}{\partial \theta} \frac{\theta}{q}$$

we define the environmental orientation of the market as

$$\eta := \frac{\varepsilon(q, \theta)}{\varepsilon(q, p)} .$$

Thus, the greater the environmental orientation the greater the ratio between 'environmental' elasticity and price elasticity and the more attractive is environmental performance as a tool to stimulate demand. In our model market demand can be written as $q = \bar{v} - v_0$. The demand elasticities with respect to environmental performance and price, respectively, are then given by $\varepsilon(q, \theta) = (p - u)/(\bar{v}\theta - p + u)$ and $\varepsilon(q, p) = p/(\bar{v}\theta - p + u)$. Hence,

$$\eta := \frac{\varepsilon(q, \theta)}{\varepsilon(q, p)} = \frac{p - u}{p} ,$$

where an increasing level of η implies a greater environmental orientation. Obviously $d\eta/du < 0$ and $d\eta/dp > 0$.

Lemma 2.1. Let a consumer's net surplus be given by $U = \max\{v\theta + u - p(\theta), 0\}$, where she purchases either one or zero units, and assume that price and environmental performance are such that the market is non-covered. Then the environmental orientation of a market decreases in baseline benefit u and increases in selling price p.

While both price and 'environmental' elasticity of demand decrease in u, the reduction is more pronounced for the 'environmental' elasticity. For a greater baseline benefit environmental performance becomes less effective than price as a means to attract the marginal consumer who is indifferent between purchasing or not and who therefore defines market size. Surprisingly perhaps the WTP for environmental performance does not feature directly in the expression for environmental orientation. However, as we would expect intuitively, and as we will establish formally below, a greater WTP for environmental performance is reflected in a higher selling price, which in equilibrium implies a greater level of environmental orientation.

Structure of the Game

There are two firms in the market, the green and brown firm, each providing a single variant of environmental performance θ_G and θ_B, respectively. The firms engage in a two-stage game of quality-then-price competition. In stage one, both firms simultaneously choose environmental performance. Observing their competitors' environmental performance they simultaneously choose prices in stage two. Using sub-game perfection as the equilibrium concept we solve the game backwards.

2.3 PRICE EQUILIBRIUM AND THE PRESENCE OF DOMINANCE

Using firms' profit functions

$$\pi_i = [p_i - (c\theta_i + c_0)]q_i(p_i, p_j, \theta_i, \theta_j); \ i, j = G, B; \quad j \neq i,$$

it is straightforward to derive the pair of Bertrand–Nash equilibrium prices

$$p_G^* = \frac{(2\bar{v}\theta_G + u)(\theta_G - \theta_B) + [c(2\theta_G + \theta_B) + 3c_0]\theta_G}{4\theta_G - \theta_B}, \qquad (2.2a)$$

$$p_B^* = \frac{(\bar{v}\theta_B + 2u)(\theta_G - \theta_B) + 3c\theta_G\theta_B + c_0(2\theta_G + \theta_B)}{4\theta_G - \theta_B}. \qquad (2.2b)$$

As a convention let us introduce $m := \bar{v} - c$ as the environmental margin and $n := u - c_0$ as the baseline margin. We can then write profit margins and demand as

$$p_G^* - c\theta_G - c_0 = \frac{(2m\theta_G + n)(\theta_G - \theta_B)}{4\theta_G - \theta_B}, \qquad (2.3a)$$

$$p_B^* - c\theta_B - c_0 = \frac{(m\theta_B + 2n)(\theta_G - \theta_B)}{4\theta_G - \theta_B}, \qquad (2.3b)$$

and

$$q_G^* = \frac{2m\theta_G + n}{(4\theta_G - \theta_B)}, \qquad (2.4a)$$

$$q_B^* = \frac{(m\theta_B + 2n)\theta_G}{(4\theta_G - \theta_B)\theta_B}. \qquad (2.4b)$$

We have argued before that it appears unreasonable to presume that products are only sold because of the benefit consumers derive from their environmental performance. In the light of this it is justified to assume a non-negative baseline margin, $n \geq 0$.[18] However, the same need not be true for the environmental margin. If consumers do not value environmental performance by a sufficient amount as opposed to the cost, then the environmental margin is negative. The following assumption guarantees non-negative output and mark-up for both firms:

$$m > -n/2\theta_G \qquad (2.5)$$

Profits can now be written as functions of environmental performance alone[19]

$$\pi_G^*(\theta_G, \theta_B) = \frac{(2m\theta_G + n)^2(\theta_G - \theta_B)}{(4\theta_G - \theta_B)^2}, \qquad (2.6a)$$

$$\pi_B{}^*(\theta_G,\theta_{BL}) = \frac{(m\theta_B + 2n)^2 \theta_G(\theta_G - \theta_B)}{(4\theta_G - \theta_B)^2 \theta_B}. \tag{2.6b}$$

Note that the presence of a positive baseline margin allows firms to sell their product at a profit even if the environmental margin is negative.

Market Share and Profit Dominance

We now derive the conditions under which the B firm attains market share and/or profit dominance. For convenience we define

$$\zeta := \theta_G/\theta_B$$

as the degree of product differentiation. Using $\theta_G = \zeta\theta_B$, we obtain from (2.4a) and (2.4b) and (2.6a) and (2.6b):

$$q_B{}^* > q_G{}^* \Leftrightarrow m < n(2\zeta - 1)/(\zeta\theta_B) =: m_q(\zeta,\theta_B), \tag{2.7}$$

$$\pi_B{}^* > \pi_G{}^* \Leftrightarrow m < n/\left(\theta_B\sqrt{\zeta}\right) =: m_\pi(\zeta,\theta_B) \tag{2.8}$$

As is easily checked, $m_q(\cdot) > m_\pi(\cdot)$. Using (2.7) and (2.8), we can characterise dominance on the part of the brown firm.

Proposition 2.1 (i) The B firm dominates with regard to market share if and only if $m < m_q(\cdot)$. (ii) The B firm dominates with regard to profit if and only if $m < m_\pi(\cdot)$. (iii) B profit dominance implies market share dominance but not vice versa.

The pattern of dominance is thus crucially determined by the relative importance of the environmental margin, m, as opposed to the baseline margin, n. The lower the environmental margin as opposed to the baseline margin, the stronger the competitive position of the B firm and the more likely its dominance. The B firm can acquire profit dominance only by becoming price leader and capturing the major share of the market. It is of course still true in our model that the B firm can lead only on the basis of an advantage in marginal cost. Here, the B firm's cost advantage increases with the environmental cost rate, c, but falls with the baseline marginal cost c_0.[20]

Any given cost advantage held by the B firm is then leveraged by the baseline benefit, u, which captures the degree of price sensitivity on the part of consumers. Thus, for a reduction in the environmental orientation of the market, the B firm will attain dominance first with respect to market share and then with respect to profit. Note that the G firm can maintain profit leadership even if the B firm dominates on market share. Here, the G firm draws on its niche position and extracts a sufficient amount of the high WTP consumers' surplus.[21]

2.4 ENVIRONMENTAL PERFORMANCE AND THE PATTERN OF DOMINANCE

Consider now the choice of environmental performance. Using (2.6a) and (2.6b) we obtain

$$\frac{\partial \pi_G{}^*(\theta_G,\theta_B)}{\partial \theta_G} = \frac{(2m\theta_G+n)\ r(\theta_G,\theta_B)}{(4\theta_G-\theta_B)^3}$$

$$= \frac{q_H{}^*(\theta_G,\theta_B)\,r(\theta_G,\theta_B)}{(4\theta_G-\theta_B)^2}, \qquad (2.9a)$$

$$\frac{\partial \pi_B{}^*(\theta_G,\theta_B)}{\partial \theta_B} = \frac{(m\theta_B+2n)\theta_G\ s(\theta_G,\theta_B)}{(4\theta_G-\theta_B)^3\,\theta_B{}^2}$$

$$= \frac{q_L{}^*(\theta_G,\theta_B)}{(4\theta_H-\theta_L)^2}\,\frac{s(\theta_G,\theta_B)}{\theta_B}, \qquad (2.9b),$$

where

$$r(\theta_G,\theta_B) = 2m\alpha(\theta_G,\theta_B) - n\beta(\theta_G,\theta_B), \qquad (2.10a)$$
$$s(\theta_G,\theta_B) = m\theta_G\theta_B\beta(\theta_G,\theta_B) - 2n\alpha(\theta_G,\theta_B) \qquad (2.10b)$$

with

$$\alpha(\theta_G,\theta_B) := 4\theta_G^2 - 3\theta_G\theta_B + 2\theta_B^2 > 0, \qquad (2.11a)$$
$$\beta(\theta_G,\theta_B) := 4\theta_G - 7\theta_B. \qquad (2.11b)$$

Observe that

$$\alpha(\cdot) > \max\{-\theta_G\beta(\cdot), \theta_G\beta(\cdot)\}\ \ \forall\theta_G > \theta_B. \qquad (2.12).$$

Inspection of the right-hand side (RHS) of (2.9a) and (2.9b) shows that net marginal revenue of improved environmental performance (where net refers to marginal as opposed to investment cost) can be decomposed into two parts. For further reference we introduce the following definition:

Definition 2.1: Consider (2.9a) and (2.9b), respectively. We call $\frac{q_i^*(\theta_G,\theta_B)}{(4\theta_G-\theta_B)}$; $i=G,B$, 'value of environmental performance' and $r(\cdot)$ and $s(\cdot)\theta_B^{-1}$, respectively, the 'competitive effectiveness' of environmental performance.

Note that the 'value of environmental performance' is always positive and increases with both the environmental and baseline margin. The 'value' can be understood as the potential to gain, in terms of profit margin or output, from adjustments in performance. The 'competitive effectiveness' terms indicate the extent to which environmental performance will help the firm to improve its competitive position.

Lemma 2.2: (i) 'Competitive effectiveness' of environmental performance i can be decomposed into a direct effect (DE) and a strategic effect (SE) as follows:

$$r(\theta_G,\theta_B)=\overbrace{[m(2\theta_G-\theta_B)-n](4\theta_G-\theta_B)}^{DE}+\overbrace{3(m\theta_B+2n)\theta_B}^{SE}$$

$$s(\theta_G,\theta_B)\theta_B^{-1}=\left\{\frac{\overbrace{[m\theta_G\theta_B-n(2\theta_G-\theta_B)](4\theta_G-\theta_B)}^{DE}}{\underbrace{-3(2m\theta_G+n)\theta_B}_{SE}}\right\}\theta_G\theta_B^{-1}$$

(ii) If $\zeta>7/4$ the 'competitive effectiveness' increases with the environmental margin, m, and falls with the baseline margin, n, for both firms. (iii) If $\zeta<7/4$ the 'competitive effectiveness' of G performance increases with both m and n; while the 'competitive effectiveness' of B performance decreases with both m and n.

Proof: See Appendix A2.1.

When choosing its environmental performance a firm not only takes into account the direct effect of this on its profit but also the strategic effect that is transmitted through the change in the rival's equilibrium price. Specifically as G performance is adjusted upwards, this increases the degree of product differentiation and, thereby, softens price competition. The increase in the price charged by the B firm gives rise to a positive strategic effect on G profit. If in contrast the B firm increases performance, the lower degree of product differentiation stiffens price competition leading to a negative strategic effect on B profit.

Intuitively one would expect the 'competitive effectiveness' of environmental performance to increase with the environmental margin, m, and to fall with the baseline margin, n. This reflects changes in the relative importance of a cost vs. environmental advantage in competition. While this is true regarding the direct effect, this is modified by the strategic effect. As we have seen, the direct effect dominates as long as the degree of product differentiation, ζ, is sufficiently high. However if product differentiation is restricted, the strategic effect may give rise to the following possible 'perverse' effects.

First, the baseline margin may have a positive impact on competitive effectiveness for the G firm. While a greater baseline margin makes environmental performance unattractive as an instrument to generate demand for a given set of prices, it also strengthens the strategic effect. Here the B firm's willingness to raise price in response to greater product differentiation is enhanced to the extent that it is able to benefit from a high baseline margin. Given that price competition is intense for a low degree of product differentiation, the positive impact of a greater baseline margin on the strategic effect dominates its negative impact on the direct effect. Thus increasing performance becomes attractive for the G firm.

Second, the environmental margin may have a negative impact on competitive effectiveness for the B firm. Whereas a greater environmental margin makes environmental performance more attractive as an instrument to generate demand for a given set of prices, it also strengthens the strategic effect. Here, the G firm's willingness to raise price in response to greater product differentiation is enhanced to the extent that it benefits from a high environmental margin. Again, intense price competition for a low degree of product differentiation implies that the positive impact of a greater baseline margin on the strategic effect dominates its negative impact on the direct effect and performance cuts become attractive for the B firm.

Equilibrium in the Absence of Investment Cost

In the absence of quality investments we can sign the marginal effect of environmental performance on profit, $\partial \pi_G{}^*/\partial \theta_G$ and $\partial \pi_B{}^*/\partial \theta_B$, as

$$\text{sgn}\left(\partial\pi_G{}^*/\partial\theta_G\right)=\text{sgn}\,r(\theta_G,\theta_B)\quad\text{and}\quad\text{sgn}\left(\partial\pi_B{}^*/\partial\theta_B\right)=\text{sgn}\,s(\theta_G,\theta_B),$$

respectively. We can therefore focus on the expressions in (2.10a) and (2.10b) alone. Profit maximisation then implies

$$r\left(\theta_G{}^*,\theta_B{}^*\right)\begin{cases}>0\Rightarrow\theta_G{}^*=\bar\theta\\=0\Rightarrow\theta_G{}^*\in[\underline\theta,\bar\theta];\\<0\Rightarrow\theta_G{}^*=\underline\theta\end{cases}$$

$$s\left(\theta_G{}^*,\theta_B{}^*\right)\begin{cases}>0\Rightarrow\theta_B{}^*=\bar\theta\\=0\Rightarrow\theta_B{}^*\in[\underline\theta,\bar\theta].\\<0\Rightarrow\theta_B{}^*=\underline\theta\end{cases}$$

Note that inequality in condition (2.5) is satisfied if

$$m>-n/2\underline\theta,\qquad(2.5')$$

which is sufficient to guarantee a non-negative profit for both firms. The following can be shown:

Lemma 2.3. In the set-up without investment cost an interior equilibrium in which the firms choose $\theta_B{}^*$ and $\theta_G{}^*$ such that $\underline\theta<\theta_B{}^*\le\theta_G{}^*<\bar\theta$ does not exist.

Proof: See Appendix A2.1.

This leaves three candidate equilibria.

- lower boundary equilibrium, where $\underline\theta=\theta_B{}^*\le\theta_G{}^*<\bar\theta$;
- maximum differentiation equilibrium, where $\underline\theta=\theta_B{}^*<\theta_G{}^*=\bar\theta$;
- upper boundary equilibrium, where $\underline\theta<\theta_B{}^*\le\theta_G{}^*=\bar\theta$.

In the following, we establish the three types of equilibria depending on the environmental margin, m. As a prerequisite assume that

$$(7/4)\underline\theta<\bar\theta<(13/4)\underline\theta.\qquad(2.13)$$

This assumption guarantees the existence of a unique equilibrium. Moreover define

$$m_l := n\left[\beta(\bar{\theta},\underline{\theta})/2\alpha(\bar{\theta},\underline{\theta})\right], \tag{2.14a}$$

$$m_h := n\left[2\alpha(\bar{\theta},\underline{\theta})/\bar{\theta}\,\underline{\theta}\,\beta(\bar{\theta},\underline{\theta})\right]. \tag{2.14b}$$

Given $n \geq 0$ it is easily verified from (2.12) that $m_l \leq m_h$. We can now establish the equilibrium in environmental performance.

Proposition 2.2. (i) A unique lower boundary equilibrium is realised if and only if $m < m_l$. Here, $\theta_G^* \in \left(\underline{\theta};(7/4)\underline{\theta}\right]$ if $m \in \left(-(n/2\underline{\theta});0\right]$ and $\theta_G^* \in \left((7/4)\underline{\theta};\bar{\theta}\right)$ if $m > 0$. (ii) A unique maximum differentiation equilibrium is realised if and only if $m \in [m_l, m_h]$. (iii) A unique upper boundary equilibrium is realised if and only if $m > m_h$. Here, $\theta_B^* \in \left(\underline{\theta};(4/7)\bar{\theta}\right)$. (iv) The comparative static properties are as given in Table 2.1.

Table 2.1 Comparative static properties of environmental performance

	$d\theta_G^*$	$d\theta_B^*$
dm	UB and MD: $= 0$ LB: > 0	UB: > 0 LB and MD: $= 0$
dn	UB and MD: $= 0$ LB: $\begin{array}{l} < 0 \Leftrightarrow m > 0 \\ \geq 0 \Leftrightarrow m \leq 0 \end{array}$	UB: < 0 LB and MD: $= 0$

Notes: UB: Upper bound, MD: Maximum differentiation, LB: Lower bound.

Proof: See Appendix A2.1.

Corollary P2.2. The lower (upper) boundary equilibrium implies B (G) market share and profit dominance.

Proof: See Appendix A2.1

We have, thus, established a set of three equilibria, which for a given baseline margin n and a given range of feasible performance levels $[\underline{\theta}, \bar{\theta}]$ depend on the environmental margin, m. Figure 2.1 gives an overview of the equilibria and the associated pattern of leadership.

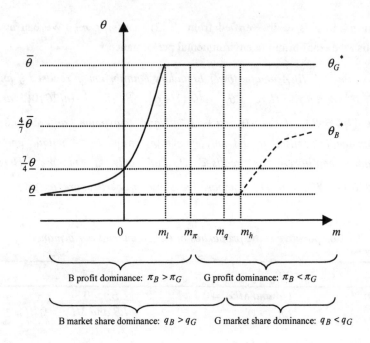

Figure 2.1 Equilibria and dominance

The pattern of dominance follows immediately from the arguments in the preceding section. Notice that the lower and upper boundary equilibria are fully associated with B and G dominance, respectively. The switch of leadership occurs under maximum differentiation, where, for a decreasing level of WTP, the B firm acquires leadership first in market share and then in profit.

It is easy to see how the regimes relate to the notion of environmental orientation of the market. In equilibrium, $\eta = \left(p_B^* - u \right) / p_B^*$. We can then establish the following proposition:

Proposition 2.3. The environmental orientation measured in equilibrium increases in the WTP for environmental performance, $\bar{v}$, and decreases in the baseline benefit u .

Proof: See Appendix A2.1.

It is then easy to see that the lower and upper boundary equilibria correspond to markets with a low and high environmental orientation, respectively. Generally firms have an incentive to maintain product differentiation in order to stifle price competition. This incentive is curbed if environmental orientation tends to extreme values. If environmental orientation is low, consumers are not much concerned about environmental performance and perceive the variants as good substitutes. Thus, price competition is intense even under product differentiation. In order to remain competitive on price, the G firm has to reduce variable cost by cutting its environmental performance.[22] If environmental orientation is high, consumers are willing to pay a substantial 'green' premium. Here, the B firm has an incentive to raise environmental performance in order to capture some of the surplus that consumers receive from green consumption, even if this is at the expense of stiffer competition. If the market configuration is indeterminate, the incentive to stifle competition dominates and maximum product differentiation arises.

The comparative static properties are summarised in Table 2.1. For $m > 0$ they are straightforward. Recall that in the absence of environmental investments, marginal revenue of environmental performance is governed by its competitive effectiveness. Since positive margins imply a degree of product differentiation $\zeta^* = \theta_H{}^*/\theta_L{}^* > 7/4$, the impact of the environmental margin, m (baseline margin, n) on competitive effectiveness is positive (negative) for both variants. Hence, a producer of an interior level of environmental performance raises it in response to an increase in m and lowers it in response to an increase in n .

For $m < 0$ we obtain a form of minimum differentiation at the low end of the environmental performance spectrum. As an increase in environmental performance is then associated with a negative contribution to profit, the G firm lowers performance beyond the benchmark level of $(7/4)\underline{\theta}$ even though this stiffens price competition. Now an increase in the baseline margin, n , induces the G firm to raise its environmental performance. As we have detailed in the discussion of Lemma 2.2, the B firm's strong propensity to raise price in response to a greater degree of product differentiation drives the G firm to increase performance despite the more severe cost disadvantage.

2.5 EQUILIBRIUM IN THE PRESENCE OF INVESTMENT COST

Consider now the choice of environmental performance when this is associated with investments in (capacity-independent) abatement technology or R&D. The first-order conditions of quality choice are now given by

$$R(\theta_G,\theta_B) := \frac{\partial \pi_G(\theta_G,\theta_B)}{\partial \theta_G} - F'(\theta_G) = \frac{q_G(\theta_G,\theta_B)r(\theta_G,\theta_B)}{(4\theta_G - \theta_B)^2} - F'(\theta_G)$$

$$= \frac{[2m\theta_G + n]r(\theta_G,\theta_B)}{(4\theta_G - \theta_B)^3} - F'(\theta_G) = 0, \qquad (2.15a)$$

$$T(\theta_G,\theta_B) := \frac{\partial \pi_B(\theta_G,\theta_B)}{\partial \theta_B} - F'(\theta_B) = \frac{q_B(\theta_G,\theta_B)s(\theta_G,\theta_B)}{(4\theta_G - \theta_B)^2 \theta_B} - F'(\theta_B)$$

$$= \frac{[m\theta_B + 2n]\theta_G \, s(\theta_G,\theta_B)}{(4\theta_G - \theta_B)^3 \theta_B^2} - F'(\theta_B) \leq 0, \qquad (2.15b),$$

where $r(\theta_G,\theta_B)$ and $s(\theta_G,\theta_B)$ are given by (2.10a) and (2.10b), respectively. Two types of equilibrium can arise. An interior equilibrium, where $\underline{\theta} < \theta_B{}^* < \theta_G{}^*$ and a boundary equilibrium, where $\underline{\theta} = \theta_B{}^* < \theta_G{}^*$. The following proposition characterises the equilibria.

Proposition 2.4

(a) A boundary equilibrium with $\underline{\theta} = \theta_B{}^* < \theta_G{}^*$ exists and is unique if the following conditions are satisfied. (i) Investment is sufficiently costly, $k > \bar{k}_1$; (ii) either the B firm dominates in profit, $m < m_\pi\left(\theta_G^*,\underline{\theta}\right)$, or G environmental performance does not decrease by too much in baseline benefit, $\frac{d\theta_G^*}{dn} \geq \varepsilon_1; \varepsilon_1 < 0$; (iii) the G firm makes a non-negative profit, i.e. (2.5′) holds; and (iv) the environmental margin is sufficiently low, $m \leq m_h{}'$.

(b) An interior equilibrium with $\underline{\theta} < \theta_B{}^* < \theta_G{}^*$ exists and is unique if (i) investment is sufficiently costly, $k > \bar{k}_2$; (ii) G environmental performance increases or does not decrease too much in baseline benefit, $\frac{d\theta_G^*}{dn} \geq \varepsilon_2; \varepsilon_2 < 0$; and (iii) the environmental margin is sufficiently high, $m > m_h{}'$.[23]

Proof: See Appendix A2.2.

Conditions (ai) and (aii) are technical and guarantee a concave profit function for the G firm and concavity of the reaction functions (in the interior regime), respectively. The conditions in (aii) and (bii), respectively, rule out leapfrogging on the part of the B firm. Finally, the conditions in (aiv) and (biii) govern whether a boundary or interior equilibrium is realised. Here, the boundary value is defined by

$$m_h' = \hat{m}_h(\underline{\theta}, m, n, k) = m_h[b_G(\underline{\theta}, m, n, k), \underline{\theta}, n],$$

where $b_G(\underline{\theta}, m, n, k)$ is the G firm's best response. It is then true that $s[b_G(\cdot), \underline{\theta}] = mb_G(\cdot)\underline{\theta}\beta[b_G(\cdot), \underline{\theta}] - 2n\alpha[b_G(\cdot), \underline{\theta}] \leq 0 \Leftrightarrow m < m_h'$. Hence the competitive effectiveness of environmental performance for the B firm is positive if and only if the environmental margin exceeds the boundary value m_h'. In this regard, m_h' differs from the boundary value m_h defined in (2.14b) for the case without investment only in that it takes into account the best-response $b_G(\underline{\theta}, m, n, k)$. Note that it therefore depends on all of the parameters including the environmental margin m itself.

The equilibrium structure can be illustrated with the help of figures 2.2a and 2.2b, which depict the two best-response functions $b_G(\theta_B, m)$ and $b_B(\theta_G, m)$ in (θ_B, θ_G)-space. Note that the B firm's best-response consists of the two segments $b_B(\theta_G, m) = \underline{\theta}$ for $\theta_G \leq \theta_G^0(m)$ and $b_B(\theta_G, m) > \underline{\theta}$ for $\theta_G > \theta_G^0(m)$ with a kink at $\theta_G = \theta_G^0(m)$.

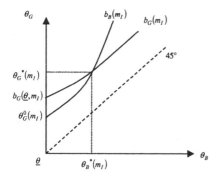

Figure 2.2a Interior equilibrium

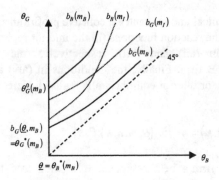

Figure 2.2b Boundary equilibrium

Figure 2.2a is drawn for an environmental margin m_I that satisfies $m_I > m_h'$. Here the G firm's best response $b_G(\underline{\theta}, m_I)$ exceeds a boundary level $\theta_G^0(m_I)$ that corresponds to the degree of product differentiation that is sufficient for the B firm to raise its performance above the minimum. Concavity of the reaction function is then sufficient for an interior equilibrium.[24] The G firm's best-response shifts upwards with the environmental margin, m. Similarly, the B firm's best response and with it the boundary level $\theta_G^0(m)$ shift downward in m. This implies the existence of a critical level of m_h', for which product differentiation is just sufficient for the B firm to be willing to raise quality above the minimum.

Figure 2.2b represents a boundary equilibrium arising for an insufficient environmental margin $m_B < m_h'$. Here, at the boundary the G firm's best response $b_G(\underline{\theta}, m_B)$ falls short of the level $\theta_G^0(m_B)$ necessary for the B firm to raise performance above the minimum. As concavity of the reaction functions implies that they are sloped away from each other, an interior equilibrium does not exist and the equilibrium is given by the pair $\{b_G(\underline{\theta}, m_B), \underline{\theta}\}$.

We now turn to some comparative static results. Here we make use of the boundary values between B and G market share dominance, $m_q' = \hat{m}_q(\underline{\theta}, m, n, k)$, and the boundary and interior equilibrium m_h' as defined above.

Corollary P2.4. In the presence of quality investment the comparative static properties of qualities and the degree of differentiation $\zeta := \theta_G^* / \theta_B^*$ are given as in Table 2.2.

Proof: See Appendix A2.

Table 2.2: Comparative static properties of equilibrium with investment cost

	$d\theta_G^*$	$d\theta_B^*$	$d\zeta$
dm	I: > 0 B: > 0	I: > 0 B: $= 0$	I: < 0 if $\frac{\partial b_B}{\partial \theta_G} \to \frac{b_B}{\theta_G}$ • B: > 0
dn	I: ambiguous > 0 if $n = 0$ B: > 0 if $m \in \lfloor m_q', m_h' \rfloor$ or $\beta \leq 0$	I: ambiguous < 0 if $n = 0$ B: $= 0$	I: > 0 B: > 0 if $m \in \lfloor m_q', m_h' \rfloor$ or $\beta \leq 0$
dk	I: < 0 B: < 0	I: < 0 B: $= 0$	I: < 0 if $m \to (m_h')^+$ B: < 0

Notes:

I: interior equilibrium, B: boundary equilibrium.

• $\frac{\partial b_B}{\partial \theta_G} \to \frac{b_B}{\theta_G}$ is implied by $m \to (m_h')^+$ and $k \to \bar{k}_2^+$, where $\bar{k}_2$ is defined in (A2.18). See the proof to the Corollary in the Appendix.

Consider the boundary equilibrium first. As for the case without investment cost (see Table 2.1), a higher environmental margin allows the G firm to enhance its environmental performance. Indeed recall from Lemma 2.2 that both value and competitive effectiveness of environmental performance increase in m. The effect of the baseline margin n is less straightforward. While n has a positive direct effect on the value of environmental performance, it has an indeterminate effect on the effectiveness. This effect is positive if and only if product differentiation is low such that $\beta < 0$. As discussed before, in this case the strategic effect of an increase in B price makes greater environmental differentiation attractive.

If $\beta > 0$, an increase in n reduces the competitive effectiveness of environmental performance and the overall impact becomes ambiguous. The positive effect triggered through the increase in demand dominates if the G firm holds the greater market share, i.e., if $m > m_q'$. However it cannot be excluded that for a low G market share the negative effect on competitive effectiveness dominates so that G quality falls in n. Obviously G quality falls in the investment rate k.

In an interior equilibrium both firms adjust environmental performance in reaction to exogenous changes. The implied changes in product differentiation give rise to a strategic effect on the marginal revenue from environmental effort. Environmental performance levels are strategic complements. Seeking to maintain product differentiation either firm will raise environmental performance in response to an increase in their rival's performance. As an increase of the environmental margin provides a firm with an incentive to raise environmental performance, this effect is then reinforced through the rival's response. Again, things are more complicated with respect to the baseline margin. Here, in an interior equilibrium an increase in n raises the marginal revenue of environmental performance for the G firm but lowers it for the B firm. But then the direct effect and the strategic effect offset each other and the overall effect is undetermined. If the baseline margin is small, i.e. if $n \to 0$, the own effect dominates the strategic effect. In such a case, θ_G increases and θ_B falls in n. The negative effect of the investment rate, k, on both levels of environmental performance is straightforward.

Finally it is interesting to study the effect of the parameters on the degree of product differentiation ζ. The effects are straightforward in a boundary regime. Ambiguity arises in an interior regime with respect to m and k, as they trigger changes in the same direction for both performance levels. A strong best-response of the B firm, i.e. $\frac{\partial b_B}{\partial \theta_G} \to \frac{b_B}{\theta_G}$, is sufficient to guarantee that product differentiation decreases with the environmental margin, m. In this case, the convexity of the cost function implies that quality adjustments by the G firm are smaller in absolute value than those undertaken by the B firm. If $\frac{\partial b_B}{\partial \theta_G} < \frac{b_B}{\theta_G}$, which is true for $k > \bar{k}_2$, product differentiation decreases in the investment rate k if, for $m \to (m_h')^+$, the B firm's performance approaches the baseline level, $\theta_B^* \to \underline{\theta}$. In this case, the B firm's marginal investment cost, $k(\theta_B^* - \underline{\theta})$ approaches zero so that changes in k trigger an almost zero reaction in B performance. As the G firm lowers performance, product differentiation falls. In contrast to their effect on environmental performance, the baseline margin n has an unambiguous positive impact on the degree of product differentiation.[25]

We conclude this section by establishing for further reference the following proposition regarding dominance in the setting with investment cost.

Proposition 2.5. (i) B dominance in terms of market share and, a fortiori, operating profit implies a boundary equilibrium. (ii) There exists a pair of unique boundary values $m_q' = \hat{m}_q(\theta, m, n, k)$ and $m_\pi' = \hat{m}_\pi(\theta, m, n, k)$, $m_\pi' < m_q'$. The B firm dominates with respect to market share if and only if $m < m_q'$, dominates with respect to market share but not operating profit if and only if $m \in [m_\pi', m_q')$, and dominates with respect to operating profit if and only if $m < m_\pi'$.

Proof: See Appendix A2.2.

It is hardly surprising that the structure of dominance with regard to market share and operating profit is the same as in the absence of investment cost. Note however that, in contrast to the case without investment cost, the boundary values m_q' and m_π' are now functions of all of the parameters including m. This is because environmental performance $\theta_G^* = b_G(\theta, m, n, k)$ is endogenously determined by the G firm's best-response, whereas in the absence of investment cost, $\theta_G^* = \bar{\theta}$ for the relevant levels of m. Finally, note that in the presence of investment costs there exists a further boundary value m_Π such that the G firm dominates with regard to total profit $\Pi = \pi - F(\theta)$ if and only if $m > m_\Pi$. Naturally, dominance with regard to operating profit is a necessary condition, implying $m_\Pi > m_\pi$.[26]

2.6 DOMINANCE IN MGPF'S MODEL

In this section we consider the approach by MGPF (2002), where consumer heterogeneity does not trace back to differences in income but stems from differences in environmental awareness.[27] We present this approach in some detail not only because we believe it is of similar validity to our own but also because it generates a range of strikingly different results. These concern positive issues, such as the question of dominance and emission levels, and the effects of environmental policies, such as unit-emission standards (section 4.3), investment subsidies (section 6.4) and taxes (section 7.5). It is thus important to understand where these differences arise from and how they can be traced through the market interaction of the firms.

Consider two products that are differentiated in their unit emission levels e_G and e_B, with $e_G \le e_B$. Gross surplus from unit consumption is given by $u - ve$ where all consumers receive a baseline benefit u but suffer a private disutility ve from the level of emission generated by their consumption.[28] Now v is a direct measure of environmental awareness, which is distributed across the population according to a uniform distribution on the support $[\underline{v}, \overline{v}]$ with density 1, implying $\overline{v} - \underline{v} = 1$.[29] The demand functions in a non-covered market are then given by

$$q_G^{MPF} = \frac{u - p_G}{e_G} - \frac{p_G - p_B}{e_B - e_G}, \qquad q_B^{MPF} = \frac{p_G - p_B}{e_B - e_G} - \underline{v}.$$

In contrast to our specification, the market is not covered at the upper end of the preference spectrum, where the consumers with the greatest concern for the environment abstain from purchasing the product. Obviously this, too, is in line with intuition. The difference fom our approach lies in consumers perceiving emissions as a 'bad' rather than perceiving abatement as a good.

Firms choose emission levels, with the sunk cost of production being a decreasing function $F(e)$, $F'(e) < 0$. This is no crucial difference, as we can easily transform the gross surplus function to $u - v[e(\theta)]$, where θ is the level of environmental effort. Under appropriate assumption regarding the functions $v(\cdot)$, $e(\cdot)$ and $F[\cdot]$ their model can be rewritten in terms of θ. The duopolists choose emission levels first and then prices. The equilibrium levels of demand are given by

$$q_G^{MPF} = \frac{e_B(2u - \underline{v}e_G)}{e_G(4e_B - e_G)}; \tag{2.16a}$$

$$q_B^{MPF} = \frac{u - 2\underline{v}e_B}{4e_B - e_G}. \tag{2.16b}$$

The corresponding levels of operating profit are

$$\pi_G^{MPF} = \frac{(e_B - e_G)e_B(2u - \underline{v}e_G)^2}{(4e_B - e_G)^2 e_G}\; ; \qquad (2.17a)$$

$$\pi_B^{MPF} = \frac{(e_B - e_G)(u - \underline{v}e_B)^2}{(4e_B - e_G)^2}\; . \qquad (2.17b)$$

It is easy to check that the green firm always dominates in market share and profit. This strong result with regard to dominance arises for two reasons. First, under MGPF's preferences the baseline benefit and the provision of environmental performance, i.e. lower emissions, are complements in generating utility. Consumers enjoy the baseline benefit of a product more the cleaner the product. In our model, the baseline benefit is a substitute for quality in the consumer's utility function. Here, consumers are indifferent between a dirty product with a high baseline benefit and a clean variant with a lower baseline benefit. This is reflected in the environmental orientation of the market, η. In our model, $\eta = (p_B - u)/p_B$ is decreasing in the baseline benefit, u. This is because for a greater baseline benefit, the market becomes relatively more price elastic. A consequence of this is that depending on the degree of quality orientation, there is scope for both high and low quality dominance. In contrast to this, the environmental orientation for MGPF's model is given by $\eta^{MPF} = \left(u - p_G^{MPF}\right)/p_G^{MPF}$ which is increasing in baseline benefit. It is thus obvious, that a greater baseline benefit always enhances the clean firm's quality advantage and contributes to its dominance. Second, the environmental concern on the part of consumers $\underline{v}$ has a stronger negative impact on the equilibrium price and output of the dirty variant.[30]

At this point we do not wish to reconcile MGPF's and our preference specifications. We do believe that both specifications have some intuitive appeal and the matter is essentially an empirical one. MGPF's specification appears to be more relevant when consumer heterogeneity with regard to their concern about the environment is more pronounced than consumer heterogeneity with regard to income, whereas our specification has the greater appeal in the opposite case. In the light of anecdotal empirical evidence there is however an issue as to whether the strong form of the clean firm's dominance with regard to market share is a likely case. With notable exceptions clean products hold just a minor market share due to consumers' limited willingness to pay for environmentally related product improvement. Finally, let us stress again the important distinction between the two models with regard to dominance. As will become clearer in subsequent chapters, this is the case because the effects of environmental policy instruments on emission levels and on welfare are strongly correlated with the presence of high or low quality dominance in the market.

2.7 CONCLUSIONS

In this chapter, we have interpreted the model of vertical differentiated duopoly in the environmental economics context. We believe that our framework captures a number of features of an environmentally differentiated industry more appropriately than the previous literature. First, together with some of the literature we explain a non-covered market at the lower end by referring consistently to consumers' lack of income rather than concern for the environment. Second, and in contrast to all previous work, our model allows for dominance by either the clean or the dirty firm. Dominance is explained by the interplay between a cost advantage and a quality advantage. A cost advantage held by the dirty firm then translates into dominance if it is played out in a market with a low environmental orientation, i.e. a market in which the price elasticity of demand outweighs the environmental elasticity.

These findings are important in several respects. First, they give a formal underpinning to environmentally related business strategies. These are formed as part of a trade-off between pursuing leadership on quality or cost and easing competition by way of product differentiation. If the environmental orientation in a market is weak, then even the clean firm has a disincentive to raise its environmental performance as the ensuing cost disadvantage would be heavily punished in this regime of strong price competition. In markets with high environmental orientation the dirty firm is forced to raise its environmental performance even at the expense of product differentiation and its cost advantage in order to preserve demand from consumers who are environmentally aware throughout. For intermediate environmental orientation the incentive to maximise product differentiation dominates.

Second, the scope for dominance on the part of the dirty firm has important implications for the structure of emissions at firm and industry level as well as for environmental policies, as will be discussed in chapters 3 to 7. As we will see the impact on industry surplus and industry emissions of environmental product standards, green subsidies and environmental taxation will depend critically on the environmental orientation and the associated configuration of the market. Indeed, a number of policies lead to opposite effects for markets with high and low environmental orientation.

Third, the issue of dominance has implications for advanced analyses. For instance, it determines the evolution or otherwise of environmental product innovation, the scope for collusion as well as the strategic use of environmental policies in trade. We will raise these more advanced issues in greater detail in chapter 9.

The model is open to a range of obvious extensions. Wauthy (1996) has demonstrated that there is a close inter-linkage between the distribution of preferences, the degree of product differentiation, and the degree of market coverage. The more widespread the distribution of willingness to pay for quality, the more likely is a setting in which the market is non-covered under a relatively lower degree of product differentiation. Kuhn (2000b) has studied the relationship between preferences, product differentiation, market coverage and dominance in an extension to the model presented in this chapter. We defer further discussion to section 9.3. In many situations firms choose qualities/environmental performance sequentially rather than simultaneously (Aoki and Prusa 1996, Lehmann-Grube 1997), an issue we consider in section 9.4. Finally, while we would expect our results to carry over to the case of Cournot competition, there is scope for confirming this.

NOTES

1. For reasons of variety we will use these expressions as synonyms.
2. See the evidence reported in section 1.5.
3. The idea extends straightforwardly to the case of positive but quality-independent marginal cost.
4. The markets for cars, consumer electronics, furniture, food or clothing are examples of markets in which the producers of the highest quality do not usually hold the greatest market share.
5. The introduction of a baseline benefit is not new. It is sometimes used to justify a covered market setting, where the baseline benefit is assumed to be so large that all consumers purchase the product (e.g. Cremer and Thisse 1994a, 1994b, 1999). However in a covered market the baseline benefit does not have any impact on firms' behaviour, market share, profit or welfare.
6. Other self-standing quality attributes are product safety, a car's or microprocessor's speed, the packaging, etc.
7. Kuhn (2000a) examines in greater detail some of the industrial economics issues.
8. A different approach is taken by Constantatos and Sartzetakis (1995) and Myles and Uyduranoglu (2002). In these models quality and environmental friendliness are negatively related. Examples include luxury products manufactured from parts of endangered species, furniture made from tropical timber, or products for which there is a technical trade-off

between product pollution and some quality attribute (e.g. the power and fuel consumption of automobile engines). Consumers are heterogeneous with respect to income. See also section 9.2.

9. Cremer and Thisse (1999) and Amacher et al. (2004) study covered market solutions where all consumers buy the product. With marginal cost being quadratic in quality/environmental performance the green and dirty firms attain the same market share and profit in equilibrium. Amacher et al. (2004) allow firms to differ in an environmental quality independent part of marginal cost depending on previous investment. Market shares may then shift accordingly but in a way unrelated to the environmental performance of the firms.

10. We discuss this further in section 5.1.

11. Strictly speaking, the consumer has preferences over bundles of 'goods', which are composed of quality and the numeraire/income. Preferences are then described by the MRS between quality and income. When there are two variants in the differentiated market, the consumption decision is over three bundles: one containing one unit of the high quality variant, one containing one unit of the low quality variant, and one containing neither. A consumer who buys the high quality variant then prefers a bundle composed of a relatively large share of quality and small share of income, and so on. Consumer heterogeneity implies the purchase of different bundles, which translates into a positive demand for both variants. In a non-covered market some consumers also choose the third bundle consisting of income alone.

12. A formal derivation of the relationship between the income distribution and the distribution of v is given in the derivation of (2.1) in Appendix A2.1.

13. Examples are agricultural products where the content of pesticides affects physical quality and the environmental impact of a product. High quality handcrafted products may be another case at hand as they are produced in a labour-intensive fashion as opposed to manufactured variants produced in an energy-intensive way.

14. See Appendix A2.1 for a formal derivation of (2.1).

15. Since $\underline{v} - c < 0$ this consumer would not prefer any higher environmental performance either.

16. We provide some comments on the covered market case in section 9.3.

17. The derivation of a consumer's net surplus $v\theta + u - p(\theta)$ for the case in which the distribution of WTP $[\underline{v}, \overline{v}]$ is related to the distribution of income $[\underline{Y}, \overline{Y}]$ is given in the Appendix A2 (Derivation of (2.1)).

18. In a more general context of quality the baseline margin may of course be negative. Kuhn (2000a) includes this case.

19. Note that for $c = c_0 = u = 0$, such that $m = \overline{v}$ and $n = 0$, equilibrium profits correspond to those in the standard formulation by Choi and Shin (1992).

20. It is readily verified that $\operatorname{sgn} m_q(\cdot)|_{c=0} = \operatorname{sgn} m_\pi(\cdot)|_{c=0} = \operatorname{sgn} n$. Furthermore for $c = 0$ partial market coverage requires $n < 0$. But this would imply clear dominance on the part of the G firm.

21. In a more general model of quality differentiation these business strategies can be interpreted as aiming at dominating a mass market (the low quality provider) or at establishing a value market (the low quality firm).

22. Note the analogy to the Dorfman–Steiner rule (Dorfman and Steiner 1954) according to which the R&D (in quality) to sales ratio equals the ratio of the quality and price elasticity of market demand. The lower this ratio, the less attractive is quality in shifting demand. Our model generalises this rule by taking into additional account the incentive to differentiate products.

23. The boundaries $\bar{k}_1$ and $\bar{k}_2$ are defined in (A2.14) and (A2.18), respectively, in Appendix A2.2.

24. If firms are not assigned a performance level a priori, the best-response function of each firm is composed of a low and high segment, with a discontinuity between them (see e.g. Aoki and Prusa 1996, Lutz 1997). Since the associated equilibria are symmetric and since we do not consider the issue of policy induced leapfrogging, we only focus on one of the segments.

25. Notice the difference to those models in which $n \equiv 0$ and investment cost $G(\theta) = \theta^\gamma$ is a homogenous function (e.g. Motta 1993, MGPF 2002). It is easily checked that in these models the degree of product differentiation $\zeta(\gamma)$ is a decreasing function of the degree of homogeneity, γ, alone. In our model, this is different for two reasons. First, and this is trivial, the investment cost function $F(\theta) = \frac{k}{2}(\theta - \underline{\theta})^2$ is obviously not homogeneous. Second and more importantly, a baseline margin $n > 0$ destroys the symmetry. As we have seen, the degree of product differentiation then becomes a function of the various exogenous parameters. While this renders the analysis perhaps more tedious and less elegant, we would maintain that it is rather unlikely that product differentiation is solely determined by the properties of the investment cost.

26. As a matter of note, $m_\Pi > m_h{}'$ can be shown. Hence, G dominance with regard to total profit implies an interior equilibrium.

27. Crampes and Ibanez (1996) were the first to introduce this preference specification. We concentrate our discussion on MGPF (2002) as the issues addressed in their model are closer to ours.

28. For the sake of consistency we have adapted the notation to the one used in this work.

29. For the sake of consistency we have slightly modified MGPF (2002). They assume a support of the distribution $[0, \bar{v}]$, implying $\underline{v} = 0$ and density $1/\bar{v}$.

30. Since MGPF (2002) assume $\underline{v} = 0$, this second effect does not contribute towards dominance. It is beyond the scope of this work to explore the possibility of low quality dominance in MGPF's model in the presence of a quality dependent marginal cost. Note that even in the presence of a quality-dependent marginal cost the baseline benefit would still work in favour of the high quality firm.

3. Emissions, market structure and dominance

3.1 INTRODUCTION

In this chapter we develop the environmental properties of the model of vertically differentiated duopoly. We take into particular account the likely presence of low quality leadership. We also highlight the differences between our set-up and that of Moraga-González and Padrón-Fumero (MGPF) (2002). MGPF (1997, 2002) study aggregate emissions at product/firm level, which are determined by a variant's unit emissions and its quantity.[1] They find that despite its lower unit emissions, the environmentally friendly variant is always associated with higher aggregate emissions. This counter-intuitive result is driven by the green firm's market share dominance in their models. In contrast to this, we find that the dirty product gives rise to higher overall emissions in the case of low quality market share dominance and, indeed, even in some cases of high quality market share dominance. The inter-linkage between market structure and industry emissions strongly depends on the form of the emission and/or damage function at industry level as well as on the functional relationship between unit abatement and unit emissions. This poses a severe problem for policy analysis as the impact of some policies is highly sensitive to the shape of the unit emission or cost function. For example, Motta and Thisse (1993) show that a maximum standard on unit emissions always reduces industry emissions, whereas MGPF (2002) show for a different specification that the converse is true.

MGPF (1997, 2002) point out that the relationship between market structure and industry emission level is determined by two factors: the products' unit emissions and the degree of product differentiation, which by affecting the degree of price competition determines the level of product and industry demand. More specifically, as a greater degree of product differentiation is associated with higher prices and lower output for both variants, industry emissions unambiguously decrease in product differentiation. Hence, an increase in the clean (dirty) firm's abatement effort then tends to reduce (raise) industry emissions by way of the volume effect.

We show that things are somewhat more complicated when taking into additional account the presence of a baseline benefit. In this case, increased abatement by the dirty firm still tends to raise demand by reducing product differentiation. However there is now an offsetting effect, as some consumers with a low WTP for environmental performance may refrain from purchasing. Hence in contrast to MGPF (2002) as well as the standard versions of the model of vertical differentiation (e.g. Ronnen 1991), the low quality/dirty firm's output is not necessarily an increasing function of its own quality/environmental effort. Indeed if the environmental orientation of the market is sufficiently low, the dirty firm's output will fall in its environmental performance. As this product is associated with greater unit emissions, it is obvious that industry emissions can fall as the dirty firm's performance improves even if product differentiation is reduced. We identify a bound on the environmental margin (or the environmental orientation of the market) below which an increase in the dirty product's environmental performance unambiguously lowers industry emissions. This result is appealing in that it holds irrespective of any assumptions regarding the unit emissions or cost function. Only if environmental orientation is high, does an increase in the dirty product's performance raise industry output. In this case the overall effect is ambiguous and depends on the particular shape of the unit emission function. We can thus describe industry emissions under laissez-faire as a function of the environmental orientation of the market. The analysis in this chapter will provide a framework for the analysis of the environmental effects of unit emission standards in the next chapter, environmentally related investment subsidies in chapter 6, and environmental taxation in chapter 7.

The remainder of the chapter is organised as follows. The next section examines the impact of the determinants of market structure on emissions at product level, section 3.3 performs the same task at firm level, section 3.4 considers industry emissions and section 3.5 concludes. One proof is relegated to Appendix A3.

3.2 UNIT EMISSIONS OF PRODUCTS

We assume that unit emissions from a variant of the differentiated product decrease in the environmental performance θ according to a function

$$e(\theta); \quad e'(\theta) \leq 0.$$

This could be a linear function but we prefer a more general specification in order to capture the increasing ($e'' < 0$) or decreasing ($e'' > 0$) returns of environmental abatement effort. Consider then the levels of unit emissions, which for the green (G) and brown (B) variant are given by $e_G := e(\theta_G)$ and $e_B := e(\theta_B)$, respectively. Obviously the green variant is associated with a (relatively) low level of unit emissions $e_G \le e_B$. In the previous chapter, we reported the dependence of the levels of environmental effort θ_G and θ_B on the exogenous parameters; in Proposition 2.2, part (iv) (Table 2.1) for the set-up without investment cost; and in Corollary P2.4 (Table 2.2) for the set-up with investment cost. The implications for unit emissions are straightforward and we do not comment on them in any great detail. Note however that both θ_G and θ_B increase in m, and e_G and e_B fall by implication. Clearly if consumers are willing to pay more for environmental performance this raises both the value and the competitive effectiveness of environmental performance (see definition 2.1) and it pays firms to cut the unit emissions of their products. For an interior equilibrium in the presence of investment costs this effect is reinforced by strategic interaction, where quality levels are strategic complements.

The positive dependence of unit abatement on environmental awareness, as measured by $\underline{\nu}$, is not always given in the set-up chosen by MGPF (2002). From (2.17a) and (2.17b) we obtain

$$\frac{\partial \pi_G^{MPF}}{\partial e_G} = \frac{-q_G^{MPF}}{(4e_B - e_G)^2 e_G} \left(2u\alpha^{MPF} + \underline{\nu}e_G e_B \beta^{MPF} \right) < 0, \qquad (3.1a)$$

$$\frac{\partial \pi_B^{MPF}}{\partial e_B} = \frac{-q_B^{MPF}}{(4e_B - e_G)^2} \left(u\beta^{MPF} + 2\underline{\nu}\alpha^{MPF} \right) < 0, \qquad (3.1b)$$

with

$$\alpha^{MPF} = 4e_B^2 - 3e_B e_G + 2e_G^2 > 0;$$
$$\beta^{MPF} = 4e_B - 7e_G.$$

The terms in (3.1a) and (3.1b) correspond to the marginal revenue of abatement (a reduction in e) for the two firms, which in equilibrium equals the marginal investment cost. Here the first and second factors in (3.1a) and (3.1b) again correspond to the 'value' and 'competitive effectiveness' of abatement as defined in definition 2.1. Provided a sufficient degree of differentiation, such that $\beta^{MPF} \geq 0$, an increase in $\underline{v}$ increases the competitive effectiveness of abatement. The firms have an incentive to lower emissions in order to mitigate the discount for dirty products that is asked for by environmentally concerned consumers. However by reducing demand for both variants (see (2.16a) and (2.16b)) a greater degree of awareness $\underline{v}$ also lowers the value of abatement. Within a shrinking market both firms may be unable to generate sufficient economies of scale to offset the abatement or R&D costs and may therefore have to increase unit emissions.[2]

As one might expect the models also tend to differ in the effect of baseline benefit, u, on unit emissions. Recall from Proposition 2.2 (Table 2.1) that in the variable cost version of our model interior levels of environmental performance (either G or B) fall in u as long as the quality margin m is non-negative. A greater baseline benefit corresponds to a lower environmental orientation of the market, which in turn implies that environmental performance is less attractive as an instrument to attract consumers and is therefore reduced. If investment costs matter, the negative effect of u on the competitive effectiveness just described is however offset by a positive effect on the value of environmental performance. The overall effect is then ambiguous. While for the dirty variant unit emissions still tend to rise with baseline benefit, they may fall for the clean variant. Assuming again $\beta^{MPF} \geq 0$, it follows from (3.1a) and (3.1b) for the MGPF set-up that unit emissions of each variant unambiguously fall with the level of baseline benefit. We have argued above that in their model a greater baseline benefit enhances the environmental orientation of the market. Thus as environmental performance becomes more important as a tool in attracting demand, firms reduce unit emissions.

3.3 AGGREGATE PRODUCT (FIRM) EMISSIONS

Aggregate emissions from the clean (G) and dirty (B) variants are given by

$$E_i = e_i q_i; \quad i = G, B.$$

The aggregate emissions from each variant are determined by its unit emissions and the quantity produced or consumed. Note that this aggregation is inappropriate if consumers use durable consumption goods, such as cars or electrical appliances, and differ in their pattern of use. In order to maintain tractable solutions we follow the literature here in assuming that consumers do not vary in their consumption patterns.[3] Given our assumption of unit demand, e_i then captures the emissions per product and consumer. As the brown variant is always associated with greater unit emissions, it follows immediately that brown dominance in market share is sufficient to guarantee $E_B > E_G$.

This contrasts with MGPF's finding that the green variant always gives rise to greater aggregate emissions.[4] In their model, market share dominance by the green variant is so pronounced that the volume effect outweighs the lower unit emissions. To see this more clearly, we can compare the emission ratio E_G/E_B both for our model and for MGPF (2002). Using the equilibrium demand levels for our model

$$q_G^* = \frac{2m\theta_G + n}{4\theta_G - \theta_B}, \qquad q_B^* = \frac{(m\theta_B + 2n)\theta_G}{(4\theta_G - \theta_B)\theta_B},$$

we obtain

$$E_G = \frac{e_G(2m\theta_G + n)}{4\theta_G - \theta_B}, \qquad E_B = \frac{e_B(m\theta_B + 2n)\theta_G}{(4\theta_G - \theta_B)\theta_B},$$

from which we can write the ratio

$$\frac{E_G}{E_B} = \frac{e_G}{e_B}\frac{q_G^*}{q_B^*} = \frac{e_G}{e_B}\frac{[2m\theta_G + n]\theta_B}{[m\theta_B + 2n]\theta_G}.$$

Observing $\frac{de_i}{d\theta_i} = e'(\theta_i) < 0$, $i = G,B$ and from Table 2.2, $d\theta_B^*/du \leq 0$, it is easily checked that the ratio falls in baseline benefit if $d\theta_G^*/du \geq 0$ or small in absolute value. It is interesting however that even in the presence of strong dominance on the part of the G firm the clean variant may be associated with lower overall emissions. Letting $n = 0$ and $m > 0$, we obtain

$$\frac{E_G}{E_B}\bigg|_{n=0} = \frac{e_G}{e_B}\frac{2m\theta_G\theta_B}{m\theta_B\theta_G} = \frac{2e_G}{e_B}.$$

This ratio is greater than one if and only if $e_G > e_B/2$. Whether or not this is satisfied depends on the properties of the function $e(\theta)$ as well as on the equilibrium levels of environmental performance, θ_G and θ_B. An unambiguous statement cannot be made. Consider for example the function

$e(\theta) = \bar{e}/\theta$, where $\bar{e}$ is an exogenous measure of emission intensity. In this case $(E_G/E_B)_{n=0} = 2/\zeta$, with $\zeta = \theta_G/\theta_B$. Here the G variant is associated with greater total emissions if and only if the degree of product differentiation is sufficiently low. For the model without investment cost we obtain $\theta_G = \bar{\theta}$ and $\theta_B = (4/7)\bar{\theta}$, implying $\zeta = 7/4$, which satisfies $(E_G/E_B)_{n=0} > 1$. For models with an investment cost $G(\theta) = \theta^\gamma$; $\gamma > 1$ it can be shown that product differentiation $\zeta(\gamma)$ is a decreasing function of γ. It follows that the G variant is then associated with greater emissions if and only if the cost function is sufficiently convex, i.e. if and only if γ is sufficiently high. Lombardini-Riipinen (2002) and Bansal and Gangopadhyay (2003) specify $e(\theta) = \bar{e} - \theta$; $\bar{e} \geq \bar{\theta}$. For this case, too, it can be verified that the emission ratio $(E_G/E_B)_{n=0}$ falls in the degree of product differentiation. However clear-cut statements can no longer be made, not even for the case where $\zeta = 7/4$.

Using (2.16a) and (2.16b) to calculate the firm emission ratio for MGPF (2002) we obtain

$$\left(\frac{E_G}{E_B}\right)^{MPF} \geq \left(\frac{E_G}{E_B}\right)^{MPF}\Bigg|_{\underline{v}=0} = \frac{e_G}{e_B}\frac{q_G^{MPF}}{q_B^{MPF}} = \frac{e_G}{e_B}\frac{2u\frac{e_B}{e_G}}{u} = 2.$$

Hence, the clean firm emits at least twice as much as its dirty rival. Once more this clear-cut result arises from the preference specification which in MGPF's model implies G dominance of a stronger degree. In their model the degree of product differentiation as measured by the ratio $e_B/e_G > 1$ tends to enhance the G firm's dominance. Thus the ratio of market shares, for $\underline{v} = 0$ given by $q_G^{MPF}/q_B^{MPF} = 2e_B/e_G$, increases in the degree of differentiation. This effect cancels out with the ratio of unit emissions $e_G/e_B < 1$, leaving the ratio of aggregate emission to be determined by the G firm's dominant market share. In our model with $n = 0$, the ratio of market shares is independent of the degree of product differentiation $q_G^*/q_B^* = 2$. As the ratio of unit emissions is given by $e_G/e_B < 1$ the ratio of aggregate emissions remains undetermined.

3.4 INDUSTRY EMISSIONS

Aggregate emissions in the duopolistic industry are given by

$$E = E_G + E_B = e_G q_G + e_B q_B \qquad (3.2),$$

In the following, it is convenient to express the output of each variant as a function of the degree of product differentiation $\zeta = \theta_G / \theta_B$ and the level of unit abatement by the brown firm θ_B,

$$q_G{}^* = \frac{2m\zeta + \frac{n}{\theta_B}}{4\zeta - 1}, \qquad (3.3a)$$

$$q_B{}^* = \frac{\left[m + 2\frac{n}{\theta_B}\right]\zeta}{4\zeta - 1}. \qquad (3.3b)$$

We can then expand (3.2) to

$$E = \frac{[2e_G + e_B]m\zeta + [e_G + 2e_B\zeta]\frac{n}{\theta_B}}{4\zeta - 1}, \qquad (3.4)$$

with

$$\frac{\partial E}{\partial \zeta} = \frac{-[2e_G + e_B]\left[m + 2\frac{n}{\theta_B}\right]}{[4\zeta - 1]^2} < 0, \qquad (3.5a)$$

$$\frac{\partial E}{\partial \theta_B}\bigg|_{\zeta = \bar{\zeta}; e_B = \bar{e}} = \frac{-[e_G + 2e_B\zeta]n}{[4\zeta - 1]\theta_B{}^2}. \qquad (3.5b)$$

For given levels of unit emissions e_G and e_B, these derivatives give the impact on industry emissions of a change in the degree of product differentiation and the level of brown environmental performance, as channelled through changes in industry output. A greater degree of product differentiation tends to reduce emissions, as competition is stifled and each firm's output is reduced. For a given degree of product differentiation, an increase in the environmental effort of the dirty firm tends to reduce the firm's own output at the lower end since some consumers refrain from purchasing the product at a higher price.

We can then write the total effect of a change in the clean firm's abatement on industry emissions as

$$\frac{dE}{d\theta_G} = e'(\theta_G)q_G{}^*(\zeta,\theta_G) + \frac{1}{\theta_G}\frac{\partial E}{\partial \zeta} < 0, \qquad (3.6a)$$

where the sign follows immediately from $e'(\theta_G) < 0$ and (3.5a). An increase in G unit abatement lowers industry emissions both directly by reducing the clean variant's unit emissions (the first term) and indirectly by increasing product differentiation and reducing sales of both variants.

The total effect of a change in the B firm's unit abatement is given by

$$\frac{dE}{d\theta_B} = e'(\theta_B)q_L{}^*(\zeta,\theta_B) - \frac{\zeta}{\theta_B}\frac{\partial E}{\partial \zeta} + \frac{\partial E}{\partial \theta_B}\bigg|_{\zeta=\bar{\zeta};e_B=\bar{e}}. \qquad (3.6b)$$

where the sign is a priori undetermined.[5] Again the first term on the RHS gives the direct effect from reduced unit emissions, which is negative. The second and third term give the effect of a reduced degree of product differentiation and the direct effect of B abatement on the output structure, respectively. Inspection of (3.5a) and (3.5b) shows that the last two terms on the RHS of (3.6b), describing the output-related effect on emissions of an increase in θ_B, increase in the environmental margin, m. It can now be shown that the level of m governs the sign of (3.6b) in the following way. Define

$$m_E := m\left|\frac{dq_G{}^*}{d\theta_B} + \frac{dq_B{}^*}{d\theta_B}\right| = 0,$$

as the level of the environmental margin for which a change in θ_B leaves industry output constant. It is readily checked that $m \le m_E$ implies $\frac{dq_G{}^*}{d\theta_B} + \frac{dq_G{}^*}{d\theta_B} \le 0$ and $\frac{dq_G{}^*}{d\theta_B} \le \frac{dq_G{}^*}{d\theta_B}$. But then an increase in the dirty firm's environmental performance, θ_B, leads to a reduction in industry output and a shift in market share from the dirty to the green firm. Since $e_G \le e_B$ this implies that industry emissions fall irrespective of the direct reduction in unit emissions, $e'(\theta_B)$. Therefore

$$m \le m_E \Rightarrow dE/d\theta_B < 0 \ \forall \ e'(\theta_B) \le 0.$$

must be true. The following Lemma characterises m_E further.

Lemma 3.1. For the set-up without investment cost there exists a unique m_E, with $m_E > m_q$. (ii) For the set-up with investment cost there exist $\underline{k}$ and $\hat{k}$, where $0 < \underline{k} < \hat{k}$. Then if the investment rate satisfies $k < \underline{k}$ there exists a unique $m_E > m_h'$, and if it satisfies $k > \hat{k}$ there exists a unique $m_E \in [m_q, m_h']$.

Proof: See Appendix A3.

Remark: If the investment rate satisfies $k \in [\underline{k}, \hat{k}]$, there exist three values $\underline{m}_E$, $\tilde{m}_E$ and $\overline{m}_E$, where $m_q' < \underline{m}_E < \tilde{m}_E < m_h' < \overline{m}_E$. In this case, $dE/d\theta_B < 0$ if $m \leq \underline{m}_E$ or if $m \in [\tilde{m}_E, \overline{m}_E]$. For the sake of brevity and intuitive clarity, we omit this more complex case from further discussion, focusing on either low investment rates $k < \underline{k}$ or high investment rates $k > \hat{k}$.

We can therefore make some general statements about the relationship between industry emissions and market structure. As $m_q' < m_E$ the following must be true.

Corollary L3.1. B market share dominance is sufficient for $dE/d\theta_B < 0$.

Furthermore the boundary value falls into the upper bound/interior equilibrium, i.e. $m_E > m_h'$, if and only if the degree of product differentiation realised in equilibrium is sufficiently large, specifically if it satisfies $\zeta > 2.5$.[6] In the absence of investment cost, the relevant degree of product differentiation is determined by the technological spread $\overline{\theta}/\underline{\theta}$. In the presence of investment cost it depends on the investment rate k. If investment in upgrading the environmental performance is 'cheap', i.e. if k is low, this tends to allow a high equilibrium degree of product differentiation, allowing $m_E > m_h'$. If in contrast investment is very costly, this tends to constrain product differentiation resulting in $m_E < m_h'$. As competition is rather stiff to begin with, improvements in the dirty variant's performance tend to trigger increases in volume.

If $m > m_E$ the reduction in product differentiation implied by an increase in θ_B tends to expand output. In this case the tendency towards a price increase of the dirty variant due to higher marginal cost is more than offset by the increase in competition under a lesser degree of product differentiation. As one extreme example consider $n \to 0$. It is readily checked from (3.5a) and (3.5b) that[7]

$$\lim_{n \to 0}\left[-\frac{\zeta}{\theta_B}\frac{\partial E}{\partial \zeta} + \frac{\partial E}{\partial \theta_B}\bigg|_{\zeta=\bar\zeta\,:e_B=\bar e} \right] = -\frac{\zeta}{\theta_B}\lim_{n \to 0}\frac{\partial E}{\partial \zeta} > 0.$$

In this case the effect of an increase in the environmental performance of the dirty product on the output of both variants is positive so that emissions tend to increase (MGPF 1997, 2002). Note from (3.6b) that even so industry emissions increase only if the volume effect is strong enough to over-compensate the direct reduction in the dirty variant's unit emissions.

Reconsider the unit emission function, $e(\theta) = \bar e/\theta$. Employing this in (3.6b) together with (3.5a) and (3.5b) one can easily check that $dE/d\theta_B < 0$ for any level of the environmental and baseline margin. The same applies for the specification $e(\theta) = \theta^{-0.5}$ as chosen by Motta and Thisse (1993). For $e(\theta) = \bar e - \theta;\ \bar e \geq \bar\theta$, it can be checked that $\bar e < 2\theta_G$ is sufficient for $dE/d\theta_B < 0$. However if the baseline margin n is zero and $\bar e > 2\theta_G$, the volume effect is positive and dominates the direct effect so that $dE/d\theta_B > 0$. Hence, if even the G variant is relatively dirty, an increase in B environmental effort raises industry emissions. Obviously the greater the unit emissions from the G variant the stronger the effect on aggregate emissions for the increase in G output that is induced by stronger competition. The fundamental difference between the two specifications $e(\theta) = \bar e/\theta$ and $e(\theta) = \bar e - \theta$ lies in the different marginal effects of abatement on unit emissions. For $e(\theta) = \bar e/\theta$ the marginal impact of abatement is given by $e'(\theta) = -(\bar e/\theta^2)$. Here emission intensive products with high levels of $e(\theta)$ are also characterised by large marginal effects of abatement such that the direct effect of unit abatement dominates. For $e(\theta) = \bar e - \theta$ we have $e'(\theta) = -1$. In this case, high levels of G unit emissions, i.e. $\bar e > 2\theta_G$, imply that the volume effect dominates.

MGPF (1997, 2002) avoid the choice of a specific functional form for $e(\theta)$ by assuming that firms choose unit emissions directly. But even then the model remains sensitive to the assumption made on whether unit emissions, e, are bounded from above or not. MGPF (2002) assume no bound and consider a homogeneous investment cost function $F(e)$, $F'(e) < 0$. They find that industry emissions depend only on the degree of product differentiation and are thus an increasing function of B performance. MGPF (1997) assume an exogenous upper bound on unit emissions, such that $e < \bar{e}$, and use a non-homogeneous cost function $F(e) = \frac{k}{2}(\bar{e} - e)$. It is easily checked that for this case $dE/de_B > 0 \Leftrightarrow \bar{e} > 2e_G$. Thus a decrease in unit emissions from the dirty variant – or, in our interpretation, an increase in abatement – reduces industry emissions if unit emissions from the G variant are sufficiently low. This parallels the finding for a unit emission function $e(\theta) = \bar{e} - \theta$. Hence even if firms choose unit emissions the overall effect of B abatement on industry emissions is sensitive to the form of the investment cost function. These ambiguities are clearly unsatisfactory. However our analysis shows that the following more general conclusions can be drawn.

Proposition 3.1 (i) Industry emissions fall in G unit abatement. (ii) Industry emissions fall in B unit abatement if the environmental orientation is sufficiently low.

Proof: Immediate from (3.6a) and Lemma 3.1.

If the condition in Lemma 3.1 holds we know that industry emissions fall in unit abatement from either of the variants irrespective of the functional forms of $e(\theta)$ and $F(\theta)$. In particular this is always the case under B dominance in market share. If the G firm dominates in market share and dominance is sufficiently strong an increase in B unit abatement raises industry output. In this case the effects on unit emissions and volume offset each other and the overall effect depends on the specific assumptions about the relationship between unit abatement and unit emissions as well as on the cost function.

We have discussed the effects of unit abatement on industry emissions in such great detail as they crucially determine the outcome of the product-related environmental policies that are the topic of the subsequent chapters. They also play a role in determining the laissez-faire levels of industry emissions. Consider the comparative static effects on industry emissions of a change in the environmental margin m:

$$\frac{dE}{dm} = \overbrace{\frac{\partial E}{\partial m}}^{>0} + \overbrace{\frac{dE}{d\theta_G}}^{<0}\overbrace{\frac{d\theta_G^*}{dm}}^{\geq 0} + \frac{dE}{d\theta_B}\overbrace{\frac{d\theta_B^*}{dm}}^{\geq 0},$$

where $\partial E/\partial m > 0$ follows immediately from (3.4), where $dE/d\theta_G < 0$ and $dE/d\theta_B$ is given by (3.6a) and (3.6b), and where $d\theta_G^*/dm \geq 0$ and $d\theta_B^*/dm \geq 0$ follow from the proofs of Proposition 2.3, part (iv) and Corollary P2.4, respectively. Thus a greater environmental margin tends to

- lower industry emissions through cuts in unit emissions for both variants,
- raise industry emissions directly by raising each variant's output, and
- change emissions through changes in industry output triggered by changes in product differentiation.

Due to the interaction of a substantial number of effects no general statement can be made. The following examples describe some limiting situations.

(i) $\left|e(\theta_i)dq_i\right| << \left|e'(\theta_i)q_i d\theta_i\right|$, $i = G, B$ and $d\theta_G^*/dm > 0$ or $d\theta_B^*/dm > 0$.

For each variant, the direct impact of environmental performance on unit emissions is strong relative to the impact from changes in output. In the limit $\frac{dE}{dm} \approx e'(\theta_G)q_G^* \frac{d\theta_G^*}{dm} + e'(\theta_B)q_B^* \frac{d\theta_B^*}{dm} < 0$. A greater environmental margin reduces industry emissions if it significantly raises the environmental performance of at least one duopolist and if the resulting reduction in emissions from this variant is strong relative to the impact from changes in output or market share. This situation reflects industries with substantial scope for clean-up activities that has not been exploited due to a low environmental orientation. In this situation even a small increase in the environmental margin induces an improvement in firms' environmental performance yielding a significant reduction in industry emissions.

(ii) $\qquad\qquad\qquad d\theta_G^*/dm \to 0$ and $d\theta_B^*/dm \to 0$.

Here changes of the environmental margin do not lead to any significant change in the firms' environmental performance. In the limit $\frac{dE}{dm} = \frac{\partial E}{\partial m} > 0$. This reflects an industry in which there is little or no scope for technological improvement in environmental performance. This is the case when firms prefer to maximise product differentiation. Alternatively it could be due to a high investment rate k. A greater environmental margin only stimulates industry output then and industry emissions increase.

(iii) $e'(\theta_i) \rightarrow 0$ $i = B, G$, $d\zeta/dm \leq 0$ and $m >> n$

The direct impact of abatement on unit emissions is weak, product differentiation is reduced, and the baseline margin is low relative to the environmental margin. In this case $\text{sgn} \frac{dE}{dm} = \text{sgn}\left(\frac{\partial E}{\partial m} + \frac{\partial E}{\partial \zeta}\frac{d\zeta}{dm}\right) = 1$. A greater environmental margin raises unit abatement but in a way that reduces product differentiation. Generally this reflects a situation in which the G variant cannot be improved by much while there is an upgrading in the environmental performance of the dirty product. If the environmental margin is then large relative to the baseline margin, the upgrading of the dirty variant will boost industry output. This leads to greater industry emissions if the direct effect of reduced unit emissions is small, i.e. if the technological scope for emission reductions is limited.

Alternatively $e'(\theta_B) \rightarrow 0$ could describe a situation in which the dirty firm engages in persuasive advertising to promote a 'green image', where θ_B reflects the level of this activity. While it suits the firm to enhance demand and effectively reduce product differentiation, there is no effect of such activity on unit emissions. Thus the promotion of pseudo-green variants enhances competition and may, by stimulating industry output, have a negative impact on the environment.

3.5 CONCLUSIONS

This chapter has developed in detail the environmental impact of environmental product differentiation at product level, firm level (aggregate product level), and at industry level.

Under the dominance of the dirty firm with respect to market share, the dirty product is naturally associated with a greater level of overall emissions. Under the dominance of the clean variant, greater pollution from the dirty variant can still arise if the difference between unit emissions is sufficiently strong. If this is not the case, the clean product is associated with greater aggregate emissions. In this regard our model allows for a richer and, in a sense, more natural set of results than the received literature, which allows for dominance by the clean firm only.

We also consider the impact of changes in a variant's unit abatement on industry emissions. This is directly determined by the change of unit emissions and indirectly by an adjustment in the variant's output to changes in the degree of competition. Additionally, in our model, output adjusts to abatement-induced changes in marginal cost. An increase in unit abatement by the clean firm unambiguously reduces industry emissions. This is because it lowers unit emissions and because it stifles competition and curtails industry output. However in contrast to the previous literature, which finds that an increase in the brown firm's unit abatement always enhances industry emissions by stimulating output, our model allows for a richer set of possibilities. In particular we have shown that if environmental orientation is low an increase in the dirty firm's environmental effort lowers both its own output and unit emissions to such an extent that industry emissions fall. This is always the case in the presence of B dominance, which is, thus, a good predictor for this effect. If environmental orientation is high, a clear-cut statement about the impact of brown environmental effort on industry emissions can no longer be made. In this case industry emissions may increase with the dirty firm's environmental effort.

While it remains essentially an empirical question whether the clean or dirty variant dominates in environmentally differentiated duopoly, the following crude predictions can be made from the analysis of dominance in the previous chapter. We have seen that dominance on the part of the dirty firm can arise only if clean production is associated with a greater marginal cost. This is likely to be the case in all instances in which green production is associated either with a substantially greater input of labour or if it involves the use of costly clean materials or intermediate inputs. Empirical studies suggest that the WTP for environmental friendliness is relatively low (see section 1.5). Hence if the dirty firm holds a significant advantage in marginal cost, we would expect it to be dominant, at the least in terms of market share. In this case, a policy which forces the dirty firm to enhance its environmental effort helps to curb industry emissions. In contrast to this, the presence of quality investment does not bear on the duopolists' market shares and, by implication, the emission structure. Hence if a product's unit emissions are determined by product design but not by variable inputs, the clean firm can evolve as the market share leader. One prominent example is the market for domestic refrigerators, where the production of the CFC-free fridge was a matter of product design but not input choice. Here the traditional dirty variants have been entirely replaced, indicating an extreme case of dominance by the clean product.

Before continuing with an analysis of environmental policies in the subsequent chapters, let us sound the following note of caution. Our analysis has been limited to a partial equilibrium, and therefore fails to take into account the effects on emissions of outside consumption. In a different context and with a different model Kuhn (1999) shows under which conditions outside effects offset the direct impact of an industry-specific environmental policy. In the context of the present model, both a change in market coverage and a change in the variants' prices give rise to a change in aggregate disposable income for outside purchases. If the share of the differentiated good's emissions in economy-wide emissions is large relative to the average share of income spent on the differentiated good, then we should expect the change in emissions from the differentiated good to be dominant and a partial analysis is justified. However one can envisage a setting in which the share of the differentiated industry's emissions is small relative to the share of income spent in this industry. In this case the impact on economy-wide emissions from a variation in outside consumption may over-compensate for the change in industry emissions. In ignoring the effects of outside consumption the following policy analysis is based on the assumption that the differentiated good is dominant in its 'environmental effects'. This is a reasonable assumption, as a rational policy maker should consider the introduction of environmental policies only for such product groups as have a significant impact on the environment. It should be borne in mind however that there is the scope for countervailing outside effects of environmental policies.

NOTES

1. See also Motta and Thisse (1993), Lombardini-Riipinen (2002), Bansal and Gangopadhyay (2003) and Amacher et al. (2004).
2. MGPF (2002) find an unambiguously positive effect of environmental awareness on unit emissions (their Proposition 4). They claim that this is due to a lower average willingness to pay. This is not entirely true as, for their distribution $[0, \bar{v}]$, prices can be shown to be independent of $\bar{v}$, the measure of awareness they use. Their findings result from the fact that demand for both products increases with the density of consumers, $1/\bar{v}$. Then a greater $\bar{v}$ implies lower levels of demand and, in turn, lower marginal revenue from abatement.
3. As an exception Myles and Uyduranoglu (2002) model the intensity of use explicitly.
4. This is evident from (3.5) in MGPF (2002).
5. For the unit emission function $e(\theta) = \bar{e}/\theta$ it can be shown that $dE/d\theta_B < 0$ holds unambiguously. However this result clearly lacks generality.
6. See Proof of Lemma 3.1 in Appendix A3.
7. It can be shown that $n = 0 \Leftrightarrow \underline{k} = \hat{k} = 0$. In this case $m_E = m_h{}' = 0$ is satisfied for any k.

4. Environmental product standards

4.1 INTRODUCTION

In many industries and for many product groups environmental standards are applied as the main policy tool. In principle we can distinguish performance standards and design standards (e.g. Besanko 1987, Sterner 2003: chapter 6).[1] The former usually impose a ceiling on total emissions from a firm or industry, whereas the latter regulate emissions per unit of output or input or prescribe a certain 'clean' technology. In the following we consider a design standard that imposes a ceiling on the unit emissions of a product. Intuitively one would expect a performance standard to be superior, as it leaves the firm more scope to achieve the intended emission level at minimum cost by adjusting unit emissions and output.[2] However when pollution arises mainly from consumption, a performance standard becomes unfeasible, because aggregate emissions depend on individual consumers' intensity of use. Hence the attainment of a certain target with respect to total emissions is beyond the direct control of the firm. Likewise, it is prohibitively costly to monitor consumption behaviour. This leaves a design standard as the only viable alternative.[3]

Prominent examples of environmental product (design) standards include the following:

- Vehicle emission standards: Emissions from individual vehicles are notoriously difficult to regulate. Whereas one approach is to tax fuel or the vehicle according to its unit emissions, many governments rely on the imposition of emission standards.[4] An example is the Californian Air Resources Board (CARB) standards that impose maximum emission requirements on a specified (and increasing) share of newly produced vehicles. The mandatory installation of catalytic converters in the US and in European countries and the banning of certain dirty engine classes constitute examples where a minimum performance technology is directly prescribed. Finally, the Corporate Average Fuel Efficiency (CAFE) standard that has been used in the US since 1975 imposes a minimum level of fuel efficiency across a producer's fleet.

- Energy efficiency standards: The US National Appliance Energy Conservation Act of 1987 imposes minimum energy efficiency standards on air-conditioners and gas water heaters (e.g. Newell et al. 1999).

The CAFE and energy efficiency standards do not regulate unit emissions directly but rather impose a minimum requirement on technology. However, use of appropriate conversion scales would allow a translation into unit emission requirements at least in principle. Incidentally, the energy/fuel efficiency examples provide one illustration of the private benefit from green consumption. In this case the benefit relates to a lower usage cost of running the product.

The two examples given relate to regulation of the environmental features of the product itself. Other examples include standards on packaging (e.g. a ban on metal containers for drinks) or the chemical composition of products (e.g. the ban on CFCs in sprays or refrigerators). In many cases, however, design standards also relate to the process of production.

- Best available technology regulation: The European Union council directive 96/61/EC (30 October 1996) regulates the licensing of plants for most production industries. Here it is mandated that licences are granted only if the plant conforms to a best available technology requirement. These requirements are laid out in detail in industry-specific documentation (e.g. European Commission (2003a, 2003b) on the best available technology for the textiles and the intensive livestock industries). As they specify the production technology, they can, in essence, be interpreted as a design standard implying a maximum emission level per unit output.

The first part of our analysis focuses on the effects of an environmental product standard on consumer surplus, profits and industry surplus. In this regard, a (maximum) unit emission standard can be interpreted as a minimum quality standard.[5] We should stress that our results therefore generalise to any industry in which quality matters. The literature has identified two quality distortions in the presence of market power that may justify quality regulation.[6]

(i) A firm that is unable to discriminate between consumers can extract the surplus only of the marginal consumer with the lowest willingness to pay for quality. As there is no incentive then to provide quality in excess of the marginal consumer's valuation, quality is under-provided relative to the taste of the average consumer (e.g. Spence 1975 and Sheshinski 1976).[7]

(ii) In a vertically differentiated oligopoly, product differentiation gives rise to an additional distortion of quality. Here quality tends to be distorted upwards at the high quality end and downwards at the low quality end in order to stifle competition (Ronnen 1991).

Our findings qualify the result by Ronnen (1991) that, at the margin, the standard raises consumer surplus and industry surplus. We show that under dominance of the dirty (low quality) firm a standard reduces aggregate consumer surplus if the willingness to pay is sufficiently small. This is mainly due to the low emphasis placed by consumers on environmental performance (quality) as opposed to price. Even if the standard reduces product differentiation and enhances price competition, absolute prices increase if environmental performance raises marginal cost to a sufficient degree. Then if consumers are relatively price sensitive, their surplus diminishes. Crampes and Hollander (1995) find a similar potential for a minimum quality standard to lower consumer surplus in a covered market. In their model, too, it is the increase in variable cost and absolute price which may curtail consumer surplus. However, this occurs only if the high quality producer reacts to the standard by raising her quality and thereby mitigates the increase in price competition to some extent. In our model, aggregate consumer surplus may be reduced even in the absence of any reaction by the clean (high quality) producer. In contrast to Ronnen (1991) and Crampes and Hollander (1995) the standard always harms both firms. This is because under dominance of the dirty (low quality) firm, this firm optimally chooses the lowest feasible performance (quality). Boom (1995) arrives at a similar result with regard to profits. Her analysis focuses on a covered market or a corner configuration, where in both configurations the low quality firm chooses the lowest feasible quality. We also find that a standard reduces industry surplus if willingness to pay for environmental performance falls below a certain boundary, and always if the dirty firm dominates in profit. While Crampes and Hollander (1995) and Scarpa (1998) find a negative welfare effect for a standard within a covered market and a triopoly, respectively, their results are not driven by the structure of preferences.

In the second part of this chapter we study the conditions under which a unit emission standard helps to curb industry emissions. In so doing we follow a number of previous studies. Arora and Gangopadhyay (1995) is limited in addressing the effect of the standard on unit emissions alone. The findings by Motta and Thisse (1993), Moraga-González and Padrón-Fumero (MGPF) (1997, 2002), and Lombardini-Riipinen (2002) are somewhat inconclusive. Motta and Thisse (1993) and Lombardini-Riipinen (2002) show that a standard unambiguously reduces industry emissions; in MGPF (1997) the impact of the standard curbs emissions if and only if the investment cost in environmental performance is not too convex; whereas in MGPF (2002) the standard always raises industry emissions. The latter result is highly counterintuitive. As it turns out, all of these results are highly sensitive to the assumptions about the relationship between environmental effort and unit emissions (Motta and Thisse 1993, Lombardini-Riipinen 2002) or investment cost (MGPF 1997, 2002), a problem already identified in the last chapter.

In contrast to this literature our concern lies more with the role of preferences (and marginal cost) on the effects of the standard. In particular we show that if willingness to pay for quality is sufficiently low the standard unambiguously reduces industry emissions. The mechanism is to an extent the flip side of the welfare effect. If willingness to pay for environmental performance is low, some consumers react to an increase in the dirty product's abatement effort by withdrawing from consumption. While the resulting drop in industry output tends to lower welfare it also helps to curb industry emissions. Notably we obtain this result irrespective of any assumptions about investment cost or the unit emission function. If willingness to pay for environmental performance is high, the impact of the standard on industry emissions becomes more ambiguous. Perverse effects of a unit emission standard become possible. The chapter concludes by noting that a trade-off between environmental policy goals and the maximisation of industry surplus exists for low levels and possibly high levels of the environmental margin. However for intermediate levels of the environmental margin the introduction of a standard unambiguously raises welfare by simultaneously enhancing industry surplus and curbing emissions.

The remainder of the chapter is organised as follows. The next section discusses the impact of a product standard on consumer surplus, profit and industry surplus. Section 4.3 discusses the environmental properties of the standard and section 4.4 comments on the potential trade-off between emission reductions and maximisation of industry surplus. The last section concludes. Proofs are relegated to Appendix A4 at the end of this work.

4.2 ENVIRONMENTAL PRODUCT STANDARD: EFFECTS ON INDUSTRY SURPLUS

In the following we consider a standard that imposes a ceiling on the unit emissions of a product. It is easy to see that a unit emission standard is nothing other than a minimum quality standard in our model of vertical differentiation. Given a product's unit emission $e(\theta)$, $e'(\theta) < 0$, an upper bound on product emissions $e(\theta) \le e_{max}$ implies a minimum abatement requirement, $\theta_{min} = e^{-1}(\theta_{min}) = e_{max}^{-1}$, where $e^{-1}(\theta)$ is the inverse unit emission function. We can therefore apply the common place analysis of a minimum quality standard (e.g. Ronnen 1991) to discuss the effects of the maximum emission standard on product and industry emissions.

Consider the following game. In stage one, the regulator commits to an environmental product standard ('standard' for short); in stage two, the firms simultaneously choose qualities subject to the regulatory constraint; and in stage three, they choose prices. The following analysis is devoted to the welfare implications of a standard policy. We consider a marginal standard, which is set at the laissez-faire level of the dirty firm's performance and is then raised by a small amount. In order to simplify, we initially confine our analysis to the setting without investment cost and then generalise this.

The Model without Investment

Environmental performance is chosen from an interval $\theta \in [\underline{\theta}, \overline{\theta}]$, where we assume $(7/4)\underline{\theta} < \overline{\theta} < (13/4)\underline{\theta}$ as in (2.13). First, consider the effect of the standard on the choice of environmental performance. We then move on to study the impact on consumer surplus and profits and finally on welfare. Assume that the standard is set such that $\theta_{min} = \theta_B^{*}$. Obviously, $d\theta_B^{*}/d\theta_{min} = 1$. The impact of the standard on G performance depends on the type of equilibrium. For the lower boundary equilibrium, where $\theta_G^{*} < \overline{\theta}$ we have to consider the reaction

$$\frac{d\theta_G^{*}}{d\theta_{min}}\bigg|_{\theta_G^{*} < \overline{\theta}} = \frac{db_G}{d\theta_B} = -\frac{r_B}{r_G} = \frac{2m(3\theta_G^{*} - 4\theta_{min}) - 7n}{-2m(8\theta_G^{*} - 3\theta_{min}) + 4n},$$

where the derivatives $r_i = \partial r/\partial \theta_i$; $i = G, B$ can be found from (2.10a). One can easily establish that

$$\frac{d\theta_G^{*}}{d\theta_{min}}\bigg|_{\theta_G^{*} < \overline{\theta}} > \frac{\theta_G^{*}}{\theta_{min}}.$$

As in Ronnen (1991) and Crampes and Hollander (1995) the G producer reacts to a standard by raising environmental performance. This is in order to alleviate tighter competition.[8] However, in contrast to above work, the response is over-proportionate, implying that product differentiation increases. Obviously $d\theta_G^*/d\theta_{min} = 0$ for the maximum differentiation and upper boundary equilibrium.[9]

Industry surplus is given by the non-weighted sum of consumer surplus S and profits $W = S + \pi_G + \pi_B$. Consumer surplus can be written as

$$S = \int_{v_0}^{v_1} (v\theta_B + u - p_B)dv + \int_{v_1}^{\bar{v}} (v\theta_G + u - p_G)dv$$

$$= q_B\left[\frac{(v_0 + v_1)\theta_B}{2} + u - p_B\right] + q_G\left[\frac{(v_1 + \bar{v})\theta_G}{2} + u - p_G\right], \quad (4.1)$$

which is the weighted sum of average surplus from each variant, with quantities used as weights.

Lemma 4.1. (i) The impact of the standard on consumer surplus is given by

$$\frac{dS}{d\theta_{min}} = q_B^* \psi_B + q_G^* \psi_G, \quad (4.2)$$

where

$$\psi_B := \frac{3(m\theta_{min} + 2n)\theta_{min}}{\left(4\theta_G^* - \theta_{min}\right)^2}\left(\frac{\theta_G^*}{\theta_{min}} - \frac{d\theta_G^*}{d\theta_{min}}\right) + \frac{m\theta_G^*\theta_{min} - 2n\left(\theta_G^* + \theta_{min}\right)}{2\theta_{min}\left(4\theta_G^* - \theta_{min}\right)} \quad (4.3a)$$

$$\psi_G := \frac{3(2m\theta_G^* + n)\theta_{min}}{\left(4\theta_G^* - \theta_{min}\right)^2}\left(\frac{\theta_G^*}{\theta_{min}} - \frac{d\theta_G^*}{d\theta_{min}}\right) + \frac{2m\left(\theta_G^* + \theta_{min}\right) - n}{2\left(4\theta_G^* - \theta_{min}\right)}\frac{d\theta_G^*}{d\theta_{min}}. \quad (4.3b)$$

(ii) $\psi_B < \psi_G$. Hence for a small increase in the standard the net change in average surplus is always greater for the G variant.

Proof: See Appendix A4.

In the absence of quality investment, the sign of the first terms on the RHS of (4.3a) and (4.3b), respectively, depends on the equilibrium regime. In the lower boundary regime they are negative, which follows from (2.5) and $\theta_G^*/\theta_{min} < d\theta_G^*/d\theta_{min}$. By triggering an increase in product differentiation the standard stifles price competition and thereby gives rise to a loss in average consumer surplus. The opposite is true in the maximum differentiation and upper boundary regime. As $d\theta_G^* / d\theta_{\min} = 0$ now, the standard lowers product differentiation, enhances price competition and powers an increase in consumer surplus.

The second terms on the RHS of (4.3a) and (4.3b), respectively, give the direct impact of changes in environmental performance on a variant's average surplus. For $m > n = 0$, both terms are strictly positive, implying an under-provision of environmental performance or quality more generally (Ronnen 1991). This is because firms target their performance at the marginal and not the average consumer as a social planner would. However the direct impact of performance on surplus is negative if $m < 0$ or if $n > 0$ and sufficiently large. In the absence of competition, a firm would raise price with an increase in environmental performance (or quality more generally). When environmental orientation is low (i.e. when n is large) this harms consumers as they are concerned about low prices rather than environmental performance.

Part (ii) of the lemma establishes an important intermediate result, which follows from direct comparison of ψ_B and ψ_G. On average the consumers of the clean variant are more prone to benefit from a standard policy. For $\psi_B < 0 < \psi_G$, the standard reduces average consumer surplus from the dirty variant and raises that from the clean variant.[10] Even though average consumer surplus may decrease in the model of Crampes and Hollander (1995) an asymmetry cannot arise. The asymmetry helps to explain the realistic situation in which (on average) the high-income consumers of the green product are in favour of environmental regulation whereas consumers of brown products are opposed to it.

Proposition 4.1. Consider a small increase in the standard over the laissez-faire level of B performance. (i) In the lower boundary regime, where $m < m_l$, this reduces aggregate consumer surplus. (ii) In the maximum differentiation regime with B profit dominance, where $m \in (m_l, m_\pi)$, this reduces (increases) consumer surplus if m is sufficiently close to m_l (m_π). (iii) Under G profit dominance, this raises consumer surplus.

Proof: See Appendix A4.

In the lower boundary regime, as realised under low environmental orientation of the market, consumers' relative concern for the environment is so limited that the increase in absolute price outweighs the increase in environmental performance. Aggregate consumer surplus thus decreases under a standard. Market coverage is also reduced. These findings contrast with Ronnen (1991), Boom (1995) and Scarpa (1998), where, in the absence of a baseline benefit, consumers always benefit from the standard. Crampes and Hollander (1995) identify a potentially negative impact of the standard on consumer surplus in a covered market. Their result however is driven by increases in variable cost alone. They find that consumer surplus is reduced if and only if the increase in competition is softened by a sufficiently strong reaction $d\theta_G{}^*/d\theta_{\min} > 0$, i.e. if the cost function is not too convex. In our model the reduction of consumer surplus through the standard cannot be explained on grounds of cost alone. Indeed Ronnen shows that the standard unambiguously raises welfare if marginal cost is linear in quality. The negative impact of a standard on consumer surplus in our model reflects the low relative preference for environmental performance/quality.

For the maximum differentiation regime with B profit dominance the impact of a standard is ambiguous. This reflects the intermediate level of environmental orientation that is associated with the maximum differentiation regime. If baseline benefit is sufficiently large the standard still lowers consumer surplus. Remarkably, this is the case even if for $d\theta_B{}^*/d\theta_{\min}\big|_{m\in[m_l,m_\pi]} = 0$ the increase in competition between the variants is not cushioned. The contrast between this and Crampes and Hollander's findings illustrates that our result is driven by preferences rather than by cost. In the maximum differentiation regime, green consumers' surplus is unambiguously raised.[11] As tighter competition from the brown variant leads to a drop in price, green consumers' surplus increases. While for a relatively low WTP for environmental friendliness the increase in G consumers' surplus is still overcompensated by the decrease in B consumers' surplus, this is reversed if WTP becomes sufficiently large. Then, the standard increases aggregate consumer surplus even in a market with B dominance.[12] Finally, in the presence of G dominance, as indeed always in the upper boundary regime, the standard unambiguously raises aggregate consumer surplus. This goes hand in hand with a high environmental orientation of the market, where environmental attributes are under-provided relative to the average consumer's tastes.

Now consider the impact of the standard on profits. From (2.6a)

$$\frac{d\pi_G{}^*}{d\theta_{\min}} = \frac{\partial \pi_G{}^*}{\partial \theta_B} = -\frac{\left(2\theta_G{}^* + \theta_{\min}\right)\left(2m\theta_G{}^* + n\right)q_G{}^*}{\left(4\theta_G{}^* - \theta_{\min}\right)^2} < 0, \qquad (4.4a)$$

which follows under use of the envelope theorem. The standard reduces the green firm's profit as products become less differentiated and competition increases. From (2.6b), we obtain

$$\frac{d\pi_B{}^*}{d\theta_{min}} = \frac{\partial \pi_B{}^*}{\partial \theta_B} + \frac{\partial \pi_B{}^*}{\partial \theta_G} \frac{d\theta_G{}^*}{d\theta_{min}} = \frac{\lambda q_B{}^*}{\left(4\theta_G{}^* - \theta_{min}\right)^2 \theta_G{}^* \theta_{min}} \quad (4.4b)$$

$$\lambda := \theta_G{}^* s\left(\theta_G{}^*, \theta_{min}\right) + \left(2\theta_G{}^* + \theta_{min}\right)\theta_{min}^2 \left(m\theta_{min} + 2n\right)\left(d\theta_G{}^*/d\theta_{min}\right). \quad (4.5)$$

Obviously, $\mathrm{sgn}\left(d\pi_B{}^*/d\theta_{min}\right) = \mathrm{sgn}\,\lambda$. A priori, λ cannot be signed unambiguously. Intuitively this is because a reaction $d\theta_G{}^*/d\theta_{min} > 0$ tends to increase B profit, while the direct impact of the standard is non-positive given the B firm's optimal performance. The following applies.

Lemma 4.2. $d\pi_B{}^*/d\theta_{min} \leq 0$.

Proof: See Appendix A4.

Thus the standard reduces the brown firm's profit under B dominance. This occurs due to a reduction in the mark-up and a loss of demand at the bottom end, as consumers with a low WTP refrain from buying the product at the higher absolute price.[13] B profit is unaffected in the case of an upper boundary regime. This result does not generalise as it rests on the assumption that the G firm cannot raise its performance beyond the upper bound $\bar\theta$ (see Proposition 4.3 below).

We now establish the impact of the standard on industry surplus as

$$\frac{dW}{d\theta_{min}} = \frac{dS}{d\theta_{min}} + \frac{d\pi_G{}^*}{d\theta_{min}} + \frac{d\pi_B{}^*}{d\theta_{min}}, \quad (4.6)$$

where the derivatives are given by (4.2), (4.4a) and (4.4b). Recall from (2.7) and (2.14b) the boundary values $m_\pi\left(\bar\theta, \theta_{min}\right) = n/\sqrt{\bar\theta\theta_{min}}$ and $m_h = 2n\alpha\left(\bar\theta, \theta_{min}\right)/\left[\bar\theta\theta_{min}\beta\left(\bar\theta, \theta_{min}\right)\right]$.

Proposition 4.2. There exists a unique boundary value $m_W \in \left(m_\pi, m_h\right)$ such that an increase in the standard raises industry surplus if and only if $m > m_W$.

Proof: See Appendix A4.

Hence, a standard raises industry surplus if and only if the environmental margin is sufficiently high. Specifically, it always reduces industry surplus in a situation of B profit dominance. While the standard raises welfare in a situation in which the B firm chooses an interior performance level $\theta_B^* > \underline{\theta}$, the case depicted by Ronnen (1991), his conclusion of an unambiguously positive welfare impact of a standard must obviously be qualified.

Usually environmental regulation – and safety, or quality regulation more generally – relates to a particular feature of the product (Arora and Gangopadhyay 1995). Given that the regulated feature is of relatively minor importance for the consumption decision, i.e. given a low environmental (quality) margin, a standard triggers a reduction in welfare. If we take dominance of the more polluting firm as an indicator of such a situation it is clear that in many empirical cases we should expect the standard to have a negative effect. While the presence of externalities associated with the product may still warrant regulation, one should be careful to avoid a justification on the grounds of its effects on industry surplus alone.

The Model with Investment

In the following we consider the model with investment cost, as developed in section 2.5. As previously we assume that the regulator commits to a standard before the firms engage in the performance-then-price game. For a marginal standard set at $\theta_B^* = \theta_{\min}$, the green firm adjusts θ_G^* according to its best response function

$$\frac{d\theta_G^*}{d\theta_{\min}} = \frac{\partial b_G}{\partial \theta_B} \in \left[0, \frac{\theta_G^*}{\theta_{\min}} \right]. \tag{4.7}$$

Remark: Note that Lemma A2.5 part (i) (in the Appendix A2.2) guarantees $\partial b_G / \partial \theta_B < \theta_G^* / \theta_{\min}$ only for an interior equilibrium. For a boundary equilibrium (4.7) holds if the investment rate k is sufficiently large.

The impact on industry surplus $W = S + \pi_G^* - F(\theta_G^*) + \pi_B^* - F(\theta_B^*)$ of the standard is now given by

$$\frac{dW}{d\theta_{\min}} = \frac{dS}{d\theta_{\min}} + \frac{d\pi_G^*}{d\theta_{\min}} + \frac{d\pi_B^*}{d\theta_{\min}} - F'\left(\theta_G^*\right)\frac{d\theta_G^*}{d\theta_{\min}} - F'\left(\theta_{\min}\right)$$

$$= \left\{ \begin{array}{l} \overbrace{\dfrac{\partial S}{\partial \theta_B} + \dfrac{\partial \pi_G^*}{\partial \theta_B} + \left(\dfrac{\partial \pi_B^*}{\partial \theta_B} - F'\left(\theta_{\min}\right)\right)}^{\leq 0} \\[4mm] + \left[\underbrace{\dfrac{\partial S}{\partial \theta_G} + \dfrac{\partial \pi_B^*}{\partial \theta_G} + \dfrac{\partial \pi_G^*}{\partial \theta_G} - F'\left(\theta_G^*\right)}_{=0} \right] \dfrac{d\theta_G^*}{d\theta_{\min}} \end{array} \right\}.$$

The welfare change is then composed of the effect of the standard on consumer surplus as well as on the two firms' operating profits net of investment cost. The impact of the standard on consumer surplus is as discussed previously, the only difference being that in this case the standard always reduces product differentiation and thus helps to enhance consumer surplus through stiffer price competition. This notwithstanding, consumer surplus may still fall if the environmental orientation of the market is too low.

Proposition 4.3. (i) The standard always reduces the clean firm's profit. (ii) It increases the dirty firm's profit if an interior regime obtains for $m \geq m_h'$ and it lowers the dirty firm's profit if this firm dominates in market share for $m \leq m_q'$.

Proof: See Appendix A4.

By committing it to a higher environmental performance a marginal standard bestows Stackelberg leadership on the dirty firm which it can use to gain a competitive advantage over its rival. While this always leads to a reduction in the clean firm's profit, it contributes towards an increase in the dirty firm's profit as long as the environmental orientation is sufficiently high. Consider the effect of the standard on the dirty firm's profit when environmental orientation is strong enough to support an interior equilibrium. Although the standard directly raises the dirty producer's cost, this is only a second-order effect. It is swamped by the first-order increase in the B firm's profit arising from an increase in G performance and the relaxation of price competition it entails. Surprisingly enough we should then expect the dirty rather than the green firm to lobby for a regulatory standard, albeit a relatively mild one. Note that the presence of strategic effects overturns the Salop and

Scheffmann (1983) story of raising rivals' cost, where (clean) high cost producers try to disadvantage their (dirty) low cost rivals by advocating environmental or social standards. If a boundary regime arises for lower levels of environmental orientation the direct negative effect of the standard assumes a first-order nature as well. A degree of environmental orientation that is low enough to support the dominance of the dirty firm in terms of market share is then sufficient for the direct effect to outweigh the strategic effect. In this case both firms suffer from the introduction of the standard.

While the sign of the welfare change $dW/d\theta_{min}$ is generally ambiguous, we are able to state the following result.

Proposition 4.4. Suppose the G firm's best response in the presence of investments is given by (4.7). Then a small increase in the standard above the laissez-faire level of B environmental performance lowers industry surplus if $m \leq m_{\pi}'$, i.e. in the presence of B dominance (with regard to operating profit) and raises industry surplus if $m \geq m_h'$, i.e. in the case of an interior equilibrium.

Proof: See Appendix A4.

The proposition extends our earlier findings to the case where investment costs are present. This result is straightforward but not trivial, as the G firm responds to the standard by raising environmental performance, whereas it fails to do so in the absence of investments in the maximum differentiation or upper boundary regime. The proposition shows that for low levels of the environmental margin, as revealed by dominance of the dirty firm in operating profit, a standard adds little benefit to the average consumer, or positively harms them.[14] Then the fall in profit always dominates and gives rise to a reduction in industry surplus. As in Ronnen (1991) the standard raises industry surplus within an interior equilibrium and this despite the green firm's effort to dampen competition.

4.3 ENVIRONMENTAL IMPACT OF A STANDARD

We continue to consider a marginal standard set close to the laissez-faire level of the dirty firm's unit emissions, such that $\theta_{min} = \theta_B^*$. The impact of the standard on overall emissions is given by

$$\frac{dE}{d\theta_{\min}} = \frac{dE}{d\theta_{\min}} + \overbrace{\frac{dE}{d\theta_G}}^{<0} \overbrace{\frac{d\theta_G^*}{d\theta_{\min}}}^{\geq 0}, \qquad (4.8)$$

where $dE/d\theta_{\min} = dE/d\theta_B$ and $dE/d\theta_G$ are given by (3.6b) and (3.6a), respectively. We can immediately state the following.

Proposition 4.5. The standard reduces industry emissions if $m \leq m_E$, as defined in Lemma 3.1.

Proof: Follows directly from Lemma 3.1.

By enforcing a lowering of unit emissions of the dirty product the standard directly contributes towards lower industry emissions. If the environmental margin is sufficiently low, i.e. for $m \leq m_E$ the increase in unit abatement θ_B additionally lowers industry output and shifts market share to the green firm. Hence industry emissions are curbed even further, no matter whether the clean firm's output increases or decreases. If the clean firm responds with greater abatement effort there is a further fall in industry emissions. Noting that $m_E > m_q{}'$, the presence of market share dominance of the dirty variant gives a clear indication that a unit emission standard is effective in reducing industry emissions.

This effect of an emission standard is straightforward and indeed what we would expect intuitively. It is worth stressing however that the literature has so far ignored it. In Motta and Thisse (1993) a unit emission standard always reduces industry emissions. However this is owing to their specification of the emission function and, as we have shown earlier, is by no means general. Similarly the potentially emission-reducing effect of a standard identified by MGPF (1997) is not robust with respect to a generalisation of the investment cost function. Finally, MGPF (2002) find that the standard unambiguously raises industry emissions. This result turns on their assumption of a homogeneous investment cost function. In contrast to this literature our result is solely motivated by the presence of a baseline benefit which is sufficiently high relative to WTP for environmental performance, and is therefore independent of any assumptions regarding the unit emission function or investment cost function.

For $m > m_E$, the effect of a standard on industry emissions becomes ambiguous. In this case, the increase in B abatement, θ_B, enhances competition to an extent that industry output increases. As we have discussed in the context of Lemma 3.1, the tendency towards an enhancement in industry output is the stronger the greater the environmental orientation. Moreover it is obvious from (4.8) that an emission-boosting effect is the more likely the weaker the reaction $d\theta_G^*/d\theta_{min}$. As discussed in the previous chapter the overall effect still depends on the properties of the function $e(\theta)$. However it is now possible to find specifications of $e(\theta)$ for which the standard raises industry emissions. As one extreme example consider a situation in which $e'(\theta_i) \to 0$; $i = G, B$ such that from (4.8) and (3.6a) and (3.6b)

$$\frac{dE}{d\theta_{min}}\bigg|_{e'(\theta_i) \to 0} = \overset{<0}{\frac{\partial E}{\partial \zeta}} \overset{<0}{\frac{d\zeta}{d\theta_{min}}} + \frac{\partial E}{\partial \theta_B}\bigg|_{\zeta=\bar{\zeta}},$$

with $\zeta = \theta_G^*/\theta_{min}$. Here,

$$\frac{d\zeta}{d\theta_{min}} = \frac{1}{\theta_{min}}\left(\frac{d\theta_G^*}{d\theta_{min}} - \zeta\right) < 0$$

follows from (4.7). Equations (3.5a) and (3.5b) can then be used to establish the existence of a boundary value m_{EE}, with $m_{EE} > m_E$, such that $m > m_{EE} \Leftrightarrow dE/d\theta_{min} > 0$.[15] Hence a perverse effect of an emission standard may arise if the environmental margin is high relative to the baseline margin and if further abatement effort does not reduce unit emissions by too much. This may be the case in a market in which a high environmental orientation has induced abatement effort on the part of both the clean and dirty firm up to the point that the technological scope for emission reductions is exhausted. In this case a standard is counterproductive from an environmental point as it merely boosts competition. The relevance of such a scenario is an empirical matter. However our earlier findings suggest that, in contrast to MGPF (2002), we can be confident that in many situations a unit emission standard is an appropriate tool to achieve a reduction in industry emissions.

4.4 SOCIAL WELFARE REVISITED

Following MGPF (2002) we complement industry surplus with a measure of the social cost of emissions in order to arrive at a more comprehensive welfare measure.

$$W^+ = W - \delta E,$$

where $\delta > 0$ measures the social damage from emissions.[16] We can study the effect of the unit emission standard by considering the derivative

$$\frac{dW^+}{d\theta_{\min}} = \frac{dW}{d\theta_{\min}} - \delta \frac{dE}{d\theta_{\min}}.$$

From our previous results we know that a trade-off arises under B profit dominance. Recall from Propositions 4.2, 4.3 and 4.4 that $m \le m_\pi' \Rightarrow \{dW/d\theta_{\min} < 0; dE/d\theta_{\min} < 0\}$. The standard then lowers both industry surplus and emissions. It raises comprehensive welfare W^+ if and only if

$$\delta > \frac{dW/d\theta_{\min}}{dE/d\theta_{\min}}.$$

Thus only if environmental concerns have sufficient weight over the creation of industry surplus should the standard be introduced. In this regard firms and consumers share a common interest against the standard.[17] The following proposition shows that there is scope for situations where a trade-off does not arise.

Proposition 4.6. Consider the introduction of a marginal unit emission standard. (i) For the set-up without investment cost there exists an interval $[m_W, m_E]$ *such that* $m \in [m_W, m_E] \Rightarrow \{dW/d\theta_{\min} > 0; dE/d\theta_{\min} < 0\}$. *(ii) For the set-up with investment cost there exist* $\underline{k}$ *and* $\hat{k}$, *where* $0 < \underline{k} < \hat{k}$, *as defined in Lemma 3.1. If the investment rate satisfies* $k < \underline{k}$, *then there exists an interval* $[m_W, m_E]$. *If it satisfies* $k > \hat{k}$, *then* $m_E < m_W$.

Proof: See Appendix A4.

Hence under some circumstances the introduction of a standard leads to an unequivocal welfare improvement as industry surplus is enhanced and emissions are curbed at the same time. Fundamentally this requires the environmental margin to fall into an intermediate range $[m_W', m_E]$. This parameter range always exists in the absence of investment cost, whereas it exists in the presence of investment cost only if a low investment rate, k, guarantees that a potential increase in emissions for $m > m_E$ can only incur in the interior regime. As we know from Proposition 4.4, industry surplus increases unambiguously within an interior regime.

If however investment is costly (a high k), this implies stiff competition and in these circumstances the pro-competitive effect of an increase in θ_B is very strong and leads to an increase in output even for modest levels of the environmental margin, as implied by $m_E < m_W$. In this case the existence of an interval $[m_{EE}, m_W]$ cannot be ruled out, where $dE/d\theta_{min} > 0$ for $m > m_{EE}$ and $dW/d\theta_{min} < 0$ for $m < m_W$. A standard then unambiguously reduces welfare for $m \in [m_{EE}, m_W]$.

Finally, $m > \max\{m_W, m_{EE}\} \Rightarrow \{dW/d\theta_{min} > 0; dE/d\theta_{min} > 0\}$. Here the introduction of a standard gives rise to a trade-off between an increase in industry surplus and an increase in emissions whenever the environmental margin is high. The standard should be introduced then if and only if

$$\delta < \frac{dW/d\theta_{min}}{dE/d\theta_{min}},$$

i.e. if and only if the social cost of pollution is sufficiently low. This corresponds to the result found by MGPF (2002). The standard is used as an industrial policy even at the expense of an increase in industry emissions.

There is an interesting aside to the trade-off between the welfare and emission impact of the standard arising for high and low values of environmental orientation. Namely the trade-off represents a more general dilemma of environmental policies. Traditional Pigouvian policies are designed to correct externalities and therefore occasion an increase in allocative efficiency.[18] Improved efficiency entails an increase in economic activity which, under some circumstances, may give rise to a greater level of pollution than in the presence of 'less efficient' policies. Despite its marginal nature the environmental standard in our model gives rise to a similar trade-off. With the primary effect being a reduction in unit emissions, the standard increases efficiency by enhancing competition if the environmental margin is sufficiently high. The boost in output offsets some of the initial reductions in pollution. Thus from an environmental point of view, the standard is 'too efficient'. If the environmental margin is low, e.g. if $m < m_\pi$, the standard reduces allocative efficiency. The ensuing reduction in industry output has an additionally mitigating effect on pollution.

4.5 CONCLUSIONS

In this chapter we have studied the effects of a unit emission standard on welfare and on industry emissions. We have shown that the standard reduces consumer surplus, and a fortiori, industry surplus if consumers are unprepared to pay for environmental performance as opposed to the baseline features of the product. In this respect we add a preference based explanation for a negative welfare impact by a quality standard to the cost based explanation offered by Crampes and Hollander (1995) and the explanation by Scarpa (1998) that points to an over-proportional decrease in profit levels in a triopoly. Our result underlines concerns about regulation, and in particular environmental regulation, where consumers' willingness to pay for environmental friendliness is likely to be low. While it would be wrong to dismiss standard setting solely on the grounds of our narrow concept of industry surplus, there is no longer an unambiguous case for it as suggested by Ronnen (1991).

Our analysis shows that the emission standard unambiguously reduces industry emissions if environmental orientation of the market is sufficiently low. This pertains irrespective of any specific functional forms. In particular, if the dirty firm holds the majority market share, the standard curtails industry emissions. There is more ambiguity if the environmental orientation is high. In this case the standard may raise industry emissions if the reaction of the clean firm is relatively weak and if the direct effect of abatement on unit emissions is not too pronounced.

We have not considered a normative setting in which a welfare-maximising level of the emission standard is derived. Such an analysis is difficult, as it involves non-marginal levels of the standard that may lie significantly above the laissez-faire level of B quality. Even if we do not consider quality investment, problems arise from the fact that the second-order derivatives $d^2W/d\theta_{min}^2$ and $d^2E/d\theta_{min}^2$ are difficult to sign and non-convexity of the objective function cannot be excluded. Due to these problems and due to the lack of generality implied by the use of specific functional forms for the unit emission and damage functions we refrain here from an analysis of optimal standard setting.

In a model in which firms have to invest in quality further discontinuities can arise because of leapfrogging and because of a violation of the non-negativity condition on long-run profit. For example, Motta and Thisse (1993, 1999) find that an optimal standard involves a corner solution in which the dirty firm receives zero long-run profit. This is because the industry surplus unambiguously increases with the standard, whereas industry emissions unambiguously decrease for the specification of the aggregate emission function chosen by Motta and Thisse (1993). In a model where industry emissions may increase with the standard, Lombardini-Riipinen (2002) finds scope for an interior solution provided that marginal environmental damage is sufficiently high. Here the optimal standard balances the increase in consumer surplus from greater competition and greater levels of environmental performance against the reduction in industry profits and the increase in environmental damage. It should be stressed that all of the above results obtain for models with $n = 0$, implying G dominance in market share and profit. Furthermore the findings are highly sensitive to assumptions about the emission and damage function. They should therefore be interpreted with caution.

NOTES

1. In reality the variety of standards is even greater, including standards regulating output or certain inputs. Helfand (1991) compares the effects of different forms of standards within a competitive industry.
2. Besanko (1987) compares the properties of design and performance standards for a homogeneous goods Cournot oligopoly. He shows that only a performance standard allows the attainment of a target emission level at minimal cost. However, as this usually involves a reduction in industry output, a design standard is preferable if the regulator is not only concerned about curtailing pollution but also about the surplus of the industry.
3. Obviously this does not establish whether a standard is preferable to a tax, a question we do not attempt to answer here.
4. See Goldberg (1998) and Sterner (2003: chapters 21 and 22) for a more detailed discussion.
5. Examples of minimum quality standards that do not directly relate to the environment include product safety standards for manufactured products, e.g. for electrical devices or automobiles, contents requirements for textiles, food or pharmaceuticals, and occupational licensing for professional services.
6. Other quality distortions arise due to price-quality discrimination by multi-product firms (e.g. Mussa and Rosen 1978, Donnenfeld and White 1988) or in the presence of asymmetric information (Akerlof 1970, Leland 1979, Shapiro 1986) or due to externalities.
7. For an overview, see Tirole (1988: section 2.2).

8. The reaction is quite different in a triopoly (Scarpa 1998). See section 8.3 for a discussion.

9. Notice that the standard lowers the boundary level m_l implying an increased range of maximum differentiation equilibria. We do not formally analyse the regime switch as this would not provide further insights.

10. It should be noted that the argument relates to average consumer surplus. While it is straightforward to show that the net effect of the standard on individual consumer's surplus from a given variant decreases with income, the effects are not unambiguously ordered across variants. The lowest income purchaser of the G variant obtains a lesser net benefit from the standard than the highest income purchaser of the B variant.

11. This is easily checked from (4.3b), where $d\theta_G^* / d\theta_{min} = 0$.

12. It can be shown that for $m = m_\pi$ and $\bar{\theta} \to (7/4)\theta_{min}$ the standard raises even the B consumers' average surplus.

13. It is easily checked that $dv_0\left(\theta_G^*, \theta_{min}\right) / d\theta_{min}\big|_{m \le m_\pi} > 0$.

14. The effect of the standard on consumer surplus is less clear-cut if we take into account the sunk costs of environmental improvements. As the calculations involved are tedious and do not add much insight, we omit them here. It can be checked that if the environmental margin is sufficiently low, the standard reduces consumer surplus.

15. This is verified, for instance, when $n = 0$ implies $m_E = m_{EE} = 0$.

16. For simplicity we assume a linear damage from emissions. The use of a more general damage function would not have a bearing on our results here as long as these functions are continuously differentiable.

17. This is certainly true for $m \le 0$ where all consumers would suffer a loss in surplus from the introduction of the standard.

18. See Baumol and Oates (1988) for a classic treatment of Pigouvian environmental policies.

5. Environmental labelling

5.1 INTRODUCTION

In many markets the introduction of environmentally friendly product variants is obstructed by problems of asymmetric information. In many instances environmental attributes are difficult for consumers to ascertain. For instance, consumers lack the know-how and the equipment to measure the content of toxic substances contained in textiles or organic produce, neither are they able to assess vehicle emissions. Likewise it is usually impossible for consumers to obtain information on the process of production and whether or not it is carried out in an environmentally benign way. In these cases, the environmental features of a product are credence attributes that cannot be ascertained by consumers, either by inspection of the product at the point of sale or by experience in the course of consumption.[1] We should note that in some cases the informational problems are less severe. For instance, upon inspection consumers are able to ascertain the amount of packaging (waste) or the inclusion of certain clean technologies such as catalytic converters in cars. However in order to make reliable decisions consumers may have to incur considerable search costs. The fuel efficiency of an engine or the energy efficiency of an appliance can be judged from experience. In this case consumers may commit costly errors with their initial purchase which cannot be rectified until a repeat purchase occurs. Either way consumers are therefore likely to be exposed to considerable informational costs. Many of them are likely to prefer to remain uninformed, especially if their willingness to pay for environmental performance is relatively low to begin with.

If consumers are imperfectly informed about quality, the firm has an incentive to under-provide it in order to save cost (Akerlof 1970). This can be in a context of adverse selection (Leland 1979) or moral hazard (Shapiro 1986).[2] Consumers are then unwilling to pay an environmental premium even if they are environmentally aware. Environmental product differentiation then relies on a mechanism that credibly signals the relevant information to consumers. One prominent example of such a signal is an environmental label.[3]

In theory and in practice one can distinguish two main forms of labelling. Type 2 labels are provided by the firm itself, and type 1 labels are awarded to the firm by a third party if the product meets certain environmental requirements (OECD 1997).[4] Type 2 labelling that is initiated by a firm provides a credible signal to consumers of the true environmental performance only if credibility is conferred upon the label by an independent expert or by the firm's own reputation for honesty. In the latter case the label is not really distinct from a trade-mark which consumers associate with quality.[5] Either way the signalling of quality usually involves investment that increases with quality (e.g. Shapiro 1986). A full-scale model of the usually complex information structures is beyond the scope of this work, but we may note that the investment cost $F(\theta)$ could be justified as the investment a firm has to incur in order to signal credibly to consumers its environmental performance θ. The analysis of a differentiated duopoly in which firms employ their own label would then follow closely the basic model with investment cost (see section 2.5).

Crampes and Ibanez (1996) model type 2 labelling in a signalling framework along the lines of Milgrom and Roberts (1986). They show within a framework of price-setting consumers that a separating equilibrium exists, in which only a true green firm acquires the label. Obviously the assumption of price-making consumers limits the applicability of the model and there remains considerable scope for research in the properties of signalling of environmental performance.

Alternatively, a credible third party may award a label to interested firms provided they meet a labelling requirement, specified as a minimum level of environmental performance or a maximum level of unit emissions. Examples include the German Blue Angel, the Nordic Swan, the US Green Seal, or the European Eco-Flower.[6] Kuhn (1999), Rege (2000) and Mason (2001) examine the effects of an eco-label on the provision of clean and polluting products in an environmentally differentiated industry.[7] Rege (2000) considers a label which perfectly separates green from non-green producers. She shows that the presence of the label mitigates the problem of adverse selection and allows for a greater supply of green products. Kuhn (1999) and Mason (2001) consider imperfect testing technology, where the label may also be acquired by non-green firms. Thus, the label separates the market only imperfectly. Kuhn (1999) is able to obtain explicit comparative static results, assuming that the labelling authority can strengthen the requirements for award of the label, implying that it becomes relatively more costly for cheaters to obtain the label. As it turns out, this does not always improve the market allocation. Depending on the particular properties of the representative consumers' utility function and the cost schedule for obtaining the label, more stringent criteria for attainment of the label may reduce entry by true green firms and may trigger additional entry by non-green firms with or without label.[8] Mason (2001) reveals a similar potential for adverse welfare effects.

This literature has focused on the informational aspects of labelling and its effect on market structure within a competitive industry, with firms being price takers. In this chapter we will disregard most of the informational problems related to labelling in order to concentrate on the effects of a label on competition within an environmentally differentiated duopoly. As the dirty firm could always opt not to sign up to the voluntary label, the requirement can then be understood as an environmental standard that applies locally, i.e. only to the clean firm. If a firm cannot use its own label, environmental performance in excess of the labelling requirement will not be recognised and will not be rewarded by consumers. For this reason the clean firm provides exactly the environmental performance specified by the requirement. As the requirement is therefore always binding we can apply an analysis analogous to the analysis of the environmental standard.

Our main findings are that, as with a standard, the introduction of an eco-label raises industry surplus only if the environmental orientation of the market is sufficiently high. The scope for a negative effect on industry surplus is more pronounced than in the case of a standard as the introduction of the label tends to increase rather than decrease product differentiation and is therefore anti-competitive. Nonetheless, if environmental orientation is high, it is optimal to set a labelling requirement even in excess of the level the clean firm would choose. Finally, as the label reduces product differentiation and therefore leads to a decrease in demand for both variants, it always curbs industry emissions.

Amacher et al. (2004) provide a related analysis of environmental labelling within a vertically differentiated duopoly with a covered market. They consider a marginal cost $MC_i = c\theta_i^2 + c_{0i}$, $i = G, B$, where firms may differ with regard to their baseline cost c_{0i}. The award of a label to the clean firm leads to an improvement in the environmental performance of both firms if meeting the requirement raises the baseline cost of the green firm relative to the brown firm so that $c_{0G} > c_{0B}$.[9] As the clean firm now tends to have a disadvantage vis-à-vis the dirty firm, it has a greater incentive to employ environmental performance as a tool to improve its market position. The greater degree of product differentiation allows the dirty firm to follow suit and improve its own performance in turn.[10]

The next section provides an analysis of a third-party eco-label and the following section concludes. One proof is relegated to the appendix A5 at the end of this work.

5.2 A MODEL OF THIRD-PARTY ECO-LABELLING IN ENVIRONMENTALLY DIFFERENTIATED DUOPOLY

The model of a standard outlined in the previous chapter is easily adapted to capture the impact of third-party environmental labelling on duopoly competition, industry surplus and the emission level. Here, we abstract from some of the more complex and salient informational aspects of labelling by assuming that a firm can sell a green product at a premium if and only if a third-party administered environmental label lends credibility. This provides the third-party institution with the scope to set an aspiration level θ_{max}, $\theta_{max} \geq \underline{\theta}$, and award the label only to firms with environmental performance in excess of θ_{max}. Consumers observe the label and believe that a labelled product is associated with performance θ_{max}. As no additional premium will be paid for performance levels $\theta > \theta_{max}$ and no label is awarded for $\theta < \theta_{max}$ the green firm will chose performance $\theta_G = \theta_{max}$. Provided there is just a single label with criterion θ_{max} available, the dirty firm will then choose $\theta_B = \underline{\theta}$. Any performance $\theta_B \in (\underline{\theta}, \theta_{max})$ would not attract a premium as it remains uncertified and is therefore non-credible to consumers. The game then effectively boils down to two stages, where the third-party chooses G performance $\theta_G = \theta_{max}$ in the first stage and the two firms choose prices in stage two. For the case with investment costs, the change in industry surplus can then be written as

$$\frac{dW}{d\theta_{max}} = \frac{\partial S}{\partial \theta_G} + \frac{\partial \pi_B^*}{\partial \theta_G} + \frac{\partial \pi_G^*}{\partial \theta_G} - F'(\theta_{max})$$

Let θ_{max}^* denote the aspiration level of the label that maximises industry surplus and θ_G^* the level of environmental performance the green firm would choose if it could set the criterion. The allocation that maximises industry surplus can then be characterised as follows.

Proposition 5.1. Let $m, n > 0$ and k be sufficiently large. Then there exist $\underline{m}$ and $\overline{m}$, with $0 < \underline{m} < \overline{m}$ such that $\theta_{max}^* = \underline{\theta}$ if and only if $m \leq \underline{m}$; $\theta_{max}^* \in (\underline{\theta}, \theta_G^*]$ if and only if $m \in (\underline{m}, \overline{m}]$; and $\theta_{max}^* > \theta_G^*$ if and only if $m > \overline{m}$.

Proof: See Appendix A5.

Figure 5.1 illustrates. Here the $\Sigma(m,\theta_G) \equiv 0$ schedule is the locus in (θ_G,m) space for which $\partial S/\partial\theta_G + \partial\pi_B^*/\partial\theta_G + \partial\pi_G^*/\partial\theta_G = 0$, whereas $\partial S/\partial\theta_G + \partial\pi_B^*/\partial\theta_G + \partial\pi_G^*/\partial\theta_G < 0$ holds for all points below the schedule. This implies that $\theta_{max}^* > \underline{\theta}$ can only be true in the area above the $\Sigma(\cdot) \equiv 0$ schedule. If the investment rate k is sufficiently high, this guarantees the existence of a continuous equilibrium schedule $\theta_{max}^*(m,k)$, passing to the left of the maximum of the $\Sigma(\cdot) \equiv 0$ schedule as depicted in Figure 5.1.[11] Then an interior level of the criterion $\theta_{max}^*(\cdot) > \underline{\theta}$ is optimal if and only if the environmental margin is sufficiently high, i.e. if and only if $m > \underline{m}$.

The $\sigma_G(m,\theta_G) \equiv 0$ schedule depicts the locus of points where $\partial S/\partial\theta_G + \partial\pi_B^*/\partial\theta_G = 0$ holds, whereas $\partial S/\partial\theta_G + \partial\pi_B^*/\partial\theta_G < 0$ for all points below $\sigma_G(\cdot) \equiv 0$. This implies that $\theta_{max}^* > \theta_G^*$ can only be true above the $\sigma_G(\cdot) \equiv 0$ schedule. For completeness, we have included the $\theta_G^*(m,k)$ schedule, depicting the equilibrium choice by the G firm. Obviously, the $\theta_G^*(\cdot)$ and $\theta_{max}^*(\cdot)$ schedules intersect at a point on $\sigma_G(\cdot) \equiv 0$ with $\theta_{max}^*(\cdot) < \theta_G^*(\cdot)$ for all $m < \overline{m}$.

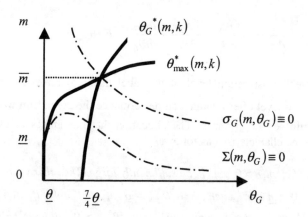

Figure 5.1 Socially optimal labelling

The intuition is similar to the case of the product standard. Low values of the environmental margin (corresponding to a low environmental orientation) imply that consumers are more concerned about low prices than about environmental performance. With the green firm increasing its environmental performance away from the minimum level in response to an increase in the labelling criterion, this has a positive impact on the prices of both variants. The price of the green variant increases because production becomes more costly and because the greater differentiation stifles competition. The latter effect also leads to a higher selling price of the brown variant. Although both firms' profits increase through labelling, the negative effect on consumer surplus more than offsets this and renders the introduction of a label sub-optimal as far as industry surplus is concerned. For levels of the environmental margin $m \in [\underline{m}, \overline{m}]$, the introduction of the label raises industry surplus as long as the labelling requirement is set at a moderate level. Specifically, this implies that the requirement should be set below the environmental performance the green firm would favour. This reflects a situation in which the negative effect on industry surplus of excessive product differentiation outweighs the negative effect of an under-provision of green environmental performance that is targeted at the marginal rather than the average G consumer. This is reversed for high levels of the environmental margin $m > \overline{m}$, where the social value of greater G performance as such outweighs the negative effect of even weaker price competition. While we have modelled a setting in which a green variant could not be differentiated in the absence of a third-party label, this latter finding extends to a situation where the green firm can differentiate its product by way of a firm-specific label. Here, the under-provision of environmental performance would warrant the replacement of the firm label by a more ambitious third-party label.

The impact of a label on industry emissions is easily shown to be positive. With $\theta_G = \theta_{\max}$ and $\theta_B = \underline{\theta}$, we have $dE/d\theta_{\max} = dE/d\theta_G > 0$ where the inequality follows from (3.6a). An emission reduction is effected through lower unit emissions from the green firm and through the reduction in industry output under weaker price competition. From a perspective of total welfare $W^+ = W - \delta E$, this implies of course that the introduction of an environmental label may be called for even for $m < \underline{m}$ if the social cost of emissions δ is sufficiently high. For $m > \underline{m}$ the consideration of industry emissions in the labelling requirement implies a stiffer criterion for which industry surplus lies below its maximum.

5.3 CONCLUSIONS

In this chapter we have shown that an analysis similar to the one for an environmental standard can be applied to examine the effects on industry surplus and emissions of a third-party eco-label. By varying the criterion for award of the label, the policy-maker can more or less directly choose the clean firm's performance level. For the case of a single label the dirty firm will provide the minimum level of environmental performance. The effects of labelling are then similar to those associated with a standard with the one marked difference that labelling expands product differentiation. This anti-competitive effect tends to lower industry surplus and industry emissions alike.

In reality, eco-labels are sometimes graded in order to allow for a distinction of different performance levels. For example, the energy-efficiency labelling of household appliances introduced by the EU in 1995 (EU directive 92/75/EC) involves energy ratings on a scale from A (most efficient) to G (least efficient). In the case of a graded label, the policy-maker wields an additional instrument to influence the performance of the dirty firm, whenever this firm has an incentive to choose an interior performance $\theta_B^* > \underline{\theta}$. It then follows immediately from the analysis of the environmental standard that a small increase in the labelling requirement targeted at the brown firm from $\theta_{min} = \theta_B^*$ leads to a further increase in industry surplus. Furthermore, as long as θ_{min} and θ_{max} are chosen such that product differentiation does not decrease, this allows for a simultaneous decrease in industry emissions. A second-best allocation can thus be attained.[12] The same applies to a set-up where a mandatory standard is targeted at the dirty firm and a (voluntary) eco-label at the green firm.

NOTES

1. For an introduction to search, experience and credence goods see Tirole (1988: section 2.3).
2. For an overview, see Tirole (1988: sections 2.3–2.6).
3. Other signals of environmental attributes may be the price in the case of repeat purchases (e.g. Milgrom and Roberts 1986), the reputation of the firm (e.g. Shapiro 1986), the resale of the product through informed and reputable intermediaries such as supermarket chains (e.g. Biglaiser and Friedman 1994, Garella and Peitz 2000) or information provided by reputable consumer groups or environmental activists (Fedderson and Gilligan 2001).
4. In practice, a third form of labelling, type 3, is characterised by the provision of raw data without further interpretation.

5. Examples here are the reputable trade-marks of some purveyors of (organic) foods.

6. OECD (1991,1997) provides detailed descriptions of these schemes. See also Sterner (2003: chapter 10).

7. See also Mattoo and Singh (1994), Kirchhoff (2000) and Swallow and Sedjo (2000).

8. Dosi and Moretto (2001) consider the effect of an eco-label being awarded to a green product line of a multi-product monopolist. They show that the award of the label may perversely trigger an increase in industry output if the reputation for the green product line spills over to the non-green line, thereby inducing the monopolist to invest more in the polluting activity.

9. This is intuitive if labelling is associated with royalty fees per unit of output. For many eco-labels, fees tend to be a royalty related to revenue (OECD 1997).

10. Amacher et al. (2004) turn to a more complicated and less intuitive argument to make this point. They assume that firms can undertake an investment I that lowers baseline marginal cost c_0 but has no effect on the quality-related marginal cost. They conclude that eco-labelling improves the environmental performance if it raises the clean firm's investment cost. This would obviously raise the clean firm's baseline cost and, thereby, cause the effect discussed in the main text. However, as investment is undertaken in a form of process innovation entirely unrelated to the environmental performance of the product, it remains unclear why this should be affected by the eco-label.

11. The $\theta_{max}^*(\cdot)$ schedule is drawn in bold and follows the abscissa on the interval $[0, \underline{m}]$, where $\theta_{max}^* = \underline{\theta}$.

12. Prices remain distorted due to market power.

6. Subsidising innovation in green product design

6.1 INTRODUCTION

A different means for the regulator to stimulate a greening of the market is the use of subsidies that are designed to reduce unit emissions of the product variants. In principle subsidies may take three forms. Environmentally motivated subsidies could be paid on each unit produced or consumed. Since volume-related subsidies can be modelled as negative taxes, we defer their treatment to the next chapter, which deals with environmentally related product taxation. Alternatively the subsidy can aim at lowering a firm's investment in the development of clean products or processes. This may amount to subsidising the installation of end-of-pipe technologies. In recent years however most governments have shifted the bulk of subsidies to the development of integrated technologies. Usually such green R&D subsidies are provided in the form of government-sponsored grants (OECD, 1999a: table 3.25). Examples include the following:

- Denmark: grants for the promotion of cleaner products and waste-recycling projects; 2000–2001: budget DKK 77 million (€ 10.32 million) p.a.;
- Greece: subsidy to promote environmentally sound and clean technologies and new and innovative products; ≤ 40% of cost;
- Netherlands: subsidy to promote the development of clean products; 40% of cost but ≤ DFL 0.5 (1) million per case (company); budget DFL 5.5 million (€ 2.5 million); and
- Norway: grant for the development of environmentally friendly technologies.

When subsidising investment cost the regulator hopes for an improvement in the product's environmental performance. As we have seen in the previous chapter, a regulatory intervention usually affects the degree of product differentiation and competition as a side-effect.[1] The associated changes in market shares and industry output may then enhance or offset the direct effects of the policy. This chapter uses the model of environmentally differentiated duopoly to study how a subsidy on investment cost impinges on the quality structure in the industry and what this implies for welfare and industry emissions. In so doing we follows Arora and Gangopadhyay (1995) and Moraga-González and Padrón-Fumero (MGPF) (1997, 2002).

Considering an equilibrium in which both firms choose interior levels of quality/unit abatement these authors find that a subsidy always raises quality/unit abatement of both firms.[2] MGPF (1997, 2002) proceed to study the effect of the subsidy on industry emissions. As it turns out, this depends on the properties of the investment cost function. Working with a non-homogeneous function, MGPF (1997) show that subsidisation reduces industry emissions. In contrast to this MGPF (2002) find that in the presence of a homogeneous investment cost function, the subsidy does not change the level of industry emissions. The effect from lower unit emissions is exactly offset by an increase in industry output arising from a reduction in product differentiation. This is notwithstanding the fact that the subsidy raises consumer and industry surplus by mitigating the under-provision of environmental performance as well as by enhancing competition and market coverage.

We re-consider the case for an investment subsidy paid to both firms when allowing for a baseline margin that is unrelated to the products' environmental performance. By raising the environmental performance of the clean variant and thereby enhancing product differentiation the subsidy may serve as a device to induce a switch from a boundary to an interior equilibrium, in which the dirty firm raises its environmental performance from the baseline level. However for a marginal subsidy this is the case only if the boundary equilibrium under laissez-faire is close to the switching point. As with an environmental standard the subsidy reduces industry surplus in the market if consumers have an insufficient willingness to pay for environmental friendliness and in particular when the dirty firm dominates. Notably this is the case even for a subsidy that is associated with only a second-order effect on public funds. In an interior equilibrium the subsidy raises consumer and industry surplus. Finally we find that subsidisation curbs emissions in a boundary equilibrium and in an interior equilibrium if the environmental margin is not too high. We also consider an asymmetric subsidy. This always enhances industry surplus and lowers industry emissions if paid to the clean firm, but it may increase industry emissions if paid to the dirty firm.

The remainder of the chapter is organised as follows. The next section discusses the effects of different forms of subsidies on the firms' choices of environmental performance. Sections 6.3 and 6.4 consider the impact on industry surplus and industry emissions, respectively, and section 6.5 concludes.

6.2 EFFECT OF R&D SUBSIDIES ON ENVIRONMENTAL PERFORMANCE

Subsidisation of green R&D can be modelled as a reduction in the firm's investment cost at a rate $1 - x_F \in [0,1]$, thus giving rise to a modified fixed cost function $x_F F(\theta)$. Obviously,

$$x_F F(\theta) \le F(\theta); \quad x_F F'(\theta) \le F'(\theta); \quad x_F F''(\theta) \le F''(\theta)$$

where the subsidy reduces the investment cost of quality but also its marginal change in quality. Suppose that the regulator decides on subsidising firm i, $i = G, B$ at rate $1 - x_F^i \in [0,1]$, respectively, before the firms engage in a game of performance-then-price competition. The first-order conditions of environmental choice are now given by

$$R\left(\theta_G, \theta_B, x_F^G\right) = \frac{\partial \pi_G^*\left(\theta_G, \theta_B\right)}{\partial \theta_G} - x_F^G F'\left(\theta_G\right)$$

$$= \frac{[2m\theta_G + n]r\left(\theta_G, \theta_B\right)}{\left(4\theta_G - \theta_B\right)^3} - x_F^G F'\left(\theta_G\right) = 0 \qquad (6.1a)$$

$$T\left(\theta_G, \theta_B, x_F^B\right) = \frac{\partial \pi_B^*\left(\theta_G, \theta_B\right)}{\partial \theta_B} - x_F^B F'\left(\theta_B\right)$$

$$= \frac{[m\theta_B + 2n]\theta_G s\left(\theta_G, \theta_B\right)}{\left(4\theta_G - \theta_B\right)^3 \theta_B^2} - x_F^B F'\left(\theta_B\right) \le 0 \qquad (6.1b)$$

where $r\left(\theta_G, \theta_B\right)$ and $s\left(\theta_G, \theta_B\right)$ are given by (2.10a) and (2.10b).[3] Note that each firm's first-order condition depends directly on the level of the own subsidy alone. However, there is an indirect effect from the subsidy paid to the rival, which is transmitted through the rival's choice of performance θ. As previously, we distinguish a boundary and interior equilibrium.

Boundary Equilibrium: $m \leq m_h{}'$

Here, $T\left(\theta_G^*, \theta_B^*, x_F^B\right) < 0$ and $R\left(\theta_G^*, \theta_B^*, x_F^G\right) = 0$ implying $\underline{\theta} = \theta_B^* < \theta_G^*$. Consider, first, the marginal effect of a symmetric subsidy, i.e. a reduction in $x_F^G \equiv x_F^B$, or of the subsidy paid to the G firm, i.e. a reduction in x_F^G.

Proposition 6.1.1. Consider a marginal subsidy offered to the G firm or both firms. (i) Under B market share dominance ($m \leq m_q{}'$) this leads to an increase in G performance but not B performance. (ii) If the environmental margin m is sufficiently close to the switching level between boundary and interior regime, $m_h{}'$, the subsidy leads to a switch to the interior regime and induces both firms to raise environmental performance.

Proof: See Appendix A6.

While the direct effect of a subsidy offered to the green firm (or both firms) always triggers an increase in G performance, the implied change in product differentiation has an indirect effect (and an indirect effect only) on the marginal revenue of quality $\partial \pi_B / \partial \theta_B$ of the brown firm. As it turns out this effect is negative if the B firm dominates on market share. Here the competitive effectiveness $s(\cdot)$ (see definition 2.1) of B performance is lowered even further so that the B firm sticks to the lowest environmental performance. In contrast an increased degree of product differentiation allows the B firm to raise performance when the environmental margin is close to the switching level, $m_h{}'$. Here the increase in product differentiation raises the competitive effectiveness of B performance to a positive level and induces the firm to improve the environmental performance of its product.

Now consider a subsidy offered to the B firm alone so that $x_L^B < 1 = x_F^G$. Since marginal revenue of environmental performance, $\partial \pi_B / \partial \theta_B$, is non-positive for a boundary equilibrium, the regulator cannot induce the B firm to raise its performance to an interior level by paying a marginal subsidy. Even if the full R&D cost is subsidised ($x_F^B = 0$) the B firm may in some cases fail to increase performance. This is because the effectiveness of environmental performance $s(\cdot)$ is negative due to an insufficient degree of product differentiation. If $m \to m_h{}'$, the B firm would increase performance but only in response to an increase in product differentiation. Strategic complementarity of the performance levels implies that the G firm in turn would raise θ_G but only in response to an increase in θ_B. In this case a co-ordination problem arises, where in equilibrium either both firms improve their environmental performance or neither does. It is not clear a priori which equilibrium is realised, although the one in which both firms raise performance is profit dominant.

Interior Equilibrium

Here $T\!\left(\theta_G^*,\theta_B^*,x_F^B\right)=0$ and $R\!\left(\theta_G^*,\theta_B^*,x_F^G\right)=0$ in (6.1a) and (6.1b) so that $\underline{\theta}<\theta_B^*<\theta_G^*$.

Proposition 6.1.2. Both firms improve environmental performance in response to the subsidy irrespective of whether it is symmetric or paid to a single firm alone.

Proof: See Appendix A6.

The proposition follows immediately from the fact that the levels of environmental performance are strategic complements. Here, the direct effect of the subsidy consists of a reduction in the marginal R&D cost. The indirect effect via the increase in the competitor's performance raises marginal revenue of own performance and thus contributes further to the incentive to enhance environmental performance.[4]

6.3 IMPACT ON INDUSTRY SURPLUS OF GREEN SUBSIDIES

In the presence of a symmetric subsidy, $x_F^G = x_F^B = x_F$ industry surplus can be written as

$$W = \left\{ \begin{array}{l} S+\pi_G^* +\pi_B^* -x_F\left[F\!\left(\theta_G^*\right)+F\!\left(\theta_B^*\right)\right] \\ -(1+\Psi)(1-x_F)\left[F\!\left(\theta_G^*\right)+F\!\left(\theta_B^*\right)\right] \end{array} \right\},$$

where the last term on the RHS gives the taxpayers' burden with $\Psi \geq 0$ denoting the shadow cost of public funds.[5] A variation in x_F then gives rise to a change in welfare as given by

$$\frac{dW}{dx_F} = \left\{ \begin{bmatrix} \frac{\partial S}{\partial \theta_G} + \overbrace{\left(\frac{\partial \pi_G^*}{\partial \theta_G} - x_F F'\left(\theta_G^*\right) \right)}^{=0} \\ + \frac{\partial \pi_B^*}{\partial \theta_G} - (1+\Psi)(1-x_F)F'\left(\theta_G^*\right) \end{bmatrix} \frac{d\theta_G^*}{dx_F} \\ + \begin{bmatrix} \frac{\partial S}{\partial \theta_B} + \left(\frac{\partial \pi_B^*}{\partial \theta_B} - x_F F'\left(\theta_B^*\right) \right) \\ + \frac{\partial \pi_G^*}{\partial \theta_B} - (1+\Psi)(1-x_F)F'\left(\theta_B^*\right) \end{bmatrix} \frac{d\theta_B^*}{dx_F} \right\} - \Psi\left[F\left(\theta_G^*\right) + F\left(\theta_B^*\right) \right], \quad (6.2)$$

where the term in bracelets gives the change in welfare as transmitted by a change in G and B environmental performance, respectively and where the last term gives the change in the net social cost of the budget. This arises from the gap between social and private evaluation of public funds, $\Psi > 0$.[6]

Consider a boundary equilibrium where $d\theta_B^*/dx_F = 0$. Then the expression[7] in (6.2) simplifies to

$$\frac{dW}{dx_F} = \left[\frac{\partial S}{\partial \theta_G} + \frac{\partial \pi_B^*}{\partial \theta_G} - (1+\Psi)(1-x_F)F'\left(\theta_G^*\right) \right] \frac{d\theta_G^*}{dx_F} - \Psi F\left(\theta_G^*\right). \quad (6.3)$$

where $\partial S/\partial \theta_G + \partial \pi_B^*/\partial \theta_G$ is the net change of industry surplus in G performance. In analogy to the case of eco-labelling (Proposition 5.1 and Figure 5.1) we can define a boundary value

$$\overline{m} := m \big| \partial S/\partial \theta_G + \partial \pi_B^*/\partial \theta_G = 0 \text{ for } \theta_G = \theta_G^*(m)$$

such that $\partial S/\partial \theta_G + \partial \pi_B^*/\partial \theta_G < 0 \Leftrightarrow m < \overline{m}$. It then follows for $m < \overline{m}$ that the expression in (6.3) is unambiguously positive, suggesting that even a marginal subsidy lowers industry surplus. This is because by inducing the G firm to upgrade its performance the subsidy has an anti-competitive effect. The subsidy particularly harms the poor consumers. As competition is stifled the dirty variant sells at a higher price. Meanwhile these consumers do not benefit from an improved environmental performance of their product and are thus worse off. At the same time market coverage falls. If the environmental margin is low this effect more than offsets any gains from increased quality.

If $m > \overline{m}$, the introduction of a marginal subsidy, i.e. a lowering of x_F from $x_F = 1$, raises industry surplus if Ψ is sufficiently close to 0 or if $F\left(\theta_G^*\right)$ is low. An infra-marginal subsidy at $x_F < 1$ gives rise to an additional welfare loss $\Psi\left(1 - x_F\right)F'\left(\theta_G^*\right)$ due to a negative externality the firm imposes on society. When raising performance under the subsidy, the firm does not take into account that this expands the regulator's budget and therefore forces additional distortions on the economy.

For an interior equilibrium, we have to take into additional account the effect of a change in B performance on gross surplus as given by $\partial S/\partial \theta_B + \partial \pi_G^*/\partial \theta_B$. In the proof of Proposition 4.4 we have shown that an interior equilibrium implies $\partial S/\partial \theta_B + \partial \pi_G^*/\partial \theta_B > 0$ and $\partial S/\partial \theta_G + \partial \pi_B^*/\partial \theta_G > 0$. Thus the introduction of a marginal subsidy at $x_F \to 1$ raises welfare if Ψ is sufficiently close to 0. The intuition is the same as in the case of a standard. In an interior equilibrium environmental performance is under-provided for both variants. This is mitigated by the subsidy.[8] We summarise:

Proposition 6.2. Consider the introduction of a (marginal) subsidy on investment cost. (i) This lowers industry surplus if the environmental margin is sufficiently low. (ii) This raises industry surplus in an interior equilibrium, if the shadow cost of public funds is sufficiently close to zero.

From the earlier Proposition 6.1.2, we know that in an interior equilibrium, the payment of a subsidy to a single firm also raises the rival's quality. Since the result in the Proposition 6.2 relies only on the direction of the change in performance but not on the relative change, we can extend our result to the case of an asymmetric subsidy.

Corollary P6.2. In an interior equilibrium an asymmetric subsidy paid to either of the firms raises welfare.

6.4 ENVIRONMENTAL IMPACT OF GREEN SUBSIDIES

We have seen that subsidising the R&D of green technologies contributes to a reduction in unit emissions, at the least from the clean variant. What is the impact of subsidisation on industry emissions? Again, consider a symmetric subsidy, $x_F^G = x_F^B = x_F$. Using (3.5a) and (3.5b), we can write its effect on industry emissions as

$$\frac{dE}{dx_F} = \left\{ \left(\overbrace{e'\left(\theta_B^*\right)q_B^* + \frac{\partial E}{\partial \theta_B} \Big|_{\zeta=\bar{\zeta}:e\left(,\theta_B^*\right)=\bar{e}}}^{<0} \right) \overbrace{\frac{d\theta_B^*}{dx_F}}^{\leq 0} + \overbrace{e'\left(\theta_G^*\right)q_G^* \frac{d\theta_G^*}{dx_F}}^{>0} + \overbrace{\frac{\partial E}{\partial \zeta} \frac{d\zeta}{dx_F}}^{\leq 0} \right\} . (6.4)$$

Hence, the subsidy has an impact on industry emissions through four channels. By reducing the G firm's and possibly the B firm's unit emissions subsidisation tends to lower aggregate emissions directly. When raising B unit abatement the subsidy tends to reduce the B firm's and industry output at the low end of demand. Finally, by changing the degree of product differentiation and competition, the subsidy affects industry emissions via changes in the firms' market shares and industry output. Industry emissions decrease in the rate of subsidy if the RHS of (6.4) is positive. Lemma 3.1 together with $d\theta_G^*/dx_F < 0$ and $d\theta_B^*/dx_F \leq 0$ then implies the following:

Proposition 6.3.1 Consider the introduction of a marginal and symmetric subsidy of investment cost. This unambiguously reduces emissions if the environmental margin is sufficiently low, i.e. if $m < m_E$.

Recall that industry emissions unambiguously fall in G unit abatement both via the direct effect and the reduction in industry output under greater product differentiation. From Lemma 3.1, we know that $m < m_E$ implies that industry emissions also fall in the level of B unit abatement irrespective of any possible reduction in product differentiation. As the subsidy raises unit abatement of either the G firm or of both firms it lowers industry emissions.

As in the case of a standard the effect of the subsidy is more ambiguous if the environmental margin is high relative to the baseline margin. In this case, the change in industry output is then determined by the change in product differentiation. In contrast to an emission standard, which in the presence of investment costs always leads to a reduction in differentiation, a subsidy may effectively raise product differentiation. While a general result cannot be derived analytically, the following limiting case is instructive.

Proposition 6.3.2. Consider the introduction of a marginal and symmetric subsidy of investment cost. This unambiguously raises product differentiation and thereby reduces emissions if $m \gg n$.

Proof: See Appendix A6.

With its greater investment level the G firm offers a greater basis for subsidisation. It therefore tends to benefit more from the transfer both absolutely and marginally. It follows that the green firm responds to a symmetric increase in the rate of subsidy with a greater increase in environmental performance than the dirty firm. Product differentiation is enhanced and industry output and emissions fall. Numerical simulation indicates that this result is likely to extend beyond the limiting case considered in the proposition. Consider the following table which can be developed by calculating the pair $\left(\theta_B^*, \zeta^*\right)$ as a numerical solution to the system (6.1a) and (6.1b), where $m = 3.191; k = \underline{\theta} = 1$ and where n and x_F assume the values given in Table 6.1.

Table 6.1 Effect of marginal subsidy on product differentiation

| | $n = 0$ | | $n = 1$ | |
	$x_F = 1$	$x_F = 0.9$	$x_F = 1$	$x_F = 0.9$
θ_B^*	1.3158	1.3677	1.0	1.0489
ζ^*	2.7988	2.9015	3.6588	3.7612
$\Delta\zeta^*$	0.1027		0.1024	

Note: Numerical results for $m = 3.191; k = \underline{\theta} = 1$. $\Delta\zeta^* := \zeta^*\big|_{x_F=0.9} - \zeta^*\big|_{x_F=1}$.

The results listed for $n = 0$ correspond to a market with a very high environmental orientation. Note that the dirty firm then chooses an interior level of environmental performance even in the absence of a subsidy. Subsidisation, modelled as a 10 percent reduction in the investment cost, then leads to an increase in all performance levels and in the degree of product differentiation, ζ^*. This is the finding we would expect according to the analytical result reported in the proposition. Contrast this with a market with a lower environmental orientation, where for $n = 1$ a boundary equilibrium is just realised (interior equilibrium if and only if $n > 1$). We know from Table 2.2 that product differentiation tends to be greater in such a market. However, as we see, the introduction of the subsidy induces an increase in the degree of product differentiation in this case as well. Indeed the same result can be found for any $n \in [0,1]$. Thus we can predict with reasonable confidence that the introduction of investment subsidies lowers industry emissions in most cases in which an interior equilibrium is realised.[9]

This finding mirrors a result by MGPF (1997) and shares with it the caveat that it relies on the non-homogeneity of the investment cost function $F(\theta)$. As was noted in the introduction, the result is in contrast to a finding by MGPF (2002), who show for a homogeneous investment cost function that an undifferentiated subsidy has no impact on industry emissions.

The analysis of an asymmetric subsidy is straightforward. Recall that in an interior regime, both firms react to the subsidy by raising their environmental performance. However the reaction of the firm that does not receive the subsidy is governed by the indirect effect only. This firm's performance increases along the best response function together with the rival's quality. Since for either firm $i = G, B$ the slope of the best response function $b_i(\theta_j)$ to the rival's performance θ_j satisfies $\partial b_i(\theta_j)/\partial \theta_j \leq b_i(\theta_j)/\theta_j$ (Lemma A2.5 in the Appendix A2.2) this implies an increase (reduction) in the degree of differentiation if the G (B) firm is the recipient of the subsidy.

Corollary P.6.3. Consider an interior equilibrium. (i) A (marginal) subsidy paid to the G firm alone increases product differentiation and lowers emissions. A (marginal) subsidy paid to the B firm alone reduces product differentiation, and (ii) lowers emissions if $m < m_E'$, but (iii) increases emissions if $m \gg n$ and if the direct effect of abatement $e'(\theta_i)$, $i = G, B$ is sufficiently small.

Proof: See Appendix A6.

By raising product differentiation, a subsidy paid to the G firm always contributes to a reduction in industry emissions. The picture is less clear for a subsidy paid to the B firm as this lowers product differentiation. If the quality margin is high relative to the baseline margin, the increase in competition boosts output. If the volume effect dominates the direct effect of unit abatement then industry emissions increase with a subsidy.

6.5 CONCLUSIONS

In this chapter, we have studied the effects of investment subsidies on the environmental performance of vertically differentiated products and the implications for industry surplus and on industry emissions. The bottom line is similar to that of the previous chapter; namely that the welfare and environmental effects of the policy tend to depend very much on the environmental orientation of the market. If this is low, subsidising green R&D may fail to induce an improvement of the dirty product. This is the case because the subsidy reduces marginal investment cost, but does not directly affect (net) marginal revenue from quality. If the competitive effectiveness of environmental performance is negative under laissez-faire, subsidisation does not provide an incentive to improve the environmental performance of the brown product unless the subsidy induces a sufficiently strong improvement in the clean product. Only if competition is relaxed to a sufficient degree by greater product differentiation, will the dirty firm raise its own performance. As the success of the policy therefore crucially hinges on an increase in the clean product's performance this suggests that in these cases a subsidy offered to the clean firm is more appropriate than a subsidy offered to the dirty firm.

This issue may be particularly pertinent when steep investment costs constrain the environmental performance of the clean variant to a low level even when the environmental orientation of the market is high. The substantial market potential for green products would induce even the dirty firm to improve its environmental performance above the minimum level in the absence of competition. However, the need to differentiate its product then prevents it from undertaking even small improvements. Such a situation may well be present in those industries, in which traditional product variants can be greened to a limited extent, but substantial improvements require the development of new technologies. For instance, whereas the fuel efficiency of traditional Otto and diesel engines can be improved to some extent, more significant gains can be expected from the fuel cell. Likewise the availability of solar panelling at economical prices is likely to alter the pattern of domestic energy supply. Here, investment costs in developing these technologies for the market are likely to be high, in particular if the considerable risk is factored in. In such a situation, only a (non-marginal) subsidy may induce the clean firm to develop the breakthrough technology. The associated relaxation of price competition after the innovation would then allow even the dirty firm to improve its product, e.g. by rendering a conventional engine/energy supply more efficient. Our analysis shows that subsidisation aimed at the introduction of breakthrough technologies can entail substantial improvements at the dirty end of the industry.

In case of a low environmental orientation, the subsidy tends to reduce welfare. As in the case of an environmental product standard consumers are willing to forego upgrades in the environmental performance of the dirty variant – and possibly even the high quality variant – in order to benefit from a low purchasing price. If for a low environmental margin the subsidy triggers an improvement in the clean variant alone, this widens product differentiation and directly harms consumers of the dirty variant, as they have to pay a higher price, without benefiting from any improvements. But even consumers of the clean variant may be harmed if their willingness to pay for environmental performance is sufficiently weak. Provided that public funds are not too costly, the subsidy enhances welfare if the environmental orientation of the market is sufficiently high, and it always does so in an interior equilibrium. In this case consumers sufficiently appreciate the cleaning-up of the product they purchase. This holds irrespective of whether or not the subsidy enhances or reduces product differentiation.

As in the case of an environmental standard, an almost converse pattern emerges regarding the effects of the subsidy on industry emissions. If environmental orientation is low, the reduction in industry output contributes to a fall in emissions in addition to the direct drop in unit emissions from the clean variant, or sometimes from both variants. If the environmental orientation is high the volume effect of the subsidy depends crucially on whether it enhances or mitigates product differentiation. While a symmetric subsidy enhances product differentiation and thereby curtails industry output, this is different in the case of a subsidy that is paid to the dirty firm alone. In the latter case, output increases and industry emissions rise if the volume effect over-compensates the direct effect on unit emissions.

As with the analysis in the previous chapter, consider a comprehensive welfare measure $W^+ = W - \delta E$, which comprises gross surplus W and the disutility from emissions δE. Without a formal analysis, it is easy to see that a trade-off between maximising industry surplus and minimising emissions can arise, both for low and high levels of environmental orientation. If environmental orientation is low the subsidy reduces industry surplus and emissions, and therefore enhances welfare if and only if the marginal societal cost of emissions δ is sufficiently high. The reverse case may arise for high levels of environmental orientation if the subsidy leads to an increase in emissions. However as it always entails a reduction in industry emissions, a marginal subsidy paid to the clean firm alone can bring about an unambiguous increase in welfare under these circumstances.

NOTES

1. More generally, the literature on R&D distinguishes between innovation and adoption (or diffusion). For an overview see Jaffe et al. (2000). In our model these distinctions are difficult to disentangle.
2. Herguera and Lutz (1997) and Rothfels (2000) consider leapfrogging as induced by subsidies.

3. We do not address the technical aspects of this equilibrium in this section. A more detailed characterisation is given in section 2.5. One requirement is that subsidisation should not violate the convexity of the profit functions in environmental performance (compare Lemmas A2.1 and A2.5). This places a lower bound on the level of x_F^i, $i = G, B$. As we are considering marginal subsidies, for which $x_F^i \to 1$, this requirement is unproblematic.

4. Herguera and Lutz (1997) study a situation where a subsidy offered to the dirty (low quality) firm alone induces this firm to leapfrog its rival. In this case, both performance levels tend to lie above the levels that would be realised under the subsidy but in the absence of leapfrogging.

5. A value $\Psi > 1$ reflects the fact that subsidies have to be financed through taxation or public debt. As the levying of public funds is usually associated with a welfare-reducing distortion, the subsidy is not a neutral transfer. The loss to the regulator is greater than the private benefit of the firm. For a more detailed discussion see Laffont and Tirole (1993: section 3.9).

6. Recall that an increase in x_F implies a reduction in the subsidy.

7. Recall that in the lower boundary regime $(1 - x_F)F(\theta) = 0$ and $\Psi F(\theta) = 0$.

8. If $\Psi > 0$, subsidisation gives rise to a first-order welfare loss from the provision of public funds. This is because the subsidy is not only paid on the improvements in quality but also at non-marginal levels of investment $F(\theta_G^*) > 0$ and $F(\theta_B^*) \geq 0$. This introduces a discontinuity into the welfare function. A way around this problem is to consider a shadow price $\Psi(g)$ depending on the level of the budget g, where $\Psi'(g) \geq 0$, $\Psi''(g) > 0$, $\Psi(0) = \Psi'(0) = 0$.

9. The level $m = 3.191$ has been chosen conveniently so that a boundary equilibrium is realised for $n = 1$. It is easily checked however that similar results obtain for other levels of m when n is bounded from above to allow for an interior equilibrium.

7. Environmental taxation

7.1 INTRODUCTION

Many countries have recently witnessed a rekindling of the debate on environmental taxation. This has arisen in the light of many industrial countries implementing or planning to implement substantial carbon taxes in order to fulfil their commitments to curbing greenhouse gas emissions (EEA 2000, OECD 2000a). Critics generally refer to the allegedly negative consequences of environmental taxation on competitiveness, employment and consumer surplus. Environmentalists claim the environmental merits of such taxes to lie in lower consumption (a controversial point), in the incentives for consumers to substitute towards clean products, and the incentives for firms to introduce green products either by using clean inputs and processes or by developing products with superior environmental performance. With much of the debate stemming from gut reactions the present chapter seeks to shed some light on the merits of the various arguments in a setting of environmental product differentiation.

The following paragraphs provide an overview of taxes and charges with an environmental impact.[1] Confining our attention to taxation related to consumption goods, we can roughly distinguish between the environmental properties of general taxes, in particular ad-valorem taxes, and a number of specific taxes related to the environmental properties of products.

Environmental Properties of Ad-valorem Taxation

As the environmental properties of ad-valorem taxation have been widely discussed in the literature (see below), we only present a brief summary in this work. There are two environmental aspects of ad-valorem taxes. First, an ad-valorem tax has an impact on industry emissions through its impact on market size and the market shares of the two variants and through its effect on the incentives for firms to reduce unit emissions. Second, a number of countries have started to use value added (i.e. ad-valorem) taxes as an environmental policy tool by introducing reduced rates for environmentally preferable products and product variants. Examples include the following.

- Belgium: 0 percent instead of 21 percent on certain recovered materials and by-products;
- Czech Republic: 5 percent instead of 22 percent on several environmentally preferable and/or energy-efficient products;
- Portugal: 5 percent instead of 17 percent on solar power and alternative energy sources;
- Switzerland: 0 percent instead of 7.5 percent on reusable containers and certain second-hand goods;
- Turkey: 8 percent instead of 15 percent on natural gas;
- United Kingdom: 5 percent instead of 17.5 percent on certain energy saving materials.[2]

Arora and Gangopadhyay (1995), Moraga-González and Padrón-Fumero (MGPF) (1997, 2002) and Bansal and Gangopadhyay (2003) all consider the choice of environmental performance within a vertically differentiated duopoly.[3] By reducing marginal revenue from quality an ad-valorem tax reduces both firms' investments in environmental performance. Performance levels being strategic complements, both firms lower their investment even if the tax is levied on one of the variants only. Arora and Gangopadhyay (1995) conjecture from this that ad-valorem taxation (subsidisation) is harmful (beneficial) from an environmental point of view. However MGPF (1997, 2002) rightly point out that the tax contributes to a reduction in industry emissions by curtailing industry output. As it turns out, a uniform tax tends to raise or, at best, leave constant industry emissions while tax discrimination in favour of the clean variant brings down industry emissions. Due to a reduction in market coverage industry surplus tends to be reduced under any form of ad-valorem taxation.[4] Thus an environmentally differentiated ad-valorem tax may improve total welfare if marginal emission damages is relatively large. When ad-valorem taxation is usually employed to generate revenue for reasons not included in the model, the environmental differentiation of the tax rate provides an extra environmental benefit. We should caution once again that these results have been obtained within a model where a baseline margin of zero implies strict dominance on the part of the clean firm.

Specific Environmental Product Taxes

Throughout this chapter we focus on specific product taxes bearing a distinct relationship to the environmental performance of a product. The following examples show a surprising variety in the applications of environmentally related taxes and charges, which in scope and importance goes well beyond the case of energy taxes. We group them roughly into three types, mainly for the purpose of introducing them into our model of vertically differentiated duopoly later on.

Type 1: Product related taxes or charges targeted at consumers

(i)   vehicle excise taxes with differentiated rates: most OECD countries, e.g. Austria (engine power); Denmark (fuel consumption); Germany (weight and emission class); Hungary (catalytic converter or not); UK and US (fuel efficiency);

(ii) duties on retail containers and one-way products: e.g. Belgium, Czech Republic, Denmark, Germany, Hungary, Norway, Poland;[5]

(iii) duties on chemical substances (e.g. solvents, CFCs, polyvinylchlorides (PVCs), volatile organic compounds (VOCs)): Belgium, Czech Republic, Denmark, Switzerland

(iv) duty on Nickle-Cadmium (NiCd)-batteries: Denmark.[6]

The regulator employs these taxes in order to mitigate externalities arising in the process of consumption (i), or with the disposal of the product (ii)–(iv). Monitoring being impractical, these taxes are not directly related to externalities nor even to emissions but rather take the form of a lump-sum tax levied on each unit with some degree of environmental differentiation in the rate.

Type 2: Charges levied on complementary energy input (or waste disposal as complementary input to consumption) of consumption and targeted at consumers

(v)   duty on cabon dioxide (CO_2): e.g. Denmark, Sweden (levied on quantity of fuel);

(vi) duty on mineral oil (per litre or other quantity measures): e.g. Denmark, Germany, UK;

(vii) duty on electricity (per kWh): Germany.

Here the regulator's objective is threefold. Apart from the generation of revenue, there may be two environmental objectives. First, the tax may induce a direct reduction in energy consumption; and second, it may generate a demand for energy-efficient investment goods. Most empirical studies suggest a low short-run price elasticity both for domestic energy and for fuel (OECD 2000b: tables 2 and 3). This suggests that these taxes have the potential to generate revenue rather than induce a direct reduction in energy use. However the tax burden associated with energy use should then provide consumers with a strong incentive to demand energy-efficient investment goods. Here the significantly greater long-run price elasticity reported for gasoline suggests a potential for such a demand-pull effect for the innovation of energy-efficient vehicles.[7]

Type 3: Production or product-related tax targeted at producers

    (viii) emission-related taxes: e.g. Czech Republic (sulphur dioxide (SO_2), nitrogen oxides (NO_X)), France (atmospheric emissions including CO_2 from 2001), Italy (SO_2, NO_X), Poland (SO_2, CO_2), Sweden (NO_X);

    (ix)   surplus manure tax: Belgium and the Netherlands;

    (x)   tax on pesticides: Scandinavian countries;

    (xi)   energy taxes paid by producers (taxation of gas, coal, oil, electricity): e.g. Denmark, Germany, Italy, Norway.

This is the classical form of emission taxation. These taxes can be linked to the emissions themselves (viii), to output (ix), and in many instances to inputs (x) and (xi). While the regulator's objective lies in a reduction in industry emissions, this may be achieved either by a reduction in output or preferably by an improvement in emission abatement. These taxes are relevant within an environmentally differentiated industry, if consumers care not only about consumption externalities but also about production externalities.

The analysis of environmental taxation goes back to Pigou (1938). For long the analysis was confined to optimal environmental taxation within perfectly competitive industries (e.g. Baumol and Oates 1988). As is well known a Pigouvian tax equates the marginal cost of pollution prevention with the marginal environmental damage. This optimally internalises the externalities imposed on society by the polluting firm. Buchanan (1969) was the first to point out that a strict Pigouvian tax is not optimal in the presence of market power.[8] This is because by raising marginal cost the tax tends to depress the monopolist's output from a level that is too low already from a social perspective. Therefore, he concludes, the tax rate should be set below marginal environmental damage if other instruments are unavailable to the regulator. The tax cut serves as an implicit subsidy on output, which at the margin helps to mitigate the under-provision of output. In a second-best setting it is thus optimal to under-internalise and forego some environmental benefits in order to mitigate a second distortion. Buchanan (1969) was subsequently generalised to study the impact of environmental taxation in oligopoly (e.g. Ebert 1991/92, Conrad and Wang 1993, Requate 1993, Simpson 1995, Katsoulacos and Xepapadeas 1996, Lange and Requate 1999 and Carlsson 2000).[9] The result of under-internalisation in the presence of market power carries over to a fixed numbers homogeneous and horizontally differentiated oligopoly as long as industry output and/or product variety decreases under the tax.[10]

This literature is limited by embracing neither the notion of environmental innovation nor that of environmental product differentiation. The issue of environmental innovation is considered by Requate (1995), who uses an N firm oligopoly to derive the pattern of adoption of a low pollution technology under taxation and in the presence of a permit market. The clean technology is associated with a cost-disadvantage, which is however offset due to a lower tax burden. Generally both technologies can be associated with inefficient adoption patterns. Carraro and Soubeyran (1996b) consider a duopoly in which firms can introduce environmental innovation in order to compare the efficiency properties of taxes as opposed to subsidies on investment cost. Petrakis (1999) studies strategic adoption of clean technologies within a duopoly with exogenous horizontal differentiation. None of the models involves consumers who have a willingness to pay for environmental friendliness.

In this chapter, we include in our model of environmentally differentiated duopoly the scope for the regulator to levy a specific tax (or subsidy) on each unit of output, the rate of which decreases (increases) in a firm's environmental performance. We analyse the impact of this tax on firms' competitiveness (for given levels of performance), on the choices of environmental performance, and, following from this, on industry surplus and emissions. While the complexity of the model rules out the derivation of an optimal tax rule, our positive analysis yields some interesting normative implications. To our knowledge the suggested form of specific taxation has not yet been considered in the literature in spite of its practical importance (see examples).

The literature dealing with the impact of taxation in the presence of consumers with a willingness to pay for environmental friendliness is rather limited. We have already discussed the work on ad-valorem taxation within an environmentally differentiated duopoly. Lombardini-Riipinen (2002) considers the effects of a lump-sum tax on unit emissions (but not on output) in a vertically differentiated duopoly. An increase in the tax rate induces both firms to cut their unit emissions with the dirty firm reducing them by more. The associated reduction in product differentiation leads to stronger competition and an expansion of the market. While this boosts industry surplus, the reductions in unit emissions overcompensate for the effect of market growth on industry emissions. Lombardini-Riipinen also considers the combined use of a lump-sum tax on unit emissions with an ad-valorem tax. Within a covered market framework where firms face a marginal cost that is quadratic in emission abatement a social optimum with regard to industry surplus and pollution damage can be attained by appropriate combination of the two taxes. Neither the work on ad-valorem taxation nor the form of emission taxes considered by Lombardini-Riipinen (2002) embraces the 'traditional' model of an environmental tax as a specific tax levied on each unit of the product.

The following principal distinction between a specific environmental tax and an ad-valorem tax leads to appreciably different effects on industry surplus and emissions. While the models of an ad-valorem tax suggest a reduction in the marginal revenue from environmental performance/quality, this is not necessarily the case for a specific environmental tax. Indeed if environmental performance is associated with higher variable cost a specific tax that decreases with environmental performance raises marginal revenue from performance. Firms then respond to an increase in the tax rate with an upgrading rather than a downgrading of their environmental performance. This has immediate consequences for the effect of the tax on industry output, which may in some cases increase rather than decrease under taxation. Consequently welfare and the level of industry emissions levels may be affected quite differently by a specific environmental tax as opposed to an ad-valorem tax. We will highlight some of these differences in the course of analysis.[11]

Conrad (1996) studies the impact of energy taxation on the provision of an energy-efficient investment good. While consumers are not directly concerned about the environment, they care about the energy efficiency of the durable, as this determines operating cost. A monopolist chooses price and energy-efficiency of the durable. Conrad then asks how a change in energy taxation affects the level of energy efficiency and, via demand, overall energy consumption. As a bottom line, energy efficiency is raised as long as the price elasticity of demand (for the durable) is sufficiently low. In this case industry emissions fall under the assumption that the introduction of the tax always raises the effective price of the durable, i.e. the reduction in selling price is more than offset by the increase in discounted operating cost. If the price elasticity is high the monopolist reacts with a reduction in energy efficiency in order to sustain a price cut. In this case the effect of the tax on industry emissions is ambiguous. Conrad (1996) also considers a duopoly with exogenous horizontal differentiation of the durable. The duopolists compete on energy efficiency and price. By raising the elasticity of a firm's demand with respect to energy efficiency, the tax triggers an increase in energy efficiency. This holds true for simultaneous and sequential choices of energy efficiency and prices. However in a sequential setting in which firms choose energy efficiency and then prices, firms are more reluctant to improve the energy efficiency of their product, as they try to dampen price competition. Assuming a damage function that increases with energy consumption, Conrad (1996) shows that an optimal tax implies under-internalisation if energy consumption decreases with the tax rate. The reason is once more that industry output and industry surplus fall with the tax rate.[12]

As expected the main differences between our model and that of Conrad (1996) lies in our assumption of consumer heterogeneity with respect to their willingness to pay for the energy-efficient durable. In Conrad (1996) consumers are homogeneous with regard to their willingness to pay for energy efficiency and therefore firms choose symmetric levels of energy efficiency. The asymmetric pattern of quality choices in the presence of vertical differentiation as such does not cause a significant difference. Neither does the asymmetry imply that firms react to the energy tax in different ways. In our model firms raise energy efficiency in response to a tax if and only if the environmental orientation is not too low corresponding to a relatively low price elasticity of demand, the same requirement as in Conrad. A substantial difference with important normative implications arises however in regard to the welfare impact of taxation. Similarly to Conrad (1996) the tax lowers industry surplus if environmental orientation is low but the opposite is true if environmental orientation is high. Here a tax mitigates the under-provision of environmental performance from the average consumer's point of view and induces stronger competition. This implies a case for over-internalisation where the tax rate is set above the level of marginal damage.[13]

Myles and Uyduranoglu (2002) consider the use of vehicle excise duties and a fuel tax within a quality differentiated car market. They assume that high quality cars are larger and more powerful and, therefore, associated with lower fuel efficiency. Consumers choose the brand of car and then the mileage they wish to travel. Assuming a competitive market with prices reflecting the quality-dependent marginal cost, they demonstrate that under plausible conditions it may be socially efficient to tax the high quality but dirty vehicle at a lower rate. This counter-intuitive result is driven by two distortions. First, for the general preference specification they are using, marginal utility from income is decreasing in income but is increasing in quality. This is the case as consumption of the higher quality product is associated with a higher total cost (purchasing price and total fuel cost). The consequence is a discontinuity in the marginal utility of income for the marginal consumer who is indifferent between the high and low quality variant. Given this consumer's income, the marginal utility of income for high quality consumption is higher than for low quality. Efficiency would then dictate a lower tax on the high quality variant. Second, for a given income a consumer travels a greater mileage with the low quality car. But then if the difference in fuel efficiency between the two variants is not too large the operation of a high quality car is associated with lower overall emissions. The consumption of high quality cars should then be encouraged on environmental grounds by a tax reduction.[14]

There are a number of obvious differences between their approach and ours. First, they assume a trade-off between quality and environmental performance (in terms of unit emissions). If environmental performance and quality were correlated their model would suggest an unambiguous tax bias in favour of the clean variant. Second, while their model is more general in considering an endogenous usage pattern and a more general preference structure, they do not consider the competitive interaction between firms in terms of prices and fuel efficiency where both variables are exogenous.[15] Thus the focus of the paper turns out to be rather different and the findings are difficult to compare.

Subsidisation of Green Consumption

Our model lends itself to the analysis of subsidies on the purchase of environmentally friendly products. A number of countries subsidise the purchase of environmentally superior products, mostly investment goods, with the purpose of promoting demand for such variants. Such subsidies can be analytically treated as inverse product-related taxes of type 1, and we can conveniently extend our model to analyse the implications of this instrument. Some examples of such variable subsidies are the following (OECD, 1999a: table 3.25):

- Germany: subsidisation of the installation of solar panels for the generation of household energy;
- Japan: grant to promote low emission vehicles; 50 percent of price differential with conventional vehicles (budget: ¥ 450 million);
- Sweden: grant to house owners on purchase of fuel tanks with reduced emissions (max. 30 percent of cost);
- Turkey: promotion of lead-free gasoline by lowering sales prices.

Our analysis of a subsidy provides yet another example of how the presence of vertical differentiation can give rise to unexpected policy effects. Namely an environmentally related subsidy paid to both the clean and dirty variants can contribute to a reduction in industry emissions and this is true even if firms do not alter their abatement effort. Even more surprisingly emissions fall although the subsidy triggers an increase in industry output. Underlying this result is the effect of the subsidy on the firms' relative competitiveness. By reducing its cost disadvantage the subsidy helps the clean firm to capture market share from its rival. If this substitution from the dirty towards the clean variant is sufficiently strong, industry emissions fall.

One part of the subsequent analysis will be devoted to a comparison between the effects of taxation and subsidisation on welfare and industry emissions. As one might suspect, subsidisation is welfare superior to taxation if willingness to pay for environmental performance is low. The conditions under which taxes as opposed to subsidies are more effective in reducing industry emissions are less clear-cut.

Conrad (1993) models the impact of an abatement subsidy, which is similar to our variable subsidy, within a Cournot duopoly. He shows that (i) the subsidy has an output raising effect and thereby helps to improve welfare; (ii) that a combined tax-subsidy scheme increases abatement per unit of polluting input by more than a pure tax. His conclusion that the policy thereby 'contributes to improving [the] global environment' (p. 130) however must clearly be subjected to the notion that the increase in abatement per unit input must over-compensate the increase in input demand as triggered by the (relatively) greater output. He does not explicitly prove this point and one can easily imagine circumstances under which the output (and input) raising effect of an abatement subsidy dominates the increase in abatement.

The remainder of the chapter is organised as follows. In the following section, we draw up a simple model of a quality (i.e., environmentally) related transfer and analyse its impact on the price equilibrium and the firms' competitive position. Section 7.3 endogenises environmental performance. Section 7.4 contains a welfare analysis and in section 7.5 we study the impact of the transfer on industry emissions. Section 7.6 concludes. A number of proofs are relegated to Appendix A6.

7.2 A MODEL OF AN ENVIRONMENTAL TAX-SUBSIDY-SCHEME

In the following we introduce a tax-subsidy scheme into our model of environmentally differentiated duopoly and relate it to the three cases of environmentally related product taxes that were identified earlier.

Type 1: Product-related tax or subsidy targeted at consumer

We assume throughout that the tax-subsidy scheme is such that the unit rate of the tax (subsidy) decreases (increases) with the environmental performance of the product. Specifically suppose the regulator imposes the following two-part transfer on each unit of the differentiated product, which has to be borne by consumers:

$$t \cdot (\theta - \rho); \; \rho \geq \underline{\theta} \qquad\qquad (7.1),$$

where $t > 0$ is the tax/subsidy rate, θ is environmental performance and ρ is a performance target set by the regulator. Here $e(\rho)$ can be viewed as the corresponding emission target. While the net transfer from the regulator increases with performance, θ, the lump-sum part $-t\rho$ determines whether it constitutes a tax or a subsidy. Obviously for $\rho = \underline{\theta}$ the transfer constitutes a unit subsidy on the provision of environmental performance. For $\rho > \underline{\theta}$ the transfer is hybrid and it depends on the variant's performance whether the transfer is a subsidy or a tax. Let $\{\theta_B^*, \theta_G^*\}$ denote the set of equilibrium performance levels in the presence of the transfer. It is then straightforward to see that for $\rho < \theta_B^*$, the transfer constitutes a subsidy for both variants; for $\rho \in [\theta_B^*, \theta_G^*]$, it constitutes a tax on the B variant but a subsidy on the G variant; and for $\rho > \theta_G^*$, it constitutes a tax on both variants.[16]

Unless the unit emission function $e(\theta)$ is linear, the tax-subsidy scheme in (7.1) is not a proper emission tax.[17] We have chosen a linear specification not only for its analytical convenience, but also because we believe it to better represent real world schemes of environmental taxation. The examples provided in the introduction show that most taxes are not directly related to unit emissions but rather to technological aspects of the product that correlate with unit emissions. The obvious advantage of linking the tax to the design properties of the product is a lower cost of measurement.

Type 2: Charge levied on complementary energy input

Here, we presume the differentiated product to be a durable which, as in Conrad (1996), requires a complementary energy input. Obvious examples are automobiles and petrol or household appliances and electricity. In such a setting we can interpret $t(\rho - \theta)$, $\rho \geq \underline{\theta}$, as the discounted value of expenditure on the energy input, e.g. the discounted value of expenditure on petrol, used over the durable's lifetime. Then t is a measure of the cost to the consumer of the input comprising the market price and a tax rate on energy. The term $\rho - \theta$ expresses energy consumption over the lifetime of the product where ρ denotes gross energy consumption. Here θ captures the energy efficiency of the durable. Since even energy-efficient equipment usually consumes at least some amount of energy we would generally expect $\rho > \theta$.[18] We make the following simplifying assumptions:

- Consumers are homogeneous with regard to their patterns of using the product so that ρ is representative for all consumers.
- Gross energy demand ρ is inelastic with respect to t. The only way the consumer can react to changes in t is by revising her purchasing decision with regard to the durable. On the one hand this implies that the regulator in our model can only hope to affect energy consumption by stimulating substitution either towards the energy-efficient variant of the durable or entirely away from the durable. On the other hand an improvement in energy efficiency θ may stimulate more intense usage of the car and thus an increase in ρ. Like Conrad (1996), we ignore this so-called 're-bound' effect.[19]

The market price components of the input cost t are constant and normalised to zero. Hence t entirely reflects the tax rate as chosen by the regulator.

Again duties on energy consumables such as the duty on mineral oil or energy are related to input measures rather than emissions.[20] Obviously the impact of these duties on consumers' purchasing decisions regarding the durable are then reflected not in unit emissions but technical properties such as energy or fuel efficiency θ.

For both type 1 and 2 taxes, the consumer faces an effective price

$$\varphi(\theta) = p(\theta) + t(\rho - \theta). \tag{7.2}$$

Then a consumer with WTP v for environmental performance realises a net surplus from consumption $U(\theta) = v\theta + u - \varphi(\theta) = (v + t)\theta + u - p(\theta) - t\rho$. The demand functions are, thus, given by $q_G = \bar{v} - v_1$ and $q_B = v_1 - v_0$ with

$$v_1 = \frac{p_G - p_B}{\theta_G - \theta_B} - t \; ; \qquad v_0 = \frac{p_B - (u - t\rho)}{\theta_B} - t \, .$$

Type 3: Production- or product-related tax or subsidy targeted at producer

Here the transfer in (7.1) occurs between the regulator and the firm. As for type 1, we interpret $t \geq 0$ as the tax rate and $\rho \geq \underline{\theta}$ as an abatement target, where the regulator can choose both variables. Using (7.1) a firm's marginal cost can then be written

$$(c - t)\theta + c_0 + t\rho \, .$$

For type 3 the indices of marginal consumers continue to be given by $v_1 = (p_G - p_B)/(\theta_G - \theta_B)$ and $v_0 = (p_B - u)/\theta_B$. Recall the consumer distribution on the interval $[\underline{v}, \overline{v}]$. A covered market with $v_0 > \underline{v}$ is then guaranteed for types 1–3 if $c - t > \underline{v}$ and $n - t\rho + (\underline{v} - c + t)\underline{\theta} < 0$, where $n = u - c_0$, hold for all relevant $t \geq 0$. This is what we assume throughout. Furthermore, let us maintain our assumption that $n - t\rho \geq 0$ implying that the baseline margin net of the 'baseline part' of the transfer is non-negative. This reflects the presumption that consumers would not purchase the product on the basis of its environmental properties alone.

Price Equilibrium and Competitiveness

Consider a game in which the regulator commits to a tax-subsidy scheme $\{t, \rho\}$ before the firms engage in a game of quality-then-price competition. It is straightforward to derive the price equilibrium, which is characterised as follows:

$$p_G^{12^*} = \frac{[2(\overline{v} + t)\theta_G + u - t\rho](\theta_G - \theta_B) + [c(2\theta_G + \theta_B) + 3c_0]\theta_G}{4\theta_G - \theta_B}, \quad (7.3a)$$

$$p_B^{12^*} = \frac{[(\overline{v} + t)\theta_B + 2(u - t\rho)](\theta_G - \theta_B) + 3c\theta_G\theta_B + c_0(2\theta_G + \theta_B)}{4\theta_G - \theta_B} \quad (7.3b)$$

for types 1 and 2, and

$$p_G^{3^*} = \frac{[2\overline{v}\theta_G + u](\theta_G - \theta_B) + [(c - t)(2\theta_G + \theta_B) + 3(c_0 + t\rho)]\theta_G}{4\theta_G - \theta_B}, \quad (7.4a)$$

$$p_B^{3^*} = \frac{[\overline{v}\theta_B + 2u](\theta_G - \theta_B) + 3(c - t)\theta_G\theta_B + (c_0 + t\rho)(2\theta_G + \theta_B)}{4\theta_G - \theta_B} \quad (7.4b)$$

for type 3. Again using $m = \overline{v} - c$ and $n = u - c_0$ we obtain for all types

$$q_G^*(\theta_G, \theta_B, t, \rho) = \frac{[2(m + t)\theta_G + n - t\rho]}{(4\theta_G - \theta_B)}, \quad (7.5a)$$

$$q_B^*(\theta_G, \theta_B, t, \rho) = \frac{[(m + t)\theta_B + 2(n - t\rho)]\theta_G}{(4\theta_G - \theta_B)\theta_B}, \quad (7.5b)$$

$$\pi_G^*(\theta_G, \theta_B, t, \rho) = \frac{[2(m+t)\theta_G + n - t\rho]^2 (\theta_G - \theta_B)}{(4\theta_G - \theta_B)^2}, \qquad (7.6a)$$

$$\pi_B^*(\theta_G, \theta_B, t, \rho) = \frac{[(m+t)\theta_B + 2(n - t\rho)]^2 \theta_G (\theta_G - \theta_B)}{(4\theta_G - \theta_B)^2 \theta_B}. \qquad (7.6b)$$

It is readily verified from (7.3a)–(7.4b) that

$$p_i^{3*} = p_i^{12*} + t(\rho - \theta_i) = \varphi_i^*; \quad i = G, B, \qquad (7.7)$$

where φ_i as in (7.2) is the effective purchasing price under the transfer. As consumers face the same effective price irrespective of the addressee of the tax, the firms' market shares, mark-ups and operating profits do not depend on the addressee of the transfer. This symmetry helps to facilitate our analysis by reducing the number of cases to be considered. Using (7.5a), (7.5b), (7.6a) and (7.6b), it is easy to check that

$$\rho < \frac{1}{t}[2(m+t)\theta_G + n] \qquad (7.8)$$

is sufficient to guarantee $\{q_i^*, \pi_i^*\} > 0, i = G, B$. If (2.7) holds so that both firms produce positive output under laissez-faire, then the condition in (7.8) is satisfied for any ρ if the tax rate t is sufficiently low. In the following, assume (7.8) to be satisfied. From (7.5a), (7.5b), (7.6a) and (7.6b), respectively,

$$\left\{\frac{\partial q_G^*}{\partial t}, \frac{\partial \pi_G^*}{\partial t}\right\} > 0 \Leftrightarrow 2\theta_G > \rho; \quad \left\{\frac{\partial q_B^*}{\partial t}, \frac{\partial \pi_B^*}{\partial t}\right\} > 0 \Leftrightarrow \theta_B > 2\rho \quad (7.9a)$$

$$\left\{\frac{\partial q_G^*}{\partial \rho}, \frac{\partial \pi_G^*}{\partial \rho}, \frac{\partial q_B^*}{\partial \rho}, \frac{\partial \pi_B^*}{\partial \rho}\right\} < 0. \qquad (7.9b)^{21}$$

For the subsequent analysis we introduce the following convention.

Definition 7.1 (i) The transfer constitutes an implicit subsidy to (an implicit tax on) the B variant, if $2\rho < \theta_B$ ($2\rho > \theta_B$). (ii) The transfer constitutes an implicit subsidy to (an implicit tax on) the G variant if $\rho < 2\theta_G$ ($\rho > 2\theta_G$).

Then, (7.9a) and (7.9b) imply the following.

Proposition 7.1. (i) Taxation of both variants ($\rho > \theta_G$) always lowers B output and profit but lowers G output if and only if it is an implicit tax on the G variant. (ii) Subsidisation of both variants $\rho < \theta_B$ always raises G output and profit but raises B output if and only if it is an implicit subsidy. (iii) An increase in the degree of taxation, i.e. an increase in the target ρ reduces output and profit of both firms.

The B firm's potential loss of market share and operating profit even under a subsidy – and likewise the G firm's increase in market share and profit even under a tax – arise from the interaction of two effects. First, an increase in t has a direct impact on the firm's demand, profit margin, and operating profit. In the case of a subsidy ($\rho < \theta$) the transfer tends to increase demand and the profit margin and vice versa in the case of a tax ($\rho > \theta$). Second, an increase in t improves the competitive position of the G firm as opposed to its rival. Thereby it allows the G firm to improve its market share and operating profit even under a tax, $\rho \geq \theta_G$, as long as the direct effect of taxation is not too strong, i.e. as long as $\rho < 2\theta_G$. Taking the change in competitiveness into account, an implicit tax for the G firm then implies a true tax, but not vice-versa. Similarly the loss of competitiveness implies that even under a subsidy, $\rho \leq \theta_B$, the B firm may lose market share and operating profit. An implicit subsidy for the B firm implies a true subsidy, but not vice versa.

The change in competitiveness itself is subject to two forces. Recall that in a non-covered market, the B firm has to defend its market share at both ends. At the high end it competes head on with the G firm, whereas at the low end it has to attract consumers from the group who do not buy the differentiated product at all. Inspection of (7.6a) and (7.6b) shows that the transfer reduces the B firm's advantage in marginal cost by an amount $t(\theta_G - \theta_B)$. Thus, the B firm loses competitiveness at the high end. More surprisingly perhaps, a substantial part of the G firm's gain in competitiveness can be attributed to the lump-sum part of the transfer $t\rho$. Inspection of (7.3a) and (7.3b) shows that the lump-sum part improves the G firm's competitive position by allowing it to set a relatively higher price than the competitor. This is because the lump-sum transfer reduces the B firm's profitability at the low end of the market, where the firm can pass the lump-sum burden to the consumers only to a much more limited extent than the G firm. The effect of the transfer on dominance in market share and profit is immediate. Since

$$q_G^* \ge q_B^* \iff m \ge m_q(t,\rho) := -t + (n-t\rho)(2\theta_G - \theta_B)/(\theta_G\theta_B) \quad (7.10)$$

$$\pi_G^* \ge \pi_B^* \iff m \ge m_\pi(t,\rho) = -t + (n-t\rho)/\sqrt{\theta_G\theta_B} \ , \quad (7.11)$$

the following is immediate:

Corollary P7.1. The introduction of an environmentally related tax or subsidy favours dominance on the part of the G firm.

We can now proceed to study how the transfer affects the choice of environmental performance.

7.3 CHOICE OF ENVIRONMENTAL PERFORMANCE

In order to keep the analysis simple let us focus for the moment on the case without investment in environmental improvements. As will be seen, a number of substantial issues arise even within this simpler setting. Much of the intuition carries over to the case in which firms invest in environmental improvements. We comment on the investment cost case where appropriate.

In the presence of the tax-subsidy scheme (7.1) the marginal revenue (net variable cost) of environmental performance is given by

$$\frac{\partial \pi_G^*(\theta_G,\theta_B,t,\rho)}{\partial \theta_G} = \frac{q_G^*(\theta_G,\theta_B,t,\rho)}{(4\theta_G-\theta_B)^2} r(\theta_G,\theta_B,t,\rho), \quad (7.12a)$$

$$\frac{\partial \pi_B^*(\theta_G,\theta_B,t,\rho)}{\partial \theta_B} = \frac{q_B^*(\theta_G,\theta_B,t,\rho)}{(4\theta_G-\theta_B)^2} \frac{s(\theta_G,\theta_B,t,\rho)}{\theta_B}, \quad (7.12b)$$

where

$$r(\theta_G,\theta_B,t,\rho) = 2(m+t)\alpha(\theta_G,\theta_B) - (n-t\rho)\beta(\theta_G,\theta_B), \quad (7.13a)$$
$$s(\theta_G,\theta_B,t,\rho) = (m+t)\theta_G\theta_B\beta(\theta_G,\theta_B) - 2(n-t\rho)\alpha(\theta_G,\theta_B), \quad (7.13b)$$

with $\alpha(\theta_G,\theta_B) := 4\theta_G^2 - 3\theta_G\theta_B + 2\theta_B^2 > 0$ and $\beta(\theta_G,\theta_B) := 4\theta_G - 7\theta_B$. Recalling our assumption $(7/4)\underline{\theta} < \overline{\theta} < (13/4)\underline{\theta}$ and using the definitions

$$m_l(t,\rho) = -t + (n-t\rho)\left[\beta(\overline{\theta},\underline{\theta})/2\alpha(\overline{\theta},\underline{\theta})\right], \quad (7.14a)$$
$$m_h(t,\rho) = -t + (n-t\rho)\left[2\alpha(\overline{\theta},\underline{\theta})/\overline{\theta}\,\underline{\theta}\beta(\overline{\theta},\underline{\theta})\right], \quad (7.14b)$$

the following can be established by analogy with Proposition 2.2.

Proposition 7.2. (i) A unique lower boundary equilibrium is realised if and only if $m < m_l(t, \rho)$. Here, $\theta_G^* \in (\underline{\theta}; (7/4)\underline{\theta}]$ if $m \in (-t - (n - t\rho)/2\underline{\theta}; 0]$ and $\theta_G^* \in ((7/4)\underline{\theta}; \overline{\theta}]$ if $m > -t$. (ii) A unique maximum differentiation equilibrium is realised if and only if $m \in [m_l(t, \rho), m_h(t, \rho)]$. (iii) A unique upper boundary equilibrium is realised if and only if $m > m_h(t, \rho)$. Here, $\theta_B^* \in (\underline{\theta}; (4/7)\overline{\theta}]$.

Corollary P7.2. The comparative static properties shown in Table 7.1 apply with regard to the transfer rate t and the environmental target ρ.

Proof: See Appendix A7.

Table 7.1 Comparative static effects of transfer

	$d\theta_G^*$	$d\theta_B^*$
dt	UB and MD: $= 0$ LB : $> 0 \Leftarrow m + t \geq 0$ $< 0 \Leftrightarrow \begin{cases} m + t < 0 \text{ and} \\ \rho > -\dfrac{2\alpha(\theta_G^*, \underline{\theta})}{\beta(\theta_G^*, \underline{\theta})} > 2\theta_G^* \end{cases}$ *	UB: > 0 LB and MD: $= 0$
$d\rho$	UB and MD: $= 0$ LB: $\begin{array}{l} > 0 \Leftrightarrow m + t > 0 \\ \leq 0 \Leftrightarrow m + t \leq 0 \end{array}$	UB: > 0 LB and MD: $= 0$

Notes:

UB: Upper bound, *MD*: Maximum Differentiation, *LB*: Lower bound.

* Observe that in the absence of investment cost $m + t < 0 \Leftrightarrow \beta(\theta_G^*, \underline{\theta}) < 0$. It is easily verified that the inequality $\rho > -2\alpha(\theta_G^*, \underline{\theta})/\beta(\theta_G^*, \underline{\theta})$ violates neither (7.8) nor $n \geq t\rho$ if (2.5) holds and if t is sufficiently small.

The impact of the transfer on the firms' choices of environmental performance is straightforward as long as the transfer-adjusted environmental margin $m + t$ is non-negative. In this case, an increase in transfer rate t

triggers an increase in the clean and dirty firm's performance in the lower and upper boundary equilibrium, respectively. Furthermore, taxation (as opposed to subsidisation) tends to provide a stronger incentive to enhance environmental performance as implied by the positive effect of the target ρ on the firms' performance levels. We will discuss some of the more counter-intuitive effects below.

In the presence of investment costs the following complications arise. Reconsider the expressions in (7.12a) and (7.12b) for the marginal (net) revenue from environmental performance $\partial \pi_i / \partial \theta_i$, $i = G, B$, which in equilibrium has to equal the marginal investment cost $F'(\theta_i)$. According to our definition 2.1 we have labelled the first term, $q_i^*(4\theta_G - \theta_B)^{-2}$, as the 'value' of environmental performance and the second terms, $r(\cdot)$ and $s(\cdot)\theta_B^{-1}$, respectively, as the 'competitive effectiveness' of environmental performance.

In the presence of investment costs, the transfer then affects the incentive to provide environmental performance through changes in the 'value' and in the 'competitive effectiveness' of performance. The effect on competitive effectiveness is presented in Table 7.1. The effect of the transfer on the 'value' of environmental performance is given by its (weighted) impact on output. The sign of this effect is captured in (7.9a) and (7.9b). According to (7.9a) the transfer increases the value of environmental performance if and only if it constitutes an implicit subsidy to the respective firm. According to (7.9b) a tax is always associated with a lower value of quality as opposed to a subsidy. It is obvious that the effects of the transfer on value and competitive effectiveness can interact in a number of offsetting or reinforcing ways.

For a boundary equilibrium the transfer only affects the performance incentives of the clean firm. However, and this is the second complication, for an interior equilibrium, the performance incentive for both firms is affected simultaneously. As qualities are strategic complements there is no problem as long as the transfer changes the marginal (net) revenue $\partial \pi_i / \partial \theta_i$, $i = G, B$ for each firm in the same direction. In this case strategic interaction reinforces the direct impact. However the impact of the transfer on environmental performance becomes even more ambiguous if it provides opposing incentives to the two firms. An analytical solution is intractable but we will report some numerical results below.

Reduction in G Performance under Taxation

Consider a market with a low environmental orientation as expressed by a negative environmental margin, $m < 0$. In this case the clean firm will have reduced its environmental performance to a low level, whereas the performance of the dirty product is at the baseline level. Now suppose the regulator introduces a marginal tax on both variants, where the transfer rate t is varied from zero while $\rho > 2\theta_G^*$. As $m < 0$ implies a lower boundary equilibrium the introduction of a marginal transfer will not have an impact on the performance of the dirty firm.

Consider thus the effect on the performance incentive for the green firm. From (7.12a),

$$\frac{\partial^2 \pi_G^*\left(\theta_G^*, \underline{\theta}, t, \rho\right)}{\partial \theta_G \partial t} = \frac{q_G^*(\cdot) r_t(\cdot)}{\left(4\theta_G^* - \underline{\theta}\right)^2} + \frac{\left(2\theta_G^* - \rho\right) r(\cdot)}{\left(4\theta_G^* - \underline{\theta}\right)^3} \qquad (7.15).$$

In the absence of investment costs the first-order condition implies $r(\cdot) = 0$ so that the second term on the RHS drops out. The effect of the tax on G performance then depends on the sign of the derivative $r_t(\cdot)$. It is easily checked that $r_t(\cdot) < 0$ if ρ is sufficiently large. In this case the G producer responds to the introduction of the tax by reducing the environmental performance of the product. To understand this, consider the two effects of the transfer on the competitive effectiveness of G performance. In accordance with Lemma 2.2 we can write

$$r(\theta_G, \theta_B, t, \rho) = \left\{ \begin{array}{c} \overbrace{[2(m+t)(2\theta_G - \theta_B) - (n - t\rho)]}^{DE} \\ \underbrace{+ 3[(m+t)\theta_B + 2(n - t\rho)]\theta_B}_{SE} \end{array} \right\},$$

where the first term on the RHS gives the direct effect (DE) on profit of an increase in θ_G and the second term gives the strategic effect (SE) through the softening of the B firm's price response. By inspection it is obvious that the tax always increases the direct effect of θ_G. This is because the tax strengthens environmental performance as a source of competitive advantage. By improving the environmental features of its product the clean firm can reduce the tax burden borne either by itself (type 3) or by its consumers (types 1 and 2). In the former case this lowers marginal cost and allows the firm to sell additional units; in the latter case this lowers the effective price faced by consumers and thus generates additional demand.

In contrast the effect of the tax on the strategic effect is negative. This follows immediately as $\rho > 2\theta_G > \theta_B/2$. As the tax erodes the dirty firm's competitive position and market share, this also limits a firm's incentive to raise price in response to a greater degree of product differentiation. Hence under environmental taxation competition remains stiff even under a greater degree of product differentiation. This in turn curbs the clean firm's incentive to improve the environmental performance of its product. As it turns out, the negative impact of an environmental tax on the incentive to provide greater environmental performance dominates when a low environmental orientation (as captured by a negative environmental margin) implies a low degree of product differentiation to begin with. Here the clean firm uses its enhanced competitive position not to draw on its inherent (quality) advantage but rather to attack more aggressively on price. In order to do this the firm cuts environmental performance. We can summarise.

Proposition 7.3.1. The introduction of a (marginal) environmental tax on both variants may induce a reduction in the clean product's environmental performance for strategic reasons if the environmental orientation is sufficiently low and the tax is an implicit tax on both variants.

What is interesting about this result is that it relies entirely on the impact of taxation on the nature of competition as captured in competitive effectiveness. In the presence of investment costs, the tendency for the tax to cause a reduction in G performance is even stronger. As the tax reduces competitive effectiveness only if $\rho > 2\theta_G$ and since $r(\cdot) > 0$ in the presence of investment costs, the second term in (7.15) is unambiguously negative. By curbing G output and squeezing the profit margin an implicit tax reduces the value of environmental performance and curbs even further the incentive to provide a clean product.

In some cases the regulator could avoid the perverse effect of taxation on the clean product's performance by adjusting the quality target downwards and thereby reducing the bite of the tax. However this is not possible when ρ is an exogenous technological parameter as in the context of energy taxation (type 2). In this case we have interpreted ρ as a measure of the (maximal) energy intensity of the product, with t the tax rate on energy. The above argument then shows that the regulator may face a serious dilemma when considering the introduction of an energy tax. Regulatory measures are most warranted under the following circumstances. Products are highly energy intensive, i.e. feature a high ρ, and firms have no market incentives to improve the energy efficiency as is the case for a negative environmental margin. However these are the very circumstances under which the introduction of an energy tax is likely actually to reduce the clean variant's level of energy efficiency.

Taxation versus Subsidisation

Consider an increase in ρ for $t > 0$.[22] From Table 7.1, we see that in the absence of an investment cost the environmental performance of both variants increases if the environmental margin is positive, i.e. if $m + t > 0$. This implies that a tax is more effective in enhancing environmental friendliness.

In the presence of investment costs a trade-off arises for an increase in the target ρ, i.e. for a shift towards taxation.[23] Given a positive environmental margin, it follows from Table 7.1 that a tax tends to be associated with a greater competitive effectiveness of environmental performance for either of the firms. However by depressing output a tax (as opposed to a subsidy) tends to reduce the value of environmental performance as a competitive tool. Either effect may dominate now and it can no longer be said whether a tax or a subsidy is more effective in stimulating environmental performance. For an illustration consider the effect of the target ρ on the clean firm's marginal revenue from environmental performance

$$R_\rho := \frac{\partial^2 \pi_G^*\left(\theta_G^*, \underline{\theta}, t, \rho\right)}{\partial \theta_G \partial \rho} = \frac{q_G^*(\cdot) r_\rho(\cdot)}{\left(4\theta_G^* - \underline{\theta}\right)^2} - \frac{r(\cdot)}{\left(4\theta_G^* - \underline{\theta}\right)^3}. \qquad (7.16)$$

The following can then be shown

Proposition 7.4. If the investment rate k is sufficiently low, then there exists an interval $\lfloor \underline{m}_\rho, \overline{m}_\rho \rfloor$ such that $R_\rho > 0 \Leftrightarrow m \in \lfloor \underline{m}_\rho, \overline{m}_\rho \rfloor$. Here, $\overline{m}_\rho < m_h{}'$ for all k, implying $R_\rho < 0$ within an interior regime.

Proof: See Appendix A7.

Hence, if investments into environmental performance are not too costly at the margin then a tax is more effective in raising the G firm's environmental performance for a range of intermediate values of the environmental margin.

In the case of a negative environmental margin, $m + t < 0$, the environmental performance of the G variant decreases in ρ. The stronger the tax character of the instrument, the more the G firm's competitive position is enhanced. But as we have outlined above, in the presence of a negative environmental margin, the G firm has an incentive to use the gain in competitiveness in order to compete more vigorously on price and thus to reduce performance. In this case a subsidy is the more effective instrument in

stimulating environmental performance. This holds a fortiori in the presence
of investment costs.

Numerical Results

An analytical derivation of the effects of a tax on performance choices within
the interior equilibrium is too cumbersome. In order to gain an idea of the
likely impact, we provide some numerical results. Consider Tables 7.2a and
7.2b, which can be developed by obtaining the pair $\left(\theta_G^*,\theta_B^*\right)$ as a numerical
solution to the system:

$$\partial\pi_i^*(\theta_G,\theta_B,t,\rho)/\partial\theta_i - F'(\theta_i)=0, \quad i=G,B,$$

where $\partial\pi_i^*(\theta_G,\theta_B,t,\rho)/\partial\theta_i$ are as given in (7.12a) and (7.12b),
respectively, and where $F'(\theta_i)=k(\theta_i-\underline{\theta})$. For the purpose of calculations
we have set $m=3.191; k=\underline{\theta}=1$. The variables n, t and ρ assume the
values given in the tables.

Table 7.2a Effect of tax on environmental performance: $n=0$

	$t=0$	$t=0.1$ $\rho=\theta_G^*$	$t=0.1$ $\rho=\hat{\rho}=6.116$	$t=0.1$ $\rho=\overline{\rho}=16.483$
θ_G^*	3.6827	3.8318	3.8192	3.7124
$\Delta\theta_G^*$		0.1491	0.1365	0.0297
θ_B^*	1.3158	1.3771	1.3817	1.0544
$\Delta\theta_B^*$		0.0613	0.0659	-0.2614
ζ^*	2.7988	2.7825	2.7641	3.5209
$\Delta\zeta^*$		-0.0163	-0.0347	0.7221

Table 7.2b Effect of tax on environmental performance: $n = 1$

	$t = 0$	$t = 0.1$ $\rho = \theta_G^*$	$t = 0.1$ $\rho = \hat{\rho} = 16.116$	$t = 0.1$ $\rho = \overline{\rho} = 26.455$
θ_G^*	3.6588	3.8486	3.8192	3.7077
$\Delta\theta_G^*$		0.1898	0.1604	0.0489
θ_B^*	1.0	1.2219	1.3817	1.0
$\Delta\theta_B^*$		0.2219	0.3817	0
ζ^*	3.6588	3.1497	2.7641	3.7077
$\Delta\zeta^*$		-0.5091	-0.8947	0.0489

Notes: Numerical results for $m = 3.191$; $k = \underline{\theta} = 1$. $\Delta\theta_G^*$, $\Delta\theta_B^*$ and $\Delta\zeta^*$ report the differences between the variable value in the respective column and the value of the same variable when $t = 0$ (reported in column 2). $\hat{\rho} := \arg\max \theta_B^*$ and $\overline{\rho} := \min\left\{\rho \,\middle|\, \pi_B^*\left(\theta_G^*, \theta_B^*, t, \rho\right) \le 0\right\}$.

Here we consider two possible regimes, one with high environmental orientation ($n = 0$) (Table 7.2a) and one with a lower level of environmental orientation for which a boundary solution just obtains ($n = 1$) (Table 7.2b). For each of these regimes the pair of environmental performance levels $\left(\theta_G^*, \theta_B^*\right)$ are reported as well as the associated degree of differentiation ζ^* in the absence of taxation, $t = 0$ (column 2 of the respective table), and for different scenarios of taxation. Specifically we consider a (marginal) tax rate $t = 0.1$ and explore the impact of different levels of the target ρ. Column 3 reports the impact of the 'weakest' possible tax on both variants, where the target is fixed at the performance level of the clean firm $\rho = \theta_G^*$. It can be shown that for the chosen combination of parameters $d\theta_G^*/d\rho < 0$, implying that increasing degrees of taxation unambiguously curb G performance. This is not true for θ_B^* which increases in ρ up to a level $\hat{\rho} = \arg\max \theta_B^*$. The performance levels at this point are reported in column 4. Recall from (7.9b) that profit levels decrease in ρ. Column 5 reports the outcome for the target level $\overline{\rho}$ at which the dirty firm makes a zero profit.[24] For ease of reference we report for each of the taxation scenarios the changes $\Delta\theta_G^*$, $\Delta\theta_B^*$ and $\Delta\zeta^*$ vis-à-vis the respective laissez-faire levels. The following observations are of interest.

(a) A moderate tax (column 3) increases both performance levels and reduces product differentiation vis-à-vis laissez-faire, which is reassuring from a policy perspective.

(b) For $\rho \leq \hat{\rho}$, strengthening the tax raises B performance but deteriorates G performance and therefore reduces product differentiation (column 4). This notwithstanding that G performance is always greater than under laissez-faire.

(c) For $\rho \in [\hat{\rho}, \overline{\rho}]$ a stronger tax reduces both performance levels (column 5). While G performance exceeds the laissez-faire level even at $\rho = \overline{\rho}$, B performance is lower or at best equal to its laissez-faire level. Hence for a high tax product differentiation is greater than under laissez-faire.

(d) The environmental incentives for the dirty firm – but not for the clean firm – generated by a tax decrease in the degree of environmental orientation. For $n = 0$, B performance increases only by 0.0613 for a tax at $\rho = \theta_G^*$ as compared to 0.2219 for $n = 1$. The scope for a stronger tax to provide further incentives to the B firm is more limited. For an increase in the target from $\rho = \theta_G^*$ to $\hat{\rho}|_{n=0}$ B performance increases only by 0.0046 for $n = 0$ as opposed to 0.1598 for $n = 1$. Finally, for $n = 0$ a strong tax at $\rho = \overline{\rho}$ leads to a reduction in the performance of the dirty variant relative to its performance under laissez faire, whereas for $n = 1$ the dirty variant exhibits the same performance as under laissez-faire. Note the contrast to the incentives provided to the G firm, where a tax induces a significant increase in performance irrespective of environmental orientation. The rather limited scope for taxes to improve the environmental performance of the dirty firm in markets with strong environmental orientation can be explained by the lack of product differentiation within this regime. In a market with high environmental orientation the dirty firm is compelled for competitive reasons to provide a high degree of environmental performance even in the absence of taxation. It is then hardly surprising that the introduction of the tax provides few additional incentives or even negative incentives.

We conclude our numerical analysis with a brief consideration of the effects of subsidisation at $\rho = \theta_B^*$ (a weak subsidy, effectively paid to the clean firm only) and $\rho = \underline{\theta}$ (a strong subsidy, paid to both firms). It is again instructive to compare a regime with high environmental orientation ($n = 0$) to one with lower environmental orientation ($n = 1$). The remaining parameters are set at the same level as in the previous tables.

Table 7.3a Effect of subsidy on environmental performance: $n = 0$

	$t = 0$	$t = 0.1$ $\rho = \theta_B^*$	$t = 0.1$ $\rho = \underline{\theta} = 1$
θ_G^*	3.6827	3.8421	3.8432
$\Delta\theta_G^*$		0.1594	0.1605
θ_B^*	1.3158	1.3601	1.3566
$\Delta\theta_B^*$		0.0443	0.0408
ζ^*	2.7988	2.8249	2.833
$\Delta\zeta^*$		0.0261	0.0342

Table 7.3b Effect of subsidy on environmental performance: $n = 1$

	$t = 0$	$t = 0.1$ $\rho = \theta_B^*$	$t = 0.1$ $\rho = \underline{\theta} = 1$
θ_G^*	3.6588	3.8366	3.8358
$\Delta\theta_G^*$		0.1778	0.177
θ_B^*	1.0	1.1162	1.1103
$\Delta\theta_B^*$		0.1162	0.1103
ζ^*	3.6588	3.4372	3.4547
$\Delta\zeta^*$		-0.2216	-0.2041

Notes: Numerical results for $m = 3.191$; $k = \underline{\theta} = 1$. $\Delta\theta_G^*$, $\Delta\theta_B^*$ and $\Delta\zeta^*$ report the differences between the variable value in the respective column and the value of the same variable when $t = 0$ (reported in column 2).

The following observations can be made.

(e) A subsidy provides an incentive for both firms to improve their environmental performance. For the clean firm this incentive is similar to the incentive under a tax. However, it is significantly weaker for the dirty firm when compared to a tax. As a consequence, a subsidy gives rise to a greater degree of product differentiation. When comparing different levels of the subsidy, the stronger subsidy at $\rho = \underline{\theta}$ tends to provide the weaker incentive for the dirty firm.

(f)   As with a tax a greater environmental orientation tends to weaken the environmental incentive for the dirty firm. Subsidisation then increases rather than reduces product differentiation.

Our results are robust with regard to intermediate levels of environmental orientation as captured by $n \in [0,1]$. Higher levels of n are not admissible as they would imply a boundary equilibrium. Variations in the environmental margin m for a given n are equivalent to changes in environmental orientation, as discussed already. Finally, we do not believe that changes in the investment rate k will have a significant qualitative impact on our findings as long as k is constrained to values that permit a well-behaved interior equilibrium. We therefore conclude with some confidence that the findings reported here can be generalised.

Relation to the Literature on Environmental Ad-valorem Taxation

It is instructive to compare our results for a quality-related specific tax to some findings in the literature regarding ad-valorem taxation and quality-unrelated specific taxes. Cremer and Thisse (1994b), Arora and Gangopadhyay (1995), MGPF (2002) and Bansal and Gangopadhyay (2003) study the effects on the provision of quality/environmental performance in a vertically differentiated duopoly. Their work shows that quality/performance levels unambiguously fall with the tax rate, irrespective of whether or not it is differentiated with respect to quality/performance. This is obviously so as the tax unambiguously reduces marginal revenue from quality/performance. It should be noted however that while some of the above work allows for a differentiation of the tax rate with respect to quality, the tax rate as such is inelastic with respect to quality. We would expect a positive effect of ad-valorem taxation on quality provision to be feasible if the tax rate were a continuous, differentiable and decreasing function in quality.

A more fundamental difference lies in the impact the tax has on the choice of environmental performance – or quality more generally – through altering the competitive effectiveness of quality. For the sake of comparison consider the effect on competitive effectiveness of a uniform and flat-rate specific tax, $t_S \geq 0$, as opposed to a uniform and flat-rate ad-valorem at rate, $1 - t_V \geq 0$. Write firm i's operating profit as $\pi_i^S = (p_i - MC_i - t_S)q_i$, $i = G, B$, in the case of a specific tax and $\pi_i^V = [t_V p_i - MC_i]q_i$ in the case of an ad-valorem tax, where $MC_i = c\theta_i + c_0$, $q_G = \overline{v} - v_1$ and $q_B = v_1 - v_0$. Using the optimal prices in the second stage we can then write profits as functions of qualities

$$\pi_G{}^S = \frac{\left[2m\theta_G + n - t^S\right]^2(\theta_G - \theta_B)}{(4\theta_G - \theta_B)^2}, \quad \pi_B{}^S = \frac{\left[m\theta_B + 2(n - t^S)\right]^2\theta_G(\theta_G - \theta_B)}{(4\theta_G - \theta_B)^2\theta_B},$$

$$\pi_G{}^V = \frac{\left[2m_V\theta_G + n_V\right]^2(\theta_G - \theta_B)}{(4\theta_G - \theta_B)^2}, \quad \pi_B{}^V = \frac{\left[m_V\theta_B + 2n_V\right]^2\theta_G(\theta_G - \theta_B)}{(4\theta_G - \theta_B)^2\theta_B},$$

where $m_V = t_V m - c$ and $n_V = t_V u - c$. The competitive effectiveness of θ_G and θ_B in the respective cases is then given by

$$r^S = 2m\alpha(\cdot) - (n - t_S)\beta(\cdot), \qquad s^S = m\theta_G\theta_B\beta(\cdot) - 2(n - t^S)\alpha(\cdot),$$
$$r^V = 2m_V\alpha(\cdot) - n_V\beta(\cdot), \qquad s^V = m_V\theta_G\theta_B\beta(\cdot) - 2n_V\alpha(\cdot),$$

with $\alpha(\theta_G,\theta_B) > 0$ and $\beta(\theta_G,\theta_B)$ as in (7.13a) and (7.13b).

Suppose $m,n \geq 0$. It is now easy to see that both r^S and s^S are increasing in t^S, implying that an increase in the specific rate unambiguously increases the competitive effectiveness of both firms' performance levels. The reason is that a specific tax erodes the baseline margin and the relative cost advantage of the dirty firm. As the tax tends to make environmental performance (quality) as opposed to cost a better source of competitive advantage this provides both firms with an incentive to raise performance.

In contrast to this, the effect of the ad-valorem tax on competitiveness is ambiguous and given by

$$dr^V/dt_V = 2\bar{v}\alpha(\cdot) - u\beta(\cdot), \qquad ds^V/dt_V = \bar{v}\theta_G\theta_B\beta(\cdot) - 2u\alpha(\cdot).$$

Here the impact of the tax on competitive effectiveness depends on the relative importance of the willingness to pay for environmental performance, $\bar{v}$, and baseline benefit, u, as sources of a firm's revenue. An increase in the ad-valorem tax lowers the competitive effectiveness of performance for both variants if $\bar{v} \gg u$.[25] In this case the tax reduces the attractiveness of environmental performance as the main source of competitive advantage. As the firms shift their focus towards price as a competitive instrument, they lower their environmental performance in order to sustain a low marginal cost. The opposite is true for $\bar{v} \ll u$. Here both firms have an incentive to substitute a cost advantage for an environmental/quality advantage in competition as the revenue flowing from serving consumers with the baseline functions is now taxed. There is also an intermediate case where the clean firm (dirty firm) lowers (raises) environmental performance under taxation. This is because the clean firm tends to receive a greater share of its revenue from the provision of environmental performance. In this regard, the tax tends to level out the two firms' particular sources of competitive advantage. These differences between specific and ad-valorem taxation illustrate once again the importance of the interaction between (environmental) quality and cost as sources of competitive advantage.[26]

7.4 IMPACT OF THE TAX-SUBSIDY SCHEME ON INDUSTRY SURPLUS

Industry surplus can be written as

$$W = S + \pi_G^* - F(\theta_G^*) + \pi_B^* - F(\theta_B^*) - t\left[q_G^*(\theta_G^* - \rho) + q_B^*(\theta_B^* - \rho)\right],$$

where the last term represents the budgetary impact of the tax-subsidy scheme. For the sake of simplicity we have normalised the shadow cost of public funds to zero. Moreover

$$S = q_G^*\left[\frac{\left(v_1^* + \bar{v}\right)\theta_G^*}{2} + u - \varphi_G^*\right] + q_B^*\left[\frac{\left(v_0^* + v_1^*\right)\theta_B^*}{2} + u - \varphi_B^*\right],$$

$$\pi_i^* = \left[\varphi_i^* - t(\rho - \theta_i^*) - c\theta_i^* - c_0\right]q_i^*; \quad i = G, B,$$

where $q_G^* = \bar{v} - v_1^*$, $q_B^* = v_1^* - v_0^*$, $v_1^* = (\varphi_G^* - \varphi_B^*)/(\theta_G^* - \theta_B^*)$ and $v_0^* = (u - \varphi_B^*)/\theta_B^*$, and where the effective price φ_i^*, $i = G, B$ is characterised by the relationships in (7.2) and (7.7). It is now readily verified that

$$\frac{dW}{dt} = \frac{\partial W}{\partial t} + \kappa_B^t \frac{d\theta_B^*}{dt} + \kappa_G^t \frac{d\theta_G^*}{dt}, \qquad (7.17)$$

where

$$\frac{\partial W}{\partial t} = \frac{\partial S}{\partial t} + \frac{\partial \pi_G^*}{\partial t} + \frac{\partial \pi_B^*}{\partial t} + \left[\left(q_G^* + t\frac{\partial q_G^*}{\partial t}\right)\left(\theta_G^* - \rho\right) + \left(q_B^* + t\frac{\partial q_B^*}{\partial t}\right)\left(\theta_B^* - \rho\right)\right]$$

$$= \left[\varphi_G^* - c\theta_G^* - c_0\right]\frac{\partial q_G^*}{\partial t} + \left[\varphi_B^* - c\theta_B^* - c_0\right]\frac{\partial q_B^*}{\partial t}, \qquad (7.18)$$

and where

$$\kappa_B^t = \frac{\partial S}{\partial \theta_B} + \frac{\partial \pi_G^*}{\partial \theta_B} + \frac{\partial \pi_B^*}{\partial \theta_B} - F'\left(\theta_B^*\right) + t\left[\left(\rho - \theta_B^*\right)\frac{\partial q_B^*}{\partial \theta_B} - q_B^* + \left(\rho - \theta_G^*\right)\frac{\partial q_G^*}{\partial \theta_B}\right]$$

$$= q_B^*\left(\frac{v_0^* + v_1^*}{2} - c\right) + \frac{\partial q_B^*}{\partial \theta_B}\left(\varphi_B^* - c\theta_B^* - c_0\right) + \frac{\partial q_G^*}{\partial \theta_B}\left(\varphi_G^* - c\theta_G^* - c_0\right), (7.19a)$$

$$\kappa_G^t = \frac{\partial S}{\partial \theta_G} + \frac{\partial \pi_B^*}{\partial \theta_G} + \frac{\partial \pi_G^*}{\partial \theta_G} - F'\left(\theta_G^*\right) + t\left[\left(\rho - \theta_G^*\right)\frac{\partial q_G^*}{\partial \theta_G} - q_G^* + \left(\rho - \theta_B^*\right)\frac{\partial q_B^*}{\partial \theta_G}\right]$$

$$= q_G^*\left(\frac{v_1^* + \bar{v}}{2} - c\right) + \frac{\partial q_G^*}{\partial \theta_G}\left(\varphi_G^* - c\theta_G^* - c_0\right) + \frac{\partial q_B^*}{\partial \theta_G}\left(\varphi_B^* - c\theta_B^* - c_0\right). (7.19b)$$

The term in (7.18) gives the direct effect of the transfer on industry surplus, while the terms in (7.19a) and (7.19b), respectively, give the effect transmitted through changes in the environmental performance of the two variants. In analogy we find

$$\frac{dW}{d\rho} = \frac{\partial W}{\partial \rho} + \kappa_B^t \frac{d\theta_B^*}{d\rho} + \kappa_G^t \frac{d\theta_G^*}{d\rho} \qquad (7.20)$$

$$\frac{\partial W}{\partial \rho} = \left[\varphi_G^* - c\theta_G^* - c_0\right]\frac{\partial q_G^*}{\partial \rho} + \left[\varphi_B^* - c\theta_B^* - c_0\right]\frac{\partial q_B^*}{\partial \rho} < 0 \qquad (7.21)$$

for the effect of the performance target on industry surplus. The inequality in (7.21) follows immediately under observation of (7.9b). We begin by considering the direct and performance-transmitted effects of the transfer in isolation. From (7.18) and (7.21) we see that the transfer has a direct impact on social surplus via the change in the output of the two variants.

Proposition 7.5.1. Consider an increase in the transfer rate t from t = 0. For given levels of environmental performance, this (i) raises industry surplus if the transfer is a subsidy for both variants and the G firm dominates *in market share, and (ii) lowers welfare if the transfer is a tax on both variants and the B firm dominates in market share. (iii) The net welfare increase is always greater for a subsidy (i.e. welfare decreases in ρ).*

Proof: See Appendix A7.

The proposition suggests that in the presence of a negligible shadow cost of public funds, subsidisation is welfare superior to taxation. This reflects the usual problem of under-supply of quantity under imperfect competition, which is worsened by a tax and ameliorated by a subsidy. In the light of this the following result is more interesting.

Proposition 7.5.2. For given levels of environmental performance, a (weak) marginal tax on both variants, with $\rho = \theta_G^*$, enhances industry surplus if the environmental margin is sufficiently high relative to the baseline margin. This requires G market share dominance.

Proof: See Appendix A7.

A tax on both variants enhances welfare as long as it provides a sufficient amount of implicit subsidisation of the green variant. This is because under laissez-faire, there is a misallocation of consumers between the two variants. Due to the green firm's greater market power under G dominance, consumption of the G variant is too low from a social perspective.[27] While the tax raises the effective prices of both variants, it lowers the relative price of the G variant.[28] The resulting increase in G consumption raises industry surplus by so much that it outweighs the loss of industry output at the bottom end.[29]

The transfer has an additional effect on industry surplus through the induced changes in environmental performance.

Lemma 7.1. $m < m_l(0,\rho) \Rightarrow \kappa_G^t < 0$; $m > m_h(0,\rho) \Rightarrow \{\kappa_G^t, \kappa_B^t\} > 0$.

Proof: See Appendix A7.

This Lemma reapplies previous findings to the case of taxation. Namely if the environmental margin is low, and always for $m < m_l(0,\rho)$, an increase in G performance reduces welfare. This is because the average G consumer's willingness to pay for environmental performance, $\left(v_1^* + \bar{v}\right)/2$, falls short of the cost rate of environmental performance or does not exceed it by much. As there is always a loss in surplus due to a stifling of competition the net effect is negative. Conversely if the environmental margin is sufficiently high, and always for $m > m_h(0, \rho)$, an increase in B performance has a positive impact on industry surplus.

Consider now the overall effect of the transfer on industry surplus for the case that investment costs are absent. In this case the following clear-cut result can be derived.

Proposition 7.6.1. Consider a marginal increase in the transfer rate from $t = 0$. This reduces (raises) industry surplus in the lower (upper) boundary regime.

Proof: See Appendix A7.

Irrespective of whether the transfer is a subsidy or a tax it always curbs welfare if WTP for environmental performance is low and a lower-boundary equilibrium arises. This is immediately intuitive if the transfer constitutes a tax on both variants and works to raise the clean firm's performance. Then it follows from Proposition 7.5.1 and Lemma 7.1 that both the direct impact and the impact transmitted through changes in the performance levels are negative. However the above findings show that the deterioration in industry surplus extends to the following cases.

The introduction of a marginal subsidy has a direct positive effect on industry surplus. However, this is more than offset by the increase in the prices of both variants. Prices rise as the improvement in G performance entails a direct cost increase and further as it stifles competition. Notice that such a counter-intuitive effect of subsidisation cannot arise in homogeneous product duopoly and is unlikely to arise under symmetric horizontal product differentiation. This result highlights once more the distinct mechanics of competition under vertical differentiation and should serve as a note of caution to the policy maker.

In the presence of a negative environmental margin, the introduction of a marginal tax lowers G performance if ρ is sufficiently high (see Table 7.1). Although this pro-competitive effect tends to enhance industry surplus, the direct reduction arising under the implicit taxation of both variants dominates so that welfare is reduced once again.

A similarly unambiguous finding applies in the case of a high environmental margin, as is present for an upper-boundary equilibrium. Here the introduction of the transfer raises the industry surplus. Again from Proposition 7.5.1 and Lemma 7.1 this is immediate for a subsidy but the finding embraces a welfare increase for a tax on both variants. In this case the social benefit from an improved performance of the dirty variant more than outweighs the negative impact of a tax.

In order to assess the relative merits of subsidies as opposed to taxation, it is instructive to consider a change in the target ρ, which determines the 'degree of taxation'.

Proposition 7.6.2 For a transfer rate t sufficiently close to zero, subsidisation (taxation) is associated with a higher industry surplus in the lower (upper) boundary regime.

Proof: See Appendix A7.

Because of its positive impact on industry output one would expect a subsidy to give rise to a greater net increase in industry surplus. This is the rationale behind the under-internalisation argument, according to which in the presence of market power environmental taxes are optimally set below their Pigouvian levels as a means of implicit subsidisation. As we see in the presence of vertical product differentiation, this is the case only within the lower boundary regime. In contrast to the received wisdom taxation tends to be welfare superior in the upper boundary regime. This can be explained with reference to the effect of the transfer on performance levels. Recall from Table 7.1, that if the environmental margin is positive, both firms' performance levels increase at the target level ρ, implying that a tax provides the stronger incentive to improve the environmental attributes of a product. As we see from Lemma 7.1, an increase in B performance enhances welfare in the upper boundary regime. This is in part due to the stiffening of competition under lower product differentiation. But then the reduction in industry output that is usually associated with a tax is mitigated through the pro-competitive effect. With the negative impact of taxation thus being (partially) offset, there remains the direct benefit to consumers from environmental improvements in the dirty variant. But this favours taxation as it provides the stronger performance incentive. In contrast to this, if taxation triggers an increase in G performance the anti-competitive effect of the tax is exacerbated due to the slackening of competition under greater product differentiation.[30]

The scope for a welfare gain from taxation parallels a finding by Cremer and Thisse (1994b), who show that a marginal ad-valorem tax raises industry surplus in a covered market duopoly when firms face a variable cost of quality. As in our model the market is plagued by excessive product differentiation. The mechanism by which the welfare gain is achieved is the reverse of the one in our model. By lowering marginal revenue from quality an ad-valorem tax reduces both levels of quality. The welfare gain arises as high quality is reduced to a greater extent so that product differentiation falls and stiffer competition leads to a price cut that more than outweighs the under-provision of quality.[31] Both Cremer and Thisse (1994b) and our work differ from MGPF (2002). These latter authors show for a non-covered market and in the absence of a variable cost of quality that an ad-valorem tax lowers industry surplus. Absent variable costs of quality, a symmetric ad-valorem tax lowers both levels of quality but leaves equilibrium prices unaffected. Under strong dominance on the part of the green/high quality firm they consider, quality is then under-provided for both variants and consumption is reduced at the low end of the market.[32] In our model the tax may increase the (absolute) price of the low quality/dirty variant. However the underlying increase in quality/environmental performance is sufficiently strong to give rise to an expansion in market coverage.

The results laid down in Propositions 7.6.1 and 7.6.2 apply directly only to the case without investment costs. A full analysis for the model with investment costs is tedious and will lead to ambiguous findings. Therefore, we merely point out the circumstances under which similar results are likely. In the presence of investment costs a boundary equilibrium, with only the G firm responding to the transfer, arises for $m < m_h(0, \rho)$. For this case we can find in analogy to Proposition 5.1 a boundary value $\overline{m}$, $\overline{m} \in [m_l(0, \rho), m_h(0, \rho)]$, where an increase in G performance curbs industry surplus if and only if $m < \overline{m}$. If this condition holds, the negative impact of an increase in t then carries over to the following cases.

The transfer is a subsidy and the G firm reacts with a strong increase of its environmental performance/quality.[33] However if the induced change in performance is small, as it may be for high levels of the investment rate k, the direct effect of the subsidy may dominate so that welfare increases in t.

The transfer is a tax and the G firm raises environmental performance or does not lower it by too much. Again as long as the tax constitutes an implicit subsidy, the G firm reacts with a performance upgrade. As the direct effect of taxation is negative so is the overall effect. If, for being an implicit tax, the transfer leads to a strong degradation of G performance it cannot be ruled out that the pro-competitive effect outweighs the negative effect of taxation.

The negative welfare effect of an increase in ρ carries over as long as the tax provides a stronger incentive to increase performance than a subsidy. Since a tax reduces the value of environmental performance, however, it may lead to a downgrading of G performance. If a tax then leads to a significantly lower level of θ_G than a subsidy the pro-competitive effect of this may overturn the welfare superiority of a subsidy. For $m \in [\overline{m}, m_h(0, \rho)]$ a subsidy has a positive impact on industry surplus, whereas a tax that leads to a deterioration of G performance has a negative impact. The effect of a tax that raises B performance, when acting as an implicit subsidy, is ambiguous.

For $m > m_h(0, \rho)$ an interior equilibrium obtains, where we have to consider the effect of the transfer not only on G but also on B performance. Recall from Lemma 7.1 that industry surplus then tends to increase in both performance levels. The numerical results reported in Tables 7.2a and 7.2b suggest that a marginal tax tends to induce both firms to raise their performance as long as the target ρ is not too high. However the welfare gain from better performance needs to offset a possible direct welfare loss.

Table 7.4a Welfare effects of taxation/subsidisation: $n = 0$

	$t = 0$	$t = 0.1$ $\rho = \theta_G^*$	$t = 0.1$ $\rho = \hat{\rho} = 6.116$	$t = 0.1$ $\rho = \theta_B^*$	$t = 0.1$ $\rho = \underline{\theta} = 1$
W	12.442	12.6866	12.5158	12.837	12.8558
ΔW		0.2446	0.0738	0.395	0.4138

Table 7.4b Welfare effects of taxation/subsidisation: $n = 1$

	$t = 0$	$t = 0.1$ $\rho = \theta_G^*$	$t = 0.1$ $\rho = \hat{\rho}$ $= 16.116$	$t = 0.1$ $\rho = \theta_B^*$	$t = 0.1$ $\rho = \underline{\theta} = 1$
W	15.6471	16.0574	14.9421	16.1621	16.1664
ΔW		0.4103	-0.705	0.515	0.5193

Notes: Numerical results for $m = 3.191$; $k = \underline{\theta} = 1$. ΔW reports the difference between the level of industry surplus in the respective column and its level when $t = 0$ (reported in column 2). $\hat{\rho} = \arg\max \theta_B^*$.

Tables 7.4a and 7.4b present for the two cases of high environmental orientation ($n = 0$) and low environmental orientation ($n = 1$) the industry surplus that is realised for laissez-faire and the levels of taxation considered earlier in Tables 7.2a/b and 7.3a/b, respectively. Industry surplus is computed as

$$W = q_G^* \left[\frac{(v_1^* + \bar{v})\theta_G^*}{2} + n \right] + q_B^* \left[\frac{(v_0^* + v_1^*)\theta_B^*}{2} + n \right] - F(\theta_G^*) - F(\theta_B^*)$$

$$= \left\{ \begin{array}{c} \frac{[2(m+t)\theta_G^* + n - t\rho]\left[2m(3\theta_G^* - \theta_B^*)\theta_G^* + n(7\theta_G^* - 2\theta_B^*) - t\theta_G^*(2\theta_G^* - \rho)\right]}{2(4\theta_G^* - \theta_B^*)^2} \\ + \frac{[(m+t)\theta_B^* + 2(n-t\rho)]\theta_G^* \left\{ (m\theta_B^* + 2n)(3\theta_G^* - 2\theta_B^*) - t[5\theta_G^*\theta_B^* - 2\rho(\theta_G^* + \theta_B^*)] \right\}}{2(4\theta_G^* - \theta_B^*)^2 \theta_B^*} \\ - \frac{k}{2}(\theta_G^* - \underline{\theta}) - \frac{k}{2}(\theta_B^* - \underline{\theta}) \end{array} \right\},$$

where the equilibrium values (θ_G^*, θ_B^*) that arise for the different tax scenarios are taken from Tables 7.2a/b. Column 2 in the respective table reports as a benchmark the industry surplus that is realised in the absence of policies. Column 3 reports the welfare that is realised under a 'weak' (marginal) tax with the rate set at $t = 0.1$ and the target $\rho = \theta_G^*$. Column 4 reports the surplus that is realised for the tax that maximises the performance of the dirty variant. Column 5 reports the surplus for the weakest subsidy with $\rho = \theta_B^*$, whereas column 6 reports the surplus for the strongest subsidy with $\rho = \underline{\theta}$. For ease of reference, the change in surplus ΔW relative to the benchmark is also provided. The following observations are due.

For the chosen parameters a (marginal) tax at rate $t = 0.1$ and $\rho = \theta_G^*$ contributes towards an increase in industry surplus over the laissez-faire level with $t = 0$. However, the welfare gain diminishes and turns negative when taxes become 'stronger', as indicated by a higher ρ.[34] The impact of environmental orientation on the scope for welfare increasing taxation is ambiguous. On the one hand, lower environmental orientation (i.e. a higher n) implies that the scope for welfare increases is exhausted at a lower ρ (compare ΔW in column 4 between Table 7.4a and 7.4b). On the other hand, the welfare gain from weak taxation, e.g. with $\rho = \theta_G^*$, tends to be more pronounced for low levels of environmental orientation (compare ΔW in column 3 between Table 7.4a and 7.4b). This may be due to a strong initial pro-competitive effect of taxation. Recall from Tables 7.2a and 7.2b that the tax leads to a decrease in product differentiation that is much more significant in the case of low environmental orientation. As this applies to a higher degree of product differentiation to begin with, the pro competitive effect is likely to trigger a more significant improvement in welfare as compared to a situation with high environmental orientation.

Subsidies tend to give rise to greater welfare gains irrespective of the degree of environmental orientation. Here the directly positive impact on surplus of a subsidy (as compared to the negative impact of a tax) outweighs the gains from environmental improvements in the dirty variant and the associated pro-competitive effect that tend to be stronger under a tax.

We should caution against these results on the basis that they are likely to be more sensitive to changes in the parameters than our findings on the performance incentives reported in Tables 7.2a/b and 7.3a/b. Another caveat relates to the shadow cost of public funds. Obviously the finding that a subsidy tends to be welfare superior relies on the assumption that the shadow cost is negligible. In the presence of distortionary taxes there is a case for the introduction of environmental taxes as a substitute for other taxes in the generation of public revenue. Indeed as the empirical evidence suggests, environmental taxation is far more frequently applied in practice than variable subsidisation (e.g. OECD 1999a).[35]

7.5 ENVIRONMENTAL IMPACT OF THE TAX-SUBSIDY SCHEME

Industry emissions in the presence of the tax-subsidy scheme (7.1) are given by

$$
\begin{aligned}
E &= e\!\left(\theta_G^*\right)\!q_G^*\!\left(\zeta^*,\theta_B^*,t,\rho\right)+e\!\left(\theta_B^*\right)\!q_B^*\!\left(\zeta^*,\theta_B^*,t,\rho\right)\\
&= \frac{\left[2e\!\left(\theta_G^*\right)+e\!\left(\theta_B^*\right)\right]\!\left(m+t\right)\!\zeta^*+\left[e\!\left(\theta_G^*\right)+2e\!\left(\theta_B^*\right)\!\zeta^*\right]\frac{(n-t\rho)}{\theta_B^*}}{4\zeta^*-1},
\end{aligned}
\tag{7.22}
$$

where $\zeta^*=\theta_G^*/\theta_B^*$ is the equilibrium degree of product differentiation. For subsequent reference recall

$$
\frac{\partial E}{\partial \zeta}=\frac{-\left[2e\!\left(\theta_G^*\right)+e\!\left(\theta_B^*\right)\right]\!\left[\left(m+t\right)+2\frac{(n-t\rho)}{\theta_B^*}\right]}{\left(4\zeta^*-1\right)^2}<0,
\tag{7.23a}
$$

$$
\frac{\partial E}{\partial \theta_L}\bigg|_{\zeta^*=\bar\zeta\,;\,e\!\left(\theta_B^*\right)=\bar e}=\frac{-\left[e\!\left(\theta_G^*\right)+2e\!\left(\theta_B^*\right)\!\zeta^*\right]\!\left(n-t\rho\right)}{\left(4\zeta^*-1\right)\theta_B^{*2}}.
\tag{7.23b}
$$

By its impact on output levels, the transfer has the following direct effect on industry emissions:

$$\frac{\partial E}{\partial t} = \frac{\left[2e\left(\theta_G^*\right)+e\left(\theta_B^*\right)\right]\zeta^* - \left[e\left(\theta_G^*\right)+2e\left(\theta_B^*\right)\zeta^*\right]\frac{\rho}{\theta_B^*}}{4\zeta^* -1} \qquad (7.24)$$

$$\frac{\partial E}{\partial \rho} = \frac{-\left[e\left(\theta_G^*\right)+2e\left(\theta_B^*\right)\zeta^*\right]t}{\left(4\zeta^* -1\right)\theta_B^*} < 0. \qquad (7.25)$$

Hence, the impact of an increase in the transfer rate at a given target ρ is ambiguous, while an increase in the target always lowers emissions. This reflects the impact of the two instruments on output, as in (7.9a) and (7.9b). From (7.24),

$$\frac{\partial E}{\partial t} < 0 \Leftrightarrow \rho > \frac{\left[2e\left(\theta_G^*\right)+e\left(\theta_B^*\right)\right]\zeta^*}{e\left(\theta_G^*\right)+2e\left(\theta_B^*\right)\zeta^*}\theta_B^*. \qquad (7.26)$$

Observing $e\left(\theta_G^*\right) \le e\left(\theta_B^*\right)$, the following can then easily be verified.

Proposition 7.7. (i) An implicit subsidy on the B (and G variant), i.e. a transfer with $\rho < \theta_B^*/2$ raises emissions. (ii) A transfer with $\rho \in \left[\theta_B^*/2\right),\theta_B^*\right]$, i.e. a subsidy, which constitutes an implicit tax on the B variant, lowers industry emissions if the spread between unit emissions is sufficiently wide, i.e. if $e\left(\theta_B^*\right) > \left[2-\left(1/\zeta^*\right)\right]e\left(\theta_G^*\right)$. (iii) A tax on both variants, i.e. a transfer with $\rho > \theta_G^*$, always lowers industry emissions. (iv) Taxation is always more effective in lowering industry emissions.

Parts (iii) and (iv) of the proposition are hardly surprising. By curtailing industry output and by shifting market share from the dirty to the clean firm taxation contributes towards a reduction in emissions. The surprising result is captured in part (ii). Contrary to intuition, a subsidy may directly lower industry emissions even if firms do not adjust environmental performance. This is the more surprising, as a subsidy on both variants increases industry output.[36] While in a symmetric oligopoly this would imply an unambiguous increase in industry emissions, the impact of the transfer on the firms' competitive positions has to be taken into account under vertical differentiation. By shifting market share from the B to the G firm a 'weak' subsidy still contributes to a reduction in B output. Then the reduction in industry emissions arising from substitution of the dirty for the clean variant over-compensates the emission increase from additional consumption if the dirty variant is associated with significantly higher unit emissions. If the subsidy is strong enough to be an implicit subsidy for the B firm it raises the output of both variants. In this case the expected increase in industry emissions occurs.

Lower Boundary Regime

When studying the overall impact of the transfer on industry emissions, additional account needs to be taken of the induced changes in the firms' environmental performance. Let us consider first the equilibrium in which the dirty firm chooses the lowest feasible performance $\theta_B^* = \underline{\theta}$ and does not adjust its performance in response to the transfer. The impact of the transfer on emissions is then characterised by

$$\frac{dE}{dy} = \frac{\partial E}{\partial y} + \frac{dE}{d\theta_G} \frac{d\theta_G^*}{dy}$$

$$= \overset{<0}{\overbrace{e'\left(\theta_G^*\right)}} q_G^*\left(\zeta^*, \underline{\theta}, t, \rho\right)\frac{d\theta_G^*}{dy} + \left(\frac{\partial E}{\partial y} + \frac{1}{\underline{\theta}} \overset{<0}{\overbrace{\frac{\partial E}{\partial \zeta}}} \frac{d\theta_G^*}{dy}\right), \quad y = t, \rho, \qquad (7.27)$$

where the second equality follows under use of (7.23a). Inspection of (7.27) shows that the impact on emissions of a change in the transfer parameter can be separated into two distinct effects: the change in the clean product's unit emissions and the change in emissions from a change in the volume and composition of industry output (the second term in (7.27)). The output-related effect is composed of the direct effect of the transfer and the impact of changes in the degree of product differentiation. It is difficult to sign these different effects at general level. While a tax tends to directly reduce output and emissions the clean firm may respond with a reduction in its environmental performance. In this case an offsetting effect arises both through greater unit emissions but also through the stiffening of competition under a lesser degree of product differentiation.

   In the light of these ambiguities we focus on a number of specific cases. For the set-up without investment costs the following effects of the transfer can be found in the case of a lower boundary equilibrium [$m < m_I(t, \rho)$].

Proposition 7.8. (i) The output related effect of an increase in the transfer rate reduces industry emissions. (ii) A tax is always more efficient through the output effect. (iii) The transfer reduces overall emissions if G performance does not fall by too much.

Proof: See Appendix A7.

Regardless of the direction of the direct effect and the change in product differentiation, the introduction of the transfer always lowers industry emissions through its impact on output. This is intuitive as the following argument demonstrates. Suppose the transfer lowers unit abatement by the G firm and thereby enhances competition and industry output. We know that this can only be the case if the transfer is a strong tax. But a strong tax curbs industry output directly and to such an extent that it over-compensates the effect from enhanced competition. Conversely consider a subsidy on both variants that raises industry output. For this case the proposition shows that the direct effect of the subsidy on output is more than offset by the anti-competitive effect that results from an upgrading in the G firm's environmental performance. A tax tends to lower emissions by more through the output effect when compared to a subsidy. Part (ii) of the proposition illustrates that this is true even when a strong tax in the presence of a negative environmental margin $m < 0$ leads to a deterioration in G performance. With regard to the overall effect it follows from part (iii) that any tax or subsidy leads to a reduction in industry emissions if the G firm improves its environmental performance in response to the transfer. This is always true for a non-negative environmental margin and a tax is then the more powerful instrument.

Consider now the set-up with investment costs while still assuming a boundary equilibrium, where the B firm does not adjust its environmental performance in response to the transfer. This represents a more pessimistic scenario for taxation, as a potentially negative effect of a tax on the value of environmental performance renders a reduction in the clean firm's environmental performance more likely. However, the following is easy to verify.

Proposition 7.9. Environmental taxation leads to a reduction in industry emissions as long as the tax constitutes an implicit subsidy to the clean firm.

The proposition follows immediately from the observation that a tax with $\rho \in \left] \theta_G^*, 2\theta_G^* \right]$ satisfies both $\partial E/\partial t < 0$, where Proposition 7.7 part (iii) applies for $\rho > \theta_G^*$, and $d\theta_G^*/dt > 0$, with $\rho \leq 2\theta_G^*$ implying that both terms in (7.15) are positive. By shifting competitive advantage towards environmental performance a weak tax therefore provides the green firm with an incentive to raise environmental performance in order to bolster further its relative environmental advantage. Taxation then unambiguously contributes towards a reduction in industry emissions. While a subsidy would provide a stronger performance incentive to the G firm, the increase in performance $d\theta_G^*/dt$ may be very small if the investment rate k is high. Supposing a very large k implies $d\theta_G^*/dt \to 0$ for either a tax or subsidy. It becomes clear that subsidisation may now lead to an increase in industry emissions through its positive effect on industry output. To give an example, this is the case for a subsidy paid to the G firm alone, where $\rho = \theta_B^* = \underline{\theta}$ when the condition in (7.26) is not satisfied. Whenever high R&D or other investment costs limit the scope for environmental improvements, a mild tax turns out to be the best instrument for emission reductions. Whereas a high tax may cause greater emissions by stifling even the modest environmental innovation that may otherwise take place, a subsidy would give rise to greater emissions by leading to the expansion of an already dirty market.

As far as the tax or subsidy is directly linked to the product or production process, i.e. in the case of type 1 or 3 taxation, the regulator has some freedom in choosing the degree of taxation/subsidisation by adjusting the target ρ. In this case there is scope for the regulator to fine-tune the transfer in order to attain the desired reduction in emissions. This does not apply, however, for our model of an energy tax (type 2 or 3). Here, the parameter ρ captures an exogenous level of energy intensity. A high level of energy intensity $\rho >> 2\theta_G^*$ would imply that a high tax is levied even on the clean variant. As we have seen previously this may stifle investments into improving the energy efficiency of the product that would otherwise undertaken by the clean firm. As the energy intensity of the clean product then falls short of the level in the absence of taxation, energy consumption within this industry and the associated emissions may turn out to be higher.

Upper Boundary Regime

As we now see, the impact of a tax is quite different if environmental orientation is high so that the industry operates in an upper boundary regime or interior regime where the dirty firm improves the environmental performance of its product over and above the minimum. For illustrative purposes, consider an upper-boundary regime $m > m_h(t,\rho)$ in the set-up without investment costs. Here the impact of transfer is given by

$$\frac{dE}{dy} = \frac{\partial E}{\partial y} + \frac{dE}{d\theta_B}\frac{d\theta_B^*}{dy}$$

$$= \overbrace{e'(\theta_B^*)}^{<0} q_B^* \frac{d\theta_B^*}{dy} + \left[\frac{\partial E}{\partial y} + \left(-\frac{\zeta^*}{\theta_B^*}\overbrace{\frac{\partial E}{\partial \zeta}}^{<0} + \frac{\partial E}{\partial \theta_B}\bigg|_{\zeta^* = \overline{\zeta}:e(\theta_B^*)=\underline{e}}\right)\frac{d\theta_B^*}{dy}\right],\quad y = t, \rho,$$

where the second equality follows under use of (7.23a) and (7.23b). Again the overall effect on emissions of the transfer can be separated into its impact on unit emissions and its impact on the structure of industry output. Recall that an increase in the performance of the dirty variant has two offsetting effects on output related emissions. By reducing product differentiation it tends to fuel competition, output and emissions but by raising marginal cost and selling price it tends to curb total industry output and emissions. Even the output-related impact on emissions is now difficult to sign. Indeed in contrast to the lower-boundary regime the transfer can in some circumstances give rise to an output-related increase in emissions unless it constitutes a tax on both variants.

Proposition 7.10. Suppose $n = 0$ and consider the introduction of a marginal transfer, where t is varied away from $t = 0$. (i) Suppose the spread between unit emissions is sufficiently narrow, i.e. $e(\theta_B^*)/e(\overline{\theta}) < 82$. Then, an increase in the transfer rate t lowers industry emissions by the output effect only if the transfer constitutes a tax on both variants, i.e. only if $\rho > \overline{\theta}$. (ii) A tax is more prone to decrease emissions by the output effect.

Proof: See Appendix A7.

Consider a situation in which both firms have exhausted most of the scope for environmental improvements so that further reductions in unit emissions are difficult to attain. This is captured by a low value of $e'(\theta)$ and since even the dirty firm has undertaken considerable improvements the ratio $e(\theta_B^*)/e(\overline{\theta})$ is likely to be low. If at the same time the baseline margin is low (or close to zero) relative to the environmental margin a further increase in the abatement effort by the dirty firm and the associated reduction in product differentiation only fuels industry output. In this case only the imposition of a tax can curb the resulting increase in emissions.

In the model with investment cost the analysis is again complicated by the strategic interaction between the two firms in their choice of environmental performance. Numerical analysis for the parameter constellations $m = 3.191; k = \underline{\theta} = 1$ and $n \in \{0,1\}$ shows that any tax with $t = 0.1$ and $\rho \geq \theta_G^*$ shifts market share from the dirty to the clean firm and reduces total industry output. Recall from Tables 7.2a/b that the clean firm's performance is raised by any tax with $\rho \in \left]\theta_G^*, \overline{\rho}\right]$, where $\overline{\rho} := \min\left\{\rho \middle| \pi_B^*\left(\theta_G^*, \theta_B^*, t, \rho\right) \leq 0\right\}$. In this case all taxes that induce an increase in the dirty variant's performance over and above the laissez-faire level unambiguously curb industry emissions. Indeed if environmental orientation is relatively low, where $n = 1$, this is true for any tax with $\rho \in \left]\theta_G^*, \overline{\rho}\right]$ as the dirty firm's performance cannot drop below the minimum $\underline{\theta}$ that is realised under laissez-faire. For higher levels of environmental orientation, e.g. for $n = 0$, the dirty firm's performance may deteriorate for some (high) ρ. If the ensuing increase in unit emissions is sufficiently strong, taxation may then fuel industry emissions.

For the parameters under consideration any subsidy tends to reduce dirty output. This is due to the shift in competitiveness towards the clean firm. However, for a high level of environmental orientation, subsidisation tends to increase total industry output. In this case and in this case only, the industry may emit more pollutants if unit emissions are not responsive to the firms' environmental performance and if the clean variant is not associated with significantly lower unit emissions. As we would expect, a weak tax (at $\rho = \theta_G^*$) tends to be more effective in curbing emissions than a subsidy by constraining output and by inducing stronger improvements in the dirty variant's environmental performance.

7.6 CONCLUSIONS

This chapter has studied the effects of a specific tax linked to the environmental performance of a product. In contrast to most of the present literature on environmental taxation, we incorporate into the model the notion of environmental product differentiation. From those models addressing taxation within an environmentally differentiated industry, our model is distinct in that we consider a quality-dependent specific tax rather than an ad-valorem tax or a lump-sum tax on unit emissions. We can conveniently apply the model to incorporate an analysis of environmentally related variable subsidies. Our findings add to the picture that has begun to emerge in the previous two chapters on environmental standards and investment cost subsidies: vertical product differentiation holds in store a number of effects of regulation running counter to received wisdom.

One of the main drivers behind these unexpected results is the inherent asymmetry between firms, with the dirty firm holding a cost advantage and the clean firm holding a 'quality' advantage. An environmentally related transfer, no matter whether subsidy or tax, enhances the competitive position of the clean firm by reducing its relative cost disadvantage. This has the following consequences in the case of fixed environmental performance levels.

(i)   If consumers' willingness to pay for environmental performance is high, a moderate tax on both variants enhances industry surplus. By shifting market share to the clean firm, the tax improves the match between consumers and variants, where due to the premium price there is too little consumption of the clean variant under laissez-faire. The associated increase in industry surplus more than offsets the loss through a reduction in market coverage.

(ii) By shifting market share to the clean firm a subsidy can lower industry emissions although it raises industry output. This effect arises if the substitution towards the clean variant is so strong that the dirty firm loses market share despite gaining consumers with a low willingness to pay.

(iii) There are implications for strategic trade policies. Suppose a domestic and foreign firm compete in the domestic market. If the domestic firm produces the clean product, the regulator can improve its competitive position by introducing either an environmentally related subsidy or tax on the product. Indeed, a tax is the more powerful instrument. Obviously, the reverse is true if the domestic firm produces the dirty variant.

It is worth stressing that the results in (i) and (ii) are recorded here for their counter-intuitive nature. It goes without saying that the model involves scope for the more conventional results. So taxation reduces industry surplus if willingness to pay for quality is relatively low, i.e. in a market with low environmental orientation. Likewise, subsidisation boosts industry emissions if the subsidy increases the dirty firm's market share.

A second set of results flows from the model once we allow for endogenous levels of environmental performance. In contrast to the literature on ad-valorem taxation, where the tax tends to reduce marginal revenue from environmental performance, the specific transfer has the potential to increase it. This is certainly the case for the model without investment cost. If the environmental margin is positive, both firms tend to improve the environmental performance of their product in response to the transfer. The incentive to do so is always stronger for a tax. In the set-up with investment costs there is an offsetting effect if the transfer constitutes an implicit tax on a variant, as this reduces the firm's market share and mark-up. In this case subsidisation may prove to be the more effective or indeed the only effective, tool in enhancing environmental performance. Conversely there is an additional positive impact when the transfer constitutes an implicit subsidy. Notably by enhancing the clean firm's competitive position a weak tax may in fact raise the 'value' of environmental investments and trigger an additional incentive to improve the product.

The analysis of the impact of the transfer on industry surplus and total emissions turns out to be rather complex when environmental performance is endogenous. Restricting attention to the set-up without investment costs, we find that the effects of the transfer turn on the environmental orientation of the market.

Environmental Taxation/Subsidisation when Environmental Orientation is Low

Consider a lower boundary equilibrium where a low environmental orientation induces the dirty firm to choose the baseline level of environmental performance. It then turns out that, at the margin, even a subsidy lowers industry surplus. Although a subsidy tends to raise surplus by expanding industry output, this is more than offset by the anti-competitive effect of an improvement in the clean product. As it contains the welfare loss, a subsidy is welfare superior to a tax. As we may expect, the environmental impact of the transfer turns out to be more 'positive'. Unless the clean firm reduces the environmental performance of its product, industry emissions again decrease in the transfer regardless of whether a tax or subsidy is brought to bear. A tax tends to be more effective in achieving emission reductions.

Again the complexity of the model renders fruitless the analysis of optimal policies aimed at maximising a welfare function with both industry surplus and emissions as its arguments. Any such attempt would imply the imposition of even more structure on the model, rendering the results almost arbitrary. The informativeness of these results would be reduced even further in the light of the number of possible regimes that would have to be analysed and compared. In rather broader terms, our analysis of the lower boundary regime then suggests the presence of two forms of trade-off. First, for a given instrument, e.g. an energy tax, the regulator faces a trade-off between generating industry surplus and cutting emissions. This suggests the under-internalisation of environmental damages. Second, the regulator faces a trade-off in the choice of instruments. By choosing a subsidy, she can contain the welfare loss but at the same time, she opts for weaker reductions in total emissions. The converse being true for a tax, the regulator's choice should then be governed by the marginal societal cost of emissions. Clearly a tax (subsidy) is the superior instrument if the societal cost of emissions is high (low).

An additional problem may arise for the regulator if the environmental margin is negative. In this case the clean firm reduces its abatement effort if the tax is sufficiently stringent. This is because it has an incentive to use its competitive advantage to steal market share from the dirty firm by attacking it more aggressively on price. In order to achieve this the firm reduces costly abatement. Now the introduction of a tax unambiguously reduces welfare. If the regulator is constrained to use a tax, as for instance in the case of energy taxation (type 2) this form of environmental policy becomes unfeasible. Unfortunately, from an environmental point of view, this is the case precisely in a situation where it is most needed as market incentives for environmental improvements are low (negative environmental margin) and the environmental intensity of even the clean product is high. In these circumstances the regulator would then fare better by reverting to an environmental product standard. By using this command-and-control instrument she can at least enforce an improvement in the environmental performance of the two variants and thereby implement a reduction in industry emissions, albeit at the cost of lower industry surplus.

Environmental Taxation/Subsidisation when Environmental Orientation is High

Now consider an upper boundary equilibrium where in the presence of a high environmental orientation the clean firm chooses the highest feasible level of unit abatement and even the dirty firm increases the environmental performance of its product. In this case the introduction of the transfer always improves welfare at the margin irrespective of whether it is a tax or subsidy. As the dirty firm cleans up its product, this benefits consumers directly and indirectly by enhancing competition. By providing to the dirty firm a stronger incentive for environmental improvements, the tax even turns out to be superior as compared to a subsidy. Industry emissions can always be curbed by a tax of sufficient strength. Furthermore a tax turns out to be the more effective instrument in curtailing emissions. The implications of this are clear. First, taxation is now superior to subsidisation not only on grounds of its better environmental performance but even with regard to the effect on industry surplus. Second, a case can now be made for over-internalisation, where the improvement of industry surplus accrues as a second benefit from environmental taxation. Indeed there is a triple benefit if other distortionary taxes can be replaced.[37]

There are three caveats to this strong case for environmental taxation. First, this case applies only if consumers are willing to pay a substantial premium on environmental performance. The empirical relevance of this is doubtful (see section 1.5). Second, we have not fully pursued the model for the case in which firms have to make investments into improved environmental performance. If the environmental performance of either of the products/firms deteriorates in response to a tax, this implies a negative impact on industry surplus and, depending on the unit emission function, may even lead to an increase in industry emissions. Finally, our statements regarding over- (or under-) internalisation are merely conjectures made on the basis of a marginal tax with the tax rate set close to zero. Really the over- (or under-) internalisation case refers to the optimal tax rate. We have argued already that the complexity of the model rules out the derivation of an optimal policy, and at this stage we happily leave this demanding task for future research.

NOTES

1. For further detail see Ekins (1999), EEA (2000) and OECD (2000a).
2. Examples are taken from (EEA 2000: table 3.3).
3. Cremer and Thisse (1994a, 1999) and Constantatos and Sartzetakis (1995) study the effect of an ad-valorem tax on entry into an environmentally differentiated duopoly with covered market. We discuss this work in section 9.4 on endogenous market structure. Lombardini-Riipinen (2002) examines the joint use of an ad-valorem tax and a tax on unit emissions as will be discussed below.
4. This does not hold for a setting in which vertically differentiated firms operate in a covered market and face variable costs of production. Cremer and Thisse (1994b) show an ad-valorem taxation raises social surplus by diminishing excessive product differentiation.
5. In 1995 a number of German communes introduced a tax on packaging. Apparently the scheme was highly effective in reducing one-way packaging. However the tax was withdrawn in response to legal challenges by producers.
6. Examples here and in the following from EEA (2000) and OECD (2000a).
7. Estimates of the short-run price elasticity for residential energy range from –0.05 to –0.9, with the majority of estimates lying well below –0.5. Here, the long-run elasticity is not substantially different. Indeed, it tends to fall short of the short-run level in micro-studies, but exceeds them in macro-studies. Estimates of the short-run elasticity for gasoline range from –0.12 to –1.36, the majority again being well below –0.5. Here, estimates of the long-run elasticity tend to be greater by an amount between 0.2 and 1.0.

8. The taxation of a polluting monopoly is also analysed in Barnett (1980).
9. For a summary survey of this literature, see Xepapadeas (1997: chapter 5). Similar models have been extensively used in discussing strategic environmental policies in the presence of trade (e.g. Barrett 1994, Rauscher 1995, Simpson and Bradford 1996, Ulph 1996 and Van Long and Soubeyran 1999).
10. The converse may apply in the presence of excessive entry (Katsoulacos and Xepapadeas 1995, Lange and Requate 1999).
11. The lump-sum tax on unit emissions considered by Lombardini-Riipinen (2002) has a similar effect to a subsidisation of the R&D cost of green technologies. In contrast to a specific tax it has no direct impact on price competition and market share. The impact is only indirect through induced changes in the levels of environmental performances.
12. Over-internalisation occurs if energy consumption increases with the tax rate. This is the case only where, in a very price elastic market, producers respond to the tax by lowering energy efficiency and selling price.
13. Due to the complex nature of the model we do not explicitly solve for the optimal tax rates. Nonetheless, the implications for optimal taxation are obvious from our results as long as marginal damage is low.
14. A similar argument holds for a (hypothetically) differentiated fuel tax.
15. In our model as in all standard models of vertical differentiation, marginal utility of income is assumed to be independent of quality. See (A2.3) in the Appendix and its derivation. This limits the application to cases in which price differentials due to differences in quality tend to be limited and therefore associated with negligible income effects.
16. An example of a mixed tax-subsidy-scheme is the mechanism for pollution reduction suggested by Sinn (1993), where each firm is assigned a pollution target E_{max}. Then, a firm is taxed (subsidised) at rate t if its emissions exceed (fall short of) the target. Observing that a (unit) emission target, e_{max} can be expressed by a 'quality' target $\rho = e_{max}^{-1}$, the scheme in (7.1) is analogous.
17. Under a proper emission tax, each unit output would be taxed at a rate $te(\theta)$.
18. For some goods, e.g. photo-voltaic roof tiling for the generation of household energy, surplus energy may be generated so that $\rho < \theta$ cannot be ruled out.
19. In this regard an integration of the present model and the approach taken by Myles and Uyduranoglu (2002) would be fruitful. However we leave this for future research.
20. An exception to this rule is the Danish duty on CO_2.
21. The same applies with regard to the mark-ups $p_i^* - c\theta_i^* - c_0;\ i = G, B$.
22. Obviously, a change in ρ leaves marginal (net) revenue from quality unaffected if $t = 0$.
23. Note that in the presence of investment cost a strictly positive $m + t$ is now required in order to guarantee $\beta(\cdot) > 0$, which in turn is necessary (and sufficient) for $d\theta_G^*/d\rho > 0$.
24. It can be checked that the G firm always makes a positive profit.
25. Note that an increase in the tax rate $1 - t_V$ implies a reduction in t_V.

26. Significant differences between ad-valorem and specific taxation have been established by Krishna (1990) with regard to the taxation of a quality-discriminating monopolist and by Myles (1995: section 11.5) with regard to the tax incidence under imperfect competition.

27. Note that this applies irrespective of any externalities.

28. This is easily checked from (7.4a) and (7.4b) and under observation of (7.7).

29. It is easy to see that market coverage falls. Note that industry output is given by $\bar{v} - v_o{}^* = \bar{v} - \left(\varphi_B^* - u \right)/\theta_B^*$. Using (7.7) and (7.4b) it is readily verified that $\rho \geq \theta_G^* \Rightarrow \partial \varphi_B^*/\partial t > 0$ and hence $\partial v_0{}^*/\partial t > 0$.

30. If the environmental margin is negative, G performance falls in ρ. But then the direct negative effect of an increase in ρ is still dominant.

31. Cremer and Thisse (1994b) go on to show that under certain conditions tax differentiation, whereby the greater rate is levied on the high quality variant, enhances welfare even further.

32. In contrast to Cremer and Thisse (1994b), MGPF (2002) find a loss in welfare even for a differentiated tax.

33. By raising both competitive effectiveness and the value of quality a subsidy triggers an unambiguous increase in G performance.

34. We have only reported industry surplus for $\rho = \hat{\rho}$. For a tax at $\rho = \bar{\rho}$, where the dirty firm's profit drops to zero, welfare falls below the laissez-faire level for any degree of environmental orientation.

35. Taxes on energy consumption in particular are likely to be introduced as sources of revenue rather than as environmental policy instruments. For a discussion and examples, see Ekins (1999).

36. This can easily be seen as follows. Note that industry output is determined by the lower marginal consumer with WTP $v_o{}^* = \left(\varphi_B^* - u \right)/\theta_B^*$. Observing (7.7) and using (7.4b) it can be readily verified that $\rho \leq \theta_B^* \Rightarrow \partial \varphi_B^*/\partial t < 0$ and hence $\partial v_0{}^*/\partial t = \left(1/\theta_B^* \right)\left(\partial \varphi_B^*/\partial t \right) < 0$. As additional consumers with lower WTP purchase the product, industry output increases.

37. For a brief survey of the literature on the double dividend argument for environmental taxation and its policy impact, see OECD (2000c).

8. Summary and conclusions

This chapter takes stock of the insights into competitive behaviour and policy making within an environmentally differentiated duopoly. At this point the analysis presented provides answers to the first two groups of research questions we have posited in the introduction.

- Given preferences and technology, what is the market outcome in an industry – mostly duopoly – in which firms differentiate their products with regard to the degree of environmental friendliness and compete in prices? How can we explain the market outcome, and the resulting level of industry emissions in terms of technology and preferences?
- How do a number of environmental policies at product level impinge on the firms' conduct and market outcome and what are the implications for gross surplus and emission levels?

In the following two sections we summarise our findings about policy making in an environmentally differentiated duopoly. Section 8.3 presents some of the rather scarce empirical evidence relevant to environmentally differentiated markets. The issues addressed in the third group of our research agenda,

- What are the likely implications of different assumptions with regard to market structure and behaviour, and what role is there for entry or entry deterrence?

will be addressed informally in the final chapter of this book.

8.1 ENVIRONMENTALLY DIFFERENTIATED DUOPOLY: WHAT HAVE WE LEARNED?

The analysis throughout this work has been based on a model of environmentally differentiated duopoly. The cornerstone of this market structure is a willingness to pay for environmental improvements of a product that differs across consumers. Consumer heterogeneity can be motivated by differences in income. The focus has been on a non-covered market, where the selling price even of the dirty variant is so high that some consumers with low income refrain from buying. Consumers with an intermediate income purchase the dirty product, and those with a high income, the clean product. A non-covered market is a reasonable model for consumer durables or some luxury items. The following products from within this category also have important environmental effects: private housing, which through insulation and design bears on energy consumption; automobiles, with the obvious feature of fuel consumption and exhausts; electrical and electronic appliances, which have an environmental impact through energy efficiency, waste and the harmful substances that may be contained or used in production; holiday packages, which through organisation and design have an important impact on landscape, local culture and energy consumption. Naturally, the non-covered market model is less applicable to convenience goods sold frequently over time.[1] For obvious reasons the model with a non-covered market is also applicable to developing economies and to emerging markets.

It appears unrealistic to assume that consumers purchase a product on the basis of its environmental attributes alone. Thus we take into account that consumers receive a baseline benefit from the consumption of the good that in many instances is large relative to their willingness to pay for environmental performance. The baseline benefit can be viewed as a measure of the importance consumers attach to the product itself as opposed to its environmental features. In this regard a greater baseline benefit implies not only that consumers are, on balance, less concerned about environmental properties but also that environmental differentiation between products becomes less relevant. Products with a high baseline benefit are therefore better substitutes and will be subject to stronger competition. The degree to which environmental product differentiation matters within a market is conveniently measured by environmental orientation, defined as the ratio between the demand elasticity with respect to environmental performance (or quality in general), and the demand elasticity with respect to price. Environmental orientation is linked to the underlying preference system as follows.

Result 1. The environmental orientation of a market increases with societal awareness about the environment and income and decreases with the 'essentiality' of a product (its baseline benefit).

Environmental orientation determines how attractive environmental performance is, as opposed to price, in generating additional demand. If environmental elasticity and price elasticity of demand can be measured or estimated, environmental orientation can be calculated as a good empirical predictor of competitive strategy.

We established in section 3.2 that an alternative model of the demand side assumes consumers to differ in the disutility they receive from a particular product's unit emissions. We have shown that this gives rise to a market structure, a pattern of industry emissions and a range of effects of environmental policies, which are contradictory to our model. Without detailing these differences again, we would like to draw attention to a direct empirical test between the two different models, which again relies on the environmental orientation of market demand.

Result 2. The willingness to pay for environmental performance is the more relevant approach as opposed to the disutility of unit emissions if the environmental orientation of a market increases with environmental awareness and decreases with a measure of the product's essentiality, i.e. the degree of market coverage.

In reality both models are likely to apply in parallel, with consumer heterogeneity arising from differences both in environmental awareness and in income. It is then an empirical question, which of these sources of heterogeneity is of greater importance. The above result can be interpreted as a testable hypothesis, which allows for a test of the two models on the basis of revealed preferences.

The firms' competitive behaviour and the competitive position they attain both turn on environmental orientation. Here, it is crucial to realise that under vertical differentiation the duopolists draw on asymmetric advantages. The clean firm draws on a 'quality' advantage in providing the more attractive product, whereas the dirty firm holds a cost advantage if environmental performance raises the marginal cost of production. Environmental orientation determines whether a price or quality advantage is more important in gaining market dominance. This in turn determines the environmental choices of the two firms.

The following pattern of dominance emerges. If the environmental orientation of the market is sufficiently low, even a small cost advantage held by the dirty firm is sufficient for its dominance. The alternative model, in which consumers receive a disutility from emissions, does not allow for low quality dominance. Thus, testing for market dominance on the part of the dirty firm is a straightforward test, on the grounds of which to falsify this model.

For an intermediate level of the environmental margin, the clean firm dominates in profit but not in market share, and for a high level of the environmental margin, the clean firm dominates both in market share and profit. Here, the environmental orientation of the market is sufficiently high to render the quality advantage more important than the cost advantage as a determinant of dominance. Notably, the clean firm always acquires dominance if environmental performance does not raise marginal cost. Regardless of whether the clean firm has to invest in quality or not, in the absence of a cost advantage, the dirty firm could always be priced out of the market. But this implies that the clean firm acquires dominance.

The provision of environmental performance is governed by the interplay of two forces: product differentiation as a strategy to stifle price competition; and the environmental orientation of the market, which determines whether firms rely on 'environmental leadership' or cost leadership in order to gain a competitive advantage. If the environmental orientation is low, the dirty firm chooses the lowest feasible environmental performance, in order to make maximum use of its cost advantage. The clean firm faces a trade-off between reducing its cost disadvantage and maintaining product differentiation and will no longer seek to maximise product differentiation. For intermediate levels of environmental orientation, cost and quality balance each other as sources of competitive advantage. In this case, the incentive to maximise product differentiation dominates for both firms. Finally, for a high environmental orientation the clean producer exploits its quality advantage by choosing maximal feasible environmental performance. Now, the dirty firm improves the environmental performance of its product over and above the minimum in order to reduce its environmental disadvantage.

Making use of the fact that the clean (dirty) firm unambiguously dominates under a high (low) environmental orientation, we can use a revealed profitability argument to infer the underlying preference and cost structure. Additionally, the pattern of dominance allows us to predict the environmental performance chosen by firms relative to what is the technical or regulatory minimum.

Result 3. (i) High (low) quality dominance with respect to both profit and market share implies an environmental orientation of the market which is strong (weak) relative to the cost of environmental performance, and high (low) levels of environmental performance by both firms relative to what is technically feasible. (ii) High quality dominance with respect to profit but low quality dominance with respect to market share implies an intermediate level of environmental orientation of the market and a high (low) level of environmental performance of the clean (dirty) firm relative to what is technically feasible.

Important aspects of the preference and cost structure as well as of the firms' environmental performance are therefore revealed in data on profit and market share, which should be readily available. This is a valuable source of information to a regulator when direct information about preferences and cost is unavailable or costly to gather.[2] As we will argue below, the regulator can, on the basis of the same data, make certain predictions about the impact of environmental policy measures.

We can now turn to the environmental implications. Industry emissions are determined by two factors: the level of unit emissions and the variants' market shares. Since product differentiation contributes to a reduction in competition, each firm's output tends to decrease with the degree of product differentiation. Thus industry emissions fall unambiguously with the environmental performance of the clean variant. The impact on output of an environmental improvement of the dirty product is ambiguous. Whereas the decline in product differentiation tends to boost competition and output levels, there is an offsetting effect when the increase in the dirty firm's marginal cost forces it to raise price. This leads to the contraction of the market at the low end and the shift of market share to the clean firm. We have shown that if the environmental margin is sufficiently low, this latter effect dominates and a partial increase in the dirty firm's environmental performance will reduce industry output. Since environmental performance levels are strategic complements, any policy that stimulates either of the two firms to clean up its product will then lead to an unambiguous fall in emissions. Whereas missing data on the environmental and baseline margin makes it difficult for the regulator to predict when this is indeed the case, a prediction can sometimes be based on the simple observation of market shares.

Result 4. If the dirty firm dominates in market share, an increase in its environmental performance unambiguously curbs industry emissions.

If the clean firm holds the greater market share and environmental improvements in the dirty product boost output, industry emissions may still fall through a reduction in unit emissions and induced changes in the clean variant's performance. However, in this case, a prediction can only be made on the basis of the preference and cost parameters as well as the unit emission functions, this information being less readily available to the regulator.

8.2 POLICY MAKING IN ENVIRONMENTALLY DIFFERENTIATED DUOPOLY: SOME LESSONS

We have considered three instruments that have particular practical relevance and that are of interest in involving different economic mechanisms:

- A maximum unit emission standard as a form of direct regulation of environmental performance, and an environmental labelling requirement as a variation on this policy;
- an investment subsidy, as a policy which affects marginal investment cost rather than marginal operating profit of quality; and
- a specific quality-related tax or subsidy that directly affects the marginal impact of environmental performance on operating profit.

The complexity of the model generally rules out an analytical derivation of optimal policies. We have refrained from numerical simulation as this would have generated a variety of locally optimal results with global optima then depending on the specific regimes. We believe that the richness of results would not have fostered understanding of the issues. We have therefore settled for the more modest goal of analysing the marginal effects of policies when these are introduced into an unregulated market. To the extent that real-world policies are in many cases perceived to be rather weak, our marginal approach may even benefit from being somewhat more in tune with the real world. At any rate, the main objective was to gain an understanding of the complex effects of policies within vertical industries.

As expected, the policy effects turn on the level of environmental orientation. It is helpful here to consider the nature of the distortions in the case of high and low environmental orientation. In either case the degree of product differentiation is too high from a social point of view. When environmental orientation is too low, the (baseline) performance of the dirty product is optimal as far as industry surplus (excluding the social cost of emissions) is concerned, whereas the performance of the clean product is too high. From the same perspective on industry surplus alone, the environmental performance of both variants is too low in the case of high environmental orientation.

In as far as the policies aim at increasing the environmental performance of either or both of the variants, they may be plagued by the following trade-offs. In the case of a low environmental orientation, improvements in environmental performance(s) contribute to a reduction in industry emissions, but also tend to curtail industry surplus. This suggests that they should not be introduced unless the marginal social cost of emissions is sufficiently high. Even then, an under-internalisation of damages is optimal. If environmental orientation is high, the policies contribute towards an improvement in industry surplus. This suggests a case for over-internalisation as long as the policy contributes towards a reduction in emissions. In some cases, however, the policy may lead to greater industry emissions and should then be introduced only if the social cost of damage is high.

The considerable sensitivity of policy outcomes with regard to environmental orientation places the onus on the policy maker to obtain information on the preference and cost structure of the industry. While much of this data is difficult to obtain, the regulator can, at least in principle, draw on observations of profits, market shares and the level of environmental performance in order to make non-trivial policy forecasts in certain cases. We illustrate this in the following by presenting 'strong' findings based only on readily observable data, besides the more general findings.

Unit Emission Standard

A unit emission standard can be interpreted as a minimum standard imposed on the environmental performance of the dirty variant. While this allows the regulator a direct handle on the dirty product, the standard provides an (indirect) incentive to the clean firm to raise its own performance in order to escape stiffer competition. As this response is under-proportional, one consequence of the standard is a reduction in product differentiation. The effects on industry surplus and industry emissions depend on environmental orientation as detailed above and can be summarised as follows.

Result 5.1. (i) Under a low environmental orientation, the introduction of a standard entails a reduction in industry emissions, which trades off against a reduction in industry surplus. (ii) For intermediate levels of environmental orientation, the introduction of the standard entails an unambiguous gain in welfare by enhancing industry surplus and curbing industry emissions unless investment in clean products is very costly. (iii) For a high environmental orientation, the standard enhances industry surplus and enhances industry emissions if the emissions from greater industry output are not offset by sufficient reductions in unit emissions.

In the case of a trade-off, a policy decision must be based on the marginal social costs of emissions, where under a low (high) environmental orientation the introduction of the standard is justified only if the marginal social cost of emissions is sufficiently high (low). The second finding is a reassuring result from a regulatory point of view. A problem exists, however, in identifying empirically the exact circumstances under which this situation arises. As all of the relevant parameters fall into the range of profit dominance for the clean firm, only the following prediction can be made on the basis of observed dominance.

Result 5.2.1. If the dirty firm dominates in profit, the introduction of a standard unambiguously lowers industry surplus and industry emissions.

Additional inferences may be drawn on the basis of observed environmental choices.

Result 5.2.2. If the dirty firm chooses an environmental performance over and above the minimum, then the introduction of the standard increases industry surplus.

Thus, the pattern of dominance and environmental choices on the part of firms reveal at least certain features of the underlying preferences and technology and can therefore be instrumental in informing policy decisions.

Environmental Labelling

By setting the requirements for the award of an eco-label the policy maker now has a tool to directly affect the clean product's quality. As expected the desirability of a third-party labelling scheme (and of a label owned by the clean firm) turns on environmental orientation.

Result 6. (i) If environmental orientation is low a third-party label should not be introduced and firm-owned labels should be discouraged unless emissions are sufficiently costly from a social point of view. (ii) If environmental orientation is very high a label should be introduced at an aspiration level stiffer than that of a firm-owned label.

Hence, the introduction of an environmental label yields an unequivocal welfare gain only if environmental orientation is sufficiently high. Otherwise the usual trade-off arises between environmental and industrial goals.

Subsidisation of Investment in Green Product Design

Whereas firms have to comply with a standard, they can forego the monetary incentive of a subsidy. Indeed, the dirty firm will not respond to the subsidy if the environmental orientation of the market is low. As the low quality firm faces a negative marginal profit from improved environmental performance, it has no incentive to improve its performance unless a top-up on the full investment cost of the firm is paid. Subsidisation always induces an upgrade in the clean firm's environmental performance. Whether or not the low quality firm reacts to the subsidy is easy to predict from observed profitability.

Result 7. If the dirty firm dominates in market share, a subsidy paid on the investment cost only induces the clean firm to improve its environmental performance.

The policy effects exhibit the now familiar trade-off between environmental and industrial policy goals for low environmental orientation. For high degrees of environmental orientation, however, there is now scope for unambiguous welfare improvements.

Result 8.1. (i) Under a low degree of environmental orientation, the introduction of a subsidy on investment entails a reduction in industry emissions, which trades off against a reduction in industry surplus. (ii) Under a high degree of environmental orientation, the introduction of a subsidy on investment always raises industry surplus; the subsidy lowers emissions if it does not reduce the degree of product differentiation, e.g. if an asymmetric subsidy is paid to the clean firm alone.

No clear-cut statement about policy effects under intermediate levels of environmental orientation can be made. Our results suggest, however, that, as in the case of the emission standard, the subsidy may help to improve both upon industry surplus and the environmental objective. In terms of easily observable characteristics of the industry, the following predictions can be made:

Result 8.2. (i) If the dirty firm dominates in market share or – stronger – if the dirty variant features the lowest feasible performance, a subsidy on investment lowers industry emissions. (ii) If the dirty variant's environmental performance lies above the lowest feasible level, a subsidy always increases industry surplus, and if paid to the clean firm alone, reduces industry emissions.

While observed dominance allows the regulator only to make limited predictions on the effect on industry emissions, observing improvements in the dirty firm's product even in the absence of subsidisation allows a more significant prediction of a positive welfare impact of subsidy payments towards the clean firm.

Environmentally related Taxes and Subsidies

We have considered a specific transfer that varies with the environmental performance. This transfer can be conveniently interpreted as a specific tax or variable subsidy that is related to the environmental attributes of the product.

Alternatively, it can be read as a tax on an energy input used in conjunction with a durable that is differentiated in energy efficiency. Finally, the transfer can be read as a tax on emissions related in the process of production. In modelling a specific transfer, we believe we captured the spirit of a form of environmentally related taxation that is equal in relevance but distinct in character from the environmentally adjusted ad-valorem taxation that has been studied in the literature.

In contrast to the previous two policies, a tax or variable transfer bears a direct impact on market structure by shifting firms' competitive advantage for given levels of environmental performance.

Result 9.1. If both variants are subsidised (taxed) on grounds of their environmental performance, but the dirty (clean) one only to a limited extent, market share and profit of the dirty (clean) firm decrease (increase).

While a subsidy directly raises the dirty firm's profit, this effect is over-compensated by the loss in competitiveness if this subsidy is only marginal. An analogous argument applies to a marginal tax on the clean variant. It will usually be difficult for the regulator to determine what constitutes a 'limited tax or subsidy', unless she is well informed about the environmental performance of the duopolists and how this links to the impact of the transfer on their competitive position. In one case, a prediction is possible on the basis of a simple observation.

Result 9.2. If the dirty firm chooses the lowest feasible environmental performance and, a fortiori, if it dominates in market share, the transfer reduces its market share and profit, irrespective of whether it is a subsidy paid on the clean variant or a tax levied on both variants.

The asymmetric impact of the transfer on the firms' competitive position and, in particular, the induced shift in market share from the dirty to the clean firm, has some interesting implications for the effect of the transfer on industry surplus and the emission level. While a tax (subsidy) directly reduces (increases) market coverage, both instruments shift market share to the clean firm. The two effects may obviously reinforce or offset each other in various ways when it comes to determining the impact of the transfer on emissions or industry surplus. This is nicely illustrated by the following two counter-intuitive effects for given levels of environmental performance:

- In the case of a high environmental orientation of the market, a tax on both variants, with the tax on the clean variant being limited in magnitude, can improve industry surplus despite a reduction in market coverage.

- In the case of a low environmental orientation of the market, a subsidy on both variants, with the subsidy on the dirty variant being limited in magnitude, can lower industry emissions despite an increase in market coverage.

For intermediate levels of environmental orientation, the direct effects of the instruments come to dominate the effect of shifting market share, so that taxation reduces industry surplus and subsidisation raises industry emissions. This notwithstanding, the message to the policy maker is to be wary about counter-intuitive policy effects if the market exhibits extreme levels of environmental orientation.

The impact of the tax/subsidy on the environmental choices is funnelled through three channels.

(i) A direct effect on the competitive effectiveness of environmental performance: by improving environmental performance the firm can reduce the tax burden borne by itself or its consumers and can, thereby, increase output and mark-up. Or, in other words, the transfer strengthens environmental performance as a source of competitive advantage.

(ii) A strategic effect: by shifting competitiveness towards the green firm, the transfer alters the rivals' pricing responses to changes in the environmental performance. For instance, by curtailing its competitive position, a tax will make the dirty firm compete vigorously on price even when product differentiation is increased. Thus, it indirectly reduces the incentive for the clean firm to improve its product.

(iii) A value effect: if the transfer raises (erodes) firms' market share and mark-up, this also increases (lowers) the value gained from an increase in environmental performance which has to be offset against the increase in investment cost.

The overall effect is then determined by the interaction of the three partial effects, the third effect being irrelevant in the absence of investment costs. When increasing its market share and profit margin, even a tax can increase the clean firm's incentive to provide environmental performance. For a dirty firm, the overall effect is more ambiguous. Whereas the direct effect and strategic effect tend to be positive under taxation, the value effect may be negative, as the shift in market share to the clean firm tends to destroy marginal revenue from performance even under a subsidy.

Focusing on the set-up without investment cost, our analysis provides us with a remarkably straightforward finding on the welfare impact of a tax/subsidy.

Result 10. The introduction of any subsidy or tax (i) reduces industry surplus if the environmental orientation in the market is so low that the clean firm chooses an environmental performance below the technological maximum, and (ii) raises industry surplus if the environmental orientation in the market is so high that the clean firm raises its environmental performance above the technological (or regulatory) minimum.

Notably, this result holds irrespective of whether the transfer in question is a subsidy or a tax. Hence, even a subsidy lowers industry surplus if the environmental orientation of a market is low. Conversely, even a tax raises industry surplus if environmental orientation is high. The result illustrates how the changes in environmental performance and product differentiation that are triggered by the transfer can overturn the direct effects of taxation or subsidisation. According to the result, a prediction of the policy impact on the basis of observed environmental performance of firms is possible. It should be clear, however, that the welfare effects tend to be far less straightforward in the presence of investment cost.

By curtailing industry output, a tax is more effective in reducing industry emissions than a subsidy. However, the presence of various offsetting effects on the firms' environmental performance and market shares rules out a general prediction about the environmental impact of either a tax or a subsidy, reaching beyond the following.

Result 11. If environmental orientation in the market is strong enough to induce the dirty firm to raise its environmental performance above the technological (or regulatory) minimum, industry emissions can be curtailed by a tax of sufficient strength.

Together with the positive impact of taxation on industry surplus in an environmentally oriented market, this would provide a strong case for environmental taxation. However, this result relies on the improvement of the dirty variant's environmental performance under taxation, as it occurs in the absence of quality investments. The effect of the tax on industry emissions may easily be reversed, however, if in the presence of quality investment, the dirty firm cuts its environmental performance under taxation.

A Comparison

It is tempting to conclude the policy analysis with a comparison of the different instruments, if not with regard to overall optimality at least with regard to their effects on industry surplus and emissions. Unfortunately, the complexity of the model renders even this more modest approach intractable. Nonetheless, a number of, albeit eclectic, observations can be made.

Consider first the incentives for firms to enhance the environmental performance of their products. One particular concern may be the lack of incentives for the dirty firm to upgrade its product in markets with a low environmental orientation. Here, the standard as a command-and-control measure has the advantage of allowing the regulator direct control of the dirty firm's performance, where taxes or subsidies as economic instruments may fail to provide incentives. By increasing the competitive effectiveness (i.e. the revenue-generating faculty) of environmental performance, a tax or a unit subsidy can provide an incentive to the dirty firm to improve its product if the rate is sufficiently high. This is in contrast to a subsidy on investment costs, which fails to induce upgrades when competitive effectiveness is negative. Finally, our analysis indicates that taxes, at least if they are not too high, tend to provide a greater performance incentive to the dirty firm than a subsidy on variable cost.

However, if taxation is so high as to induce an erosion of revenue, this may stifle the firms' scope to increase environmental performance in the presence of investment costs. Furthermore, if the environmental margin is negative, a tax may stifle the incentive for the clean firm to improve its product as the firm prefers to draw on the competitive advantage provided by the tax under intense price competition.

Next, consider the impact of the instrument on industry surplus and emissions when environmental orientation is low. Here, all of the instruments under consideration are plagued by a trade-off between environmental and industrial policy objectives. If the dirty variant dominates the market then increases in dirty performance would lower surplus even when taking into consideration the pro-competitive effect. Economic instruments may then be preferable to a standard in that they allow flexibility to the dirty firm to leave its performance unaltered and, thereby, avoid a deterioration of surplus. This flexibility may be particularly beneficial when the regulator is unable to assess the environmental performance of the market. In this case, the firm's response to economic incentives, or lack thereof, reveals important information on the state of environmental orientation and the cost structure. However, such flexibility may be unwanted if environmental objectives override the concern for industry surplus. In this case, a standard helps to curb emissions not only by forcing the dirty firm to cut back the unit emissions of their variant but providing a knock-on stimulus towards further environmental improvements of the clean product. The resulting reduction in market coverage provides a further impetus towards lower emissions. By directly constraining industry output and by shifting market share towards the clean variant, a tax tends to curtail industry emissions even when firms do not alter substantially the environmental performance of their products. A subsidy per unit output related to environmental improvements, in contrast, tends to dampen the trade-off between environmental and industrial policy objectives and is thus preferable if a more balanced policy is required.

In markets with a high environmental orientation, a reverse trade-off may arise between the social cost of higher emissions and the increase in industry surplus. While there is scope for such a scenario in the case of a unit emission standard, it appears to be less likely in the case of economic instruments. As we have shown, a low tax provides scope a simultaneous cut in industry emissions and an improvement in industry surplus. Likewise, a subsidy on R&D outlays required to improve further the clean variant (and this variant alone) also enhances both industry surplus and contributes towards lower emissions.

Political Feasibility

In democracies political feasibility places important constraints on environmental policies. Under majority voting and in the presence of interest groups exerting direct political pressure, a policy is the more likely to be implemented the greater the number of beneficiaries. Here, environmental policies touch upon the interests of six groups, producers and consumers of the clean and dirty variant, respectively, the recipients of environmental damage and taxpayers. Generally, policies that lead to the enhancement of a particular variant tend to raise (depress) the surplus of the consumers of this variant when environmental orientation is high (low). A further effect on consumer surplus arises from changes in the degree of product differentiation as this alters the degree of competition and the prices faced by the consumers.

Under low environmental orientation a standard tends to harm all consumers irrespective of the change in product differentiation. It also harms both firms, the dirty firm by diluting its cost advantage and the clean firm by stiffening competition. Hence, environmental interests are confronted by a grand coalition of producers and consumers. The effects are more varied in the presence of R&D subsidies. As only the dirty firm upgrades its environmental performance, this increases product differentiation and relaxes competition. Under a low degree of environmental orientation such a policy is still harming all consumers. However, because of its anti-competitive effect the subsidy is likely to find support from all producers. Such policies may then well be agreed upon if the particular interests of producers and environmentalists are better organised than those of consumers and taxpayers.

For intermediate degrees of environmental orientation a rift arises between the interests of the rich consumers of the clean and the poor consumers of the dirty variant. Consumers of the clean variant may now benefit from environmental improvements even if slacker competition implies an increase in (quality-deflated) prices. Owing to the pro-competitive effect these consumers also benefit from improvements in the dirty variant. In contrast, consumers of the dirty variant stand to lose from improvements in the clean variant due to its anti-competitive effect. If environmental orientation is not too high their willingness to pay for environmental performance is also insufficient for them to support environmental improvements of their own product when they are accompanied by a cost-driven price increase. In this case, any policy leading to environmental improvements in either of the variants will find the support of rich consumers, but will be opposed by the poor. This affects standards, R&D subsidies and taxes alike. The only policy that may enlist the support of poor consumers is an output-related subsidy for both variants that induces a decrease in the effective price of the dirty variant.

The interests of producers are prone to diverge in two instances. First, if environmental orientation is high enough to support an interior equilibrium, a standard favours the dirty firm at the expanse of the clean one. Clean producers may then find themselves to be the only group opposed to the standard as long as it does not boost emissions. If it does, interests are pitched against each other in a curious way, where environmentalists align with clean producers against the introduction of the policy and dirty producers are aligned with consumers in their support. Second, any subsidy that turns out to be an implicit tax on the dirty product and any tax that turns out to be an implicit subsidy to the green product will find the support of the clean but not the dirty firm. This is due to the competitive advantage the transfer bestows upon the clean firm. Environmental taxation is particularly likely to find political support within a domestic economy that imports the dirty good.

Finally, a 'grand' coalition, excluding only taxpayers, may arise in favour of subsidising R&D costs or the sales of cleaner products when environmental orientation is high. This provides that the subsidy tends to enhance product differentiation and thereby relax competition and, in case of a sales-related subsidy, that it does not shift too much profit from the dirty towards the clean firm.

8.3 A BOTTOM LINE

The analysis of policy making in environmentally differentiated duopoly has brought to the forefront a number of issues that can be generalised beyond the rather specific model we have used.

First, vertically – and for that matter environmentally – differentiated markets exhibit an inherent asymmetry that arises from the heterogeneity of consumers with regard to their willingness to pay not only for quality but indeed for the product itself. This asymmetry is reflected in the firm's pricing and quality choices, as well as in the distribution of market shares, profits and consumer surplus. In such an environment, both absolute changes in quality levels, and changes in the degree of product differentiation bear important effects, which may be offsetting or reinforcing each other. They stand behind many of the counter-intuitive effects of environmental policies, which are unknown to symmetric oligopoly.

Second, we have shown for the case in which environmental improvements raise marginal cost that firms are asymmetric with regard to their particular competitive advantage – environmental performance/quality or cost. In this respect, the market outcome depends crucially on what we have called the environmental – or more generally, quality – orientation of the market. If it is low (high) it favours the dirty (clean) firm and biases both firms' strategies towards the provision of dirty low-price (clean high-price) products. If the environmental orientation of the market takes on an intermediate value, both firms draw on their particular competitive advantage, and even though the firms' environmental and price strategies are asymmetric, the distribution of market power is symmetric.[3]

As one would expect, environmental orientation plays an important part in determining the effects of environmental policies. While the exact impact of the policy on industry surplus and industry emissions obviously depends on the particular policy in question, the policies we have analysed – direct regulation, and economic incentives related to investment cost, and marginal revenue of quality – share the following pattern as regards their outcomes. A trade-off between containing industry emissions and enhancing industry surplus is prone to arise in markets with low environmental orientation. Provided that the policy achieves an improvement in the environmental performance of the product variants, this helps to raise industry output under a high environmental orientation and curbs it under a low environmental orientation. As environmental performance tends to be under-supplied in a market with high environmental orientation but over-supplied in one with low environmental orientation, industry surplus is boosted by the policy in the first case and reduced in the latter. Furthermore, a policy-induced reduction in output in a market with low orientation helps to curb emission levels, whereas a possible increase in industry output in a market with high environmental orientation may boost industry emissions. For intermediate levels of environmental orientation, a situation is likely in which the introduction of the policy can both enhance industry surplus and curtail emissions.

For the policy maker, this begs the all-important question as to what is the level of environmental orientation they are likely to face in practice. Our analysis has shown that the environmental orientation of a market is revealed in the distribution of market shares and profit and in the firms' product choices relative to technological benchmarks. This proves to be helpful to a regulator who is uninformed about the underlying cost and preference structure. In some cases, this information may also be used to predict policy outcomes. Nonetheless, the complex effects of policies within environmentally differentiated industries rule out all too sweeping claims as to the effectiveness or ineffectiveness of policies without giving adequate consideration to the particular market structure. The bottom line for the regulator is the cautionary note to be wary of the intricate nature of policy making within environmentally differentiated duopoly.

NOTES

1. We discuss the implications of models with full market coverage in section 9.3 of the following chapter.
2. For an introduction to environmental regulation under incomplete information, see Xepapadeas (1997: chapter 4).
3. Recall, however, that symmetric market shares imply dominance by the high quality firm in profit, and symmetric profit implies market share dominance by the low quality firm.

9. Into the green . . . an outlook

This final chapter will be concerned with a number of issues that we deem to be important in the greening of markets, full consideration of which, however, lies beyond the scope of the present work. These include social interaction as a motivation for green consumption and the role of crowding-out effects (section 9.1); the technological relationship between environmental performance and other product features (section 9.2); different assumptions regarding market structure and conduct (section 9.3); the evolution of market structure, including inter-temporal product choice, entry and exit as well as entry deterrence (section 9.4); and a brief survey of other issues including transaction cost, green public procurement, vertical industry structure and international issues (section 9.5). As we shall see, a range of issues has already been touched upon in the literature, although not usually in the context of environmental policy. It is therefore the main objective of this chapter to survey the literature that is transferable to the issue and to demonstrate in an informal way how it can be applied to the greening of markets. Where applicable, we also point out the implications of the present work. Based on these insights or, indeed, the absence thereof, we identify issues for future research into the greening of markets. The final section 9.6 sums up and concludes this work.

9.1 REVISITING MOTIVATION: SOCIAL INTERACTION AND CROWDING OUT

In line with the existing literature on environmentally differentiated duopoly, our analysis was based on the assumption that the surplus a consumer receives from the environmental performance of a variant, $v\theta$, is unrelated (a) to her peers' environmental consumption pattern, (b) to the environmental performance of competing products and (c) to the requirements imposed by regulation. We therefore side-step both the consequences of social interaction and the feedback of environmental policies on voluntary green consumption behaviour.

One could think of at least two ways of incorporating social interaction into the model. First, consumers' benefit from green consumption may increase with the number of fellow consumers. Thus, one might consider a benefit from green consumption as given by $v\theta f[q(\theta)]$, where $f[q(\theta)]$ is an increasing function of the number of fellow consumers. Such a benefit structure implies positive feedback in the consumption of either the clean or the dirty variant, in a very similar way to a network good.[1] The greater the number of consumers favouring a particular variant the greater the incentive for further consumers to adopt it as well. In such a situation, there exists a strong tendency towards monopolisation of the market by either of the variants. Indeed this may be one explanation why it is difficult for green products to take off in some markets.

Second, social interaction may arise in the sense that consumers value their own behaviour against the yardstick of potential purchasing decisions, which they consider to be inferior or superior. Thus a benefit from green consumption may arise only with reference to non-green consumption. In this regard, a consumer's net surplus may be given either by a function $v(\theta - \theta_B)$ or by a function $v\left(\theta - \frac{\theta_G + \theta_B}{2}\right)$, $\theta \in \{\theta_G, \theta_B\}$. In both cases only consumers of the green variant receive a positive benefit, which diminishes with the dirty variant's performance. While consumers of the dirty variant do not receive a benefit in the first case, they even suffer a loss in surplus in the second case, as caused by a feeling of shame. Note that under the first set of preferences, the dirty producer never has an incentive to raise environmental performance unless he is able to leapfrog his rival. For the second specification, a gap in market coverage may occur. Here, consumers with little feeling of shame, i.e. those with a low v, purchase the dirty variant, consumers with significant social consciousness, i.e. those with high v, purchase the clean variant whereas consumers with intermediate levels of consciousness do not purchase at all. The implications of such specifications of preferences remain to be explored.

Lombardini-Riipinen (2002: chapter 5) considers a similar set-up, when she compares a situation in which green consumers receive a benefit $v\theta_G + b(\theta_G - \theta_B)q_G$, with the second term denoting the social reward from green consumption. She can then show that an increase in the strength of the norm, b, leads to an improvement in the clean firm's environmental performance, a reduction in the dirty firm's environmental performance and an increase in market coverage fuelled by stiffer competition. For an appropriate choice of the unit emission function, the presence of the social norm favouring green consumption may then lead to an increase in industry emissions: a social reward trap as the author calls it. In contrast a norm punishing the consumption of the dirty product tends to reduce market coverage and industry emissions.

Hollander (1990) and Frey (1992) show that voluntary contributions are reduced in response to the introduction of regulation or market incentives. The presence of a mechanism, which establishes an allocation without relying on an individual's best intentions in participating, reduces the benefits from voluntary behaviour. Under social interaction, this also erodes the norm and may lead to its collapse. Rauscher (1997) demonstrates in an environmental economics context that the introduction of an emission standard or an emission tax can lead to a reduction in voluntary abatement effort, which more than compensates for the effects from mandatory abatement. These findings translate to the context of green consumption. If, for example, a consumer's gross benefit from green consumption is given by $v(\theta - \theta_{min})$, the introduction of a standard effectively reduces a consumer's green glow and may, thus, trigger a downturn in green consumption.[2] Clearly there is still much scope for exploring alternative models of consumer motivation on the mechanics of an environmentally differentiated industry.

9.2 REVISITING PRODUCT FEATURES

The analysis in the present work has been built on two key assumptions regarding environmental performance as opposed to other product characteristics.

- Environmental performance is an add-on feature to the product or is increasing with the overall quality of the product. This implies that there is no inherent technological trade-off between environmental performance and other quality aspects of the product that could not be overcome by incurring some additional cost.
- Variants are only differentiated by environmental performance, implying that there are no relevant aspects of horizontal differentiation in the market.

Recall that environmental orientation serves as a measure of the relative importance consumers attach to environmental performance as opposed to other product attributes. Our model is therefore sufficiently rich to describe both industries, in which environmental performance constitutes an important element in competition, and industries in which it rather constitutes a competitive disadvantage. This notwithstanding, there exist relationships between product characteristics which are not embraced by our model. In the following, let us briefly consider the consequences of relaxing the two assumptions above.

Suppose there exists an unavoidable technological trade-off between environmental performance and the quality dimension of another product feature. As an illustration, consider the case of the fuel efficiency of an automobile which trades off against acceleration and size. The current state of technology – even if state of the art – does not yet allow this trade-off to be neutralised. Given a trade-off between environmental performance and quality along a set of other product dimensions, the form of product differentiation depends strongly on the pattern of consumer preferences. The following cases are conceivable.

Case 1: Some consumers are concerned about the environment whereas others rather value performance along other dimensions. As a unanimous ranking of the variants does not exist, even if they sell at an identical price, the products are horizontally differentiated. If the trade-off is such that environmental performance and the other quality dimension can be mixed in a continuous fashion, all possible product variants can be ordered along a line with the cleanest/low performance variant and the dirtiest/high performance variant at the poles. Assuming that consumers' tastes are distributed along this line, it is straightforward to employ the standard Hotelling type model of horizontal product differentiation (Hotelling 1929).[3] We do not wish to pursue this any further but merely point it out as one interesting issue for future research.

Case 2: Consumers are predominantly concerned about the alternative quality feature. Thus, if products sell at equal price consumers agree on ranking them in descending order of their environmental performance.[4] Maintaining our assumption that consumers are heterogeneous with respect to income, the following demand structure emerges: the richest consumers purchase the dirty/high quality variant, middle income consumers purchase the clean/low quality variant and the poorest consumers abstain from consumption. Our notion of quality orientation is still applicable to such a market. Obviously, however, a market with low quality orientation now turns out to be a market with lower industry emissions, as the clean variant now holds the majority market share. The framework we have set out within this work can be readily used for analysis if the following is observed. (a) Unit emissions are now an increasing function of quality, $e(\theta)$; $e' > 0$; (b) a unit emission standard now corresponds to $\theta_{max} \leq \theta_{high}^*$; and (c) an environmentally related tax on each unit output or on the energy input of a durable can be modelled as $t\theta$, $t > 0$.[5]

The following can be verified:

- A unit emission standard triggers a reduction in the quality of both variants. It then reduces (increases) industry surplus if the quality orientation of the market is high (low). If willingness to pay for quality is sufficiently low ($m < m_E$), the unit emission standard unambiguously raises industry output. In this case, industry emissions may increase or fall depending on the impact of the standard on unit emissions.

- An environmental tax reduces the output and profit of both firms, while shifting competitiveness towards the low quality firm. If the baseline margin is non-negative, all interior quality levels fall with the tax rate, irrespective of whether quality falls on fixed or variable cost. High quality is reduced from a corner value if the tax rate is sufficiently high. For given levels of quality, the tax always lowers welfare and industry emissions. If the high quality firm adjusts quality downwards, the associated increase in industry output may potentially lead to a reversal of these effects in a market with low quality orientation.

Now suppose there exists more than one dimension of product differentiation. Products can be viewed as bundles of those attributes which are relevant to the consumer (Lancaster 1966). A consumer can then be characterised by a vector of characteristics that describe her ideal product. Using the distribution of consumers' tastes over these vectors, including price, one can derive demand functions for an unspecified number of products, which depend on the characteristics' vectors and prices (see e.g. Caplin and Nalebuff 1991, Anderson et al. 1992, Feenstra and Levinsohn 1995). Not surprisingly the crux of these models is their complexity. While Caplin and Nalebuff (1991) and Anderson et al. (1992) provide existence and uniqueness conditions for a price equilibrium, to our knowledge, the analysis of the quality stage remains unresolved at this level of generality. A meaningful policy analysis that incorporates the impact of the policy on product specifications is then ruled out.

Simpler models allow the integration of a single horizontal and a single vertical attribute of product differentiation (e.g. environmental performance and colour). While these models are still far removed from the full complexity of interaction in numerous dimensions, they may provide important insights into the circumstances under which environmental differentiation will play a role. Economides (1989) considers a setting in which consumers differ in their preferences over the horizontal attribute but not with respect to their willingness to pay for quality. He shows that firms always have an incentive to maximise horizontal differentiation and minimise quality. Neven and Thisse (1990) extend this framework to allow for heterogeneous preferences along the quality dimension. Two equilibria can arise, involving maximum horizontal and minimum vertical differentiation or vice versa. The driving force is consumer heterogeneity. Suppose, for example, that the income distribution is wide relative to the distribution of tastes. In this case firms prefer to differentiate their product with respect to quality for the following reason. A relatively wide income distribution implies that consumers regard products as poorer substitutes with respect to quality than with respect to their horizontal dimension. In this case, quality differentiation grants greater market power to the firms. There is a tendency to use the other dimension aggressively, and, thus, minimise differentiation. Dos Santos Ferreira and Thisse (1996) consider a model in which consumers are heterogeneous with respect to both the horizontal and vertical attributes in the following way. Consumers are more concerned about product quality the greater the mismatch between the products' and their most preferred (horizontal) specification. In this case an exogenous increase in horizontal differentiation entails a reduction in vertical differentiation. Combining the two findings we can make a prediction on the relevance of environmental product differentiation.

- Environmental product differentiation is the more relevant the greater consumer heterogeneity with regard to environmental performance relative to other product dimensions.
- Environmental product differentiation is the more relevant the more restricted the firms' technological capability to differentiate products in other dimensions.

Thus the more homogeneous the products either in the view of consumers or in technological terms the greater the potential for environmental product differentiation. This should give us some prediction as to the industries or economies under which our model is applicable. For example one might predict environmental product differentiation to be relevant in markets for household appliances (which are nowadays relatively homogeneous with regard to their other aspects). In contrast to this, the incentive for automobile manufacturers to engage in environmental differentiation is likely to be lower.

9.3 REVISITING MARKET STRUCTURE AND CONDUCT

In this section we review the following generalisations of the model relating to issues of market structure and conduct: market coverage, number of firms, collusion, quantity competition, multi-product firms.

Market Coverage

We have assumed a cost structure that guarantees that the consumer with the lowest willingness to pay for quality would not purchase the product even if the dirty (low-quality) variant were available at marginal cost. As we have previously argued, this assumption is by no means justified for all classes of goods and all economies. The model of non-covered markets is a good description of industries within developing economies – think of the issue of volume-related environmental impact in China – as well as of developing industries in developed countries. However, we should believe many commodity markets to be covered in developed economies. In a model with unit demand, this obviously implies that industry output is fixed, but there are more subtle implications regarding the way firms compete.

Wauthy (1996) analyses the effects of a variation in the distribution of consumers' willingness to pay for quality $[\underline{v}, \overline{v}]$ on the equilibrium in a vertically differentiated duopoly with high quality dominance. He shows that as the relative spread of preferences, $\overline{v}/\underline{v}$, decreases, the system moves from a non-covered to a covered market. In a covered market, two equilibrium regimes are possible, an interior regime and a corner regime. Here, 'interior' and 'corner' refer to the benefit of the consumer with the lowest WTP. In an interior configuration this consumer attains a strictly positive benefit, whereas in a corner configuration her benefit is exactly zero. Wauthy (1996) shows that the incentive to differentiate products decreases in $\overline{v}/\underline{v}$ giving rise to maximum (minimum) differentiation in the covered (non-covered) market. He argues that this is a consequence of the degree of consumer heterogeneity. If the spread of preferences is wide, consumers perceive variants as poor substitutes even if they are not differentiated by much in a technological sense. Since firms have significant market power then, they can set high prices and the market is non-covered. In order to attract consumers with low willingness to pay, there is an obvious incentive for the low quality firm to improve its product, whence arises a tendency towards minimum differentiation. If, on the other hand, preferences are narrowly spread, consumers perceive the variants as good substitutes. Price competition is stiff and the market is covered. Now firms have an incentive to maximise differentiation.

Kuhn (2000b) performs a similar analysis and studies the dependence of market coverage and firm dominance on the ratio between (maximum) willingness to pay for quality and baseline benefit, $\bar{v}/u$, as an (alternative) measure for the quality orientation of the market.[6] In the presence of positive marginal cost, full market coverage provides that either baseline benefit or willingness to pay are sufficiently high. This notwithstanding, a covered market is more likely for a low environmental orientation. The lower the relative concern of consumers for environmental performance, the greater the substitutability of the variants. But then price competition is more intense and the market turns out to be covered. In a similar way to Wauthy (1996) the market can take on an interior configuration or a corner solution.

Within an interior configuration the baseline benefit no longer plays a role in determining the firms pricing decisions, and product differentiation tends to be maximised for the purpose of stifling intense price competition. In the corner configuration, however, a case of minimum product differentiation can arise. If environmental orientation, as measured by $\bar{v}/u$, is relatively low, the high quality firm lowers its performance in a predatory action against its rival. This is rational as in the corner configuration the dirty firm pegs its price to the level of baseline benefit. If there is only a small premium paid for environmental performance, the high quality producer exploits the inflexibility in its rival's pricing by cutting its environmental performance and engaging in aggressive pricing in order to capture market share.

Kuhn (2000b) also studies the effects of a minimum quality standard in a covered market. The bottom line supports the results found in the present analysis. The policy tends to reduce industry surplus when the quality orientation of the market is relatively low. The effect on industry emissions is straightforward for the interior configuration and the corner configuration as long as the clean firm chooses a high level of environmental performance. By reducing the dirty firm's cost advantage, the standard shifts market share towards the clean firm. Moreover, as unit emissions of the dirty variant are reduced directly, an unambiguous reduction in industry emissions is achieved. The market being covered, an expansion in industry output cannot occur despite the stiffening of competition under the standard. This leaves the regulator with one worry less about a possible neutralisation of her policies for mature industries exhibiting a covered market.

A somewhat different story emerges for the corner regime, if the clean firm preys upon its rival by cutting environmental performance. Oddly the clean firm responds to the improvement of its rival's performance with a further reduction in its own performance. Rigorously following its predatory pricing strategy, the clean firm responds to its rival's improved performance by slashing price even further. A reduction in environmental performance enables it to do so. While market share is again shifted towards the cleaner product and unit-emissions from the dirty product fall, there is now an offsetting effect due to the reduced environmental performance of the clean variant. This counter-intuitive result aside, the following can be summarised about the effects of a unit emission standard.

- If the environmental orientation of the market is low the trade-off between environmental and traditional industrial policy objectives arises within a covered market, too.
- If the environmental orientation of the market is high the environmental standard contributes to an improvement in both objectives.

Let us conclude this section with a caveat regarding the nature of a covered market. The fixedness of industry output is obviously due to our assumption of unit demand, or more strictly speaking, a perfectly inelastic product – as opposed to variant – demand on the part of each individual consumer. Upon relaxing this assumption we see that full market coverage, in the sense of everyone buying the product, does not imply that industry output is rigid. Consumers may well adjust the number of units they purchase of a durable in reaction to price changes.[7] Examples here are the market for automobiles or TV sets, whereas the market for household appliances may serve as an example of a covered market with true unit demand. Obviously, in those markets, in which product demand of individual consumers is price elastic, induced changes in product differentiation and competition entail volume effects as an additional source of feedback of policies on the environment.

Number of Firms

While not many real-world industries are duopolies, a reduction to small numbers oligopoly is convenient for analysis and indeed in most cases is the only way to obtain a numerical, let alone analytical solution to the quality stage. While price equilibrium in an N firm vertically differentiated duopoly can be studied in a relatively convenient way (e.g. Shaked and Sutton 1982, 1983), an explicit analysis of firm's quality choices becomes tedious once moving beyond the four firm case. Donnenfeld and Weber (1992, 1995) solve analytically for the triopoly quality structure in the absence of quality costs, Scarpa (1998) studies triopoly in the presence of sunk quality costs. Finally, Motta and Thisse (1993) apply numerical analysis to study the market configuration of up to four firms. Not surprisingly all of these models involve a ranking of the profit levels in ascending order of quality/environmental performance. Significant differences may arise however with regard to the effects of policies.

Scarpa (1998) considers the introduction of a marginal quality standard which is set close to the laissez-faire level of the lowest quality. His findings diverge greatly from the results found for a duopoly. While the intermediate quality is raised in response to the standard, the high quality is curtailed. The producer of the intermediate quality is in a dilemma, as any attempt to increase the degree of differentiation vis-à-vis the low quality producer implies a reduction in differentiation vis-à-vis the high quality producer. As an equilibrium reaction, the intermediate firm then simultaneously upgrades quality and cuts price. There are now two effects on the marginal revenue from high quality. On the one hand, the increase in intermediate quality raises the competitive effectiveness of high quality (as in duopoly). On the other hand, however, the stiffening in price competition (given quality) tends to lower the value of quality and, thus, stifles the quality incentive. Scarpa then shows by way of simulation that the latter effect dominates so that the high quality producer reacts with a reduction in quality. Numerical analysis shows that the standard has the following impact on industry surplus and emissions. All profits fall with the standard, mainly due to the increase in price competition. The profit squeeze is more pronounced in a three-firm setting as there is less scope for firms to evade price competition by differentiation. As all prices are reduced and market coverage increases, all consumers are better off. Nonetheless, aggregate welfare always sinks in response to the standard.[8] Scarpa also shows that market coverage increases and average quality in the market drops. Together this implies that an environmental standard would trigger an increase in aggregate emissions.

A standard is therefore justified neither from an environmental nor from an industrial policy perspective. Scarpa suggests that his strong results may not be robust with respect to the nature of the cost function. If quality falls on variable rather than fixed cost the cost raising effects of quality serve to dampen the increase in price competition, which may change the quality reactions of the high and intermediate quality producers. This notwithstanding, his work shows how sensitive the vertical differentiation model is with respect to assumptions about the number of market participants.

There is an obvious interest in considering a market with more firms within a framework that allows for different levels of environmental orientation. While we would expect firms' profit rankings to ascend (descend) with environmental performance levels in the presence of strong (weak) environmental orientation, the ranking remains an open question within markets with intermediate levels of quality orientation. Can the intermediate firm, by mixing quality and cost advantage, attain a position of dominance, or is the firm rather worse off, as it cannot play on any particular strength?

Scarpa's pessimistic results, which were obtained for a maximum environmental orientation (in the absence of a baseline benefit), also warrant further investigation when allowing for lower levels of environmental orientation of the market.

Collusion

Firms often seek to avoid adversary price competition by engaging in collusion. According to the folk theorem, practically any pricing pattern can be sustained as a collusive outcome if firms interact repeatedly over indeterminate time, use grim-trigger-strategies and do not discount the future by too much.[9] Two interesting questions arise in the context of our work.

- What are the incentives for firms to collude in a vertically differentiated industry and how does this affect their pattern of product choice? Furthermore, what is the pattern of industry emissions evolving from this?
- How do regulatory measures shape the incentives for firms to collude and, again, what does this imply for industry surplus and emissions?

It is well known that collusive outcomes are more difficult to sustain when firms are asymmetric.[10] This notion is confirmed by Haeckner (1994) for a vertically differentiated duopoly with high quality dominance in which quality improvements fall on sunk cost. Since the high quality firm can sustain a high level of profits even in the non-co-operative outcome, it cannot be punished effectively and, therefore, has a greater incentive to deviate. In the absence of quality-dependent variable costs, this tendency increases with the quality differential. Haeckner (1994) does not analyse the quality stage of the game. Thus, the important question remains unanswered as to whether firms choose minimal quality differentiation with a view to colluding afterwards or whether they are better off by maintaining differentiation within a non-co-operative game. An opposite result is found by Ecchia and Lambertini (1997), who consider a vertically differentiated duopoly in a covered market. Firms incur variable costs that are quadratic in quality. When choosing optimal qualities, firms attain equal profit in a non-co-operative equilibrium. But this implies that both firms can effectively punish their rival after a deviation has occurred. Under a Nash-sharing rule, there are strong incentives for collusion despite vertical product differentiation.

Our analysis suggests a similar possibility for a non-covered market setting. If the environmental/quality orientation of the market is such that the cost and quality advantages of the respective firms balance each other, the duopolists attain an equal non-co-operative profit despite providing maximally differentiated products. Punishment is equally effective for both firms, and we should expect collusion to be sustainable in spite of maximum product differentiation. Conversely, with dominance shifting to the clean (dirty) firm in the presence of high (low) environmental orientation, we should expect collusion to be less sustainable given the firms' non-co-operative environmental choices. However, we have shown that the dominated firm seeks to minimise differentiation and, thereby, opens new scope for collusion. Hence, we would predict that the dirty (clean) firm will upgrade (downgrade) its performance in order to generate collusion if the environmental orientation of the market is sufficiently high (low). It remains to be verified by a full-scale model, under which precise conditions collusion is then likely to arise. Nonetheless, we are on reasonably safe ground in making the following two predictions.

First, the prospect of collusion could be a serious impediment to the introduction of green products in a market in which environmental orientation is relatively low. Conversely it could serve as a driver behind the introduction of green products if environmental orientation is high. Second, we can easily predict the effect on industry surplus and industry emissions of collusion under maximum differentiation if each firm receives the share of joint profits attributable to its variant.[11] Since both industry output and the dirty firm's output contract in the presence of collusion, there is an unambiguous reduction both in industry surplus and industry emissions.[12] If firms adjust their environmental performance in order to generate a collusive outcome, the effects on welfare and industry emissions depend on how much the gap in environmental performance levels is being closed, and are, therefore, less straightforward to predict.

Ecchia and Lambertini (1997) study the impact of a marginal quality standard on the incentives to collude. By increasing the low quality firm's non-co-operative profit at the expense of its high quality rival, the standard introduces an asymmetry into the duopoly and, therefore, destabilises a collusive agreement. However, this result is not general. In the presence of high quality dominance, as considered by Haeckner (1994), the standard would reduce product differentiation in the non-co-operative situation, and, thereby, facilitate collusion. A similar reasoning applies in our model when the dirty firm chooses an interior level of environmental performance. For the alternative case of the dirty firm choosing the minimum feasible performance, we have shown that both firms' profits fall in the standard, and, thus, an unambiguous statement cannot be made.

Damania (1996) studies the impact of an emission tax in a homogeneous goods oligopoly, in which firms have the scope for collusion. By raising the marginal cost of output, the tax makes deviation from the agreement less profitable and, thus, enhances collusion. Consequently, firms respond to the tax by cutting output rather than increasing their abatement effort. Consider now within our set-up the effect of an environmentally related tax or subsidy when the clean and dirty firms receive an equal profit for an intermediate level of environmental orientation. We have shown that both a tax and a subsidy shift competitiveness towards the clean firm. In contrast to Damania (1996) taxation (and subsidisation) therefore destabilise collusion. A breakdown in collusion leads to the flooding of the market, and while this enhances welfare, emissions tend to increase. These intuitive arguments demonstrate once again the different mechanisms behind vertically differentiated industries and suggest some interest in pursuing the issue of collusion further.

Quantity Competition

We have assumed that firms do not face capacity constraints when competing on price. Thus, in the absence of collusion, product differentiation is the only device to keep firms from undercutting each other until marginal cost pricing evolves as equilibrium. From Kreps and Scheinkman (1983) it is well known that duopolists selling a homogeneous good effectively compete as quantity setters à la Cournot when they have to install capacity prior to pricing. Das and Donnenfeld (1989) apply this to a vertically differentiated duopoly in which firms choose capacity and quality prior to engaging in price competition. It is easily checked that the inverse demand functions implied by capacity-constrained pricing are the same as those in a direct model of a vertically differentiated Cournot duopoly as considered, for example, by Motta (1993).[13]

An issue arises as to the conditions under which vertically differentiated Cournot duopoly may be the more appropriate model of an environmentally differentiated industry. While this is ultimately an empirical question, the following arguments can be brought forth in support of the Bertrand type of model. Suppose there are increasing returns to the installation of capacity. It is then efficient for the green firm to over-invest in capacity if it expects a rising market share over time. However, as long as the environmental orientation of the market is relatively low in the initial phase of the market, the green firm can satisfy its demand with the capacity it has installed. The dirty firm could be viewed as an incumbent with a historical capacity in place. In the newly formed duopoly its market share is reduced from the monopoly level, and it can therefore satisfy demand.

Alternatively one could envisage an environmentally differentiated industry evolving out of a homogeneous goods or horizontally differentiated industry, where an innovation allows an improvement in the environmental performance of an existing product. With only minor features of the product altered, the green firm is then able to use the existing capacity. The increase in market power due to product differentiation implies again that both firms produce below their old capacity.

Of course one could also conceive of a scenario where specific capacity has to be put in place for 'green' production, so that the green firm at least is capacity constrained. The most obvious example is organic agriculture, where capacity is determined once green crops have been planted. The same applies to livestock farming. Capacity constraints also arise with regard to the area available for organic farming, where the conversion from traditional to organic farming usually requires a number of years for fertilisers and pesticides to wash out.[14] Capacity also has to be installed if the green product is new and cannot be generated by merely changing features of existing products.

It is well known that Cournot and Bertrand responses to exogenous shocks differ. There is good reason to believe that this is also true for vertically differentiated duopoly, and a re-evaluation of the impact of environmental policies becomes necessary. Das and Donnenfeld (1989) consider, in the context of trade theory, the impact of output constraints and a minimum quality standard on vertically differentiated Cournot duopoly. Their results are instructive, as they allow for an immediate interpretation in the context of environmentally differentiated duopoly. Observing that the duopolists choose quality and quantity simultaneously and face a variable cost, we can apply the model to the following scenarios.[15]

(i)   Exogenous increase in the capacity of a 'green' firm from a level below Cournot capacity

This may apply for example to the case of organic agriculture, where the green firm can only gradually increase its capacity. An increase in the supply of green products may also be implied by a voluntary industry agreement. In this case the firms react as follows.

- The dirty firm reduces output but only under-proportionately so that industry output increases; and
- both firms cut back their environmental performance.

The change in output levels are as expected from the strategic substitutability of output in Cournot oligopoly. The change in environmental performance is more surprising. In order to sell its variant to consumers with a lower willingness to pay for environmental performance the clean firm has to reduce price across the board. But then environmental performance becomes less attractive as a tool to extract consumer surplus, and the clean firm cuts back on it in order to reduce costs. The increase in industry output implies that the dirty firm, too, is selling to consumers with a lower average willingness to pay for environmental performance. Again environmental performance becomes less attractive as a tool to extract consumer surplus, and the dirty firm also cuts back on it. It is then easy to see that the following forces govern a change in industry emissions:

- the increase in industry output and the reduction in both variants' environmental performance tend to boost industry emissions;
- the shift in market share from the dirty to the clean variant tends to reduce industry emissions.

While the overall effect is undetermined, this result shows a clear potential for a green market to give rise to an increase in industry emissions if the two variants do not differ too much in their unit emissions.

(ii)   Output ceiling imposed on the production of the dirty variant

Output restrictions for the dirty firm arise from regulatory requirements such as the German requirement that the share of reusable beverage containers must not fall short of 72 percent. They may also arise from negotiated agreements between firms and the regulator. Finally, constraints on the supply of the non-green variant may arise indirectly through a restriction of pollution rights. In this case, the following can be predicted.

- The clean firm increases output but only under-proportionately so that industry output falls.
- The clean firm cuts back on environmental performance, whereas the dirty firm improves it.

The impact of the policy on the clean firm's choices is as explained before. As industry output falls, this implies that the dirty firm now sells to consumers with a greater willingness to pay for environmental performance. The firm thus improves its product in order to extract more consumer surplus. The impact of the output constraint on industry emissions is then as follows.

- The reduction in industry output, the shift in market share towards the clean firm and the improvement in the environmental performance of the dirty variants all tend to reduce industry emissions.
- The deterioration of the clean firm's environmental performance tends to raise emissions.

The latter effect can dominate only if the clean firm holds the greater market share or if its gain in market share is so substantial that environmental performance as a tool to maintain product differentiation is no longer required. This may be the case, for example, if the dirty variant is practically banned from the market. In this case, an increase in industry emissions may be the unintended consequence.

(iii) Emission standard imposed on the dirty variant

In this case, the following reactions can be expected.

- Both firms reduce output.
- The green firm improves its product's environmental performance.

Hence, the standard serves to reduce industry emissions, albeit, at the likely expense of lower industry surplus.

These examples should demonstrate the interest in a more in-depth analysis of environmental policies within a capacity-constrained industry, both in regard to the welfare implications and in regard to other policy instruments, such as taxes and subsidies. Furthermore, the literature on vertically differentiated duopoly with Cournot competition is so far entirely based on the notion of high quality dominance, which can be easily checked for these models. Thus, there is further scope for exploring the industry structure and its behaviour in the presence of low quality dominance.

Multi-product Firms

In a number of industries 'green' products are not introduced to the market by stand-alone 'green' firms but rather by traditional firms, adding a 'green' variant to their existing product line. Examples are 'eco-models' of automobiles, energy efficient models of household appliances, and 'green' electricity offered by some utilities. Price discrimination on the part of a monopolist then emerges as a second motivation for product differentiation besides the stifling of competition within oligopoly.[16]

Mussa and Rosen (1978) consider a monopolist who introduces a continuous range of qualities so as to price discriminate between consumers whose willingness to pay is continuously distributed along a line.[17] Willingness to pay being consumers' private information, the monopolist has to ensure, for price discrimination to be effective, that each consumer self-selects the quality targeted at her. In particular, the monopolist has to guarantee that consumers with high willingness to pay do not switch to lower quality variants to take advantage of their lower price. To guarantee self-selection, the monopolist distorts downwards the quality of all but the top quality variants in a way that makes the purchase of a lower than the target quality unattractive to each consumer.[18] Hence the monopoly would have an incentive to set the environmental performance of conventional product variants below the efficient level, as defined by marginal willingness to pay for environmental performance equalling marginal cost. In so doing the firm guarantees itself a premium on the green variant(s).

Besanko et al. (1988) show for a two-consumer-two-variant model that a minimum quality standard set at not too stringent a level can mitigate this distortion. While driving down the price for the high quality variant and, thus, shifting surplus from the monopolist to consumers, the standard leaves unaffected the performance of this variant. Thus for an environmental standard a simultaneous gain in welfare and a reduction in industry emissions should be expected. The authors proceed to show that if the standard is set at too strict a level, the monopolist can no longer maintain self-selection. In this case it may be profitable to drop the low quality variant from the product line and focus on the provision of high quality to a limited segment of the market. The standard then obviously entails a loss in industry surplus.[19]

9.4 INTER-TEMPORAL CHANGES IN QUALITY AND MARKET STRUCTURE

So far we have focused on an exogenous market structure. In so doing, we have overlooked the evolution of the market structure as a defining aspect of the greening of markets. The following issues play a role here: (i) inter-temporal aspects of firms' and regulatory choices; (ii) entry and exit; and (iii) entry deterrence. While obviously the three issues are closely interrelated, we address them in the suggested sequence, moving from the relatively more straightforward to the more complicated.

Inter-temporal Product Choice

We have assumed throughout our analysis that the firms make their quality choices simultaneously. However, there are good reasons to believe that quality choices are made sequentially even when entry is not an immediate issue. Sequential innovation is likely when a new product is pioneered. In this regard, a sequential move game has much intuitive appeal for the environmental context, with solar or fuel cell technology only being the most prominent examples.

Vertically differentiated duopoly with sequential quality choice is analysed by Aoki and Prusa (1996) and Lehmann-Grube (1997). The first study shows that sequential quality choice leads to smaller quality investments by both firms and to a shift in surplus from consumers to firms, while overall surplus is lower. In both studies, the reason for the downward distortion in quality lies in high quality dominance, which induces the first-mover to choose high quality but set it at a slightly lower level (as compared to a set-up with simultaneous moves) in order to gain a Stackelberg advantage. As the follower responds with a lower quality, this enhances the first-mover's profit. For a convex quality cost, the degree of product differentiation rises and stifles competition. As quality of both variants is under-provided even in the simultaneous setting, social welfare falls a fortiori. While neither of the studies is concerned with the environmental implications, it is straightforward to infer the following. While unit emissions tend to be greater as compared to the simultaneous setting, the reduction in industry output helps to curb industry emissions. This is of course the mirror image of the effects of a unit emission standard in a set-up with a zero baseline margin.

The implications of dominance on the part of the dirty (low quality) firm are easily detailed. Obviously the first-mover would now choose to produce the dirty variant. As the effects of performance choice by the dirty firm as a first-mover are equivalent to those of a standard, we can refer to Proposition 4.3, where it was stated that the standard unambiguously reduces the dirty firm's profit if this firm dominates the market. In this case there is no incentive for the dirty firm to increase its performance from the baseline level even as a first-mover, and sequential adoption has no implications for industry surplus and emissions.

Closely related to the sequencing of the firms' moves is the timing of policy-making. It becomes increasingly recognised that environmental policies just as any other policies are likely to be plagued with problems of time consistency. A policy-maker who is unable to commit to an announced policy scheme may be tempted to adjust the policy after firms have made investments in abatement or environmental product design. While policy adjustments are optimal ex post they can lead to sub-optimal outcomes ex ante when firms anticipate them. By adjusting their investments firms can then manipulate the policies to their favour. This may result in a loss of welfare relative to a situation where the policy-maker is able to commit. Petrakis and Xepapadeas (1999) analyse the impact of an emission tax on firms' abatement effort and output (a) when the regulator is able to commit to the tax before the firms invest in abatement, and (b) when she is not. In the time-consistent set-up (b) the monopolist over-invests in abatement in order to be exposed to a lower tax rate expost. Although this leads to lower emissions, greater output and greater consumer surplus, welfare is lower due to excessive innovation.[20]

Lutz et al. (2000) study the implications of time consistency for standard setting within a vertically differentiated duopoly. Specifically, the producer of the clean (high quality) variant, which dominates in profit and market share, may be able to commit to a level of environmental performance (quality) before the standard is enacted. As with the set-up of first-mover advantage studied by Aoki and Prusa (1996) and Lehmann-Grube (1997), the firm will then adjust its performance downward and thereby force the regulator to set a laxer standard. Thus the regulator's inability to commit leads to greater unit emissions and a reduction in industry surplus. Whether industry emissions increase or decrease depends on the trade-off between the reduction in unit emissions and the reduction in industry output that arises in the time-consistent set-up.

Lutz et al. (2000) cite a number of examples that illustrate the long time lag between the legislation and implementation of environmental regulation that may give rise to a problem of time inconsistency. The US National Appliance Energy Conservation Act, for instance, was passed in 1987. The Act required that energy-efficiency standards were to be met by 1990, with these standards to be established in the meantime by the Department of Energy in consultation with producers. Newell et al. (1999: p. 969) study the effects of the standards on energy efficiency and report that about 7 and 8 percent of the increase in average energy efficiency for room air-conditioners and gas water heaters, respectively, were attributable to the standard. Importantly, however, these improvements occurred mainly through an elimination of the lower tail of the distribution, i.e. through upgrades of the least efficient products. The lack of response by producers of energy-efficient appliances suggests they may have been committed to a level of efficiency. Whether efficiency would have previously been set at too low a level for strategic reasons ultimately remains an empirical question.

In contrast to the problems related to first-mover advantage the softening up of standards when the regulator is unable to commit remains a problem even when the dirty firm dominates the market. As the clean firm is always harmed by the standard it has an incentive to soften its effect irrespective of whether or not it dominates the market.

So far we have disregarded the fact that development and adoption of clean(er) technologies is usually a process that takes time and involves considerable uncertainty. This is obvious again with respect to solar or hydrogen technologies for which the development times are measured in decades rather than years. Dosi and Moretto (1995) consider a monopolist that conditions the expected date of introduction of a green technology on the degree of uncertainty with regard to market demand for the product. If stock pollution is accumulated towards a critical threshold, the introduction of the green technology may occur too late from a regulatory point of view. By offering an appropriate subsidy or the guarantee of a minimum return to the innovation, the regulator can bring the expected date of innovation forward in time. Dosi and Moretto (1996) extend their previous work to consider a waiting game played by duopolists. In addition to the uncertainty faced by each individual firm, there is a second-mover advantage manifest in a lower adoption cost.[21] The second-mover advantage increases inertia even beyond the level related to uncertainty in the monopoly case. While this insight is useful, the model is incomplete in that the authors do not consider the impact of the ex-post adoption market structure on the adopters' and non-adopters' profit. In their model, the adopters' expected pay-off is independent of the number of fellow adopters. The profit of the non-adopter is not modelled. This heavily biases the model against a possible case of first-mover advantage. Indeed, as Fudenberg and Tirole (1985) have shown in an environment with certainty, the presence of first-mover advantage leads to a pre-emption game in which rents are completely dissipated.[22]

Hoppe (2000) provides a more convincing model of a waiting game. Building on Fudenberg and Tirole (1985), she considers a game of duopolists competing on adoption dates, when the economic return from technology adoption is uncertain. Her model shows that the pre-emption result is reversed if and only if the level of uncertainty exceeds a certain threshold. Here the possibility of learning from the rival's success or failure about the state of demand gives rise to a second-mover advantage, and the firms engage in a waiting game, resulting in strategic delay in adoption by both firms.

The scope for both a waiting and a pre-emption game renders interesting an application of Hoppe's model to the introduction of green technologies. Suppose, for example, that uncertainty pertains not only with respect to the market potential of a technology but also with regard to its effectiveness in emission abatement. In this case the welfare consequences of pre-emption as opposed to waiting depend on this second form of uncertainty. Waiting would constitute a problem from a regulatory point of view if the technology is associated with a high expected value of emission reduction. However, if the environmental effectiveness of the innovation is uncertain and/or increases in time, there may exist a regulatory gain to waiting. Policy instruments, e.g. the investment subsidies considered by Dosi and Moretto (1995), would then have to be adjusted accordingly.

Hoppe (2000) assumes that irrespective of whether or not the innovation is profitable, an adopting firm cannot receive a lower return than a firm that does not adopt. In other words, the innovation gives rise to market dominance with respect to operating profit. A second-mover advantage can then emanate only from the informational spill-over. A waiting game also arises if the non-innovating firm acquires dominance with respect to operating profit. Suppose that, at the outset, both firms produce a dirty variant and receive the same (zero) profit. Environmental differentiation would allow both firms to increase their profit if one of them innovates and introduces a clean variant. However, as long as the environmental orientation is low, the dirty firm would acquire the greater share of the industry profit arising under environmental differentiation. An incentive to free-ride on the green innovator then implies a waiting game.

How the process of innovation can be entirely stifled if the environmental orientation of the market is sufficiently low can be demonstrated with reference to a model by Beath et al. (1987). They consider a vertically differentiated duopoly, in which firms acquire patents, which determine their technological capacity $\overline{\theta}_t$. A firm, holding a patent issued in period t, can then produce any environmental performance (quality) $\theta \leq \overline{\theta}_t$. New patents are being issued over time, giving rise to a sequence $\underline{\theta} = \overline{\theta}_o < ... < \overline{\theta}_{t-1} < \overline{\theta}_t$. Suppose firm 1 has purchased a patent in period $t-1$ and adopts environmental performance $\theta_1 = \min\{b_G(\theta_2), \overline{\theta}_{t-1}\}$, where $b_G(\theta_2)$ is the green firm's best response. Firm 2 has purchased a patent in period $t-x$, $x > 1$ and produces $\theta_2 = \min\{b_B(\theta_1), \overline{\theta}_{t-x}\}$ accordingly.[23] Now suppose a new patent is issued in period t and put on offer. Beath et al. (1987) consider a model in which high quality dominance is present. Recall that in this situation the clean firm always produces at the highest feasible performance/quality level. Thus in their model whichever firm acquires the patent, it produces $\theta_i = b_G(\theta_j) = \overline{\theta}_t$; $i, j = 1, 2$; $i \neq j$. In this case there is a perpetual demand for new innovation.

According to Proposition 2.4 (part i) the optimal performance choices are given by $b_G(\theta_B^*) = b_G(\underline{\theta}) < \overline{\theta}$ and $b_B(\theta_G^*) = \underline{\theta}$ if the willingness to pay for environmental performance (quality) is sufficiently low. Obviously the dirty firm has no incentive to bid for the new patent, while the clean firm bids only if $\overline{\theta}_t \leq b_G(\underline{\theta}) < \overline{\theta}$. Hence the best response $b_G(\underline{\theta})$ imposes a ceiling on the demand for environmental (product) innovation in this market, which at some point will come to a halt. Note that there is still a demand for process innovation aimed at reducing the cost rate of environmental performance, c. By increasing $b_G(\underline{\theta})$ such a complementary innovation may induce further environmental innovation. However in case of a low environmental orientation of the market, innovation is more likely to be biased towards a reduction in baseline marginal cost c_0 or towards an improvement in the product characteristics underlying the baseline benefit u. Innovation in this direction renders the provision of environmental performance even less attractive. A bias against environmental innovation may then become self-reinforcing.

Entry and Exit

We have so far neglected the role of entry and exit in the development of green markets. Entry and exit are important for the following reasons. First, by altering market shares and industry output they become important determinants of industry surplus and industry emissions. Second, by affecting the profitability of a product, changes in the number of firms bear on the incumbent firms' incentives to provide environmental performance. Finally, if the environmental orientation of the market is low, incumbent firms may fail to provide (sufficiently) green products. However, these products may be introduced by entering firms. Entry and exit themselves are determined by the underlying preference and cost structure, and importantly by the environmental policy regime. With regard to the latter it is well known that within a competitive industry subsidies and taxes are equivalent in inducing emission reductions by an individual firm. However, by raising profit, subsidies induce entry into the industry, which in turn may lead to higher overall emissions. The converse is true, of course, for taxes (see e.g. Baumol and Oates 1988, chapter 14). Similar results apply to imperfectly competitive industries. Basing their model on Mankiw and Whinston's (1986) finding of excessive entry into a Cournot industry, Katsoulacos and Xepapadeas (1995) show that an optimal environmental tax should over-internalise emissions in order to reduce the number of firms to a more efficient level.[24] In the following, we consider some particular features of vertically differentiated industries that give rise to rather surprising results when entry and exit are allowed.

Just as for any other industry the number of firms within a vertically differentiated industry is limited by the entry cost as opposed to the size of the market.[25] However, Shaked and Sutton (1983) show that a vertically differentiated industry with price-setting firms may sustain only a limited number of firms even when entry costs approach zero. A natural oligopoly, as the authors label it, arises if the 'finiteness property' is satisfied. The number of variants is finite if and only if no consumer is locally indifferent between distinct variants offered at their (variable) unit cost (Shaked and Sutton 1983).[26] In other words, the market is finite if all consumers have a unanimous ranking over all variants, given that these are offered at their variable cost.[27] If this condition is violated, then the market can sustain an infinite number of products for entry cost being close to zero. In such a case each consumer obtains his most preferred variant. If the condition holds however, the market is a natural oligopoly irrespective of the level of entry cost and the size of the market.

It is instructive to apply the concept of finiteness to our model. Recall that a consumer's gross surplus and unit cost are given by $U = v\theta + u$, with $v \in [\underline{v}, \overline{v}]$, and $MC = c\theta + c_0$. Now suppose the environmental performance of products is drawn from the spectrum $[\underline{\theta}, \overline{\theta}]$ and the respective product offered at marginal cost.[28] Then, a necessary and sufficient condition for a covered market is given by

$$c < \underline{v} + n/\underline{\theta} \qquad (9.1).$$

Given $n \geq 0$, the following is easily verified.

- *If (9.1) fails so that the market is non-covered, the finiteness property holds if and only if $\overline{v} < c$. In this case, the market is limited at the upper end of the performance spectrum, i.e. it is limited to low performance.*
- *If (9.1) holds so that the market is covered, the finiteness property holds if and only if $c \notin [\underline{v}, \overline{v}]$. The market is limited at the upper end of the performance spectrum (i.e. limited to low quality) if $\overline{v} < c$ and at the lower end of the performance spectrum (i.e. to high quality) if $c < \underline{v}$.*

To understand the idea behind the finiteness property, consider a consumer with willingness to pay $v = c$. For any θ offered at variable cost, this consumer receives the same net surplus $U|_{v=c} = v\theta + u - MC = n \geq 0$. This consumer is indifferent about the environmental performance of a product if it sells at marginal cost.[29] The existence of such a consumer is sufficient to guarantee infinite entry as long as firms charge prices slightly above marginal cost. This is immediately seen by contradiction. Suppose there is a finite number of firms. By differentiating their products, they can always maintain a price above marginal cost. Given that entry is costless, a further firm can then enter with some performance level hitherto not provided. The firm always makes a profit, as in the worst of cases it could sell its product at marginal cost to the consumer with $v = c$ (and some close neighbours). The process of entry only stops when no further firm can enter selling at a price above or equal to its marginal cost. This can be the case only if products are perfect substitutes and in an address model this implies infinite entry.

In contrast, consider $\bar{v} < c$. In this case consumers unanimously rank variants in descending order of performance if these sell at marginal cost. Likewise for $c < \underline{v}$ consumers unanimously rank variants selling at marginal cost in ascending order of quality. Note that the latter situation is ruled out if (9.1) fails. Thus, a non-covered market can be finite only at the upper end of the performance spectrum. Assume $\underline{v} + n/\underline{\theta} < \bar{v}$, which under observation of (9.1) implies the presence of a non-covered market if the cost rate of quality, c, is sufficiently high. Varying the marginal cost rate of quality, we can then trace out the following sequence of regimes.[30]

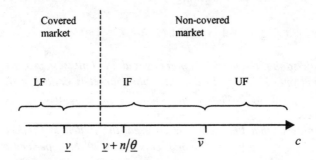

Notes: LF: Finiteness at lower end of quality spectrum; IF: infinite market; UF: Finiteness at upper end of quality spectrum.

Figure 9.1 Finiteness and market coverage

Consider $c > \bar{v}$. In this case, consumers unambiguously prefer the dirty variants. While a number of 'greenish' variants can be sold in a market dominated by dirty firms, entry by producers selling green variants is limited. This structure seems to capture well the character of many 'greening' markets, where the market is dominated by relatively dirty variants, with only a limited degree of 'green' entry. Suppose now, that either technological progress leads to a reduction in the cost rate of quality c or an increase in baseline income of the economy shifts the interval $[\underline{v}, \bar{v}]$ upwards. While this induces additional entry by greener variants to begin with, the finiteness of the market breaks down when $c \leq \bar{v}$. The number of variants and firms is then only limited by exogenous entry costs. Despite the entry of firms selling variants with high environmental performance, the switch in market structure is likely to raise industry emissions. Consider a situation in which almost infinite entry takes place, such that prices are driven down to almost marginal cost. This has two effects, both of which contribute to an increase in industry emissions:

- Industry output is boosted due to plummeting prices, and
- the market share of the variant with the poorest environmental performance increases. This surprising effect occurs as the fierce competition from entering variants forces the dominating firm to cut its price to marginal cost. However, as long as c is still very close to $\bar{v}$ most consumers prefer the variant with the lowest environmental performance, if it is sold at marginal cost. The dirty firm now captures almost the entire market.

Thus, competitive pressure forces the dirty producer to flood the market at the expense of the environment.[31] This dramatic change in market structure has its mirror image at the lower boundary between infinite and natural and infinite oligopoly. If marginal cost falls below $\underline{v}$, this induces exit by a great number of dirty firms; surprisingly, again with the effect of an increase in industry emissions. While industry output remains constant within a covered market, the provider of the clean variant now loses market share. Recall that for c just slightly above $\underline{v}$ almost everyone would prefer to buy the green variant if it sells at marginal cost. Moreover, as heavy competition forces the prices of all variants down to marginal cost, the green firm captures almost the entire market. As soon as the market turns to natural oligopoly, the green firm raises its price and loses market share to its dirty rivals, which invariably drives up emission levels. In this case, competition is beneficial to the environment by forcing the green firm into market dominance.

Cremer and Thisse (1994a, 1999) consider the effect of an ad-valorem tax on market structure and industry emissions at the lower boundary between natural oligopoly and a competitive market.[32] They argue that by slightly raising the firm's effective marginal cost the regulator can induce a shift from natural oligopoly to an infinite market structure, in which emissions fall due to the capture of almost the entire market by the green firm. In a similar spirit, the argument we presented above indicates a potential for adverse effects of both environmental taxes and subsidies. Recall from our analysis in the previous chapter that in the presence of a transfer $t(\rho - \theta)$, which could be a tax or subsidy, a firm's net cost rate of environmental performance is given by $c - t$. Thus if the gross cost rate of performance, c, is just slightly above either $\underline{v}$ or $\bar{v}$ the introduction of the transfer at some positive t may trigger a reduction in the net cost rate that is sufficient to overturn the market regime. The transfer would then turn the market into a competitive market when

$c - t < \overline{v}$ or into a natural oligopoly when $c - t < \underline{v}$. As we have shown this is detrimental to the environment in both cases.[33]

The following case might illustrate the empirical relevance of finiteness in market structure. Recall the rapid diffusion of refrigerators and freezers based on methane as a cooling agent rather than ozone-depleting CFCs. At the outset, only non-green freezers were being sold. Before the development of methane-based technology, the cost rate of environmental improvements in terms of the cooling agent was high, implying a natural 'monopoly' for the CFC-based technology as cooling agent.[34] The innovation of the methane based cooling system allowed the production of green cooling equipment at a low cost rate of environmental performance. In the event, this turned the market into a lower natural monopoly with only one, the green, variant being viable in the market. While for a few years there was competition between a variety of different systems, suggesting an infinite variety structure, practically all manufacturers introduced the methane-based variant in due course, thereby completing the switch to natural monopoly (at the low end). Incidentally, the low level of the cost rate of environmental performance is revealed by the fact that the market has switched to natural monopoly at the low end even in many developing countries, for which we would expect the lower bound to willingness to pay, $\underline{v}$, to be very low.

Let us now turn to the issue of contestability. As we have argued already, contestability forces, at the switching points between natural and infinite variety oligopoly, incumbent firms to cut price to marginal cost. This argument, however, neglects the scope for incumbent firms to adjust their environmental performance in anticipation of entry. Hung and Schmitt (1988) consider the quality choices of natural duopolists under the threat of entry. Firms face a set-up cost but no variable cost of quality. The market is covered, and in an uncontested duopoly one would expect maximum product differentiation. However, the authors show that the presence of an entry threat forces the low quality firm to increase quality to a level at which it receives zero long-run profit. This is the only viable strategy for the firm if it intends to remain in the market, as otherwise it would leave scope for entry with some higher level of quality. By matching the price of the low quality incumbent, the entrant could drive it from the market. As the incumbent loses its set-up costs, this is inferior to the zero-profit equilibrium. It follows that contestability guarantees an improvement in low quality above the minimum level. Demand levels are independent of quality within this model. When 'quality' is negatively related to unit emissions, contestability then invariably leads to lower industry emissions. As product differentiation is reduced to the minimum level for which duopoly is sustainable, social welfare is maximised.

There is then no scope for a quality/environmental standard to improve the allocation (Constantatos and Perrakis 1998).[35]

Again, it is instructive to compare this situation to one where for $\bar{v} < c$ the market is finite at the upper end. For the sake of the argument assume that the market sustains only two producers who enter sequentially at a set-up cost which they have to sink before committing to quality. By analogy to Hung and Schmitt (1988), a producer being committed to an environmental performance/quality greater than the baseline level can be driven from the market unless she has cut performance/quality to a level for which it receives a zero profit. This implies that 'contestability from below' gives rise to a degradation of environmental performance/quality. While this may raise industry surplus, such a situation is again bad news from an environmental point of view. Here, the danger of being replaced by dirtier variants rules out significant improvements in the environmental performance of a product even if, for reasons of product differentiation, these were in the interest of the producer itself. Moreover, more intense competition boosts industry output implying that contestability from below leads to unambiguously higher industry emissions. In this regard, only the imposition of regulation helps to improve the situation.

Entry Deterrence

It is natural to presume that incumbent firms have an incentive to alter their product configurations in order to deter entry even if entry would not mean the expulsion of an incumbent as in Hung and Schmitt (1988). This idea underlies the occasional claims by environmentalists that major manufacturers introduce 'pseudo-green' variants in order to deter entry by truly innovative green products. So it is argued in the context of the European automobile industry, where the introduction by major manufacturers of variants with fuel consumption of around 5.0 litres per 100 km may have blocked the introduction of the <3.0 litre car.

Lutz (1997) considers a monopolist, using quality to deter entry, and derives the conditions under which entry deterrence is feasible and profitable.[36] He assumes that the incumbent (firm 1) and entrant (firm 2) face an investment cost $k_i \theta_i^2$, $i = 1, 2$, where $k_1 \neq k_2$ allows for the presence of a cost advantage for one of the firms. If $k_1 = k_2$ no firm has an advantage in producing quality and the incumbent always deters entry if this is feasible. In this instance, the incumbent can be shown to set quality below the optimal monopoly level. While a downward distortion in environmental performance for the purpose of entry deterrence may be problematic from a welfare as well as from an environmental perspective, this obviously does not square with the idea of 'pseudo-green' variants. However, Lutz also shows that for $k_1 < k_2$, the case in which the incumbent faces a cost-disadvantage in producing quality, entry deterrence, if feasible at all, involves an upgrading of quality relative to the optimal monopoly level. By offering a relatively close substitute to the entrants' product, the incumbent threatens the entrant with a degree of price competition that renders entry unprofitable. This lends intriguing support to the environmentalists' story, particularly as the use of integrated green technologies is likely to allow for improvements in environmental performance at a cost far lower than the cost that has to be incurred for an upgrading of products based on a more conventional technology.

Lutz's analysis is based on the implicit assumption that the incumbent is committed to its quality choice. This assumption is not self-evident. Indeed, there is a strong case to view investments in quality analogously to investments in capacity.[37] Having sunk an investment in quality a firm is committed not to produce a quality in excess of its technological capability; but it cannot commit not to curtail quality. Were a firm to enter with a cleaner technology, the incumbent's best response would then be to reduce its environmental performance and accommodate entry.[38] There are a number of explanations for why the incumbent may be committed nonetheless. First, decisions involving product design may after all be irreversible. Indeed, a 5.0 litre per 100 km engine is not easily converted back into one with a 10.0 litre per 100 km engine. Second, the incumbent may have established a reputation for being tough (Kreps and Wilson 1982). Third, the incumbent may inhibit entry by incorporating patented features into her variant, which would also have to be used by the entrant. The remaining two possibilities appear to be particularly interesting from an environmental policy point of view.

One way for the incumbent to commit to a certain level of environmental performance lies in convincing the regulator to establish a minimum quality standard.[39] For instance, in 1985 the European Commission introduced vehicle emission standards that effectively prescribed the use of three-way catalytic converters. This was in response to heavy lobbying on the part of the German government and its automobile industry. It has been argued by Lévêque and Nadaï (1995) that this stopped the development of the coupling of clean engines and catalytic converters as a better technology.

A second strategy for the incumbent is to enter a voluntary agreement with the regulator. Deviation from this agreement triggers a punishment, which could be direct in the form of regulation being introduced ex post, or indirect, amounting to a loss in reputation vis-à-vis both the regulator and public opinion.[40] Commitment value is present if the loss in reputation feeds back negatively on (future) sales, its stock value or the likelihood of future regulation. While these arguments suggest the relevance of entry deterrence by pseudo-green variants, its welfare and environmental implications remain to be established.

9.5 A BROADER PERSPECTIVE

We have confined our presentation to the issues that can be addressed in one variant or other of the vertical differentiation model. This has already brought up a panoply of policy issues. Many more aspects to the greening of markets remain unaddressed as they draw on different fields of economic theory and lie beyond the scope of this work. This section provides the briefest of outlines.

Transaction costs, switching costs and network externalities: Jaffe et al. (2000) identify the importance of transaction costs in the adoption decision of energy saving-housing insulation. If green products are characterised by a complex technology that requires a different mode of operation, switching costs may play a significant role. Think of a house owner considering the installation of solar panelling as an alternative source of energy, or a local authority considering the introduction of a system of decentralised mini-power plants. Moreover, for traditional providers of utilities there is an incentive to use contracts as a device to deter entry by green providers.

Network externalities may play a significant role for durables that require a complementary input. An example from the past is the provision of lead-free petrol as a complement to a car with a catalytic converter. A corresponding example from the future may be the provision of hydrogen as a fuel. A virtual network exists, as consumers benefit from the number and dispersion of outlets of clean fuel, with the latter being an increasing function of the degree of adoption of the green engine type. The take-off of a networked technology, therefore, turns on the initial adoption decisions, and the introduction of networked 'green' technologies may then be plagued by excess inertia.[41]

Green Public Procurement: A number of commentators argue that the establishment of a green industry may be facilitated by government procurement activities embracing environmental considerations (OECD 1999b).[42] Demand from the public sector may be necessary to top up a level of private demand that is insufficient to create the degree of economies of scale in the product market, which in turn is necessary for R&D investments in green product or process design to be profitable. If private demand is insufficient in the first place, there is little cause for concern about government procurement having a crowding-out effect on private consumption. However, the question remains whether public funds may not rather be spent on subsidising private demand.

As part of his analysis of warm glow-giving, Andreoni (1990) shows that a tax-based subsidy of warm glow-giving enhances the supply of the public good over and above the level attained, were the tax used for direct purchase of the public good. The reason is that channelling a given amount of funds through individual charity increases the warm glow and, thus, induces the individual to top up the amount with private resources. This casts some doubt on a strategy of green public procurement. If individuals receive a green glow, the resources may be spent more effectively on subsidising private consumption of clean products.

Vertical industry structure: In many cases, big retail chains play a pivotal role in promoting green products. Their monopsony power allows them to provide much stronger incentives for manufacturers to improve the environmental performance of their products.[43] Moreover, scale economies in testing product quality together with their own reputation allow retail chains to take on the role of intermediaries, who guarantee to consumers the environmental performance of their green product range. Indeed, intermediation may replace a reliance of firms on their own reputation or signalling efforts (Biglaiser and Friedman 1994) or on external certification (Garella and Peitz 2000).

In a different vein, vertical relationships play an important role in the problem for the producers of green energy of access to a grid run by traditionally non-green utilities. Clearly, a range of regulatory issues arises in this regard.[44]

Durability and recycling: An important class of green products is characterised by their durability. Issues arise here relating to both the durable goods monopolist's problem and a firm's scope for shifting its activities from manufacturing to servicing. In a similar vein, recycling activities matter as does the interaction of firms in a structure of inter-linked markets for primary and secondary resources or goods.[45]

International trade and development: Throughout the present analysis, we have pointed out some consequences of environmental product differentiation for environmental policies in a global economy. In chapter 4, we analysed the effects of unit-emission standards on profits and welfare. The claim by Motta and Thisse (1993, 1999) that the unilateral introduction of unit-emission standards by one of two trading countries unambiguously grants domestic firms a competitive advantage and enhances domestic welfare clearly has to be conditioned on the environmental orientation of the market. If the assumption of a high environmental orientation of the market that is implicit in Motta and Thisse (1993, 1999) does not hold, standard setting entails a reduction in all firms' profits and, possibly, consumer surplus. Hence, a trade dividend to environmental policies should not be expected in markets with low environmental orientation. The claim that standards (Herguera and Lutz 1996, Rothfels 2000) or subsidies (Herguera and Lutz 1997, Rothfels 2000) can be used as a leapfrogging device to assist the domestic firm in acquiring a position of high quality dominance is obviously subject to a similar qualification.

As we have shown in chapter 7 both environmentally related product taxes and subsidies improve the competitive position of a clean firm. This suggests their use as a trade policy for industrialised countries to protect their, presumably cleaner, industries from dirty imports.

Kuhn (1998a, 1998b) argues that the prospect of environmental product differentiation may keep a firm from relocation when faced with unilateral environmental regulation. The presence of some consumers with a willingness to pay for green products may thus render unilateral environmental policies possible, where otherwise a regulatory race to the bottom would ensue. Finally, Rege (2000) addresses the use of environmental labelling as a trade policy.[46]

Recall that environmental orientation is determined by the income realised in an economy. Clearly, industrialised economies with high levels of income should be expected to exhibit a greater degree of environmental orientation than developing economies. It is then quite apparent from our analysis that we should expect different effects from the same policy in economies with different states of development, and should therefore expect economies to differ in their use of environmental policies.

9.6 SUMMING UP

Drawing together the insights into the functioning of a vertically differentiated market one cannot help wondering whether one will be left with one formidable Gordian knot of offsetting effects. The embarrassment of riches in terms of the possible outcomes of environmental policy making arises from two sources. (i) There are differences in the fundamental nature of industrial behaviour under different forms of market structure, relating to the choice of competitive variables, the decision on whether or not to collude, and the absence or presence of natural oligopoly. (ii) For each particular market structure, the level tuning of firms' strategies and the effects of policies depend on the particular realisation of preference and cost parameters, as captured in environmental orientation.[47] Hence, when assessing the impact of a projected environmental policy measure the regulator needs to gain a clear view of both (i) and (ii). Finally, the regulator should be aware of the potential trade-offs between environmental and industrial policy objectives that require a value judgement.

A further aspect of complexity arises from the time dimension. Policies have short run, medium run, and long run effects, where adjustment is likely to involve movements in prices, market shares and industry output in the short run; changes in environmental performance in the medium run; and entry and exit, as well as changes in the direction of technological progress, in the long run. Naturally, these stages feed back into each other. While these notions are very general and not at all confined to the problem of policy making in an environmentally differentiated industry, we feel that they are the cornerstone of a framework for understanding environmental policies in a greening industry. We hope that the present work has put some flesh on this organising structure by pointing out a number of the salient issues involved. In light of the apparent complexity of policy making in a vertically differentiated industry, our only general advice to the policy maker is to take careful account of the structural properties of the industry, the inter-temporal aspects of policy making and the possible trade-offs involved.

Let us conclude with an insight of the present work that is pointing beyond the immediate dilemmas faced by the policy maker. We have seen the important role of what we have called the environmental orientation of the market in determining the impact of environmental policies. While policies are instrumental in the greening of markets in those situations in which the environmental orientation of the market is low, their potential for further environmental improvements is much reduced in industries with a high environmental orientation. Environmental orientation depends on consumers' environmental awareness and on the income level of the economy. But then these two factors are the ultimate drivers behind the 'greening' of markets both through consumer choice in the market and through voting behaviour in a democratic process of policy making. This leaves us with the hope that at some distant point in the future economies throughout the world will bring forth the income and the awareness that renders further policy making towards 'greening' markets ineffective for the simple reason of markets being green.

NOTES

1. For an introduction to competition in the presence of network effects, see e.g. Cabral (2000a, chapter 17). See Becker (1991) for an application to restaurant pricing and Grilo et al. (2001) for a model of horizontally differentiated duopoly with network effects.

2. Note that if the standard is binding, the dirty variant does not generate any green glow for the consumer. The firm cannot charge a price above the baseline benefit then and the market is always covered. We comment on this case in section 9.3.

3. For an introduction to horizontal product differentiation see e.g. Tirole (1988: chapter 7). See d'Aspremont et al. (1979), de Palma et al. (1985) and Economides (1986) on whether minimum or maximum differentiation is realised at the stage of product choice.

4. This framework is used by Constantatos and Sartzetakis (1995) and Myles and Uyduranoglu (2002).

5. It is less straightforward to model subsidies.

6. Price and quality elasticity of market demand are no longer defined in a covered market, nor is obviously the measure η. However, as can be seen from Proposition 2.3, η is positively related to the ratio $\bar{v}/u$, which, thus, serves as proxy.

7. See Anderson et al. (1992) on how to incorporate elastic product demand into characteristic models of product differentiation. Unfortunately the resulting analytics are less than straightforward if the model is to be solved beyond the stage of product choice.

8. Motta and Thisse (1993, 1999) find that a standard raises welfare in a market with four firms. However, placing their model in the context of trade theory, the welfare expression they consider comprises the consumer surplus and profit of only the two domestic firms (in any constellation). In this regard, they underestimate the loss in profit.

9. Under grim trigger strategies any deviation from the collusive agreement is punished by a reversion to non-co-operative play for the infinite future.

10. For an excellent introduction to the determinants of tacit collusion see Cabral (2000a: chapter 8).

11. It is easy to verify that for $m = m_\pi$ the collusive profit exceeds the non-co-operative profit for each firm.

12. This can be verified in a straightforward way.

13. See Gal-Or (1983) and Bonnano (1986) for earlier contributions on Cournot competition in a vertically differentiated duopoly.

14. Incidentally, most European countries have recently witnessed an excess demand for organic food. In the UK this has led the five big supermarket chains to charge price premia on organic food in the order of 60 to 70 percent (*Independent*, 6 February 2000).

15. The three cases follow immediately from Propositions 1 to 3 in Das and Donnenfeld (1989), who consider voluntary quantity restraints for a high and low quality import, as well as a minimum quality standard on an import.

16. Many industries are characterised by oligopolistic competition with product lines. Here, the use of product differentiation for competitive reasons becomes intermingled with its use for the purpose of price discrimination (e.g. Champsaur and Rochet 1989, and De Fraja 1996). The complexity of this set-up rules out straightforward conclusions for the greening of markets.

17. Of course, the continuous quality range relies on the assumption that there are no quality related fixed costs. For an introduction to the model of quality discrimination see Tirole (1988: sections 3.3.2, 3.2.3 and 3.5.1).

18. Donnenfeld and White (1988) point out that the monopolist may also distort the quality spectrum at the upper end if consumers with a high absolute willingness to pay (which the monopolist aims at extracting) have a low marginal willingness to pay (which governs the direction of distortion). In Mussa and Rosen (1978) absolute and marginal willingness to pay are positively correlated and, thus, distortion of quality occurs at the low end. Champsaur and Rochet (1989) argue that a monopolistic firm has an incentive to attract additional consumers from a low (high) quality outside good by offering additional low (high) quality variants.

19. In a setting à la Mussa and Rosen (1978) in which the monopolist chooses a continuum of variants, we would expect the standard to raise quality of all interior variants, and cause the market to contract. Thus, while the effect on industry surplus is ambiguous, there should again be an unambiguous reduction in industry emissions.

20. Poyago-Theotoky and Teerasuwannajak (2002) analyse the same issue for horizontally differentiated oligopoly. They show that the inability to commit may lead to lower emissions and greater welfare if product differentiation is low.

21. The authors attribute the second-mover advantage somewhat unconvincingly to a network effect without explaining the nature of the network and the externalities within. Knowledge spillovers appear to be a far more plausible explanation for the lower adoption cost of the second-mover.

22. For a summary introduction to the literature on dynamic R&D competition and some of the seminal articles, see Cabral (2000b: part vi).

23. A reversal of the firms' roles is obviously unreasonable, as firm 1 would not then have purchased the patent $\bar{\theta}_{t-1}$.

24. For a similar analysis see Lange and Requate (1999), who study the effect of taxation on entry within a circular model of product differentiation.

25. When firms engage in a pre-emptive race for quality leadership, entry costs are effectively endogenous.

26. For a textbook presentation, see Beath and Katsoulacos (1991: sections 6.2 and 6.3).

27. Note the difference as compared to the definition of vertical differentiation referring to a unanimous ranking, given that variants are offered at equal *price*.

28. Shaked and Sutton (1983) is more general in its specification of variable cost, and, thus, uses unit cost.

29. The neighbours above and below, being characterised by $v > c$ and $v < c$, respectively, no longer agree on the ranking of any two variants as long as these are offered at variable cost.

30. As (9.1) is a sufficient condition for a non-covered market, the boundary between the two market segments must lie somewhere to the left of $\underline{v} + n/\underline{\theta}$.

31. Since the market shares of green firms are negligible as compared to the non-green producer, this situation corresponds more to one of contestability than actual competition.

32. A similar argument is made by Constantatos and Sartzetakis (1995) for the case that quality is negatively related to environmental performance.

33. The presence of entry costs dampens these effects by reducing the degree of competition in the intermediate market regime. If entry costs are sufficiently high, the distinction between the two regimes vanishes, and catastrophic shifts in the market regime cannot occur.

34. Here we interpret 'natural monopoly' in the sense of a single viable variant. Of course, the presence of horizontal product differentiation allows firms to maintain positive profits.

35. Incidentally, the situation is reversed in a non-covered market with high quality dominance. As there is no situation of natural oligopoly, a third firm can always enter with a low quality provided its set-up cost is not too high. Donnenfeld and Weber (1992) show for such a setting that the low quality firm reduces its quality to the minimum level, when anticipating entry. This obviously has harmful environmental consequences if low quality relates to a dirty product.

36. Other models of entry deterrence in vertically differentiated industry include Hung and Schmitt (1992) and Donnenfeld and Weber (1995). The latter consider the incentives for duopolists to deter entry by a third firm. This can obviously be achieved by an appropriate reduction in product differentiation.

37. This is for example, the assumption in the model by Beath et al. (1987) outlined above.

38. There is an obvious analogy to the model of entry deterrence by capacity (Dixit 1980).

39. With only the incumbent being directly affected by the regulation, this is a form of raising rivals' costs more subtle than the one considered by Salop and Scheffmann (1983). Here the entrant's costs are raised in so far as in order to maintain product differentiation, she would have to provide a degree of environmental performance (the 0.5 litre per 100 km engine perhaps) which is overly costly to produce.

40. This logic could be at the heart of the 1999 automobile deal struck between the German government and its automobile industry on the development of more fuel-efficient cars that was publicised with great furore.

41. For an introduction to models of switching cost see Klemperer (1995). Contracts as a barrier to entry have been analysed by Aghion and Bolton (1984). An introduction to the issue of network externalities is given in Cabral (2000a: chapter 16).

42. Obviously, public procurement touches upon a great variety of issues in regulation and contracting, a lot of which are addressed in Laffont and Tirole (1993).

43. One example is the ban which a number of leading European supermarket chains have imposed on genetically manipulated food. A number of major supermarket chains have

'greened' their purchasing strategy, e.g. 'ICA' in Sweden (OECD 1997) or 'Migros' in Switzerland (Willer and Richter, 2004).

44. For an overview on the role of intermediaries see Spulber (1999). For an accessible introduction to the access pricing problem see Armstrong et al. (1994).
45. See e.g. Fullerton and Wu (1998).
46. See Rauscher (1995) for a comprehensive study of the link between environmental policies and trade and trade policies and the environment.
47. While we feel the distinction between (i) and (ii) to be generally useful, their interdependence, possibly in both directions, should clearly be borne in mind.

Appendices

APPENDIX A1: ABBREVIATIONS AND NOTATION

Abbreviations

G   green/clean
B   brown/dirty
LHS   left hand side
RHS   right hand side
WTP   willingness to pay

Notation[1]

$b_G(\theta_B) \geq \theta_B; \quad b_B(\theta_G) \leq \theta_G$	G and B firms' best response
$\underline{b}_G(\theta_B) \leq \theta_B; \quad \overline{b}_B(\theta_G) \geq \theta_G$	G and B firms' best response from below and above, respectively
c	cost rate of environmental performance; change of marginal cost in environmental performance
c_0	baseline marginal cost
$E = e(\theta_G)q_G + e(\theta_B)q_B$	industry emissions
$e = e(\theta); \quad e'(\theta) \leq 0$	unit emissions given unit abatement θ
$F(\theta) = \frac{k}{2}(\theta - \underline{\theta})^2$	investment cost related to environmental performance
k	investment rate
$\overline{k}_1, \overline{k}_2$	critical values of investment rate
$MC = c\theta + c_0$	marginal cost
M	consumption of outside composite
$m := \overline{v} - c$	environmental margin
$m_l < m_\pi < m_q < m_h$	boundary values with respect to m

m_E — boundary value such that $m \leq m_E \Rightarrow \frac{dE}{d\theta_B} < 0$

$m_l := n\lfloor \beta(\bar{\theta},\underline{\theta})/2\alpha(\bar{\theta},\underline{\theta})\rfloor$ — boundary value between lower-bound and maximum differentiation regime

$m_h := n\lfloor 2\alpha(\bar{\theta},\underline{\theta})/\bar{\theta}\,\underline{\theta}\,\beta(\bar{\theta},\underline{\theta})\rfloor$ — boundary value between maximum differentiation and upper bound-regime (in absence of investment cost)

$m_h':= \hat{m}_h(\underline{\theta},m,n,k)$ — boundary value between interior and boundary regime in the presence of investment cost

$m_q := n(2\theta_G - \theta_B)/(\theta_G\theta_B)$ — boundary value determining market share dominance (in absence of investment cost)

$m_q':= \hat{m}_q(\underline{\theta},m,n,k)$ — boundary value determining market share dominance (in presence of investment cost)

$m_\pi := n/\sqrt{\theta_G\theta_B}$ — boundary value determining profit dominance (in absence of investment cost)

$m_\pi':= \hat{m}_\pi(\underline{\theta},m,n,k)$ — boundary value determining dominance with respect to operating profit (in presence of investment cost)

m_W — boundary value, where $m \leq m_W \Leftrightarrow \frac{dW}{d\theta_{\min}} \leq 0$

$n := u - c_0$ — baseline margin

p_i — price of variant $i = G, B$

$Q \in \{0,1\}$ — consumption of differentiated good

$q_G = \bar{v} - v_1$ — output of green/clean variant

$q_B = v_1 - v_0$ — output of brown/dirty variant

$R(\theta_G,\theta_B):= \frac{q_G r(\theta_G,\theta_B)}{(4(\theta_G-\theta_B))^2} - F'(\theta_G)$ — first-order derivative of G profit with respect to environmental performance in the presence of investment cost

$R_x(\theta_G,\theta_B) \quad x = G,B,m,n,k$ — corresponding second-order derivative

$r(\theta_G,\theta_B):= 2m\alpha(\theta_G,\theta_B) - n\beta(\theta_G,\theta_B)$ — competitive effectiveness of G environmental performance

S — aggregate consumer surplus

$s(\theta_G,\theta_B):=m\theta_G\theta_B\beta(\theta_G,\theta_B)-2n\alpha(\theta_G,\theta_B)$ — competitive effectiveness of B performance

$T(\theta_G,\theta_B):=\dfrac{q_B s(\theta_G,\theta_B)}{(4\theta_G-\theta_B)^2\theta_B^{\,2}}-F'(\theta_B)$ — first-order derivative of B profit with respect to environmental performance in the presence of investment cost

$T_x(\theta_G,\theta_B)\quad x=G,B,m,n,k$ — corresponding second-order derivative

$t\geq0$ — transfer rate

$t(\rho-\theta)$ — tax-subsidy scheme

U — individual consumer's net surplus

u — baseline benefit

$V(\theta,Q,M)=\theta Q+\hat{V}(uQ+M)$ — utility function

$v\in\left[\underline{v},\bar{v}\right]$ — WTP for environmental performance (= marginal rate of substitution between environmental performance and income)

$v_0:=\dfrac{p_B-u}{\theta_B}$ — WTP of lower marginal consumers (indifference between B variant and no purchase)

$v_1:=\dfrac{p_G-p_B}{\theta_G-\theta_B}$ — WTP of upper marginal consumers (indifference between G and B variants)

$\bar{v}$ — upper bound of distribution of v (maximum WTP)

$W=S+\pi_G+\pi_B$ — industry surplus

$1-x_F^i\in[0,1],\ i=G,B$ — rate of subsidy on investment cost

$Y\in\left[\underline{Y},\bar{Y}\right]$ — consumer's income (uniformly distributed)

$\alpha(\theta_G,\theta_B):=4\theta_G^2-3\theta_G\theta_B+2\theta_B^2>0$

$\beta(\theta_G,\theta_B):=4\theta_G-7\theta_B$

δ — marginal disutility from emissions

$\varepsilon(q,p),\ \varepsilon(q,\theta)$ — price and environmental elasticity of market demand

$\varphi_i:=p_i+t(\rho-\theta_i),\ i=G,B$ — effective price for variant i in the presence of the transfer

$\eta:=\dfrac{\varepsilon(q,\theta)}{\varepsilon(q,p)}$ — environmental orientation

$\Psi \geq 0$ shadow cost of public funds

$\Pi_i = \pi_i - F(\theta)$, $i = G, B$ long-run profit

$\pi_i = (p_i - MC)q_i$, $i = G, B$ operating profit

$\theta \in \left[\underline{\theta}, \overline{\theta}\right]$ environmental performance (quality)

$\theta_{\min}$, with $\theta_B \geq \theta_{\min}$ value of minimum performance standard

$\theta_{\max}$ with $\theta_G \geq \theta_{\max}$ criterion of eco-label

$\rho \geq \underline{\theta}$ performance target

$\zeta := \theta_G / \theta_B$ degree of product differentiation

APPENDIX A2.1

Derivation of (2.1): $U = u + v\theta - p(\theta)$

Suppose consumers' income Y is uniformly distributed on the interval $\left[\underline{Y}, \overline{Y}\right]$ with mass 1. Consumers have an identical utility function

$$V(\theta, Q, M) = \theta Q + \hat{V}(uQ + M), Q \in \{0,1\}. \qquad (A2.1)$$

Utility is thus additively separable into a benefit from consumption of the differentiated product, θQ and utility $\hat{V}(\cdot)$ from baseline consumption. Baseline consumption comprises a quantity M of the outside commodity and the unit or zero quantity $Q \in \{0,1\}$ of the differentiated product. The latter is weighted with a baseline utility factor u. Let $\hat{V}(\cdot)$ be a strictly concave function such that $\hat{V}' > 0$ and $\hat{V}'' < 0$.

A consumer's budget constraint is given by

$$Y = p(\theta)Q + M \qquad (A2.2)$$

where $p(\theta)$ denotes the price of a unit of environmental performance/quality θ purchased by the consumer. With the outside good serving as numeraire, $p(\theta)$ is measured in units of the outside good. Inserting (A2.2) into (A2.1) and observing consumers' utility maximising choice $Q^* \in \{0,1\}$ yields the indirect utility function

$$V_I(\theta, p(\theta), Y) = \theta Q^* + \hat{V}\big([u - p(\theta)]Q^* + Y\big),$$

where

$$Q^* = \begin{cases} 0 & \text{if } \max_{\theta}\{\theta + \hat{V}[u - p(\theta) + Y]\} < 0 \\ 1 & \text{if } \max_{\theta}\{\theta + \hat{V}[u - p(\theta) + Y]\} \geq 0 \end{cases} .$$

Assume $\underline{Y} \gg u - p(\theta)$. Then, a first-order Taylor expansion of $\hat{V}(\cdot)$ around Y yields

$$V_I[\theta, p(\theta), Y] \cong \{\theta + \hat{V}'(Y)[u - p(\theta)]\}Q^* + \hat{V}(Y),$$

where $\hat{V}'(Y)$ is the marginal rate of substation (MRS) between income and environmental performance and is uniformly distributed. Under use of the definition $v := 1/\hat{V}'(Y)$ the last expression can be rewritten as

$$V_I(\theta, p(\theta), Y) \cong (1/v)[v\theta + u - p(\theta)]Q^* + \hat{V}(Y), \qquad (A2.3)$$

where $\hat{V}(Y)$ is a type-specific constant. Technically, v is now uniformly distributed along $[\underline{v}, \overline{v}]$, where $\underline{v} \sim \underline{Y}$ and $\overline{v} \sim \overline{Y}$. Economically, v corresponds to the MRS between environmental performance and income. It follows naturally that willingness to pay for environmental performance increases in income.

From (A2.3), it follows immediately

$$Q^* = \begin{cases} 0 & \text{if } \max\{u + v\theta - p(\theta)\} < 0 \\ 1 & \text{if } \max\{u + v\theta - p(\theta)\} \geq 0 \end{cases}, \qquad (A2.4)$$

which is a restatement of (A2.4) in terms of the approximated indirect utility function (A2.3).

Finally, assume that $Y \geq u + v\overline{\theta}$, $Y \in [\underline{Y}, \overline{Y}]$, $v \in [\underline{v}, \overline{v}]$ such that if a unit is purchased according to (A2.4) this is always feasible according to the budget constraint (A2.2).

In order to obtain net surplus as in (2.1), which is measured in units of the numeraire, we have to re-scale the expression in (A2.3), which gives indirect utility as measured in utils. Note that we can interpret θQ as a special case of a sub-utility function $Z(\theta Q)$, which measures the utility of environmental performance. Let $Z(\theta Q) = z\theta Q$, where the parameter z measures utils/[unit of environmental performance]. Now, let $z = 1$ such that one unit of environmental performance translates into one util. In this case, θ measures environmental performance in both technological and preference terms. The MRS between environmental performance and income, $v = 1/\hat{V}'$ is measured in [units of numeraire]/util. Thus, $v\theta$ is measured in units of numeraire. The same applies for $u - p(\theta)$. Thus, the term in square brackets in (A2.3) is measured in units of numeraire, while (A2.3) is measured in utils. Re-scaling is achieved by multiplication of the RHS in (A2.3) with v, where $\hat{V}(Y)$ is dropped for being unrelated to the surplus from the differentiated product. Obviously then, marginal cost in (2.1) is measured in units of the outside good as well.

Proof of Lemma 2.2
(i) 'Competitive effectiveness' of environmental performance i can be decomposed into a direct effect (DE) and a strategic effect (SE) as follows:

$$r(\theta_G,\theta_B) = \overbrace{[m(2\theta_G - \theta_B) - n](4\theta_G - \theta_B)}^{DE} + \overbrace{3(m\theta_B + 2n)\theta_B}^{SE}$$

$$s(\theta_G,\theta_B)\theta_B^{-1} = \left\{ \frac{\overbrace{[m\theta_G\theta_B - n(2\theta_G - \theta_B)](4\theta_G - \theta_B)}^{DE}}{\underbrace{-3(2m\theta_G + n)\theta_B}_{SE}} \right\}\theta_G\theta_B^{-1}$$

(ii) If $\zeta > 7/4$ the 'competitive effectiveness' increases with the environmental margin, m, and falls with the baseline margin, n, for both firms. (iii) If $\zeta < 7/4$ the 'competitive effectiveness' of G performance increases with both m and n; while the 'competitive effectiveness' of B performance decreases with both m and n.

Using the direct profit function, we can write the marginal revenue of environmental performance (net marginal cost) as follows

$$\frac{d\pi_i(p_i,p_j,\theta_i,\theta_j)}{d\theta_i} = \frac{d[(p_i - MC_i)q_i(p_i,p_j,\theta_i,\theta_j)]}{d\theta_i}$$

$$= (p_i - MC_i)\frac{\partial q_i(\cdot)}{\partial\theta_i} - cq_i(\cdot) + (p_i - MC_i)\frac{\partial q_i(\cdot)}{\partial p_j}\frac{dp_j^*}{d\theta_i},$$

where we observe the envelope theorem. Noting from (2.3a)–(2.4b) that
$p_G{}^* - MC_G = (\theta_G - \theta_B)q_G{}^*$ and $p_B{}^* - MC_B = (\theta_B/\theta_G)(\theta_G - \theta_B)q_B{}^*$, we obtain

$$\frac{d\pi_G(\cdot)}{d\theta_G} = q_G^* \left[\overbrace{(\theta_G - \theta_B)\frac{\partial q_G(\cdot)}{\partial\theta_G} - c}^{DE} + \overbrace{(\theta_G - \theta_B)\frac{\partial q_G(\cdot)}{\partial p_B}\frac{dp_B^*}{d\theta_G}}^{SE} \right],$$

$$\frac{d\pi_B(\cdot)}{d\theta_B} = q_B^* \left[\overbrace{(\theta_G - \theta_B)\frac{\theta_B}{\theta_G}\frac{\partial q_B(\cdot)}{\partial\theta_B} - c}^{DE} + \overbrace{(\theta_G - \theta_B)\frac{\theta_B}{\theta_G}\frac{\partial q_B(\cdot)}{\partial p_G}\frac{dp_G^*}{d\theta_B}}^{SE} \right],$$

where the strategic effect refers to the impact on profit through the induced change in the rival's price. Inserting

$$\frac{\partial q_G(\cdot)}{\partial\theta_G} = \frac{p_G^* - p_B^*}{(\theta_G - \theta_B)^2} = \frac{m(2\theta_G - \theta_B) - n + c(4\theta_G - \theta_B)}{(4\theta_G - \theta_B)(\theta_G - \theta_B)};$$

$$\frac{\partial q_G(\cdot)}{\partial p_B} = \frac{\partial q_B(\cdot)}{\partial p_G} = \frac{1}{(\theta_G - \theta_B)};$$

$$\frac{\partial q_B(\cdot)}{\partial\theta_B} = \frac{p_G^* - p_B^*}{(\theta_G - \theta_B)^2} + \frac{p_B^* - u}{\theta_B^2} = \frac{\left[\begin{array}{c} m\theta_G\theta_B - n(2\theta_G - \theta_B) \\ + c(4\theta_G - \theta_B)\theta_B \end{array} \right]\theta_G}{(4\theta_G - \theta_B)(\theta_G - \theta_B)\theta_B^2};$$

$$\frac{dp_B^*}{d\theta_G} = \frac{3[m\theta_B + 2n]\theta_B}{(4\theta_G - \theta_B)^2}; \qquad \frac{dp_G^*}{d\theta_B} = \frac{-3[2m\theta_G + n]\theta_G}{(4\theta_G - \theta_B)^2};$$

yields

$$\frac{d\pi_G(\cdot)}{d\theta_G} = \frac{q_G^*}{4\theta_G - \theta_B} \left\{ \overbrace{[m(2\theta_G - \theta_B) - n](4\theta_G - \theta_B)}^{DE} \atop \underbrace{+ 3(m\theta_B + 2n)\theta_B}_{SE} \right\} = \frac{q_G^* r(\cdot)}{4\theta_G - \theta_B},$$

$$\frac{d\pi_B(\cdot)}{d\theta_B} = \frac{q_B^* \theta_G}{(4\theta_G - \theta_B)\theta_B} \left\{ \frac{\overbrace{[m\theta_G \theta_B - n(2\theta_G - \theta_B)(4\theta_G - \theta_B)]}^{DE}}{\underbrace{-3(2m\theta_G + n)\theta_B}_{SE}} \right\},$$

$$= \frac{q_B^* s(\cdot)}{(4\theta_G - \theta_B)\theta_B}$$

as given in part (i) of the Lemma. Parts (ii) and (iii) follow immediately from (2.11a) and (2.11b), where $\beta(\theta_G, \theta_B) = \beta(\zeta, \theta_B) = (4\zeta - 7)\theta_B > 0$ $\Leftrightarrow \zeta > 7/4$. ■

Proof of Lemma 2.3
In the set-up without investment cost an interior equilibrium in which the firms choose θ_B^* and θ_G^* such that $\underline{\theta} < \theta_B^* \le \theta_G^* < \bar{\theta}$ does not exist.

We prove part (i) by contradiction. Suppose an interior equilibrium exists. This requires $r(\theta_G^*, \theta_B^*) = s(\theta_G^*, \theta_B^*) = 0$. Consider the following cases:

(a) $m \le 0$: Then from (2.10a), $r(\theta_G^*, \theta_B^*)\big|_{m \le 0} = 0 \Leftrightarrow \beta(\cdot) \le 0$. From (2.10b), $s(\theta_G^*, \theta_B^*)\big|_{\beta(\cdot) \le 0} < 0$, a contradiction.

(b) $m > 0$: Then, from (2.10a) $r(\theta_G^*, \theta_B^*)\big|_{m > 0} = 0 \Leftrightarrow m = n\beta(\cdot)/2\alpha(\cdot)$. Notice that this requires $n \ne 0$. Inserting into (2.10b) gives $s(\theta_G^*, \theta_B^*) = n[\theta_G^* \theta_B^* \beta(\cdot)^2 - 4\alpha(\cdot)^2]/2\alpha(\cdot)$. From (2.12) it follows that the expression in square brackets is unambiguously negative. Thus, a contradiction. If $n = 0$, it follows from (2.10a) that $r(\theta_G^*, \theta_B^*)\big|_{n=0} > 0$, again a contradiction. Excluding the trivial case $m = n = 0$, there exists no combination of n and m for which $r(\theta_G^*, \theta_B^*) = s(\theta_G^*, \theta_B^*) = 0$.

Hence, an interior equilibrium does not exist. ■

Proof of Proposition 2.2:
(i) A unique lower boundary equilibrium is realised if and only if $m < m_l$. Here, $\theta_G^* \in (\underline{\theta}; (7/4)\underline{\theta}]$ if $m \in (-(n/2\underline{\theta}); 0]$ and $\theta_G^* \in ((7/4)\underline{\theta}; \bar{\theta})$ if $m > 0$.

(ii) A unique maximum differentiation equilibrium is realised if and only if $m \in [m_l, m_h]$. *(iii) A unique upper boundary equilibrium is realised if and only if* $m > m_h$. *Here,* $\theta_B^* \in (\underline{\theta}; (4/7)\bar{\theta})$. *(iv) The comparative static properties are as given in Table 2.1.*

We prove part (i) first and then part (iii), while presuming the absence of leapfrogging. Part (ii) follows as a 'residual'. The comparative static properties in Table 2.1 of part (iv) follow along the way. Finally, we establish that leapfrogging does not occur.

To prove part (i) we have to show that $\underline{\theta} = \theta_B^* < \theta_G^* < \bar{\theta}$ is implied by $m < m_l$. $\underline{\theta} < \theta_G^* < \bar{\theta}$ requires

$$r\left(\theta_G^*, \theta_B\right) = 2m\alpha(\cdot) - n\beta(\cdot) = 0 \qquad (A2.5),$$

or

$$m = n\left[\beta(\cdot)/2\alpha(\cdot)\right]. \qquad (A2.5')$$

We begin by noting that (2.8) and (A2.5′) cannot be simultaneously satisfied for $n < 0$. By contradiction suppose (2.8) and (A2.5′) hold for $n < 0$. Combining the expressions gives $-2n/\theta_B < m = n\left[\beta(\cdot)/2\alpha(\cdot)\right]$. Observing $n < 0$, the exterior inequality is equivalent to $-4\alpha(\cdot) > -\beta(\cdot)\theta_B$. This contradicts (2.12). In addition, (A2.5′) cannot be satisfied for $n = 0$. Thus, $n > 0$ is necessary for $\theta_G^* < \bar{\theta}$ and we can focus on this case alone.

By Lemma 2.3, $r\left(\theta_G^*, \theta_B\right) = 0 \Rightarrow s\left(\theta_G^*, \theta_B\right) < 0$ and, therefore, $\theta_B^* = \underline{\theta}$. The second-order condition for a profit maximum is then given by

$$r_G := \partial r\left(\theta_G^*, \underline{\theta}\right)/\partial\theta_G = 2\left[m\left(8\theta_G^* - 3\underline{\theta}\right) - 2n\right] < 0. \qquad (A2.6)$$

This holds for all $\theta_G^* \leq \bar{\theta}$ if

$$m < 2n/\left(8\bar{\theta} - 3\underline{\theta}\right) =: \tilde{m}. \qquad (A2.6')$$

First, consider $m > 0$. Satisfaction of (A2.5) implies $\beta\left(\theta_G{}^*, \underline{\theta}\right) = 4\theta_G{}^* - 7\underline{\theta} > 0$. Satisfaction of (A2.6′) requires

$$\max_{\theta_G{}^* \in \left((7/4)\underline{\theta}, \bar{\theta}\right)} n\left[\beta(\cdot)/2\alpha(\cdot)\right] < \tilde{m} \, . \tag{A2.6′′}$$

Using (2.11a) and (2.11b), it is easily verified that the LHS is maximized by $\theta_G{}^* = \bar{\theta}$ for all $\bar{\theta} \leq (13/4)\underline{\theta}$. Observing the definition of $\tilde{m}$ in (A2.6′) one can show that (A2.6′′) holds for all $\theta_G{}^* \leq \bar{\theta} < (13/4)\underline{\theta}$, where the second inequality is satisfied by assumption (2.13).

From (A2.5) and (A2.6)

$$d\theta_G{}^* \big/ dn = \beta(\cdot)/r_G \, , \tag{A2.7a}$$

$$d\theta_G{}^* \big/ dm = -2\alpha(\cdot)/r_G > 0 \, , \tag{A2.7b}$$

where $r_G < 0$. From these we obtain the comparative static properties, as summarised in part (iv) of the proposition. As $\beta(\cdot) > 0$ for $m > 0$, it follows that $d\theta_G{}^* \big/ dn < 0$.

From (A2.7b), there follows the existence of a boundary value m_l such that $\theta_G{}^* = \bar{\theta} \quad \forall m \geq m_l$. From (A2.5′), it follows that this boundary value is given by $m_l = n\left[\beta(\bar{\theta}, \underline{\theta})/2\alpha(\bar{\theta}, \underline{\theta})\right]$ as defined in (2.14a) in the main text. Consequently, $\theta_G{}^* \in \left((7/4)\underline{\theta}; \bar{\theta}\right]$ if and only if $m_l > m$.

Now, consider $m \in (-n/2\underline{\theta}; 0]$. Satisfaction of (A2.5′) implies $\beta\left(\theta_G{}^*, \underline{\theta}\right) = 4\theta_G{}^* - 7\underline{\theta} < 0$. Inspection of (A2.6) shows that the second-order condition is always satisfied. From (A2.7a), it then follows that $d\theta_G{}^* \big/ dn > 0$. It remains to be proved that $\theta_G{}^* > \underline{\theta}$. Recall from (2.5′) that $m > -n/2\underline{\theta}$ guarantees a non-negative profit for some $\theta_G > \underline{\theta}$. From (A2.5′), it follows that an interior equilibrium with $\theta_G{}^* > \underline{\theta}$ then exists if $-n/2\underline{\theta} < m = n\left[\beta(\cdot)/2\alpha(\cdot)\right]$. The inequality implies $\underline{\theta}\beta(\cdot) > -\alpha(\cdot)$. From (2.12), this is satisfied for $\theta_G{}^* > \underline{\theta}$. Therefore, condition (2.5′) is sufficient to guarantee the existence of an equilibrium with $\theta_G{}^* > \underline{\theta}$. Consequently, $\theta_G{}^* \in \left(\underline{\theta}, (7/4)\underline{\theta}\right]$ if $m \in (-n/2\underline{\theta}; 0]$.

For part (iii) we have to show that $\underline{\theta} < \theta_B^* < \theta_B^* = \overline{\theta}$ is implied by $m > m_h$. $\underline{\theta} < \theta_B^* < \overline{\theta}$ requires

$$s\left(\theta_G, \theta_B^*\right) = m\theta_G\theta_B^*\beta(\cdot) - 2n\alpha(\cdot) = 0 \qquad (A2.8)$$

or

$$m = n\left[2\alpha(\cdot)/\theta_G\theta_B^*\beta(\cdot)\right]. \qquad (A2.8')$$

We begin by noting that (2.5) and (A2.8') cannot simultaneously be satisfied for $m < 0$. By contradiction suppose (2.5) and (A2.8') hold for $m < 0$. Satisfaction of (2.5) requires $m > -n/2\theta_G$ and thus $n > 0$. Given this, satisfaction of (A2.8') requires $\beta(\cdot) < 0$. Combining (2.5) and (A2.8') gives $-n/2\theta_G < m = n\left[2\alpha(\cdot)/\beta(\cdot)\theta_G\theta_B^*\right]$. Observing $\beta(\cdot) < 0$, the exterior inequality is equivalent to $4\alpha(\cdot) < -\beta(\cdot)\theta_B^*$. This contradicts (2.12). In addition, (A2.8') cannot be satisfied for $m = 0$. Thus, $m > 0$ is necessary for $\underline{\theta} < \theta_B^*$ and we can focus on this case alone.

By Lemma 2.3 $s\left(\theta_G, \theta_B^*\right) = 0 \Rightarrow r\left(\theta_G, \theta_B^*\right) > 0$ and, therefore, $\theta_G^* = \overline{\theta}$. The second-order condition for B performance choice is given by

$$s_B := \partial s\left(\overline{\theta}, \theta_B^*\right)/\partial\theta_B = 2\left[m\left(2\overline{\theta} - 7\theta_B^*\right)\overline{\theta} + n\left(3\overline{\theta} - 4\theta_B^*\right)\right] < 0 . \qquad (A2.9)$$

This holds for all $\theta_B^* > \underline{\theta}$ if

$$m > +n\left(3\overline{\theta} - 4\underline{\theta}\right)/\left[\overline{\theta}\left(7\underline{\theta} - 2\overline{\theta}\right)\right] =: \widetilde{m}, \qquad (A2.9')$$

where numerator and denominator of the fraction in the middle expression are positive by virtue of (2.13). Satisfaction of (A2.8') implies $\beta\left(\overline{\theta}, \theta_B^*\right) = 4\overline{\theta} - 7\theta_B^* > 0$. Satisfaction of (A2.9') requires

$$\min_{\theta_B^* \in \left(\underline{\theta}, (4/7)\overline{\theta}\right)} n\left[2\alpha(\cdot)/\overline{\theta}\theta_B^*\beta(\cdot)\right] > \widetilde{m}. \qquad (A2.9'')$$

Using (2.11a) and (2.11b) it is easily verified that the LHS is minimised by $\theta_B^* = \underline{\theta}$ for all $\underline{\theta} \geq (4/13)\overline{\theta}$. Observing the definition of $\widetilde{m}$ in (A2.9') it is straightforward to show that the inequality in (A2.9$''$) holds for all $\theta_B{}^* \geq \underline{\theta} > (4/13)\overline{\theta}$, where the second inequality is satisfied by assumption (2.13). From (A2.8) and (A2.9)

$$d\theta_B{}^*/dn = 2\alpha(\cdot)/s_B < 0, \quad d\theta_B{}^*/dm = -\beta(\cdot)\overline{\theta}\theta_B{}^*/s_B . \quad (A2.10)$$

From these we obtain the comparative static properties, as summarised in part (iv) of the proposition. Note that for $n > 0$ we have $d\theta_B{}^*/dm > 0$ as $\beta(\cdot) > 0$. It follows that there exists a boundary value m_h such that $\theta_B{}^* = \underline{\theta} \quad \forall m \leq m_h$. From (A2.8$'$), it follows that this boundary value is given by $m_h = n\left[2\alpha(\overline{\theta},\underline{\theta})/\overline{\theta}\,\underline{\theta}\beta(\overline{\theta},\underline{\theta})\right]$ as defined in (2.14b) in the main text. Consequently, $\theta_B{}^* \in \left(\underline{\theta},(4/7)\overline{\theta}\right]$ and $\theta_G{}^* = \overline{\theta}$ if and only if $m > m_h$.

Part (ii) of the Proposition follows from the previous proofs and $m_l < m_h$.

Finally, we have to show for the boundary equilibria that firms do not have an incentive to leapfrog. Obviously, leapfrogging cannot arise in the maximum differentiation equilibrium. In the lower (upper) boundary equilibrium only the B (G) firm can leapfrog. Then, it has to be guaranteed that the equilibrium profit for the respective firm exceeds the maximum profit it could attain by leapfrogging. This is easily proved in two steps. First, we show that the B (G) firm is profit leader in the lower (upper) boundary equilibrium. As both benefit and variable cost are linear in environmental performance we can refer to the standard proof that in a lower (upper) boundary equilibrium the B (G) firm cannot improve its profit by leapfrogging (Shaked and Sutton 1982: proof of Proposition 1).

Consider $n > 0$. Then, B (G) profit leadership is given for the upper (lower) boundary equilibrium if $m_\pi \in [m_l, m_h]$. Using the definitions in (2.8) and (2.14a), $m_\pi > m_l \Leftrightarrow \beta(\overline{\theta},\underline{\theta})\sqrt{\theta_G\theta_B} < 2\alpha(\overline{\theta},\underline{\theta})$. This condition is always satisfied as $\beta(\overline{\theta},\underline{\theta})\sqrt{\theta_G\theta_B} < \beta(\overline{\theta},\underline{\theta})\overline{\theta} < 2\alpha(\overline{\theta},\underline{\theta})$, where the second inequality follows from (2.12). Similarly, using (2.14b), $m_\pi < m_h \Leftrightarrow 2\alpha(\overline{\theta},\underline{\theta})\sqrt{\theta_G\theta_B} > \overline{\theta}\,\underline{\theta}\beta(\overline{\theta},\underline{\theta})$. Again, this is always satisfied since by virtue of (2.12), $2\alpha(\overline{\theta},\underline{\theta})\sqrt{\theta_G\theta_B} > 2\alpha(\overline{\theta},\underline{\theta})\underline{\theta} > \overline{\theta}\,\underline{\theta}\beta(\overline{\theta},\underline{\theta})$. Thus, $m_\pi \in [m_l, m_h]$. For $n \leq 0$ we have G dominance (Proposition 2.1) within the upper boundary regime (part (iii) of this proposition). This completes the proof.■

Proof of Corollary P2.2
The lower (upper) boundary equilibrium involves B (G) market share and profit leadership.

The proof relating to profit dominance is part of the previous proof. Recall that $m_\pi \in [m_l, m_h]$. Since $m_\pi < m_q$, it follows that lower-bound equilibrium implies B market share dominance. The upper-bound equilibrium involves G market share dominance if $m_q < m_h$. Using (2.7) and (2.14b), this holds if and only if $2\theta_G \theta_B \alpha(\bar{\theta}, \underline{\theta}) > (2\theta_G - \theta_B)\bar{\theta}\underline{\theta}\beta(\bar{\theta}, \underline{\theta})$. This is always satisfied as $2\theta_G \theta_B \alpha(\bar{\theta}, \underline{\theta}) > 2\theta_G \bar{\theta}\underline{\theta}\beta(\bar{\theta}, \underline{\theta}) > (2\theta_G - \theta_B)\bar{\theta}\underline{\theta}\beta(\bar{\theta}, \underline{\theta})$, where the first inequality follows from (2.12). ∎

Proof of Proposition 2.3
The environmental orientation measured in equilibrium increases in the WTP for environmental performance, $\bar{v}$, and decreases in the baseline benefit u.

Consider

$$\frac{d\eta}{dv} = \frac{\partial\eta}{\partial p_B}\left(\overbrace{\frac{\partial p_B^*}{\partial \bar{v}}}^{>0} + \overbrace{\frac{\partial p_B^*}{\partial \theta_G}}^{>0}\overbrace{\frac{d\theta_G^*}{dm}}^{\geq 0} + \overbrace{\frac{\partial p_B^*}{\partial \theta_B}}^{>0}\overbrace{\frac{d\theta_B^*}{dm}}^{\geq 0}\right) > 0,$$

where the derivatives of p_B^* are found from (2.2b) and the derivatives of the equilibrium values of qualities follow from Table 2.1. Note that $d\theta_B^*/dm > 0$ implies $m > m_h$, which in turn implies $\partial p_B^*/\partial\theta_B > 0$. But then all of the terms in brackets are non-negative. Next consider

$$\frac{d\eta}{du} = \frac{1}{p_B^{*2}}\left(-p_B^* + u\frac{dp_B^*}{du}\right).$$

In a non-covered market $p_B^* \geq u$ must be true so that $dp_B^*/du < 1 \Rightarrow d\eta/du < 0$. Consider thus

$$\frac{dp_B^{\,*}}{du} = \frac{\partial p_B^{\,*}}{\partial u} + \frac{\partial p_B^{\,*}}{\partial \theta_G} \frac{d\theta_G^{\,*}}{dn} + \frac{\partial p_B^{\,*}}{\partial \theta_B} \frac{d\theta_B^{\,*}}{dn}.$$

Note that $d\theta_B^{\,*}/dn < 0$ implies $m > m_h$, which in turn implies $\partial p_B^{\,*}/\partial \theta_B > 0$. Hence the last term is non-positive and we obtain

$$\frac{\partial p_B^{\,*}}{\partial u} + \frac{\partial p_B^{\,*}}{\partial \theta_G} \frac{d\theta_G^{\,*}}{dn} = \frac{2\left(\theta_G^{\,*} - \theta_B^{\,*}\right)}{4\theta_G^{\,*} - \theta_B^{\,*}} + \frac{3\theta_B^{\,*}\left(m\theta_B^{\,*} + 2n\right)}{\left(4\theta_G^{\,*} - \theta_B^{\,*}\right)^2} \frac{d\theta_G^{\,*}}{dn} < 1 \,(A2.11)$$

as a sufficient condition for $dp_B^{\,*}/du < 1$. This is satisfied for $d\theta_G^{\,*}/dn \le 0$. Consider thus $d\theta_G^{\,*}/dn > 0$, implying $m < 0$. Using in turn (A2.7a) and (A2.5′) in (A2.11) one can verify the inequality for this case, too.∎

APPENDIX A2.2

We establish within a series of Lemmas the conditions for the interior equilibrium with $\underline{\theta} < \theta_B^* < \theta_G^*$ and the boundary equilibrium with $\underline{\theta} = \theta_B^* < \theta_G^*$, as laid down in Proposition 2.4.

From (2.15a) and (2.15b) we obtain the following second-order derivatives:

$$R_G(\theta_G, \theta_B) = \frac{\partial^2 \pi_H(\theta_G, \theta_B)}{\partial \theta_G^{\,2}} - F''$$

$$= \frac{-8q_B[m(5\theta_G + \theta_B)\theta_B - n(2\theta_G - 5\theta_B)]\theta_B}{(4\theta_G - \theta_B)^3 \theta_G} - k, \quad (A2.12a)^2$$

$$R_B(\theta_G, \theta_B) = \frac{\partial^2 \pi_G(\theta_G, \theta_B)}{\partial \theta_G \partial \theta_B}$$

$$= \frac{2q_G[2m(5\theta_G + \theta_B)\theta_B + n(8\theta_G + 7\theta_B)]}{(4\theta_G - \theta_B)^3} > 0, \quad (A2.12b)$$

$$T_G(\theta_G, \theta_B) = \frac{\partial^2 \pi_B(\theta_G, \theta_B)}{\partial \theta_G \partial \theta_B}$$

$$= \frac{2q_B[m(8\theta_G + 7\theta_B)\theta_G + 2n(5\theta_G + \theta_B)]\theta_B}{(4\theta_G - \theta_B)^3 \theta_G} > 0, (A2.12c)$$

$$T_B(\theta_G, \theta_B) = \frac{\partial^2 \pi_B(\theta_G, \theta_B)}{\partial \theta_B^2} - F''$$

$$= \frac{-2\left\{ q_B \begin{bmatrix} m(8\theta_G + 7\theta_B)\theta_G \theta_B^2 \\ -n(16\theta_G^3 - 16\theta_G^2\theta_B + \theta_G\theta_B^2 - 4\theta_B^3) \end{bmatrix} \right\} + n\theta_G s(\theta_G, \theta_B)/\theta_B}{(4\theta_G - \theta_B)^3 \theta_B^2} - k \ . (A2.12d)$$

Note that the signs of R_G and T_B are a priori undetermined. The second-order conditions require them to be negative, which we shortly show to be satisfied. Define

$$\hat{m} := \frac{2n}{5\underline{\theta}} \qquad (A2.13),$$

$$\bar{k}_1 := \frac{625(\hat{m} - m)^4}{3456[m\underline{\theta} + 2n]^2} \qquad (A2.14).$$

As before, assume that (2.5′) holds. Then the following is true.

Lemma A2.1. For all $\underline{\theta} \leq \theta_B^*$, there exists a unique optimum value θ_G^* if one of the following two conditions is satisfied: (a) $m \geq \hat{m}$ or (b) $k > \bar{k}_1$. The G firm realises a positive profit $\pi_G(\theta_G^*, \theta_B^*) - F(\theta_G^*) > 0$.

Proof: A unique optimum value θ_G^* exists if the following conditions are satisfied. (i) $R(\theta_B^*, \theta_B^*) > 0$, (ii) $\lim_{\theta_G \to \infty} R(\theta_G, \theta_B^*) < 0$, (iii) $R_G(\theta_G, \theta_B^*) < 0 \ \forall \theta_G$ and (iv) $\pi_G(\theta_G^*, \theta_B^*) - F(\theta_G^*) > 0$. We prove these conditions in turn.

(i) $R(\theta_B^*, \theta_B^*) > 0$. We have noted in the main text that $\frac{\partial \pi_G(\theta_G, \theta_B)}{\partial \theta_G} > \frac{\partial \pi_B(\theta_G, \theta_B)}{\partial \theta_B}$ is always true. Optimal B performance implies either of two possibilities: (a) $T(\theta_B^*, \theta_B^*) = \frac{\partial \pi_B(\theta_B^*, \theta_B^*)}{\partial \theta_B} - F'(\theta_B^*) = 0$, where $\theta_B^* > \underline{\theta}$. In this case $R(\theta_B^*, \theta_B^*) = \frac{\partial \pi_G(\theta_B^*, \theta_B^*)}{\partial \theta_G} - F'(\theta_B^*) > 0$. (b)

$T'\left(\theta_B^*,\theta_B^*\right)=\frac{\partial\pi_B\left(\theta_B^*,\theta_B^*\right)}{\partial\theta_B}<0$, where $\theta_B^*=\underline{\theta}$. It is readily verified from (2.15a) and (2.10a) that $R(\underline{\theta},\underline{\theta})>0$.

(ii) $\lim\limits_{\theta_G\to\infty} R\left(\theta_G,\theta_B^*\right)<0$. Repeated application of the rule of l'Hôpital gives

$$\lim\limits_{\theta_G\to\infty} R\left(\theta_G,\theta_B^*\right)=\frac{m^2}{4}-F'\left(\theta_G\right)=-\infty \ .$$

(iii) Consider the third-order derivative of the G firm's profit function, which from (A2.12a) follows as

$$R_{GG}\left(\theta_G,\underline{\theta}\right)=\frac{24q_B\underline{\theta}\left[m\left(20\theta_G+7\underline{\theta}\right)\underline{\theta}-2n\left(4\theta_G-13\underline{\theta}\right)\right]}{\left(4\theta_G-\underline{\theta}\right)^4\theta_G} \ .$$

From this, it is easily checked that

$$\theta_G^{\max}=\underset{\theta_G}{\arg\max}\, R_G\left(\theta_G,\underline{\theta}\right)=\frac{\left[7m\underline{\theta}+26n\right]\underline{\theta}}{4\left[2n-5m\underline{\theta}\right]}$$

gives rise to a unique and global maximum of $R_G\left(\theta_G,\underline{\theta}\right)$. Noting that $\theta_G^{\max}>0\Leftrightarrow m<2n/5\underline{\theta}=:\hat{m}$. It is readily checked that $R_G\left(\theta_G,\underline{\theta}\right)<0\ \forall\theta_G>0$ if this condition is not met. Thus, the sufficient condition is $m\geq\hat{m}$ as stated in part (a). Assuming now $m<\hat{m}$, we obtain from straightforward calculations:

$$R_G\left(\theta_G^{\max},\underline{\theta}\right)=\frac{\left[2n-5m\underline{\theta}\right]^4}{3456\left[m\underline{\theta}+2n\right]^2}-k=\frac{625(\hat{m}-m)^4}{3456\left[m\underline{\theta}+2n\right]^2}-k \ .$$

Obviously, $k>\frac{625(\hat{m}-m)^4}{3456\left[m\underline{\theta}+2n\right]^2}:=\bar{k}_1\Rightarrow R_G\left(\theta_G,\underline{\theta}\right)\leq R_G\left(\theta_G^{\max},\underline{\theta}\right)<0$, as stated in condition (b) in the Lemma. Thus, satisfaction of either condition (a) or (b) is sufficient for $R_G\left(\theta_G,\underline{\theta}\right)<0$.

(iv)   We can write the G firm's long-run profit as

$$\Pi_G\left(\theta_G^*,\theta_B^*\right)=\pi_G\left(\theta_G^*,\theta_B^*\right)-\tfrac{k}{2}\left(\theta_G^*-\underline{\theta}\right)$$

$$=\frac{q_G\left(\theta_G^*-\theta_B^*\right)\left[2m\theta_G^*+n\right]}{4\theta_G^*-\theta_B^*}-\frac{k}{2}\left(\theta_G^*-\underline{\theta}\right)^2 \ .$$

Inserting from the first-order condition $\frac{q_G r\left(\theta_G^*,\theta_B^*\right)}{\left(4\theta_G^*-\theta_B^*\right)^2}=k\left(\theta_G^*-\underline{\theta}\right)$ yields

$$\Pi_G\left(\theta_G^*,\theta_B^*\right)=\frac{q_G\left\{\begin{array}{l}2\left(4\theta_G^*-\theta_B^*\right)\left(\theta_G^*-\theta_B^*\right)\left[2m\theta_G^*+n\right]\\-r\left(\theta_G^*,\theta_B^*\right)\left(\theta_G^*-\underline{\theta}\right)\end{array}\right\}}{2\left(4\theta_G^*-\theta_B^*\right)^2}.$$

First, consider a boundary equilibrium, where $\theta_B^*=\underline{\theta}$. Here,

$$\Pi_G\left(\theta_G^*,\underline{\theta}\right)=\frac{q_G\left\{2\left(4\theta_G^*-\underline{\theta}\right)\left[2m\theta_G^*+n\right]-r\left(\theta_G^*,\underline{\theta}\right)\right\}\left(\theta_G^*-\underline{\theta}\right)}{2\left(4\theta_G^*-\underline{\theta}\right)^2}.$$

Given that (2.5′) holds, $\Pi_G\left(\theta_G^*,\underline{\theta}\right)>0\Leftrightarrow2\left(4\theta_G^*-\underline{\theta}\right)\left[2m\theta_G^*+n\right]-r\left(\theta_G^*,\underline{\theta}\right)>0$. Substituting from (2.10a), (2.11a) and (2.11b) into the last inequality and rearranging gives $2m\left(4\theta_G^{*2}-\theta_G^*\underline{\theta}-2\underline{\theta}^2\right)+3n\left(4\theta_G^*-3\underline{\theta}\right)>0$. Letting $\theta_G^*\to\underline{\theta}$, the RHS converges to $3\underline{\theta}\left[2m\underline{\theta}+n\right]>0$, which by virtue of (2.5′) is satisfied.

Consider now an interior equilibrium. Here $\Pi_G\left(\theta_G^*,\theta_B^*\right)>0$ if

$$\left(4\theta_G^*-\theta_B^*\right)\left(\theta_G^*-\theta_B^*\right)\left[2m\theta_G^*+n\right]-r\left(\theta_G^*,\theta_B^*\right)\theta_G^*\overset{!}{\geq}0.$$

Using the definition of $r\left(\theta_G^*,\theta_B^*\right)$ from (2.10a) this condition can be transformed into

$$2m\theta_G^{*2}\left(4\theta_G^*-7\theta_B^*\right)+n\left(12\theta_G^{*2}-17\theta_G^*\theta_B^*+\theta_B^{*2}\right)\overset{!}{\geq}0.$$

Noting that in an interior equilibrium $s\left(\theta_G^*,\theta_B^*\right)>0$ and, therefore, $4\theta_G^*-7\theta_B^*>0$, it is easily checked that this inequality is satisfied. Thus the G firm makes a positive profit in both a boundary and interior equilibrium.

It follows from (i)–(iv) that a unique optimum value $\theta_G^* > \theta_B^*$ always exists in the presence of sunk costs of environmental performance.∎

The presence of the baseline term can introduce a convexity into the G firm's profit function. A unique optimum θ_G^* exists only if the function is strictly concave. For this to be true it is sufficient that either m or the (investment) cost rate k are sufficiently high. Note from (A2.13) and (A2.14) that for $m \geq \hat{m}$, $\bar{k}_1 \leq 0$. Thus $m \geq \hat{m}$ is sufficient. The Lemma also shows that optimal choice of θ guarantees the G firm a positive long-run profit. It is sufficient to establish this for the G firm. If (2.5′) holds the B firm could always realise a positive profit by choosing $\underline{\theta}$. For the G firm this is not straightforward. In the presence of investment costs the G firm may face a situation in which for no $\theta_G > \theta_B^*$ it can realise a positive long-run profit. The Lemma shows that this case cannot arise.[3]

We now establish that leapfrogging cannot arise in our set-up if a relatively mild condition is satisfied. To begin with, recall that a firm dominating in profit has no incentive to leapfrog (Lehmann-Grube 1997). It can be shown that the G firm always dominates with regard to long-run profit. In a boundary equilibrium, the G or B firm may dominate in profit. Since for $\theta_B^* = \underline{\theta}$ under B profit leadership the case of backward leapfrogging by the G firm is ruled out, we only have to check whether the B firm has an incentive to leapfrog under G profit leadership. In the following, we establish a condition ruling this out.

Leapfrogging by the B firm does not occur if the following condition holds

$$\Pi_B\left(\theta_G^*, \theta_B^*\right) = \pi_B\left(\theta_G^*, \theta_B^*\right) - F\left(\theta_B^*\right)$$
$$\geq \pi_B\left[\theta_G^*, \bar{b}_B\left(\theta_G^*\right)\right] - F\left[\bar{b}_B\left(\theta_G^*\right)\right] = \Pi_B\left[\theta_G^*, \bar{b}_B\left(\theta_G^*\right)\right]$$

where $\bar{b}_B\left(\theta_G^*\right) \geq \theta_G^*$ is the best response to θ_G^* from above. The following lemma allows us to focus on the case with $n = 0$.

Lemma A2.2. $\quad \dfrac{d\Pi_B\left(\theta_G^*, \theta_B^*\right)}{dn} > \dfrac{d\Pi_B\left[\theta_G^*, \bar{b}_B\left(\theta_G^*\right)\right]}{dn} \quad$ *if* $\quad \dfrac{d\theta_G^*}{dn} \geq \varepsilon \quad$ *for some* $\varepsilon \leq 0$.

Proof: In order to prove this lemma as well as the following Lemma A2.3 we rely on the auxiliary lemma AL, part (i), which is presented following the present proof. Consider

$$\frac{d\Pi_B\left(\theta_G^*,\theta_B^*\right)}{dn}=\frac{\partial\pi_B\left(\theta_G^*,\theta_B^*\right)}{\partial n}+\frac{\partial\pi_B\left(\theta_G^*,\theta_B^*\right)}{\partial\theta_G}\frac{d\theta_G^*}{dn},\quad\text{(A2.15a)}$$

$$\frac{d\Pi_B\left[\theta_G^*,\bar b_B\left(\theta_G^*\right)\right]}{dn}=\frac{\partial\pi_B\left[\theta_G^*,\bar b_B\left(\theta_G^*\right)\right]}{\partial n}+\frac{\partial\pi_B\left[\theta_G^*,\bar b_B\left(\theta_G^*\right)\right]}{\partial\theta_G}\frac{d\theta_G^*}{dn},\text{(A2.15b)}$$

where the impact on $\Pi_B(\cdot)$ of $d\theta_B^*/dn$ and $d\bar b_B(\cdot)/dn$ is disregarded by virtue of the envelope theorem. Using (2.6a) and (2.6b) to determine the relevant derivatives, the expressions in (A2.15a) and (A2.15b) can be expanded to

$$\frac{d\Pi_B\left(\theta_G^*,\theta_B^*\right)}{dn}=\overbrace{\frac{4\left(\theta_G^*-\theta_B^*\right)\theta_G^*\left[m\theta_B^*+2n\right]}{\left(4\theta_G^*-\theta_B^*\right)^2\theta_B^*}}^{>0}+\overbrace{\frac{\left(2\theta_G^*+\theta_B^*\right)\theta_B^*\pi_B\left(\theta_G^*,\theta_B^*\right)}{\left(4\theta_G^*-\theta_B^*\right)\left(\theta_G^*-\theta_B^*\right)\theta_G^*}}^{>0}\frac{d\theta_G^*}{dn},$$

$$\frac{d\Pi_B\left[\theta_G^*,\bar b_B\left(\theta_G^*\right)\right]}{dn}=\overbrace{\frac{2\left[\bar b_B(\cdot)-\theta_G^*\right]\left[2m\bar b_B(\cdot)+n\right]}{\left[4\bar b_B(\cdot)-\theta_G^*\right]^2}}^{>0}+\overbrace{\frac{-\left[2\bar b_B(\cdot)+\theta_G^*\right]\pi_B\left[\theta_G^*,\bar b_B(\cdot)\right]}{\left[4\bar b_B(\cdot)-\theta_G^*\right]\left[\bar b_B(\cdot)-\theta_G^*\right]}}^{<0}\frac{d\theta_G^*}{dn}.$$

Assume $d\theta_G^*/dn\geq0$. Then $\frac{d\Pi_B\left(\theta_G^*,\theta_B^*\right)}{dn}>\frac{d\Pi_B\left[\theta_G^*,\bar b_B\left(\theta_G^*\right)\right]}{dn}$ if

$$\frac{\partial\pi_B\left(\theta_G^*,\theta_B^*\right)}{\partial n}=\frac{4\left(\theta_G^*-\theta_B^*\right)\theta_G^*\left[m\theta_B^*+2n\right]}{\left(4\theta_G^*-\theta_B^*\right)^2\theta_B^*}$$
$$>\frac{2\left[\bar b_B(\cdot)-\theta_G^*\right]\left[2m\bar b_B(\cdot)+n\right]}{\left[4\bar b_B(\cdot)-\theta_G^*\right]^2}=\frac{\partial\pi_B\left[\theta_G^*,\bar b_B(\cdot)\right]}{\partial n}.$$

We now show that the inequality is, indeed, satisfied. Define $a:=\bar b_B\left(\theta_G^*\right)/\theta_G^*$ and $b:=\theta_B^*/\theta_G^*$, where $a\geq1$ and $b\leq1$. From AL, part (i), $b\leq1/a$. Using a and b in the above inequality yields

$$\frac{\partial \pi_B\left(\theta_G^*,b\right)}{\partial n} = \frac{4(1-b)\left[mb+2\,n/\theta_G^*\right]}{(4-b)^2\,b} > \frac{2(a-1)\left[2ma+n/\theta_G^*\right]}{(4a-1)^2} = \frac{\partial \pi_B\left(\theta_G^*,a\right)}{\partial n}$$

It is easily checked that $\frac{\partial^2 \pi_B\left(\theta_G^*,b\right)}{\partial n\partial b} < 0$. Observing $b \le 1/a$, it follows that

$$\frac{\partial \pi_B\left(\theta_G^*,b\right)}{\partial n} \ge \frac{\partial \pi_B\left(\theta_G^*,a^{-1}\right)}{\partial n} = \frac{4(a-1)a\left[m+2\,na/\theta_G^*\right]}{(4a-1)^2}$$

$$> \frac{2(a-1)\left[2ma+n/\theta_G^*\right]}{(4a-1)^2} = \frac{\partial \pi_B\left(\theta_G^*,a\right)}{\partial n}$$

Here, the middle inequality is readily verified. Hence $\frac{d\Pi_B\left(\theta_G^*,\theta_B^*\right)}{dn} > \frac{d\Pi_B\left(\theta_G^*,\bar{b}_B\left(\theta_G^*\right)\right)}{dn}$ is true for $d\theta_G^*/dn \ge 0$. By continuity the result extends to $d\theta_G^*/dn \in [\varepsilon,0]$, implying that the reaction term must not be too large in absolute value. ∎

Remark: The comparative static properties of $d\theta_G^*/dn$ are discussed surrounding Corollary P2.4. Unfortunately, the sign is generally ambiguous. However, the magnitude of $\left|d\theta_G^*/dn\right|$ decreases in the investment cost parameter k. Thus, Lemma A2.2 is always satisfied if k is sufficiently large.

Lemma AL. Define $a := \bar{b}_B\left(\theta_G^*\right)/\theta_G^*$ *and* $b := \theta_B^*/\theta_G^*$. *Optimal choice of* $\bar{b}_B\left(\theta_G^*\right)$ *and* θ_G^* *implies (i)* $b \le 1/a$ *for* $n \ge 0$; *and (ii)* $a < 7/4$ *and* $b < \frac{a(7-4a)}{4a-1}$ *for* $n = 0$.

Proof: We note that $b := \theta_B^*/\theta_G^* \in [0,1]$ and $a := \bar{b}_B\left(\theta_G^*\right)/\theta_G^* \ge 1$. Writing the G firm's first-order condition in (2.15a) as a function of b, we obtain

$$k\left(\theta_G^* - \underline{\theta}\right) = \frac{\left(2m\theta_G^*+n\right)r(b)}{(4-b)^3\theta_G^{*2}}, \qquad \text{where} \qquad r(b) = 2m\alpha(b)\theta_G^* - n\beta(b) \qquad \text{with}$$

$\alpha(b) := 4 - 3b + 2b^2$ and $\beta(b) := 4 - 7b$. Similarly, we obtain the leapfrogging firm's first-order condition as

$$k\left(a\theta_G{}^* - \underline{\theta}\right) = \frac{\left(2ma\theta_G{}^* + n\right)r(a)}{(4a-1)^3\theta_G{}^{*2}}, \tag{A2.16}$$

where $r(a) = 2m\alpha(a)\theta_G{}^* - n\beta(a)$ with $\alpha(a) := 4a^2 - 3a + 2$ and $\beta(a) := 4a - 7$. The following must hold.

$$\frac{\left(a\theta_G{}^* - \underline{\theta}\right)}{\left(\theta_G{}^* - \underline{\theta}\right)} = \frac{\left(2ma\theta_G{}^* + n\right)r(a)(4-b)^3}{\left(2m\theta_G{}^* + n\right)r(b)(4a-1)^3} \overset{!}{\geq} a .$$

As $a \geq 1$, the inequality implies

$$Q(a,b) := \frac{r(a)(4-b)^3}{r(b)(4a-1)^3} \overset{!}{\geq} 1 ,$$

which imposes a restriction on a and b. Note that B leapfrogging is only relevant for $m \geq m_\pi{}' = n/\left(\sqrt{b}\theta_G{}^*\right)$. For this case it is easily checked that $\partial Q(a,b)/\partial a < 0$ and $\partial Q(a,b)/\partial b < 0$.

(i) Evaluating $Q(a,b)$ at $b = 1/a$ yields $Q\left(a, \frac{1}{a}\right) = \frac{2m\alpha(a)\theta_G{}^* - n\beta(a)}{a\left[2m\alpha(a)\theta_G{}^* - an\beta(a)\right]} \leq 1$ where the inequality is readily verified for $m \geq m_\pi{}' = n\sqrt{a}/\theta_G{}^*$ and $a \geq 1$. Hence, $Q(a,b) \geq 1 \Rightarrow b \leq 1/a$, which proves part (i).

(ii) Now consider $Q(a,b)\big|_{n=0} := \frac{\alpha(a)(4-b)^3}{\alpha(b)(4a-1)^3}$. Evaluating $Q(a,b)\big|_{n=0}$ at $a = 7/4$ yields $Q\left(\frac{7}{4}, b\right)\big|_{n=0} = \frac{(4-b)^3}{24\alpha(b)} < 1 \quad \forall b$. Evaluating $Q(a,b)\big|_{n=0}$ at $b = \frac{a(7-4a)}{4a-1}$, where $\frac{a(7-4a)}{4a-1} > 0$, yields

$$Q\left(a, \frac{a(7-4a)}{4a-1}\right)\bigg|_{n=0} = \frac{\left(4a^2 - 3a + 2\right)\left(4a^2 + 9a - 4\right)^3}{\left(32a^4 - 64a^3 + 66a^2 - 11a + 4\right)(4a-1)^4} < 1 \quad \forall a \in \left[1, \frac{7}{4}\right],$$

where the inequality follows from tedious but straightforward calculations. Thus, $Q(a,b)\big|_{n=0} \geq 1 \Rightarrow \left\{a < \frac{7}{4}; b < \frac{a(7-4a)}{4a-1}\right\}$, which proves part (ii). This completes the proof.∎

Lemma A2.2 implies that, by favouring the B producer, an increase in the baseline margin n tends to reduce the incentive for upward leapfrogging. Having ruled out $n < 0$, the strongest incentive for leapfrogging is obviously given for $n = 0$. We then find the following.

Lemma A2.3. If Lemma A2.2 holds the B firm never leapfrogs the G firm.

Proof:[4] We seek to show $\left\{\Pi_B\left(\theta_G^*, \theta_B^*\right) - \Pi_B\left[\theta_G^*, \bar{b}_B\left(\theta_G^*\right)\right]\right\}\Big|_{n=0} > 0$. Observing that $\Pi_B\left(\theta_G^*, \theta_B^*\right) > 0$ is guaranteed by condition (2.5′) it is sufficient to show that

$$\Pi_B\left[\theta_G^*, \bar{b}_B\left(\theta_G^*\right)\right]\Big|_{n=0} = \pi_B\left[\theta_G^*, \bar{b}_B\left(\theta_G^*\right)\right]\Big|_{n=0} - F\left[\bar{b}_B\left(\theta_G^*\right)\right] < 0.$$

Using $a = \bar{b}_B\left(\theta_G^*\right)/\theta_G^*$ in (2.6a) and then inserting from (A2.16) we can write

$$\Pi_B\left[\theta_G^*, \bar{b}_B\left(\theta_G^*\right)\right]\Big|_{n=0} = \Pi_B\left(\theta_G^*, a\right)\Big|_{n=0}$$

$$= \frac{4m^2(a-1)a^2\theta_G^*}{(4a-1)^2} - \frac{k\left(a\theta_G^* - \underline{\theta}\right)^2}{2} = \frac{2m^2 a\Theta\left(\theta_G^*, a\right)}{(4a-1)^3},$$

with

$$\Theta\left(\theta_G^*, a\right) = 2a(a-1)(4a-1)\theta_G^* - \left(a\theta_G^* - \underline{\theta}\right)\alpha(a)$$
$$= a^2\theta_G^*\beta(a) + \underline{\theta}\alpha(a).$$

Obviously, $\Pi_B\left(\theta_G^*, a\right)\Big|_{n=0} < 0 \Leftrightarrow \Theta\left(\theta_G^*, a\right) < 0$. Observing $\alpha(a) = 4a^2 - 3a + 2 \le a(4a-1)$ for $a \le 1$ and $\underline{\theta} \le b\theta_G^*$, where $b = \theta_B^*/\theta_G^*$, we obtain

$$\Theta\left(\theta_G^*, a\right) \le a\theta_G^*\left[a\beta(a) + (4a-1)b\right].$$

It is now easily checked that $b \le \frac{a(7-4a)}{4a-1} \Rightarrow \Theta\left(\theta_G^*, a\right) < 0$. From Lemma A2.1 part (ii) we know that the LHS inequality is satisfied. Thus $\Theta\left(\theta_G^*, a\right) < 0$ and $\Pi_B\left(\theta_G^*, a\right)\Big|_{n=0} < 0$. Leapfrogging is never profitable. ∎

This no-leapfrogging result applies both to the boundary and interior regime. Similar to Motta (1993), the result relies on the quadratic form of the cost function and does not necessarily generalise.

We can now establish the conditions for the interior equilibrium. The conditions for the boundary equilibrium then follow in a straightforward way.

Interior Equilibrium

Here $s(\theta_G^*, \theta_B^*) > 0$ and $r(\theta_G^*, \theta_B^*) > 0$ so that the first-order conditions (2.15a) and (2.15b) hold as equalities, $R(\theta_G^*, \theta_B^*) = 0$ and $T(\theta_G^*, \theta_B^*) = 0$. Recall that $s(\theta_G^*, \theta_B^*) > 0$ if and only if $m \geq m_h(\theta_G^*, \theta_B^*)$, where

$$m_h(\theta_G, \theta_B) = 2n\alpha(\theta_G, \theta_B) / [\theta_G \theta_B \beta(\theta_G, \theta_B)]. \qquad (A2.17)$$

We establish a set of conditions for an interior equilibrium as follows. First, we determine a boundary level of θ_G, for which the B firm is indifferent between choosing the corner level $\underline{\theta}$ of performance or an interior level $\theta_B > \underline{\theta}$ (Lemma A2.4). This determines the kink at which the B firm's best response to θ_G switches from the corner to an interior level. We then show that if the investment rate k is sufficiently high, both firms' best responses with regard to θ satisfy a sufficient condition for the existence of an interior equilibrium (Lemmas A2.5 and A2.6). Finally, working with the best responses, we determine a boundary value m_h', which in contrast to (A2.17) is determined only by the parameters of the model, and show that an interior equilibrium requires m to exceed a boundary value m_h' (Lemma A2.7). We can then fully characterise an interior equilibrium (part (a) of Proposition 2.4).

Let $b_G(\theta_B)$ and $b_B(\theta_G)$ denote the G and B firm's best response functions, respectively.[5] For the G firm, $b_G(\theta_B)$ satisfies $R[b_G(\theta_B), \theta_B] = 0$. For the B firm, $b_B(\theta_G)$ satisfies $T[\theta_G, b_B(\theta_G)] = 0$ if and only if $m \geq m_h[\theta_G, b_B(\theta_G)]$. We can then define

$$\theta_G^0(m) := \theta_G | m = m_h(\theta_G, \underline{\theta})$$

as the level of G performance, for which the B firm is indifferent between choosing $b_B(\theta_G^0) = \underline{\theta}$ or an interior level of performance slightly above $\underline{\theta}$.

Lemma A2.4. $\theta_G^0(m)$, $\partial\theta_G^0(m)/\partial m < 0$, *with domain* $m > 2n/\underline{\theta}$ *and range* $\theta_G^0(m) \in \left[\frac{7}{4}\underline{\theta}, \infty\right)$, *determines* a *boundary* *where* $m > m_h(\theta_G, \underline{\theta}) \Leftrightarrow \theta_G > \theta_G^0(m)$.

Proof: From (A2.17) and under observation of (2.11a) and (2.11b) it is readily checked that $m_h\left(\frac{7}{4}\underline{\theta},\underline{\theta}\right) = \infty$, $\lim_{\theta_G \to \infty} m_h(\theta_G, \underline{\theta}) = 2n/\underline{\theta}$ and $\frac{\partial m_h(\theta_G,\underline{\theta})}{\partial \theta_G} = \frac{-4n\left(8\theta_G^2 + 8\theta_G\underline{\theta} - 7\underline{\theta}^2\right)}{\theta_G^2 \beta(\cdot)^2} < 0$. It follows for $m \geq 2n/\underline{\theta}$ that there exists a unique $\theta_G^0(m) := \theta_G | m = m_h(\theta_G, \underline{\theta})$. Setting $m - m_h\left(\theta_G^0, \underline{\theta}\right) \equiv 0$ and taking the total differential, $dm - \frac{\partial m_h\left(\theta_G^0,\underline{\theta}\right)}{\partial \theta_G} d\theta_G^0 \equiv 0$ gives the slope $\frac{d\theta_G^0}{dm} = \left(\frac{\partial m_h\left(\theta_G^0,\underline{\theta}\right)}{\partial \theta_G}\right)^{-1} < 0 . \blacksquare$

Thus, the B firm's best response function consists of two segments: $b_B(\theta_G) = \underline{\theta}$ $\forall \theta_G \leq \theta_G^0$ and $b_B(\theta_G) > \underline{\theta}$ $\forall \theta_G > \theta_G^0$. The latter is intuitive and will be proved formally in Lemma A2.6 part (ii). Note that $b_B(\theta_G)$ is continuous but has a kink at $\theta_G = \theta_G^0$. The boundary level can be understood as a minimum degree of differentiation for the B firm to raise performance above the minimum level (see Figures 2.2a and 2.2b in the main text).

For $m \leq 2n/\underline{\theta}$, the function $\theta_G^0(m)$ is undefined. It can be easily verified from (A2.17) that in this case, an increase in B performance above the minimum is profitable not even if θ_G tends to infinity. In the following, assume $m > 2n/\underline{\theta}$ and $\theta_G > \theta_G^0$ such that $b_B(\theta_G) > \underline{\theta}$. The conditions for the existence of an interior equilibrium $R\left(\theta_G^*, \theta_B^*\right) = 0$ and $T\left(\theta_G^*, \theta_B^*\right) = 0$ are then given by $R_G\left(\theta_G^*, \theta_B^*\right) < 0$, $T_B\left(\theta_G^*, \theta_B^*\right) < 0$ and

$$J\left(\theta_G^*, \theta_B^*\right) = R_G\left(\theta_G^*, \theta_B^*\right) T_B\left(\theta_G^*, \theta_B^*\right) - R_B\left(\theta_G^*, \theta_B^*\right) T_G\left(\theta_G^*, \theta_B^*\right) > 0,$$

where $J(\cdot)$ is the Jacobian determinant of the system (2.15a) and (2.15b) and constitutes of the second-order derivatives (A2.12a)–(A2.12d). The slopes of the best response functions are given by

$$\frac{\partial b_G(\theta_B)}{\partial \theta_B} = \frac{-R_B[b_G(\theta_B),\theta_B]}{R_G[b_G(\theta_B),\theta_B]},$$

$$\frac{\partial b_B(\theta_G)}{\partial \theta_G} = \frac{-T_G[\theta_G,b_B(\theta_G)]}{T_B[\theta_G,b_B(\theta_G)]}; \quad \theta_G > \theta_G^0.$$

Define

$$\bar{k}_2 := \frac{8n^2\theta_G^0\left(\theta_G^0 - \underline{\theta}\right)\alpha\left(\theta_G^0,\underline{\theta}\right)}{\left(4\theta_G^0 - \underline{\theta}\right)^2 \underline{\theta}^2}. \tag{A2.18}$$

Lemma A2.5. In an interior equilibrium, (i) $\partial b_G(\theta_B)/\partial \theta_B \in [0, b_G(\theta_B)/\theta_B]$ *is always true; and (ii)* $\partial b_B(\theta_G)/\partial \theta_G \in [0, b_B(\theta_G)/\theta_G]$ *if* $k \geq \bar{k}_2$.

Proof: Part (i). Consider $\frac{\partial b_G(\theta_B)}{\partial \theta_B} = \frac{-R_B[b_G(\theta_B),\theta_B]}{R_G[b_G(\theta_B),\theta_B]}$, where from (A2.12a) and (A2.12b),

$$R_G[b_G(\theta_B),\theta_B] = \frac{-8q_B\{m[5b_G(\cdot)+\theta_B]\theta_B - n[2b_G(\cdot)-5\theta_B]\}\theta_B}{[4b_G(\cdot)-\theta_B]^3 b_G(\cdot)} - k,$$

$$R_B[b_G(\theta_B),\theta_B] = \frac{3q_G r[b_G(\cdot),\theta_B] + [4b_G(\cdot)-\theta_B]r_B[b_G(\cdot),\theta_B]}{[4b_G(\cdot)-\theta_B]^3},$$

and where $r_B[b_G(\theta_B),\theta_B] = -2m[3b_G(\cdot)-\theta_B]+7n$. In an interior equilibrium

$$m > m_h[b_G(\cdot),\theta_B] = 2n\alpha[b_G(\cdot),\theta_B]/\{b_G(\cdot)\theta_B \beta[b_G(\cdot),\theta_B]\}.$$

Using this it is readily verified that $r_B[b_G(\theta_B),\theta_B]\big|_{m>m_h[b_G(\theta_B),\theta_B]} < \frac{-m\{4\alpha[b_G(\cdot),\theta_B]+7b_G(\cdot)\theta_B \beta[b_G(\cdot),\theta_B]\}}{2\alpha[b_G(\cdot),\theta_B]} < 0$, where the last inequality follows under observation of (2.11a) and (2.11b). Hence,

$$R_B[b_G(\theta_B),\theta_B]\big|_{m>m_h(\cdot)} < \frac{3q_G r[b_G(\cdot),\theta_B]}{[4b_G(\cdot)-\theta_B]^3} \tag{A2.19}$$

Moreover,

$$R_G\big[b_G(\theta_B),\theta_B\big]\big|_{m>m_h(\cdot)} < \frac{-4q_Bm\left\{\overset{>0}{\overbrace{\begin{array}{c}2\big[5b_G(\cdot)+\theta_B\big]\alpha(\cdot)\\-\big[2b_G(\cdot)-5\theta_B\big]\beta(\cdot)\end{array}}}\right\}\theta_B^{\,2}}{\big[4b_G(\cdot)-\theta_B\big]^3 b_G(\cdot)\alpha(\cdot)} - k$$

$$< -k = \frac{-q_G r\big[b_G(\cdot),\theta_B\big]}{\big[4b_G(\cdot)-\theta_B\big]^2\big[b_G(\cdot)-\underline{\theta}\big]} < \frac{-q_G r\big[b_G(\cdot),\theta_B\big]}{\big[4b_G(\cdot)-\theta_B\big]^2 b_G(\cdot)} < 0 \quad \text{(A2.20)},$$

where the equality follows from the first-order condition. Combining (A2.19) and (A2.20) and recalling $R_B\big[b_G(\theta_B),\theta_B\big]>0$, we obtain $\partial b_G(\theta_B)/\partial\theta_B > 0$ and $\frac{\partial b_G(\theta_B)}{\partial\theta_B} = \frac{-R_B[b_G(\cdot),\theta_B]}{R_G[b_G(\cdot),\theta_B]} < \frac{3b_G(\cdot)}{[4b_G(\cdot)-\theta_B]} < 1 < \frac{b_G(\cdot)}{\theta_B}$, which completes the proof of part (i).

Part (ii). Consider $\frac{\partial b_B(\theta_G)}{\partial\theta_G} = \frac{-T_G[\theta_G,b_B(\theta_G)]}{T_B[\theta_G,b_B(\theta_G)]} \overset{!}{<} \frac{b_B(\theta_G)}{\theta_G}$. Rearranging the

inequality gives $T_G[\theta_G,b_B(\theta_G)]\theta_G \overset{!}{<} -T_B[\theta_G,b_B(\theta_G)]b_B(\theta_G)$, and after inserting from (A2.12c) and (A2.12d) this can be written as

$$\frac{2q_B\{m[8\theta_G+7b_B(\cdot)]\theta_G+2n[5\theta_G+b_B(\cdot)]\}b_B(\cdot)}{[4\theta_G-b_B(\cdot)]^3}$$

$$\overset{!}{<}\left\langle\begin{array}{c}\dfrac{2q_B\left\{\begin{array}{c}m[8\theta_G+7b_B(\cdot)]\theta_G b_B(\cdot)^2\\-n\big[16\theta_G^{\,3}-16\theta_G^{\,2}b_B(\cdot)+\theta_G b_B(\cdot)^2-4b_B(\cdot)^3\big]\end{array}\right\}}{[4\theta_G-b_B(\cdot)]^3 b_B(\cdot)}\\[2em]+\dfrac{2n\theta_G s[\theta_G,b_B(\cdot)]}{[4\theta_G-b_B(\cdot)]^3 b_B(\cdot)^2}+kb_B(\cdot)\end{array}\right\rangle.$$

After rearranging and cancelling terms we obtain

$$\frac{2q_B n\big[16\theta_G^{\,3}-16\theta_G^{\,2}b_B(\cdot)+11\theta_G b_B(\cdot)^2-2b_B(\cdot)^3\big]}{[4\theta_G-b_B(\cdot)]^3 b_B(\cdot)} - \frac{2n\theta_G s[\theta_G,b_B(\cdot)]}{[4\theta_G-b_B(\cdot)]^3 b_B(\cdot)^2}$$

$$= \frac{2q_B n\alpha[\theta_G,b_B(\cdot)]}{[4\theta_G-b_B(\cdot)]^2 b_B(\cdot)} - \frac{2n\theta_G s[\theta_G,b_B(\cdot)]}{[4\theta_G-b_B(\cdot)]^3 b_B(\cdot)^2}$$

$$= \frac{2n\{mb_B(\cdot)[\alpha(\cdot)-\theta_G\beta(\cdot)]+4n\alpha(\cdot)\}\theta_G}{[4\theta_G-b_B(\cdot)]^3 b_B(\cdot)^2}$$

$$= \frac{4n\{m[2\theta_G + b_B(\cdot)]b_B(\cdot)^2 + 2n\alpha(\cdot)]\theta_G}{[4\theta_G - b_B(\cdot)]^3 b_B(\cdot)^2} \overset{!}{<} kb_B(\cdot),$$

where the second equality follows under observation of (2.4b) and (2.10b) and the third equality follows under observation of (2.11a) and (2.11b). Thus

$$k \overset{!}{\geq} \frac{4n\{m[2\theta_G + b_B(\cdot)]b_B(\cdot)^2 + 2n\alpha(\cdot)]\theta_G}{[4\theta_G - b_B(\cdot)]^3 b_B(\cdot)^3} = \tilde{k}[\theta_G, b_B(\cdot)]. \quad \text{(A2.21)}$$

Note that satisfaction of this condition implies $T_B[\theta_G, b_B(\theta_G)] < 0$. Observing $T_G[\theta_G, b_B(\theta_G)] > 0$, $\partial b_B(\theta_G)/\partial \theta_G > 0$. Using this we find

$$\frac{d\tilde{k}[\theta_G, b_B(\cdot)]}{d\theta_G} = \frac{\partial \tilde{k}[\theta_G, b_B(\cdot)]}{\partial \theta_G} + \frac{\partial \tilde{k}[\theta_G, b_B(\cdot)]}{\partial \theta_B} \frac{\partial b_B(\theta_G)}{\partial \theta_G} < 0,$$

where

$$\frac{\partial \tilde{k}[\theta_G, b_B(\cdot)]}{\partial \theta_G} = \frac{-4n\{m[8\theta_G^2 + 12\theta_G b_B(\cdot) + b_B(\cdot)^2] + 4n[5\theta_G + b_B(\cdot)]\}}{[4\theta_G - b_B(\cdot)]^4 b_B(\cdot)} < 0,$$

$$\frac{\partial \tilde{k}[\theta_G, b_B(\cdot)]}{\partial \theta_B} = \frac{-4n\theta_G \left\{ \begin{matrix} m[8\theta_G^2 - 8\theta_G b_B(\cdot) - 3b_B(\cdot)^2] \\ +2n\left[\begin{matrix} 48\theta_G^3 - 48\theta_G^2 b_B(\cdot) \\ +23\theta_G b_B(\cdot)^2 - 8b_B(\cdot)^3 \end{matrix} \right] \end{matrix} \right\}}{[4\theta_G - b_B(\cdot)]^4 b_B(\cdot)^4} < 0 .^6$$

It follows that $\tilde{k}[\theta_G, b_B(\cdot)] \leq \tilde{k}[\theta_G^0, b_B(\theta_G^0)] = \tilde{k}(\theta_G^0, \underline{\theta})$, where θ_G^0 is as defined in Lemma A2.4. Substituting $m = m_h(\theta_G^0, \underline{\theta}) = 2n\alpha(\theta_G^0, \underline{\theta})/|\theta_G^0 \partial \beta(\theta_G^0, \underline{\theta})|$ into (A2.21) yields

$$\tilde{k}(\theta_G^0, \underline{\theta}) = \frac{8n^2 \theta_G^0 (\theta_G^0 - \underline{\theta})\alpha(\theta_G^0, \underline{\theta})}{(4\theta_G^0 - \underline{\theta})^2 \underline{\theta}^2} =: \bar{k}_2 .$$

Thus, $k \geq \bar{k}_2$ is sufficient for $\partial b_B(\theta_G)/\partial \theta_G \in [0, b_B(\theta_G)/\theta_G]$, which proves part (ii) of the Lemma. ∎

Again, the baseline term n may cause the objective functions to be convex. It is easily checked that in an interior equilibrium $m > \hat{m}$, so that the condition (a) in Lemma A2.1 is satisfied. Hence, the G firm's objective function is concave. However, the problem remains present with respect to the B firm's objective function. Inspection of (A2.12d) shows that $T_B(\theta_G, \theta_B) > 0$ for $k = 0$ and $m = m_h(\theta_G, \theta_B)$. Thus, the cost rate k has to be sufficiently large to guarantee a sufficient degree of concavity. As easily checked, $b_G(\theta_B)$ decreases in k. Then for high k we may have $b_G(\underline{\theta}) < \theta_G^0$ so that the condition $k \geq \bar{k}_2$ may rule out an interior equilibrium. However a boundary equilibrium exists even for this case. An equilibrium may fail to exist altogether only if $k < \bar{k}_2$. In the following, assume $k \geq \bar{k}_2$ to be satisfied. Since $\bar{k}_2 = 0$ for $n = 0$, an interior equilibrium is feasible if n is sufficiently small. The following lemma establishes two properties that are important for the existence of a unique interior equilibrium.

Lemma   A2.6.   Let $\partial b_G(\theta_B)/\partial \theta_B \in [0, b_G(\theta_B)/\theta_B]$ *and* $\partial b_B(\theta_G)/\partial \theta_G \in [0, b_B(\theta_G)/\theta_G]$. *Then, (i) the second-order conditions are satisfied; and (ii)* $b_B(\theta_G) > \underline{\theta} \Leftrightarrow \theta_G > \theta_G^0$.

Proof: Part (i): We have shown $R_G[b_G(\theta_B), \theta_B]\big|_{m > m_h(\cdot)} < 0$ and $T_B[\theta_G, b_B(\theta_G)] < 0$ as part of the proof of the previous lemma. Since $b_G(\theta_B^*) = \theta_G^*$ and $b_B(\theta_G^*) = \theta_B^*$, $R_G(\theta_G^*, \theta_B^*) < 0$ and $T_B(\theta_G^*, \theta_B^*) < 0$. Writing

$$J(\theta_G^*, \theta_B^*) = R_G(\cdot)T_B(\cdot) - R_B(\cdot)T_G(\cdot) = R_G(\cdot)T_B(\cdot)\left[1 - \frac{R_B(\cdot)}{R_G(\cdot)}\frac{T_G(\cdot)}{T_B(\cdot)}\right],$$

we obtain

$$J(\theta_G^*, \theta_B^*) > 0 \Leftrightarrow \left[1 - \frac{R_B(\cdot)}{R_G(\cdot)}\frac{T_G(\cdot)}{T_B(\cdot)}\right] > \left[1 - \frac{b_B(\theta_G^*)}{\theta_G^*}\frac{\theta_B^*}{b_G(\theta_B^*)}\right] \geq 0,$$

where the first inequality on the RHS of the condition follows from the previous Lemma. Hence part (i) of this Lemma.

Part (ii). Consider the total derivative

$$\frac{dm_h[\theta_G,b_B(\cdot)]}{d\theta_G} = \frac{\partial m_h[\theta_G,b_B(\cdot)]}{\partial\theta_G} + \frac{\partial m_h[\theta_G,b_B(\cdot)]}{\partial\theta_B}\frac{\partial b_B(\theta_G)}{\partial\theta_G}, \text{(A2.22)}$$

which gives the change of the boundary value $m_h[\theta_G,b_B(\theta_G)]$ for an increase in θ_G along B's best response. From the definition $\theta_G^0(m) := \theta_G | m = m_h(\theta_G,\underline{\theta})$, it follows that $m = m_h[\theta_G^0(m),\underline{\theta}] = m_h\{\theta_G^0(m),b_B[\theta_G^0(m)]\}$. But then $\frac{dm_h[\theta_G,b_B(\cdot)]}{d\theta_G} < 0$ is sufficient to guarantee $m > m_h[\theta_G,b_B(\theta_G)] \Leftrightarrow \theta_G > \theta_G^0$ and, thus, $b_B(\theta_G) > \underline{\theta} \Leftrightarrow \theta_G > \theta_G^0$ as stated in the Lemma. Using (A2.17), we obtain from straightforward calculations

$$\frac{\partial m_h[\theta_G,b_B(\cdot)]}{\partial\theta_G} = \frac{-4n[8\theta_G^2 + 8\theta_G b_B(\cdot) - 7b_B(\cdot)^2]}{\theta_G^2\beta(\cdot)^2} < 0,$$

$$\frac{\partial m_h[\theta_G,b_B(\cdot)]}{\partial\theta_B} = \frac{-2n[16\theta_G^2 - 56\theta_G b_B(\cdot) + 13b_B(\cdot)^2]}{b_B(\cdot)^2\beta(\cdot)^2}.$$

Substituting into (A2.22) yields

$$\frac{dm_h[\theta_G,b_B(\cdot)]}{d\theta_G} = \frac{-2n\left\{\begin{matrix}2[8\theta_G^2 + 8\theta_G b_B(\cdot) - 7b_B(\cdot)^2]b_B(\cdot)^2 \\ +[16\theta_G^2 - 56\theta_G b_B(\cdot) + 13b_B(\cdot)^2]\theta_G^2[\partial b_B(\cdot)/\partial\theta_G]\end{matrix}\right\}}{\theta_G^2 b_B(\cdot)^2\beta(\cdot)^2}.$$

Consider now an interior equilibrium, where $m > m_h[\theta_G,b_B(\theta_G)]$. Using $\partial b_B(\theta_G)/\partial\theta_G \le b_B(\theta_G)/\theta_G$ we can rewrite the above expression as

$$\frac{dm_h[\theta_G,b_B(\cdot)]}{d\theta_G} \le \frac{-2n\left\{\begin{matrix}2[8\theta_G^2 + 8\theta_G b_B(\cdot) - 7b_B(\cdot)^2]b_B(\cdot) \\ +[16\theta_G^2 - 56\theta_G b_B(\cdot) + 13b_B(\cdot)^2]\theta_G\end{matrix}\right\}}{\theta_G^2 b_B(\cdot)\beta(\cdot)^2}$$

$$= \frac{-2n[16\theta_G^3 - 40\theta_G^2 b_B(\cdot) + 29\theta_G b_B(\cdot)^2 - 14b_B(\cdot)^3]}{\theta_G^2 b_B(\cdot)\beta(\cdot)^2} \le 0 \qquad . \text{ (A2.23)}$$

$$\Leftrightarrow \theta_G \ge \frac{7}{4}b_B(\cdot)$$

Note that the condition is verified for $m > m_h[\theta_G, b_B(\theta_G)]$. Consider now a boundary equilibrium, where for $\theta_G < (7/4)b_B(\theta_G) \Rightarrow b_B(\theta_G) = \underline{\theta}$ and $\partial b_B(\theta_G)/\partial \theta_G = 0$. Then $\frac{dm_h[\theta_G, b_B(\cdot)]}{d\theta_G} < 0$ is also true which proves part (ii) of the Lemma. ∎

Recall that $b_B(\theta_G) > \underline{\theta}$ if and only if $m > m_h[\theta_G, b_B(\theta_G)]$. Given that this condition is satisfied, part (i) of the Lemma implies that if the reaction functions are as characterised as in Lemma A2.5, there exists a unique point of intersection. Part (ii) implies that $\theta_G > \theta_G^0$ is necessary and sufficient for an interior choice $\theta_B > \underline{\theta}$. Indeed, this is equivalent to saying that $\theta_G > \theta_G^0$ is necessary and sufficient for $m > m_h[\theta_G, b_B(\theta_G)]$. From Lemma A2.4 we know that $\theta_G > \theta_G^0(m)$ is equivalent to $m > m_h(\theta_G, \underline{\theta})$.

So far we have focused on the B firm's best response for a given value of m. Taking into account optimal performance choice by the G firm, which is a function of the exogenous parameters $\{\theta, m, n, k\}$, the condition for an interior equilibrium is given by $m > m_h[b_G(\underline{\theta}, m, n, k), \underline{\theta}, n]$, where

$$m_h[b_G(\cdot), \cdot] = \frac{2n\alpha[b_G(\cdot), \underline{\theta}]}{b_G(\cdot)\underline{\theta}\beta[b_G(\cdot), \underline{\theta}]}. \tag{A2.24}$$

The following can then be established.

Lemma A2.7. There exists a unique boundary value $m_h' = \hat{m}_h(\underline{\theta}, m, n, k)$ such that $\theta_B^* > \underline{\theta}$ if and only if $m > m_h'$.

Proof: As a preliminary, we note that $db_G(\underline{\theta}, m, \cdot)/dm > 0$, where the explicit derivative is given in the proof of Corollary P2.5. It is then easy to see that there exists a $m_\beta := m|b_G(\underline{\theta}, m, \cdot) = (7/4)\underline{\theta}$, such that $b_G(\underline{\theta}, m, \cdot) \geq (7/4)\underline{\theta} \Leftrightarrow m \geq m_\beta$. Finally, recall that $m_h((7/4)\underline{\theta}, \underline{\theta}) = \infty$. It is now convenient to define the function

$$N_h(\underline{\theta}, m, n, k) := m - m_h[b_G(\underline{\theta}, m, n, k), \underline{\theta}, n], \tag{A2.25}$$

with domain $m \geq m_\beta$. We can, thus, define $m_h' := m|N_h(m, \cdot) = 0$. In order to establish the existence and uniqueness of $m_h' = \hat{m}_h(\underline{\theta}, m, n, k)$ we have to show the following: (i) $dN_h(m,\cdot)/dm > 0$; (ii) $N_h(m_\beta,\cdot) < 0$; (iii) $\lim_{m \to \infty} N_h(m,\cdot) > 0$.

Using (A2.25) together with (A2.24), it is readily verified that

(i) $\dfrac{dN_h(m,\cdot)}{dm} = 1 - \overset{<0}{\overline{\dfrac{dm_h(\cdot)}{d\theta_G}}}\,\overset{>0}{\overline{\dfrac{db_G(\cdot)}{dm}}} > 0$, where $\dfrac{dm_h(\cdot)}{d\theta_G} = \dfrac{-4n\left(8b_G(\cdot)^2 + 8b_G(\cdot)\underline{\theta} - 7\underline{\theta}^2\right)}{b_G(\cdot)^2\,\beta(\cdot)^2} < 0$,

(ii) $N_h(m_\beta,\cdot) = m_\beta - m_h\left(\tfrac{7}{4}\underline{\theta},\underline{\theta},\cdot\right) = -\infty$,

(iii) $\lim_{m \to \infty} N_h(m,\cdot) = m + \lim_{\theta_G \to \infty} m_h(\theta_G,\underline{\theta}) = m + 2n/\underline{\theta} = +\infty$.

Thus, there exists a unique $m \in \left[m_\beta, \infty\right) \mid N_h(m,\cdot) = 0$, where $m_h' := m \mid N_h(m,\cdot) = 0$. It follows immediately from (A2.1) that $m_h' = \hat{m}_h(\underline{\theta},m,n,k)$ is an implicit function of the remaining parameters.

From $dN_h(m,\cdot)/dm > 0$, it follows that $m > m_h' \Leftrightarrow m > m_h\left[b_G(\underline{\theta},m,\cdot),\cdot\right]$, and, equivalently, $m > m_h' \Leftrightarrow s\left[b_G(\underline{\theta},m,\cdot),\underline{\theta}\right] > 0$. But then, $m > m_h' \Leftrightarrow T\left[b_G(\underline{\theta},m,\cdot),\underline{\theta}\right] > 0$ and $\theta_B^* = \underline{\theta}$ cannot be an equilibrium. Lemma A2.6 then guarantees an equilibrium with $\theta_B^* > \underline{\theta}$. Similarly, $m \leq m_h' \Leftrightarrow T\left[b_G(\underline{\theta},m,\cdot),\underline{\theta}\right] \leq 0$ so that $\theta_B^* = \underline{\theta}$ is the only equilibrium. ∎

We can now establish the existence of an interior equilibrium.

Proposition 2.4 (b) An interior equilibrium with $\underline{\theta} < \theta_B^* < \theta_G^*$ exists and is unique if (i) investment is sufficiently costly, $k > \bar{k}_2$; (ii) G environmental performance increases or does not decrease too much in baseline benefit, $d\theta_G^*/dn \geq \varepsilon_2; \varepsilon_2 < 0$; and (iii) the environmental margin is sufficiently high, $m > m_h'$.

Condition (i) guarantees concavity of the reaction functions by Lemmas A2.5 and A2.6; condition (ii) rules out leapfrogging by Lemmas A2.2 and A2.3; and condition (ii) guarantees an interior crossing of the reaction functions by Lemma A2.7.

242   The greening of markets

Boundary Equilibrium

In this case, $s\left(\theta_B^*, \underline{\theta}\right) < 0$ and, from (2.15a) and (2.15b), $R\left(\theta_B^*, \underline{\theta}\right) = 0$ and $T\left(\theta_B^*, \underline{\theta}\right) < 0$ so that $\underline{\theta} = \theta_B^* < \theta_G^*$. The conditions under which this is the case are given in the following Proposition.

Proposition 2.4 (a) A boundary equilibrium with $\underline{\theta} = \theta_B^* < \theta_G^*$ exists and is unique if the following conditions are satisfied. (i) Investment is sufficiently costly, $k > \bar{k}_1$; (ii) Either the B firm dominates in profit, $m < m_\pi\left(\theta_G^*, \underline{\theta}\right)$, or G environmental performance does not decrease by too much in baseline benefit, $d\theta_G^* / dn \geq \varepsilon_1$; $\varepsilon_1 < 0$; (iii) the G firm makes a non-negative profit, i.e. (2.5') holds; and (iv) the environmental margin is sufficiently low, $m \leq m_h'$.

Condition (i) guarantees a concave profit function by Lemma A2.1; the conditions in (ii) rule out leapfrogging, either due to B leadership as by Lemma 2.3, or, for the case of G leadership, by Lemmas A2.2 and A2.3; condition (iii) guarantees positive profit by Lemma A2.1; and condition (iv) implies the existence of a unique boundary equilibrium by Lemma A2.7.

Proof of Corollary P2.4

From (2.15a) and (2.15b) we derive the following derivatives for subsequent use.

$$R_m\left(\theta_G^*, \theta_B^*\right) = \frac{1}{\left(4\theta_G^* - \theta_B^*\right)^2}\left[\frac{\partial q_G}{\partial m} r\left(\theta_G^*, \theta_B^*\right) + q_G \frac{\partial r(\cdot)}{\partial m}\right]$$

$$= \frac{4\left[2m\alpha\left(\theta_G^*, \theta_B^*\right)\theta_G^* + n\left(2\theta_G^* + \theta_B^*\right)\theta_B^*\right]}{\left(4\theta_G^* - \theta_B^*\right)^3} > 0, \quad \text{(A2.26a)}$$

$$R_n\left(\theta_G^*, \theta_B^*\right) = \frac{1}{\left(4\theta_G^* - \theta_B^*\right)^2}\left[\frac{\partial q_G}{\partial n} r\left(\theta_G^*, \theta_B^*\right) + q_G \frac{\partial r(\cdot)}{\partial n}\right]$$

$$= \frac{2\left[2m\left(2\theta_G^* + \theta_B^*\right)\theta_B^* - n\beta\left(\theta_G^*, \theta_B^*\right)\right]}{\left(4\theta_G^* - \theta_B^*\right)^3}, \quad \text{(A2.26b)}$$

$$R_k\left(\theta_G^*\right) = -\left(\theta_G^* - \underline{\theta}\right) < 0; \quad \text{(A2.26c)}$$

and for an interior equilibrium, where $s(\theta_G^*, \theta_B^*) > 0$

$$T_m(\theta_G^*, \theta_B^*) = \frac{1}{(4\theta_G^* - \theta_B^*)^2 \theta_B^*}\left[\frac{\partial q_B}{\partial m} s(\theta_G^*, \theta_B^*) + q_B \frac{\partial s(\cdot)}{\partial m}\right]$$

$$= \frac{2\theta_G^*\left[m\beta(\theta_G^*, \theta_B^*)\theta_G^* - 2n(2\theta_G^* + \theta_B^*)\theta_B^*\right]}{(4\theta_G^* - \theta_B^*)^3 \theta_B^*} > 0, \quad \text{(A2.27a)}$$

$$T_n(\theta_G^*, \theta_B^*) = \frac{1}{(4\theta_G^* - \theta_B^*)^2 \theta_B^*}\left[\frac{\partial q_B}{\partial n} s(\theta_G^*, \theta_B^*) + q_B \frac{\partial s(\cdot)}{\partial n}\right]$$

$$= \frac{-4\theta_G^*\left[m(2\theta_G^* + \theta_B^*)\theta_B^{*2} + 2n\alpha(\theta_G^*, \theta_B^*)\right]}{(4\theta_G^* - \theta_B^*)^3 \theta_B^{*2}} < 0, \quad \text{(A2.27b)}$$

$$T_k(\theta_B^*) = -(\theta_B^* - \underline{\theta}) < 0. \quad \text{(A2.27c)}$$

Using these derivatives together with the second-order terms (A2.12a)–
(A2.12d) while observing $J(\cdot) = R_G(\cdot)T_B(\cdot) - R_B(\cdot)T_G(\cdot) > 0$, it is
straightforward to derive the following comparative static reactions.

(i)   Boundary equilibrium

$$\frac{db_G(\theta)}{dm} = \frac{-R_m[b_G(\theta), \underline{\theta}]}{R_G[b_G(\theta), \underline{\theta}]} > 0, \quad \frac{db_G(\theta)}{dn} = \frac{-R_n[b_G(\theta), \underline{\theta}]}{R_G[b_G(\theta), \underline{\theta}]},$$

$$\frac{db_G(\theta)}{dk} = \frac{b_G(\theta) - \underline{\theta}}{R_G[b_G(\theta), \underline{\theta}]} < 0,$$

where $\text{sgn}(db_G(\theta)/dn) = \text{sgn}\, R_n[b_G(\theta), \underline{\theta}]$. Noting from Proposition 2.5 that
$m > m_q' \Leftrightarrow m > m_q[b_G(\theta), \underline{\theta}]$, it is easily checked from (A2.26b) that
$m \geq m_q'[b_G(\theta, m_q'), \underline{\theta}] := \frac{n[2b_G(\theta, m_q') - \underline{\theta}]}{b_G(\theta, m_q')\underline{\theta}} \Rightarrow \text{sgn}\, R_n[b_G(\theta, m), \underline{\theta}] > 0$ and
$\beta[b_G(\theta, m), \underline{\theta}] \leq 0 \Rightarrow \text{sgn}\, R_n[b_G(\theta, m), \underline{\theta}] > 0$, implying the conditions in
Table 2.2.

(ii) Interior equilibrium

$$\frac{d\theta_G^*}{dm}=\frac{\overset{>0}{T_m(\cdot)}\overset{>0}{R_B(\cdot)}-\overset{>0}{R_m(\cdot)}\overset{<0}{T_B(\cdot)}}{J(\cdot)}>0,\quad \frac{d\theta_B^*}{dm}=\frac{\overset{>0}{R_m(\cdot)}\overset{>0}{T_G(\cdot)}-\overset{>0}{T_m(\cdot)}\overset{<0}{R_G(\cdot)}}{J(\cdot)}>0,$$

$$\frac{d\theta_G^*}{dk}=\frac{\overset{<0}{T_k(\cdot)}\overset{>0}{R_B(\cdot)}-\overset{<0}{R_k(\cdot)}\overset{<0}{T_B(\cdot)}}{J(\cdot)}<0,\quad \frac{d\theta_B^*}{dk}=\frac{\overset{<0}{R_k(\cdot)}\overset{>0}{T_G(\cdot)}-\overset{<0}{T_k(\cdot)}\overset{<0}{R_G(\cdot)}}{J(\cdot)}<0,$$

$$\frac{d\theta_G^*}{dn}=\frac{\overset{<0}{T_n(\cdot)}\overset{>0}{R_B(\cdot)}-\overset{>0}{R_n(\cdot)}\overset{<0}{T_B(\cdot)}}{J(\cdot)},\tag{A2.28a}$$

$$\frac{d\theta_B^*}{dn}=\frac{\overset{>0}{R_n(\cdot)}\overset{>0}{T_G(\cdot)}-\overset{<0}{T_n(\cdot)}\overset{<0}{R_G(\cdot)}}{J(\cdot)}.\tag{A2.28b}$$

While the signs of the last two reaction terms are ambiguous, we can establish them for the extreme case $n=0$. In this case from (A2.26b) and (A2.27b)

$$T_n\left(\theta_G^*,\theta_B^*\right)\big|_{n=0}=\frac{-4m\left(2\theta_G^*+\theta_B^*\right)\!\theta_G^*}{\left(4\theta_G^*-\theta_B^*\right)^3}=-\frac{\theta_G^*}{\theta_B^*}R_n\left(\theta_G^*,\theta_B^*\right)\big|_{n=0}.\tag{A2.29}$$

From (A2.28a) $\operatorname{sgn}\!\left(d\theta_G^*/dn\right)=\operatorname{sgn}\!\left[T_n(\cdot)R_B(\cdot)-R_n(\cdot)T_B(\cdot)\right]$. Using (A2.12b) and (A2.12d) together with (A2.29) and observing $q_B\big|_{n=0}=\tfrac{1}{2}q_G\big|_{n=0}=\frac{m\theta_G^*}{4\theta_G^*-\theta_B^*}$ this yields

$$\left[T_n(\cdot)R_B(\cdot)-R_n(\cdot)T_B(\cdot)\right]\big|_{n=0}=\frac{4m\left(2\theta_G^*+\theta_B^*\right)\!\theta_B^*}{\left(4\theta_G^*-\theta_B^*\right)^5}\begin{bmatrix}2q_B\big|_{n=0}m\left(8\theta_G^*+7\theta_B^*\right)\!\theta_G^*\\-4q_G\big|_{n=0}m\left(5\theta_G^*+\theta_B^*\right)\!\theta_G^*\\+k\left(4\theta_G^*-\theta_B^*\right)^3\end{bmatrix}$$

$$=\frac{4m\left(2\theta_G^*+\theta_B^*\right)\!\theta_B^*}{\left(4\theta_G^*-\theta_B^*\right)^4}\left[-3q_G\big|_{n=0}\theta_G^*+k\left(4\theta_G^*-\theta_B^*\right)^2\right]$$

$$=\frac{4q_G\big|_{n=0}m\left(2\theta_G^*+\theta_B^*\right)\!\theta_B^*}{\left(4\theta_G^*-\theta_B^*\right)^4\left(\theta_G^*-\underline{\theta}\right)}\left[-3\theta_G^*\left(\theta_G^*-\underline{\theta}\right)+2\alpha\left(\theta_G^*,\theta_B^*\right)\right]$$

$$= \frac{4q_G\big|_{n=0}\, m\big(2\theta_G^* + \theta_B^*\big)\theta_B^*\Big[5\theta_G^{*2} - 6\theta_G^*\theta_B^* + 4\theta_B^{*2} + 3\theta_B^*\underline{\theta}\Big]}{\big(4\theta_G^* - \theta_B^*\big)^4\big(\theta_G^* - \underline{\theta}\big)} > 0,$$

where the third equality follows under use of (2.15a) and observation that $r(\cdot)\big|_{n=0} = 2m\alpha(\cdot)$ and the fourth equality follows under use of (2.11a). Thus, $d\theta_G^*/dn\big|_{n=0} > 0$. Along a similar line, it can be verified from (A2.28b) together with (A2.29), (A2.12a), (A2.12c) that $d\theta_B^*/dn\big|_{n=0} < 0$.

(iii) Change in product differentiation ζ

The reaction is straightforward for a boundary equilibrium. Consider an interior equilibrium. Here,

$$\frac{d\zeta}{dm} = \frac{1}{\theta_B^{*2}}\left[\theta_B^*\frac{d\theta_G^*}{dm} - \theta_G^*\frac{d\theta_B^*}{dm}\right]$$

$$= \frac{1}{J(\cdot)\theta_B^{*2}}\left\{\overbrace{T_m(\cdot)}^{>0}\overbrace{R_G(\cdot)}^{<0}\theta_B^*\overbrace{\left[\frac{R_B(\cdot)}{R_G(\cdot)} + \frac{\theta_G^*}{\theta_B^*}\right]}^{>0} - \overbrace{R_m(\cdot)}^{>0}\overbrace{T_B(\cdot)}^{<0}\theta_G^*\overbrace{\left[\frac{\theta_B^*}{\theta_G^*} + \frac{T_G(\cdot)}{T_B(\cdot)}\right]}^{\geq 0}\right\},$$

where the signs of the expressions in square brackets follow from Lemma A2.5. While the expression is ambiguous, in general, we know from Lemma A2.5 part (ii) that $\lim_{m\to(m_h')^+} T_G(\cdot)/T_B(\cdot)\big|_{k=\bar{k}_2} = \theta_B^*/\theta_G^*$. Hence, $\lim_{m\to(m_h')^+} d\zeta/dm\big|_{k=\bar{k}_2} < 0$, as indicated in Table 2.2. Finally,

$$\frac{d\zeta}{dn} = \frac{1}{J(\cdot)\theta_B^{*2}}\left\{\begin{array}{l}\overbrace{T_n(\cdot)}^{<0}\overbrace{R_G(\cdot)}^{<0}\theta_B^*\overbrace{\left[\frac{R_B(\cdot)}{R_G(\cdot)} + \frac{\theta_G^*}{\theta_B^*}\right]}^{>0}\\[2em]-\overbrace{R_n(\cdot)}^{>0}\overbrace{T_B(\cdot)}^{<0}\theta_G^*\overbrace{\left[\frac{\theta_B^*}{\theta_G^*} + \frac{T_G(\cdot)}{T_B(\cdot)}\right]}^{\geq 0}\end{array}\right\} > 0, \qquad (A2.30)$$

$$\frac{d\zeta}{dk} = \frac{1}{J(\cdot)\theta_B^{*2}} \left\{ \overbrace{T_k(\cdot)}^{\leq 0}\overbrace{R_G(\cdot)}^{<0}\theta_B^* \overbrace{\left[\frac{R_B(\cdot)}{R_G(\cdot)} + \frac{\theta_G^*}{\theta_B^*}\right]}^{>0} - \overbrace{R_k(\cdot)}^{\leq 0}\overbrace{T_B(\cdot)}^{<0}\theta_G^* \overbrace{\left[\frac{\theta_B^*}{\theta_G^*} + \frac{T_G(\cdot)}{T_B(\cdot)}\right]}^{\geq 0} \right\}.$$

Observing that $\displaystyle\lim_{m\to(m_h')^+} T_k(\theta_B^*) = 0$ and $\displaystyle\lim_{m\to(m_h')^+} T_G(\cdot)/T_B(\cdot)\Big|_{k=\bar{k}_2} < \theta_B^*/\theta_G^*$,

it follows that $\displaystyle\lim_{m\to(m_h')^+} d\zeta/dk\Big|_{k>\bar{k}_2} < 0$ as indicated in Table 2.2. ∎

Proof of Proposition 2.5
(i) B dominance in terms of market share and, a fortiori, operating profit implies a boundary equilibrium. (ii) There exists a pair of unique boundary values $m_q' = \hat{m}_q(\underline{\theta}, m, n, k)$ and $m_\pi' = \hat{m}_\pi(\underline{\theta}, m, n, k)$, $m_\pi' < m_q'$. The B firm dominates with respect to market share if and only if $m < m_q'$, dominates with respect to market share but not operating profit if and only if $m \in [m_\pi', m_q'[$, and dominates with respect to operating profit if and only if $m < m_\pi'$.

Part (i) is obvious from (2.25). Part (ii) can be proved by analogy with Lemma A2.7. Define the function

$$N_q(\underline{\theta}, m, n, k) := m - m_q[b_G(\underline{\theta}, m, n, k), \underline{\theta}, n], \qquad (A2.31)$$

where $m_q(\cdot)$ is as in (2.7). Defining $m_q' := m|N_q(m, \cdot) = 0$, we can establish the existence and uniqueness of $m_q' = \hat{m}_q(\underline{\theta}, m, n, k)$ by showing (a) $\dfrac{dN_q(\cdot)}{dm}\Big|_{N_q(\cdot)=0} = 1 - \dfrac{n}{b_G(\cdot)^2}\dfrac{db_G(\cdot)}{dm} > 0$; (b) $N_q[m_\pi(\cdot), \cdot] < 0$; and (c) $N_q(m_h', \cdot) > 0$.

Substituting $db_G(\cdot)/dm = -R_m(\cdot)/R_G(\cdot)$ we obtain

$dN_q(\cdot)/dm\big|_{N_q(\cdot)=0} > 0 \Leftrightarrow \left[\theta_G^{*2} R_G(\cdot) > nR_m(\cdot)\right]\big|_{m=m_q}$. Substituting from (A2.12a) and (A2.26a) we find that the RHS inequality holds if and only if

$$\frac{4n}{\left(4\theta_G^* - \underline{\theta}\right)^3}\left[\begin{array}{l}2m\alpha(\cdot)\theta_G^* \\ + n\left(2\theta_G^* + \underline{\theta}\right)\underline{\varrho}\end{array}\right] > \frac{8(m\underline{\theta} + 2n)}{\left(4\theta_G^* - \underline{\theta}\right)^4}\left[\begin{array}{l}m\left(5\theta_G^* + \underline{\theta}\right)\underline{\varrho} \\ - n\left(2\theta_G^* - 5\underline{\theta}\right)\end{array}\right] + k$$

Inserting $k = \frac{(2m\theta_G^* + n)[2m\alpha(\cdot) - n\beta(\cdot)]}{(4\theta_G^* - \underline{\theta})^3(\theta_G^* - \underline{\theta})}$ from the first-order condition (2.15a) and

subsequently $m = m_q = n(2\theta_G^* - \underline{\theta})/(\theta_G^*\underline{\theta})$ from (2.7) one can check after tedious calculations that the above inequality is always true. Hence $dN_q(\cdot)/dm\big|_{N_q(\cdot)=0} > 0$. This proves claim (a). Claims (b) and (c) are readily verified using (A2.31) together with (2.8), and (A2.24).

Similarly, defining $N_\pi(\underline{\theta}, m, n, k) := m - m_\pi[b_G(\underline{\theta}, m, n, k), \underline{\theta}, n]$, it is easy to show that, $dN_\pi(\cdot)/dm > 0$, $N_\pi[-n/2\underline{\theta}, \cdot] < 0$, where $m = -n/2\underline{\theta}$ is the zero profit level of the environmental margin, and $N_\pi[m_q(\cdot), \cdot] > 0$. This proves part (ii) of the proposition. ∎

APPENDIX A3

Proof of Lemma 3.1
(i) For the set-up without investment cost there exists a unique m_E, with $m_E > m_q$. (ii) For the set-up with investment cost there exist $\underline{k}$ and $\hat{k}$, where $0 < \underline{k} < \hat{k}$. Then if the investment rate satisfies $k < \underline{k}$ there exists a unique $m_E > m_h'$, and if it satisfies $k > \hat{k}$ there exists a unique $m_E \in [m_q, m_h']$.

Consider

$$\frac{dE}{d\theta_B} = e'(\theta_B)q_B^*(\zeta, \theta_B) - \frac{\zeta}{\theta_B}\frac{\partial E}{\partial \zeta} + \frac{\partial E}{\partial \theta_B}\bigg|_{\zeta(\theta_G, \theta_B) = \bar{\zeta}; e(\theta_B) = \bar{e}} . \quad (3.6b)$$

Since $e'(\theta_B) \le 0$ we have $\frac{dE}{d\theta_B} < 0 \Rightarrow -\frac{\zeta}{\theta_B}\frac{\partial E}{\partial \zeta} + \frac{\partial E}{\partial \theta_B}\bigg|_{\zeta(\theta_G, \theta_B) = \bar{\zeta}; e(\theta_B) = \bar{e}} < 0$.
Inserting from (3.5a) and (3.5b) we obtain

$$-\frac{\zeta}{\theta_B}\frac{\partial E}{\partial \zeta} + \frac{\partial E}{\partial \theta_B}\bigg|_{\zeta(\theta_G, \theta_B) = \bar{\zeta}; e(\theta_B) = \bar{e}} = \frac{\begin{Bmatrix} m[2e(\theta_G) + e(\theta_B)]\zeta \\ -\frac{n}{\theta_L}[8e(\theta_B)\zeta^2 - 4e(\theta_B)\zeta - e(\theta_G)] \end{Bmatrix}}{(4\zeta - 1)^2 \theta_B} .$$

Observing $e(\theta_B) \geq e(\theta_G)$, it is then readily verified that

$$\frac{dE}{d\theta_B} < 0 \Rightarrow m \leq \frac{n\left[8\zeta^2 - 4\zeta - 1\right]}{3\theta_B\zeta} =: m_E(\zeta, \theta_B). \tag{A3.1}$$

Recall from the proof of Proposition 2.5 that $m \geq m_q' \Leftrightarrow m \geq m_q(\zeta, \theta_B)$. Using (A3.1) and (2.7) it is then readily verified that $m_E(\zeta, \theta_B) > m_q(\zeta, \theta_B) \ \forall(\zeta, \theta_B)$.

Part (i): Note

$$\frac{\partial m_E(\cdot)}{\partial \zeta} = \frac{n\left(8\zeta^2 + 1\right)}{3\theta_B\zeta^2} > 0 \tag{A3.2a}$$

$$\left.\frac{\partial m_E(\cdot)}{\partial \theta_B}\right|_{\zeta = \bar{\zeta}} = \frac{-n\left(8\zeta^2 - 4\zeta - 1\right)}{3\theta_B^2\zeta} < 0. \tag{A3.2ba}$$

Consider the function $N_E(m) := m - m_E[\zeta, \theta_B]$. We can then write

$$\frac{dN_E(m)}{dm} = 1 - \frac{dm_E(\cdot)}{dm} = 1 - \frac{\partial m_E(\cdot)}{\partial \zeta}\frac{d\zeta}{dm} - \left.\frac{\partial m_E(\cdot)}{\partial \theta_B}\right|_{\zeta\left(\theta_G^*, \theta_B^*\right) = \bar{\zeta}}\frac{d\theta_B^*}{dm}. \tag{A3.3}$$

Define $m_E := m | N_E(m) = 0$. We can now establish existence and uniqueness of m_E' by showing that the following conditions are satisfied for $n \geq 0$. (a) $dN_E(m)/dm > 0$, (b) $N_E(m_q') < 0$, and (c) $\lim_{m \to \infty} N_E(m) > 0$.

Consider them in turn.

(a)   Using (A3.3) together with (A3.2a) and (A3.2b), and observing that $d\theta_B^*/dm \geq 0$ it is clear that $dN_E/dm > 0$ holds if $d\zeta/dm \leq 0$. In the absence of investment costs it is true that $m > m_q \Rightarrow d\theta_G^*/dm = 0$. But then, $d\zeta/dm \leq 0$ must be true.

(b)   This is implied by $m_E(\zeta, \theta_B) > m_q(\zeta, \theta_B) \ \forall(\zeta, \theta_B)$ and (a).

(c) Using the definition of $m_E(\zeta, \theta_B^*)$ in (A3.1), applying the rule of l'Hôpital and observing that $\lim_{m \to \infty} \zeta = 5.551$, it is readily verified that

$$\lim_{m \to \infty} m_E(\zeta, \theta_B^*) = 0 \text{ and, therefore, } \lim_{m \to \infty} N_E(m) = m > 0.$$

Hence, there exists a unique boundary value m_E such that $m \le m_E \Rightarrow \frac{dE}{d\theta_B} < 0$. This completes the proof of part (i).

Part (ii): Evaluating $s(\zeta, \underline{\theta}, m) = [m\zeta \underline{\theta} \beta(\zeta) - 2n\alpha(\zeta)]\underline{\theta}^2$, where $\alpha(\zeta) = (4\zeta^2 - 3\zeta + 2) > 0$ and $\beta(\zeta) := 4\zeta - 7$, at $m = m_E(\zeta, \underline{\theta})$ gives $s(\zeta, \underline{\theta}, m_E(\cdot)) = n[32\zeta^3 - 96\zeta^2 + 42\zeta - 5]\underline{\theta}^2/3$. It is readily verified that $s(\zeta, \underline{\theta}, m_E(\cdot)) \le 0 \Leftrightarrow \zeta \le 2.5$, where $\zeta = 2.5$ is the maximum degree of product differentiation for which $m = m_E$ implies a boundary regime with $\theta_B^* = \underline{\theta}$.

Consider first $\zeta \le 2.5$. Within the boundary regime, the first-order condition for G performance, as measured in ζ^*, is then given by

$$R(\zeta^*, \underline{\theta}, k, m, n) = \frac{(2m\zeta^*\underline{\theta} + n)[2m\alpha(\zeta^*)\underline{\theta} - n\beta(\zeta^*)]}{(4\zeta^* - 1)^3 \underline{\theta}^2} - k(\zeta^* - 1)\underline{\theta} = 0.$$

Evaluating this at $m = m_E(\zeta^*, \underline{\theta})$ and solving $R[\zeta^*, \underline{\theta}, k, m_E(\cdot), n] = 0$ for k yields the function

$$k_b(\zeta^*, n) := k\Big|_{R[\zeta^*, \underline{\theta}, k, m_E(\cdot), n] = 0} = \frac{\left(16\zeta^{*3} - 16\zeta^{*2} + 5\zeta^* + 4\right)n^2}{9\zeta^*(\zeta^* - 1)\underline{\theta}^3}$$

on the domain $\zeta^* \in [1, 2.5]$. This function defines the locus in (ζ^*, k) space on which $m = m_E(\zeta^*, \underline{\theta})$ is realised in equilibrium. It is readily checked that $k_b(\zeta^*, n)$ is strictly convex with a minimum at $\zeta^* = 1.7202$. From this we find

$$\underline{k} := \min\{k | R[\zeta^*, \underline{\theta}, k, m_E(\cdot), n] = 0\} = k_b(1.7202, n) = 4.1883\, n^2/\underline{\theta}^3.$$

Define

$$\hat{k} := k_b(2.5, n) = 4.9333\, n^2 / \underline{\theta}^3$$

as the value of k for which $m = m_E(\zeta^*, \underline{\theta})$ is realised for $\zeta^* = 2.5$. Also note that convexity implies that $k_b(\zeta^*, n) = \hat{k}$ also holds for the lower value $\zeta^* = 1.3491$ and $k(\zeta^*, n) > \hat{k} \Leftrightarrow \zeta^* < 1.3491$.

Consider now $\zeta^* > 2.5$, implying an interior regime with $\theta_B^* > \underline{\theta}$. Here the equilibrium pair (ζ^*, θ_B^*) is jointly determined by the first-order conditions $R(\zeta^*, \theta_B^*, m) = 0$ and $T(\zeta^*, \theta_B^*, m) = 0$ as given in (2.15a) and (2.15b). Evaluating $R[\zeta^*, \theta_B^*, m_E(\cdot)] = 0$ and $T[\zeta^*, \theta_B^*, m_E(\cdot)] = 0$ now allows us to solve for the triple (ζ^*, θ_B^*, k) for which $m = m_E(\zeta^*, \theta_B^*)$ is realised as an equilibrium. Specifically we obtain

$$k_I(\zeta^*, n) := k\Big|_{R[\zeta^*,\theta_B^*,k,m_E(\cdot),n]=T[\zeta^*,\theta_B^*,k,m_E(\cdot),n]=0}$$

$$= \frac{-\left(4\zeta^{*4} - 24\zeta^{*3} + 11\zeta^{*2} + 5\zeta^* - 4\right)n^2}{36\zeta^*\left(\zeta^* - 1\right)\left(6\zeta^{*3} - 4\zeta^{*2} + 5\zeta^* + 2\right)^2}$$

on the domain $\zeta^* \in [2.5, \infty)$.[7] This function can be shown to decrease in ζ^* on the interval $[2.5, 5.551]$, where $\zeta^* \geq 5.551 \Rightarrow k_I(\zeta^*, n) \leq 0$.

Observing that $k_I(2.5, n) = k_b(2.5, n) = \hat{k}$, we can establish the continuous function

$$k_{full} = \begin{cases} k_B(\zeta^*, n) & \text{for } \zeta^* \in [0, 2.5] \\ k_I(\zeta^*, n) & \text{for } \zeta^* \in [2.5, 5.551] \end{cases}.$$

It exhibits a local minimum $k_{full} = \underline{k}$ at $\zeta^* = 1.7202$, a local maximum $k_{full} = \hat{k}$ at $\zeta^* = 2.5$, as well as a global maximum at $\zeta^* = 1$ and a global minimum at $\zeta^* = 5.551$. But then it follows that any $k < \underline{k}$ corresponds to a unique $\zeta^* > 2.5$ when $m = m_E(\zeta^*, \underline{\theta})$ is realised in equilibrium. But as

$\zeta^* > 2.5 \Leftrightarrow m_E\left(\zeta^*,\underline{\theta}\right) > m_h\left(\zeta^*,\underline{\theta}\right) > m_h{}'$ it follows that $k < \underline{k} \Rightarrow m_E > m_h{}'$
Likewise, any $k > \hat{k}$ corresponds to a unique $\zeta^* < 2.5$ for $m = m_E\left(\zeta^*,\underline{\theta}\right)$ to
be realised in equilibrium. Since $\zeta^* < 2.5 \Leftrightarrow m_E\left(\zeta^*,\underline{\theta}\right) < m_h\left(\zeta^*,\underline{\theta}\right) < m_h{}'$ in
equilibrium it follows that $k > \hat{k} \Rightarrow m_E < m_h{}'$. This completes the proof. ∎

APPENDIX A4

Proof of Lemma 4.1
(i) The impact of the standard on consumer surplus is given by

$$\frac{dS}{d\theta_{\min}} = q_B{}^* \psi_B + q_G{}^* \psi_G, \qquad (4.2)$$

where

$$\psi_B := \frac{3(m\theta_{\min} + 2n)\theta_{\min}}{\left(4\theta_G{}^* - \theta_{\min}\right)^2}\left(\frac{\theta_G{}^*}{\theta_{\min}} - \frac{d\theta_G{}^*}{d\theta_{\min}}\right) + \frac{m\theta_G{}^*\theta_{\min} - 2n\left(\theta_G{}^* + \theta_{\min}\right)}{2\theta_{\min}\left(4\theta_G{}^* - \theta_{\min}\right)} \quad (4.3a)$$

$$\psi_G := \frac{3\left(2m\theta_G{}^* + n\right)\theta_{\min}}{\left(4\theta_G{}^* - \theta_{\min}\right)^2}\left(\frac{\theta_G{}^*}{\theta_{\min}} - \frac{d\theta_G{}^*}{d\theta_{\min}}\right) + \frac{2m\left(\theta_G{}^* + \theta_{\min}\right) - n}{2\left(4\theta_G{}^* - \theta_{\min}\right)}\frac{d\theta_G{}^*}{d\theta_{\min}}. \quad (4.3b)$$

(ii) $\psi_B < \psi_G$. Hence for a small increase in the standard the net change in average surplus is always greater for the G variant.

Part (i): The impact of the standard on consumer surplus is given by the total
derivative of (4.1). For $\theta_B{}^* = \theta_{\min}$ this can be written after some
rearrangement:

$$\frac{dS}{d\theta_{\min}} = q_B{}^*\left(\frac{v_0 + v_1}{2} - \frac{dp_B{}^*}{d\theta_{\min}}\right) + q_G{}^*\left(\frac{v_1 + \overline{v}}{2}\frac{d\theta_G{}^*}{d\theta_{\min}} - \frac{dp_G{}^*}{d\theta_{\min}}\right), \qquad (A4.1a)$$

where

$$v_0 = \frac{p_B^* - u}{\theta_{min}} = \frac{\left[\begin{array}{c} m\left(\theta_G^* - \theta_{min}\right)\theta_{min} - n\left(2\theta_G^* + \theta_{min}\right) \\ + c\left(4\theta_G^* - \theta_{min}\right)\theta_{min} \end{array}\right]}{\left(4\theta_G^* - \theta_{min}\right)\theta_{min}} , \quad \text{(A4.1b)}$$

$$v_1 = \frac{p_G^* - p_B^*}{\theta_G^* - \theta_{min}} = \frac{m\left(2\theta_G^* - \theta_{min}\right) - n + c\left(4\theta_G^* - \theta_{min}\right)}{4\theta_G^* - \theta_{min}} , \quad \text{(A4.1c)}$$

$$\frac{dp_B^*}{d\theta_{min}} = \frac{\partial p_B^*}{\partial \theta_B} + \frac{\partial p_B^*}{\partial \theta_G}\frac{d\theta_G^*}{d\theta_{min}}, \quad \frac{dp_G^*}{d\theta_{min}} = \frac{\partial p_G^*}{\partial \theta_B} + \frac{\partial p_G^*}{\partial \theta_G}\frac{d\theta_G^*}{d\theta_{min}}$$

and

$$\frac{\partial p_B^*}{\partial \theta_B} = \frac{\left[\begin{array}{c} m\left(4\theta_G^{*2} - 8\theta_G^*\theta_{min} + \theta_{min}^2\right) - 6n\theta_G^* \\ + c\left(16\theta_G^{*2} - 8\theta_G^*\theta_{min} + \theta_{min}^2\right) \end{array}\right]}{\left(4\theta_G^* - \theta_{min}\right)^2} , \quad \text{(A4.1d)}$$

$$\frac{\partial p_B^*}{\partial \theta_G} = \frac{3\theta_{min}\left[m\theta_{min} + 2n\right]}{\left(4\theta_G^* - \theta_{min}\right)^2} > 0, \quad \frac{\partial p_G^*}{\partial \theta_B} = \frac{-3\theta_G^*\left[2m\theta_G^* + n\right]}{\left(4\theta_G^* - \theta_{min}\right)^2} < 0,$$

$$\frac{\partial p_G^*}{\partial \theta_G} = \frac{\left[\begin{array}{c} 2m\left(4\theta_G^{*2} - 2\theta_G^*\theta_{min} + \theta_{min}^2\right) + 3n\theta_{min} \\ + c\left(16\theta_G^{*2} - 8\theta_G^*\theta_{min} + \theta_{min}^2\right) \end{array}\right]}{\left(4\theta_G^* - \theta_{min}\right)^2} . \quad \text{(A4.1e)}$$

By (A4.1a), the marginal impact of the standard on aggregate consumer surplus is given by the change of average consumer surplus from each variant at given levels of quantities. Sequentially inserting the relevant terms into the expression in (A4.1a) then gives (4.2)–(4.3b) as reported in part (i) of the Lemma.

Part (ii): From (4.3a) and (4.b), we obtain after some transformations:

$$\psi_B < \psi_G \Leftrightarrow - \left\{ \begin{array}{c} \dfrac{m\theta_G^*\theta_{\min}\left(8\theta_G^* - 5\theta_{\min}\right) + 2n\left(4\theta_G^{*2} - \theta_{\min}^2\right)}{2\left(4\theta_G^* - \theta_{\min}\right)^2 \theta_{\min}} \\ + \dfrac{r\left(\theta_G^*, \theta_{\min}\right)}{2\left(4\theta_G^* - \theta_{\min}\right)^2} \dfrac{d\theta_G^*}{d\theta_{\min}} \end{array} \right\} < 0.$$

Since $m \geq -n/\left(2\theta_G^*\right)$, $r\left(\theta_G^*, \theta_{\min}\right) \geq 0$ and $d\theta_G^*/d\theta_{\min} \geq 0$ both terms in bracelets are non-negative and the inequality is always satisfied. ■

Proof of Proposition 4.1

Consider a small increase in the standard over the laissez-faire level of B performance. (i) In the lower boundary regime, where $m < m_l$, this reduces aggregate consumer surplus. (ii) In the maximum differentiation regime with B profit dominance, where $m \in \left(m_l, m_\pi\right)$, this reduces (increases) consumer surplus if m is sufficiently close to m_l (m_π). (iii) Under G profit dominance, this raises consumer surplus.

Part (i): We seek to establish $dS/d\theta_{\min}\big|_{m<m_l} = \left(q_B^* \psi_B + q_G^* \psi_G\right)\big|_{m<m_l} < 0$. Recall $q_B^* > q_G^*$ for $m < m_l$. By Lemma 4.1, $\psi_B < \psi_G$. Then $\left(\psi_B + \psi_G\right)\big|_{m<m_l} < 0$ is sufficient for $dS/d\theta_{\min}\big|_{m<m_l} < 0$. Observing the first order condition for G quality choice we can substitute the RHS of (A2.5′) for m in (4.3a) and (4.3b). After collection of terms this yields

$$\left(\psi_B + \psi_G\right)\big|_{m<m_l} = \dfrac{n\left\{\phi - 2\theta_{\min}\tau \dfrac{d\theta_G^*}{d\theta_{\min}}\Big|_{\theta_G^* < \bar\theta}\right\}}{4\left(4\theta_G^* - \theta_{\min}\right)^2 \theta_{\min}\alpha\left(\theta_G^*, \theta_{\min}\right)} < 0,$$

where

$$\phi := \theta_G^*\theta_{\min}\left(16\theta_G^* + 5\theta_{\min}\right)\beta(\cdot) - 4\left(4\theta_G^{*2} - 6\theta_G^*\theta_{\min} - \theta_{\min}^2\right)\alpha(\cdot) < 0,$$

$$\tau := \left(4\theta_G^* + 17\theta_{\min}\right)\alpha(\cdot) - \left[4\theta_G^{*2} - 3\theta_G^*\theta_{\min} - 4\theta_{\min}^2\right]\beta(\cdot) > 0$$

are easily verified when using $\alpha(\cdot) = 4\theta_G^{*2} - 3\theta_G^* \theta_{\min} + 2\theta_{\min}^2$ and $\beta(\cdot) = 4\theta_G^* - 7\theta_{\min}$.

Part (ii): For $m \in [m_l, m_\pi]$, we know that $q_B^* > q_G^*$ and $d\theta_G^* / d\theta_{\min}\big|_{m \in [m_l, m_\pi]} = 0$. We first prove that $dS/d\theta_{\min}\big|_{m=m_l} < 0$. Recall $m_l = n[\beta(\bar{\theta}, \underline{\theta}) / 2\alpha(\bar{\theta}, \underline{\theta})]$. We can thus write $(\rho + \psi)\big|_{m=m_l} = \dfrac{n\bar{\phi}}{4(4\bar{\theta} - \theta_{\min})^2 \theta_{\min} \alpha(\bar{\theta}, \theta_{\min})} < 0$, where $\bar{\phi} = \phi\big|_{\theta_G^* = \bar{\theta}} < 0$. By continuity, this holds for a range of $m > m_l$.

From (4.3a) and (4.3b) we calculate

$$
\frac{dS}{d\theta_{\min}}\bigg|_{m \geq m_l} = \left(q_B^* \psi_B + q_G^* \psi_G \right)_{m > m_l}
$$
$$
= \frac{\left[\begin{array}{l} m^2 \left(28\bar{\theta} + 5\theta_{\min}\right)\bar{\theta}^2 \theta_{\min}^2 + 2mn\left(20\bar{\theta} + \theta_{\min}\right)\bar{\theta}\theta_{\min}^2 \\ -2n^2\left(8\bar{\theta}^2 - 6\bar{\theta}\theta_{\min} - 5\theta_{\min}^2\right) \end{array} \right]}{2\left(4\bar{\theta} - \theta_{\min}\right)^3 \theta_{\min}^2} \quad (A4.2)
$$

Evaluating the RHS at $m = m_\pi = n / \sqrt{\bar{\theta}\theta_{\min}}$ gives

$$
\frac{dS}{d\theta_{\min}}\bigg|_{m=m_\pi} = \frac{n^2 \left[\begin{array}{l} \bar{\theta}\left(-16\bar{\theta}^2 + 40\bar{\theta}\theta_{\min} + 15\theta_{\min}^2\right) \\ + 2\theta_{\min}\left(20\bar{\theta} + \theta_{\min}\right)\sqrt{\bar{\theta}\theta_{\min}} \end{array} \right]}{2\left(4\bar{\theta} - \theta_{\min}\right)^3 \theta_{\min}^2},
$$

where the expression in the second line follows from straightforward calculation. The expression in square brackets is positive for $\bar{\theta} < (13/4)\theta_{\min}$. For a proof of part (iii) we note from (A4.2) that $dS/d\theta_{\min}$ is increasing in m. Thus, $dS/d\theta_{\min}\big|_{m \geq m_\pi} > 0.\blacksquare$

Proof of Lemma 4.2
$d\pi_B^* / d\theta_{\min} \leq 0.$

Since $d\theta_G{}^*/d\theta_{\min} = 0$ and $s(\bar\theta, \theta_{\min}) = s(\bar\theta, \theta_B{}^*) = 0$ for $m \geq m_h$, it is trivial that $\lambda = 0$ $\forall m \geq m_h$. It remains to be shown that $\operatorname{sgn} \lambda = \operatorname{sgn}(d\pi_B{}^*/d\theta_{\min}) = -1$ $\forall m < m_h$. Recall $s(\theta_G{}^*, \theta_{\min}) < 0$ $\forall m < m_h$. For $m \in (m_l, m_h)$, where $d\theta_G{}^*/d\theta_{\min} = 0$, it follows that $\lambda = \theta_G{}^* s(\theta_G{}^*, \theta_{\min}) < 0$. For $m < m_l$, we can rewrite (4.5) by substituting from (2.10b) for $s(\cdot)$ and from (2.14b) for m. After simplification this yields

$$\lambda\Big|_{m<m_l} = \frac{n}{2\alpha(\cdot)} \big[\theta_{\min}\beta(\cdot) - 4\alpha(\cdot)\big]\Big[4\theta_G{}^{*2} - 5\theta_G{}^*\theta_{\min} + \theta_{\min}^2 \Big] < 0.$$

The inequality follows as the first expression in square brackets is negative from (2.12) and the second expression in square brackets is positive. Hence, $\operatorname{sgn} \lambda = \operatorname{sgn}(d\pi_B{}^*/d\theta_{\min}) = -1$ $\forall m < m_h$. ∎

Proof of Proposition 4.2
There exists a unique boundary value $m_W \in (m_\pi, m_h)$ such that an increase in the standard raises industry surplus if and only if $m > m_W$.

First, consider $m < m_l$. From part (i) of Proposition 4.1, Lemma 4.2 and (4.4a), we have $dW/d\theta_{\min}\big|_{m<m_l} < 0$. Now, consider $m \geq m_l$. We rewrite (4.6) conveniently using the RHS expressions of (4.2), (4.4a) and (4.4b) to obtain

$$\frac{dW}{d\theta_{\min}} = \left\{ \begin{array}{l} \left[\psi_B + \dfrac{\lambda}{\left(4\theta_G{}^* - \theta_{\min}\right)^2 \theta_G{}^* \theta_{\min}}\right] q_B{}^* \\[2ex] + \left[\psi_G - \dfrac{\left(2\theta_G{}^* + \theta_{\min}\right)\left(2m\theta_G{}^* + n\right)}{\left(4\theta_G{}^* - \theta_{\min}\right)^2}\right] q_G{}^* \end{array} \right\}.$$

Inserting the definitions (4.3a), (4.3b) and (4.5) of ρ, ψ and λ, respectively, using (2.4a) and (2.4b), and observing $\theta_G{}^* = \bar\theta$ and $db_H/d\theta_{\min}\big|_{m\geq m_l} = 0$, we obtain

$$\frac{dW}{d\theta_{\min}}\Big|_{m\geq m_l} = \frac{\sigma_B(m)}{2(4\bar\theta - \theta_{\min})^3 \theta_{\min}^2},$$

$$\sigma_L(m) := \begin{bmatrix} m^2\left(20\bar\theta - 17\theta_{\min}\right)\bar\theta^2\theta_{\min}^2 + 2mn\left(4\bar\theta - 7\theta_{\min}\right)\bar\theta\theta_{\min}^2 \\ -2n^2\left(24\bar\theta^3 - 18\bar\theta^2\theta_{\min} + 5\bar\theta\theta_{\min}^2 + \theta_{\min}^3\right) \end{bmatrix}$$

Given a maximum differentiation or upper boundary regime, then assumption (2.13) and the first-order condition $s(\bar\theta,\theta_B^*) = 0$ imply $\theta_{\min} = \theta_B^* < (4/7)\bar\theta$. This, in turn, implies $\partial\sigma_B(m)/\partial m > 0$. Using $m_\pi = n/\sqrt{\bar\theta\theta_{\min}}$ and $m_h = 2n\alpha(\bar\theta,\theta_{\min})/[\bar\theta\theta_{\min}\beta(\bar\theta,\theta_{\min})]$ it is readily verified that $\sigma_B(m)|_{m<m_\pi} < \sigma_B(m_\pi) < 0 < \sigma_B(m_h) < \sigma_B(m)|_{m>m_h}$. Hence, there exists a unique boundary value $m_W \in (m_\pi, m_h)$ such that $\sigma_B(m_W) = 0$ and $\text{sgn}(dW/d\theta_{\min})|_{m>m_l} = \text{sgn}\,\sigma_B(m) = 1 \Leftrightarrow m > m_W$ as indicated in the proposition.∎

Proof of Proposition 4.3
(i) The standard always reduces the clean firm's profit. (ii) It increases the dirty firm's profit if an interior regime obtains for $m \geq m_h'$ and it lowers the dirty firm's profit if this firm dominates in market share for $m \leq m_q'$.

Part (i): Noting $\partial\pi_G^*/\partial\theta_G - F'(\theta_G^*) = 0$ from the first-order condition (2.15a) it follows that $d\pi_G^*/d\theta_{\min} = \partial\pi_G^*/\partial\theta_{\min} < 0$.

Part (ii): Consider an interior equilibrium with $m \geq m_h'$. Here, $\partial\pi_B^*/\partial\theta_{\min} - F'(\theta_{\min}) = 0$, implying $d\pi_B^*/d\theta_{\min} = (\partial\pi_B^*/\partial\theta_G)(d\theta_G^*/d\theta_{\min}) > 0$. Now consider $m \leq m_q'$. Using $\pi_B^*(\zeta^*,\theta_{\min}) = \frac{(\zeta^*-1)\zeta^*(m\theta_{\min}+2n)^2}{(4\zeta^*-1)^2\theta_{\min}}$ with $\zeta^* = \theta_G^*/\theta_{\min}$ we obtain

$$\frac{d\pi_B^*(\cdot)}{d\theta_{\min}} = \frac{\partial\pi_B^*(\cdot)}{\partial\theta_{\min}}\Big|_{\zeta^*=\bar\zeta} + \frac{\partial\pi_B^*(\cdot)}{\partial\zeta}\frac{d\zeta^*}{d\theta_{\min}}$$

$$= \frac{(\zeta^*-1)\zeta^*(m\theta_{\min}+2n)(m\theta_{\min}-2n)}{(4\zeta^*-1)^2\theta_{\min}^2} + \frac{(m\theta_{\min}+2n)^2(2\zeta^*+1)}{(4\zeta^*-1)^3\theta_{\min}}\frac{d\zeta^*}{d\theta_{\min}}.$$

Noting that $d\zeta^*/d\theta_{min} < 0$ it follows that the second term is negative. Furthermore, $m \leq m_q' \leq n(2\zeta^* - 1)/(\zeta^*\theta_{min}) < 2n/\theta_{min}$ implies that the first term is negative too. This completes the proof.∎

Proof of Proposition 4.4
Suppose the G firm's best response in the presence of investments is given by (4.7). Then a small increase in the standard above the laissez-faire level of B environmental performance lowers industry surplus if $m \leq m_\pi'$, i.e. in the presence of B dominance (with regard to operating profit) and raises industry surplus if $m \geq m_h'$, i.e., in the case of an interior equilibrium.

Using

$$\frac{dS}{d\theta_{min}} = \frac{\partial S}{\partial \theta_B} + \frac{\partial S}{\partial \theta_G}\frac{d\theta_G^*}{d\theta_{min}}$$

$$= \left\{ \begin{array}{l} q_B^*\left(\dfrac{v_0 + v_1}{2} - \dfrac{\partial p_B^*}{\partial \theta_B}\right) - q_G^*\dfrac{\partial p_G^*}{\partial \theta_B} \\[3mm] + \left[q_G^*\left(\dfrac{v_1 + \bar{v}}{2} - \dfrac{\partial p_G^*}{\partial \theta_G}\right) - q_B^*\dfrac{\partial p_B^*}{\partial \theta_G}\right]\dfrac{d\theta_G^*}{d\theta_{min}} \end{array} \right\},$$

and

$$\frac{\partial \pi_G^*}{\partial \theta_B} = \frac{\partial p_G^*}{\partial \theta_B}q_G^* + \left(p_G^* - MC_G\right)\frac{\partial q_G^*}{\partial \theta_B} < 0,$$

$$\frac{\partial \pi_B^*}{\partial \theta_G} = \frac{\partial p_B^*}{\partial \theta_G}q_B^* + \left(p_B^* - MC_B\right)\frac{\partial q_B^*}{\partial \theta_G} > 0,$$

with $MC_i = c\theta_i + c_0$; $i = G, B$, we can write

$$dW/d\theta_{min} = \kappa_B + \kappa_G\left(d\theta_G^*/d\theta_{min}\right) \quad \kappa_B \in \left\{\kappa_B^I, \kappa_B^B\right\}, \qquad (A4.3)$$

where

$$\kappa_B^B = \frac{\partial S}{\partial \theta_B} + \frac{\partial \pi_B^*}{\partial \theta_B} + \frac{\partial \pi_G^*}{\partial \theta_B}$$

$$= q_B^* \left(\frac{v_0 + v_1}{2} - c \right) + \frac{\partial q_B^*}{\partial \theta_B} \left(p_B^* - MC_B \right) + \frac{\partial q_G^*}{\partial \theta_B} \left(p_G^* - MC_G \right), \quad \text{(A4.4a)}$$

$$\kappa_B^I = \frac{\partial S}{\partial \theta_B} + \frac{\partial \pi_G^*}{\partial \theta_B} = q_B^* \left(\frac{v_0 + v_1}{2} - \frac{\partial p_B^*}{\partial \theta_B} \right) + \frac{\partial q_G^*}{\partial \theta_B} \left(p_G^* - MC_G \right), \quad \text{(A4.4b)}$$

$$\kappa_G = \frac{\partial S}{\partial \theta_G} + \frac{\partial \pi_B^*}{\partial \theta_G} = q_G^* \left(\frac{v_1 + \bar{v}}{2} - \frac{\partial p_G^*}{\partial \theta_G} \right) + \frac{\partial q_B^*}{\partial \theta_G} \left(p_B^* - MC_B \right). \quad \text{(A4.4c)}$$

It is easily checked that $\kappa_B = \kappa_B^B$ and $\kappa_B = \kappa_B^I$ in a boundary and interior equilibrium, respectively.

Consider $m \leq m_\pi'$, implying a boundary equilibrium. Using (A4.4a) and (A4.4c) together with (A4.1b)–(A4.1d) and (2.2a/b) and (2.4a/b) it can be verified after some tedious calculations that

$$\frac{dW}{d\theta_{\min}} \bigg|_{m \leq m_\pi'} = \kappa_B^B + \kappa_G \frac{d\theta_G^*}{d\theta_{\min}} = \frac{\sigma_B^B(m) + \sigma_G(m)\theta_{\min}^2 \left(d\theta_G^* / d\theta_{\min} \right)}{2 \left(4\theta_G^* - \theta_{\min} \right)^3 \theta_{\min}^2},$$

$$\sigma_B^B(m) := \begin{bmatrix} m^2 \left(20\theta_G^* - 17\theta_{\min} \right) \theta_G^{*2} \theta_{\min}^2 + 2mn\left(4\theta_G^* - 7\theta_{\min} \right) \theta_G^* \theta_{\min}^2 \\ -2n^2 \left(24\theta_G^{*3} - 18\theta_G^{*2}\theta_{\min} + 5\theta_G^*\theta_{\min}^2 + \theta_{\min}^3 \right) \end{bmatrix}, \text{(A4.5a)}$$

$$\sigma_G(m) := \begin{bmatrix} 2m^2 \left(8\theta_G^{*3} - 6\theta_G^{*2}\theta_{\min} - 3\theta_G^*\theta_{\min}^2 + \theta_{\min}^3 \right) \\ -3n\left[2m\theta_{\min} + n \right]\left(4\theta_G^* - \theta_{\min} \right) \end{bmatrix}. \quad \text{(A4.5b)}$$

Recalling from the proof of Proposition 2.5 that $m \leq m_\pi' \Leftrightarrow m \leq n / \sqrt{\theta_G^* \underline{\theta}}$, with $\theta_G^* = b_G(m, \underline{\theta})$, and observing that $\partial \sigma_B^B(m_\pi') / \partial m > 0$ and $\partial \sigma_G(m_\pi') / \partial m > 0$, we obtain

$$\sigma_B^B(m)\Big|_{m<m_\pi'} < \sigma_B^B(m_\pi') = \dfrac{-n^2\left[\left(\begin{array}{c} 48\theta_G^{*\,3} - 56\theta_G^{*\,2}\theta_{\min} \\ + 27\theta_G^*\theta_{\min}^{\,2} + 2\theta_{\min}^{\,3}\end{array}\right)\sqrt{\theta_G^*\theta_{\min}} \\ -2\left(4\theta_G^* - 7\theta_{\min}\right)\theta_G^{*\,2}\theta_{\min}\right]}{\sqrt{\theta_G^*\theta_{\min}}} < 0\,,$$

$$\sigma_G(m)\Big|_{m<m_\pi'} < \sigma_G(m_\pi') = \dfrac{-n^2\left[\begin{array}{c} 6\left(4\theta_G^* - \theta_{\min}\right)\theta_G^*\theta_{\min}^{\,2} \\ -\left(\begin{array}{c}16\theta_G^{*\,3} - 24\theta_G^{*\,2}\theta_{\min} \\ -3\theta_G^*\theta_{\min}^{\,2} + 2\theta_{\min}^{\,3}\end{array}\right)\sqrt{\theta_G^*\theta_{\min}}\end{array}\right]}{\theta_G^*\theta_{\min}\sqrt{\theta_G^*\theta_{\min}}}\,.$$

Noting that $d\theta_G^*\big/d\theta_{\min} \le \theta_G^*\big/\theta_{\min}$, we have

$$\left.\frac{dW}{d\theta_{\min}}\right|_{m\le m_\pi'} \le \frac{\sigma_B^B(m_\pi') + \sigma_G(m_\pi')\theta_G^*\theta_{\min}}{2\left(4\theta_G^* - \theta_{\min}\right)^3\theta_{\min}^{\,2}} < 0\,,$$

where the last inequality is easily verified.

Next, consider $m \ge m_h'$, implying an interior equilibrium. Using (A4.4b) and (A4.4c) together with (A4.1b)–(A4.1e) and (2.2a/b) and (2.4a/b) it is readily verified that

$$\left.\frac{dW}{d\theta_{\min}}\right|_{m\ge m_h'} = \kappa_B^I + \kappa_G\,\frac{d\theta_G^*}{d\theta_{\min}} = \frac{\sigma_B^I(m) + \sigma_G(m)\theta_{\min}^{\,2}\left(d\theta_G^*\big/d\theta_{\min}\right)}{2\left(4\theta_G^* - \theta_{\min}\right)^3\theta_{\min}^{\,2}}\,,$$

$$\sigma_B^I(m) := \left[\begin{array}{c} 3m\left[m\theta_G^* + 2n\right]\left(4\theta_G^* - \theta_{\min}\right)\theta_G^*\theta_{\min}^{\,2} \\ -2n^2\left(8\theta_G^{*\,3} - 6\theta_G^{*\,2}\theta_{\min} - 3\theta_G^*\theta_{\min}^{\,2} + \theta_{\min}^{\,3}\right)\end{array}\right]\,. \quad \text{(A4.5c)}$$

Recalling that $m \ge m_h' \Leftrightarrow m \ge 2n\alpha\big(\theta_G^*,\theta_{\min}\big)\big/\big[\theta_G^*\theta_{\min}\beta\big(\theta_G^*,\theta_{\min}\big)\big]$ from Appendix A2.2 and observing $\partial\sigma_B^I(m_h')\big/\partial m > 0$, one can verify after some tedious calculations that $\sigma_B^I(m)\big|_{m>m_h'} > \sigma_B^I(m_h') > 0$. Similarly, using

(A4.5b), we find $\partial \sigma_G(m_h')/\partial m > 0$ and $\sigma_G(m)\big|_{m>m_h'} > \sigma_G(m_h') > 0$. Hence, $dW/d\theta_{\min}\big|_{m \geq m_h'} > 0$, which completes the proof. ∎

Proof of Proposition 4.6
Consider the introduction of a marginal unit emission standard. (i) For the set-up without investment cost there exists an interval $[m_W, m_E]$ such that $m \in [m_W, m_E] \Rightarrow \{dW/d\theta_{\min} > 0; dE/d\theta_{\min} < 0\}$. (ii) For the set-up with investment cost there exist $\underline{k}$ and $\hat{k}$, where $0 < \underline{k} < \hat{k}$, as defined in Lemma 3.1. If the investment rate satisfies $k < \underline{k}$, then there exists an interval $[m_W, m_E]$. If it satisfies $k > \hat{k}$, then $m_E < m_W$.

Evaluate at $m = m_E = n\left[8\zeta^{*2} - 4\zeta^* - 1\right]\big/\left(3\zeta^*\theta_B^*\right)$ the functions $\sigma_B^B(m)$, $\sigma_B^I(m)$ and $\sigma_G(m)$ as defined in (A4.5a)–(A4.5c) for the boundary and interior regimes, respectively and note that $\sigma_B^B(m)$ is equivalent to $\sigma_B(m)$ as used in the Proof of Proposition 4.1 for the case without quality investment. Note $\partial \sigma_B^I(m_E)/\partial m > 0$, $\partial \sigma_B^B(m_E)/\partial m > 0$ and $\partial \sigma_G(m_E)/\partial m > 0$ and observe $m \geq m_E \Rightarrow m \geq n\left[8\zeta^{*2} - 4\zeta^* - 1\right]\big/\left(3\zeta^*\theta_B^*\right)$, with $\zeta^* = \zeta(m) = b_G(m,\cdot)/b_B(m,\cdot)$ and $\theta_B^* = b_B(m,\cdot)$. We then find $\sigma_B^I(m)\big|_{m>m_E} > \sigma_B^I(m_E) > 0$; $\sigma_B^B(m)\big|_{m>m_E} > \sigma_B^B(m_E)$ with $\sigma_B^B(m_E) > 0 \Leftrightarrow \zeta(m_E) > 1.3578$; and $\sigma_G(m)\big|_{m>m_E} > \sigma_G(m_E)$ with $\sigma(m_E) > 0 \Leftarrow \zeta(m_E) > 1.4262$. Recall from Proposition 4.4

$$\frac{dW}{d\theta_{\min}} = \frac{\sigma_B(m) + \sigma_G(m)\theta_{\min}{}^2\left(d\theta_G{}^*/d\theta_{\min}\right)}{2\left(4\theta_G{}^* - \theta_{\min}\right)^3 \theta_{\min}{}^2},$$

with $\sigma_B(\cdot) = \sigma_B^B(\cdot)$ and $\sigma_B(\cdot) = \sigma_B^I(\cdot)$ in a boundary and interior equilibrium, respectively.

Part (i): In the absence of investment cost $m_E > m_q > m_l$ implies that $d\theta_G{}^*/d\theta_{\min} = 0$. If $m_E > m_h$ then an upper boundary equilibrium is realised, where $\sigma_B(m_E) = \sigma_B^I(m_E) > 0$. In this case obviously $dW/d\theta_{\min}\big|_{m=m_E} > 0$, implying the existence of the interval $[m_W, m_E]$. If $m_E \leq m_h$ then a maximum differentiation is realised, where $\sigma_B(m_E) = \sigma_B^B(m_E)$. In this case $\zeta^* = \overline{\theta}/\underline{\theta} > 7/4 > 1.3578$, where the first inequality follows from (2.13). This implies, in turn, $\sigma_B^B(m_E) > 0$, $dW/d\theta_{\min}\big|_{m=m_E} > 0$ and thus the existence of $[m_W, m_E]$.

Part (ii). We have established in Lemma 3.1 that $k < \underline{k} \Rightarrow m_E > m_h'$. But then it follows that $dW/d\theta_{\min}\big|_{m=m_E} > 0$, imlpying again the existence of $[m_W, m_E]$. Now consider $k > \hat{k} \Rightarrow m_E < m_h'$, as by Lemma 3.1. Within the proof of part (ii) of the same Lemma we have also shown that $k > \hat{k} \Leftrightarrow \zeta^* < 1.3491$. But this implies $\sigma_B^B(m_E) < 0$, $\sigma_G(m_E) < 0$ and therefore $dW/d\theta_{\min}\big|_{m=m_E} < 0$. Hence, $k > \hat{k} \Rightarrow m_E < m_W$, which completes the proof.∎

APPENDIX A5

Proof of Proposition 5.1
Let $m, n > 0$ and k sufficiently large. Then there exist $\underline{m}$ and $\overline{m}$, with $0 < \underline{m} < \overline{m}$, such that $\theta_{\max}^* = \underline{\theta}$ if and only if $m \leq \underline{m}$; $\theta_{\max}^* \in \left(\underline{\theta}, \theta_G^*\right]$ if and only if $m \in (\underline{m}, \overline{m}]$; and $\theta_{\max}^* > \theta_G^*$ if and only if $m > \overline{m}$.

Consider

$$\frac{dW}{d\theta_{\max}} = \frac{\partial S}{\partial \theta_{\max}} + \frac{\partial \pi_B^*}{\partial \theta_{\max}} + \frac{\partial \pi_G^*}{\partial \theta_{\max}} - F'(\theta_{\max})$$

$$\overset{\theta_{\max}=\theta_G}{=} q_G^*\left(\frac{v_1 + \overline{v}}{2} - c\right) + \frac{\partial q_B^*}{\partial \theta_G}\left(p_B^* - MC_B\right) + \frac{\partial q_G^*}{\partial \theta_G}\left(p_G^* - MC_G\right) - F'(\theta_G)$$

$$= \frac{\Sigma(m, \theta_G)}{2(4\theta_G - \underline{\theta})^3} - F'(\theta_G),$$

where

$$\Sigma(m,\theta_G) := \begin{bmatrix} 4m^2\left(240_G{}^3 - 18\theta_G{}^2\underline{\theta} + 5\theta_G\underline{\theta}^2 + \underline{\theta}^3\right) \\ -2mn(4\theta_G - 7\underline{\theta})\underline{\theta} - n^2\left(20\theta_G - 17\underline{\theta}\right) \end{bmatrix}.$$

Furthermore, recall from (A4.4c) that

$$\frac{\partial S}{\partial\theta_{max}} + \frac{\partial\pi_B}{\partial\theta_{max}}^{*\ \theta_{max}=\theta_G} = \frac{\sigma_G(m,\theta_G)}{2(4\theta_G - \underline{\theta})^3}.$$

with $\sigma_G(\cdot)$ as defined in (A4.5b), where θ_{min} is substituted for $\underline{\theta}$. It is then readily verified that $\partial S/\partial\theta_{max} + \partial\pi_B^*/\partial\theta_{max} + \partial\pi_G^*/\partial\theta_{max} = 0$ and $\partial S/\partial\theta_{max} + \partial\pi_B^*/\partial\theta_{max} = 0$ correspond to the two loci $\Sigma(m,\theta_G) \equiv 0$ and $\sigma_G(m,\theta_G) \equiv 0$ in (θ_G, m) space (see Figure 5.1). Furthermore it is readily checked that $\partial\Sigma(\cdot)/\partial m\big|_{\Sigma(m,\theta_G)=0} > 0$, $\partial\Sigma(\cdot)/\partial\theta_G\big|_{\Sigma(m,\theta_G)=0} > 0 \Leftrightarrow \theta_G > \tilde\theta_G$, where $\tilde\theta_G \in \underline{\theta}, (7/4)\underline{\theta}[$, as well as $\partial\sigma_G(\cdot)/\partial m\big|_{\sigma_G(m,\theta_G)=0} > 0$ and $\partial\sigma_G(\cdot)/\partial\theta_G\big|_{\sigma_G(m,\theta_G)=0} > 0$. It follows that

(a) $dm/d\theta_G\big|_{\Sigma(m,\theta_G)=0} < 0 \Leftrightarrow \theta_G > \tilde\theta_H$ and $\Sigma(m,\theta_G) < 0 \Leftrightarrow m < m^-(\theta_G)$,
     where $m^-(\theta_G) := m\big|\Sigma(m,\theta_G) \equiv 0$, as well as

(b) $dm/d\theta_H\big|_{\sigma_G(m,\theta_G)=0} < 0$ and $\sigma_G(m,\theta_G) < 0 \Leftrightarrow m < m^+(\theta_G)$, where
     $m^+(\theta_G) := m\big|\sigma_G(m,\theta_G) \equiv 0$.

This implies the shapes and location of the $\sigma_G(\cdot) \equiv 0$ and $\Sigma(\cdot) \equiv 0$ loci as depicted in Figure 5.1. In particular, $m^+(\theta_G) > m^-(\theta_G)$ is always true. Furthermore it is easily checked that $\underline{m} := m^-(\underline{\theta}) > 0$. Now assume that

$$k \geq \max \frac{d}{d\theta_G}\left[\frac{\Sigma(m,\theta_G)}{2(4\theta_G - \underline{\theta})^3}\right].$$

This implies that $d^2W/d\theta_{max}{}^2 < 0$ for all θ_{max} and is therefore sufficient for the existence of a unique $\theta_{max}^*(m,k) = \arg\max W(\theta_{max})$. Let

$\theta^-(m) = \min\{\theta | \Sigma(m, \theta_G) \equiv 0\}$. $d^2W/d\theta_{max}{}^2 < 0$ for all θ_{max} then implies that $\theta^*_{max}(m, k) < \theta^-(m)$ for all relevant m as depicted in Figure 5.1. As is readily verified, $d\theta^*_{max}(\cdot)/dm \geq 0$, where $d\theta^*_{max}(\cdot)/dm > 0 \Leftrightarrow m \geq \underline{m}$. We can then define $\overline{m} := m^+ \big|\theta^*_{max}(m^+, k)\big|$. It is then easy to see that $\theta^*_{max}(\cdot) = \underline{\theta} \Leftrightarrow m \leq \underline{m}$; $\qquad \theta^*_{max}(\cdot) \in \big(\underline{\theta}, \theta^*_G(\cdot)\big] \Leftrightarrow m \in (\underline{m}, \overline{m}]$ and $\theta^*_{max}(\cdot) > \theta^*_G(\cdot) \Leftrightarrow m > \overline{m}$ as stated in the proposition. $\blacksquare$

APPENDIX A6

Proof of Proposition 6.1.1
Consider a marginal subsidy offered to the G firm or both firms. (i) Under B market share dominance ($m \leq m_q'$) this leads to an increase in G performance but not B performance. (ii) If the environmental margin m is sufficiently close to the switching level between boundary and interior regime, m_h', the subsidy leads to a switch to the interior regime and induces both firms to raise environmental performance.

As is easily checked,

$$\frac{d\theta^*_G}{dx^G_F} = \frac{F'(\theta^*_G)}{R_G(\cdot)} < 0,$$

where $R_G(\theta^*_G, \theta^*_B, x^G_F) < 0$ follows from the second order condition. Hence, an increase in the rate of subsidy $1 - x^G_F$ raises the performance of the G product.

Since $s(\theta^*_G, \underline{\theta}) \leq 0$ the subsidy can trigger an increase in B performance only if $ds(\theta^*_G, \underline{\theta})/dx^G_F = s_G(\theta^*_G, \underline{\theta})d\theta^*_G/dx^G_F < 0$. From (2.10b) we obtain

$$s_G(\theta^*_G, \underline{\theta}) = \partial s(\cdot)/\partial\theta_G = m(8\theta^*_G - 7\underline{\theta})\underline{\theta} - 2n(8\theta^*_G - 3\underline{\theta})$$

While this expression cannot be signed unambiguously, it is easily verified that $\qquad m \leq m_q' \leq n(2\theta^*_G - \underline{\theta})/(\theta^*_G, \underline{\theta}) \Rightarrow s_G(\theta^*_G, \underline{\theta}) < 0 \qquad$ and

$m = m_h' = 2n\alpha(\theta_G^*,\underline{\theta})/\beta(\theta_G^*,\underline{\theta}) \Rightarrow s_G(\theta_G^*,\underline{\theta}) > 0$. This implies the statements in part (i) and part (ii) of the Proposition.∎

Proof of Proposition 6.1.2
Both firms improve environmental performance in response to the subsidy irrespective of whether it is symmetric or paid to a single firm alone.

First, consider the symmetric case, where $dx_F^G = dx_F^B = dx_F > 0$. It is easily checked from (6.1a) and (6.1b) that

$$\frac{d\theta_G^*}{dx_F} = \frac{F'(\theta_G^*)T_B - F'(\theta_B^*)R_B}{J} < 0, \quad (A6.1a)$$

$$\frac{d\theta_B^*}{dx_F} = \frac{F'(\theta_B^*)R_G - F'(\theta_G^*)T_G}{J} < 0, \quad (A6.1b)$$

where the second-order derivatives $R_G < 0$, $R_B > 0$, $T_G > 0$, $T_B < 0$ are defined in analogy to (A2.12a)–(A2.12d), while observing that the last term in (A2.12a) and (A2.12d), respectively, is now $x_F k$ rather than k. The determinant is given by $J = R_G T_B - R_B T_G > 0$.

Next, consider an asymmetric change in the subsidy to the G firm, such that $dx_F^G > dx_F^B = 0$. Then from (6.1a) and (6.1b)

$$\frac{d\theta_G^*}{dx_F^G} = \frac{F'(\theta_G^*)T_B - F'(\theta_B^*)R_B}{J} < 0, \quad (A6.2a)$$

$$\frac{d\theta_B^*}{dx_F^G} = \frac{-F'(\theta_G^*)T_G}{J} < 0. \quad (A6.2b)$$

Finally, for a change in the subsidy to the B firm, such that $0 = dx_F^G < dx_F^B$,

$$\frac{d\theta_G^*}{dx_F^B} = \frac{-F'(\theta_B^*)R_B}{J} < 0, \quad (A6.3a)$$

$$\frac{d\theta_B^*}{dx_F^B} = \frac{F'(\theta_B^*)R_G - F'(\theta_G^*)T_G}{J} < 0. \quad (A6.3b)$$

Hence, in an interior regime, performance is raised in all instances.∎

Proof of Proposition 6.3.2
Consider the introduction of a marginal and symmetric subsidy of investment cost. This unambiguously raises product differentiation and thereby reduces emissions if $m \gg n$.

Consider the effect of the subsidy on product differentiation

$$\frac{d\zeta}{dx_F} = \frac{1}{\theta_B^{*2}} \left(\theta_B^* \frac{d\theta_G^*}{dx_F} - \theta_G^* \frac{d\theta_B^*}{dx_F} \right). \tag{A6.4}$$

Substituting for the reaction terms from (A6.1a) and (A6.1b) yields

$$\frac{d\zeta}{dx_F} = \frac{F'\left(\theta_G^*\right)\left(\theta_B^* T_B + \theta_G^* T_G\right) - F'\left(\theta_B^*\right)\left(\theta_B^* R_B + \theta_G^* R_G\right)}{\theta_B^{*2} J}$$

$$= \frac{x_F k \left[\left(\theta_G^* - \underline{\theta}\right)\left(\theta_B^* T_B + \theta_G^* T_G\right) - \left(\theta_B^* - \underline{\theta}\right)\left(\theta_B^* R_B + \theta_G^* R_G\right)\right]}{\theta_B^{*2} J}.$$

Now insert from (A2.12a)–(A2.12d) for the second-order R_G, R_B, T_G, T_B, while observing that the last term in (A2.12a) and (A2.12d) is now $x_F k$ rather than k. Into these expressions substitute $n \equiv \phi m$, where $\phi := n/m$. We can now factor m out of the expressions. Furthermore, since $m \gg n \Leftrightarrow \phi \approx 0$ the terms associated with the baseline margin n vanish from the derivatives in (A2.12a)–(A2.12d). For instance,

$$R_G\left(\theta_G^*, \theta_B^*\right) = \frac{-8m^2\left(\theta_B^* + 2\phi\right)\left[\left(5\theta_G^* + \theta_B^*\right)\theta_B^* - \phi\left(2\theta_G^* - 5\theta_B^*\right)\right]}{\left(4\theta_G^* - \theta_B^*\right)^4} - k$$

$$\overset{\phi \to 0}{=} \frac{-8m^2\left(5\theta_G^* - \theta_B^*\right)\theta_B^{*2}}{\left(4\theta_G^* - \theta_B^*\right)^4} - k$$

and similarly for R_B, T_G and T_B. After tedious but straightforward calculations it can be verified that $\left(\theta_B^* T_B + \theta_G^* T_G\right)_{m \gg n} \approx -x_F k \theta_B^*$ and $\left(\theta_B^* R_B + \theta_G^* R_G\right)_{m \gg n} \approx -x_F k \theta_G^*$. Hence

$$\frac{d\zeta}{dx_F}\bigg|_{m>>n} \approx \frac{-(x_F k)^2 \left(\theta_G^* - \theta_B^*\right)\theta}{\theta_B^{*2} J} < 0.$$

Observing that $d\theta_G^*/dx_F < 0$, $d\theta_B^*/dx_F < 0$, it then follows from (6.4) that $dE/dx_F\big|_{m>>n} < 0$.∎

Proof of Corollary P6.3
Consider an interior equilibrium. (i) A (marginal) subsidy paid to the G firm alone increases product differentiation and lowers emissions. A (marginal) subsidy paid to the B firm alone reduces product differentiation, and (ii) lowers emissions if $m < m_E'$, but (iii) increases emissions if $m >> n$ and if the direct effect of abatement $e'(\theta_i)$, $i = G, B$ is sufficiently small.

Part (i): Inserting from (A6.2a) and (A6.2b) into (A6.4) it is readily verified that $d\zeta/dx_F^G < 0$. It then follows immediately from (6.4) that $dE/dx_F^G > 0$. Part (ii) follows immediately from Lemma 3.1. Part (iii): Inserting from (A6.3a) and (A6.3b) into (A6.4), it is readily verified that $d\zeta/dx_F^B > 0$. Since

$$\lim_{e'(\theta_i)\to 0,\ i=B,G} \operatorname{sgn} \frac{dE}{dx_F^B}\bigg|_{m>>n} = \operatorname{sgn}\left(\frac{\partial E}{\partial \zeta}\frac{d\zeta}{dx_F^B}\right) = -1, \qquad \text{the subsidy raises}$$

emissions.∎

APPENDIX A7

Proof of Corollary P7.2
The comparative static properties shown in Table 7.1 apply with regard to the transfer rate t and the quality target ρ.

Using the first-order terms

$$r\left(\theta_G^*, \underline{\theta}, t, \rho\right) = 2(m+t)\alpha\left(\theta_G^*, \underline{\theta}\right) - (n - t\rho)\beta\left(\theta_G^*, \underline{\theta}\right) = 0,$$
$$s\left(\overline{\theta}, \theta_B^*, t, \rho\right) = (m+t)\overline{\theta}\theta_B^*\beta\left(\overline{\theta}, \theta_B^*\right) - 2(n - t\rho)\alpha\left(\overline{\theta}, \theta_B^*\right) = 0,$$

for the lower and upper boundary equilibrium, respectively, the following derivatives are readily derived:

$$\frac{d\theta_G^*}{dt} = \frac{-r_t\left(\theta_G^*,\underline{\theta},t,\rho\right)}{r_G\left(\theta_G^*,\underline{\theta},t,\rho\right)} = \underbrace{\frac{-\left[2\alpha\left(\theta_G^*,\underline{\theta}\right)+\rho\beta\left(\theta_G^*,\underline{\theta}\right)\right]}{2\left[(m+t)\left(8\theta_G^*-3\underline{\theta}\right)-2(n-t\rho)\right]}}_{<0}, \quad \text{(A7.1a)}$$

$$\frac{d\theta_G^*}{d\rho} = \frac{-r_\rho\left(\theta_G^*,\underline{\theta},t,\rho\right)}{r_G\left(\theta_G^*,\underline{\theta},t,\rho\right)} = \underbrace{\frac{-t\beta\left(\theta_G^*,\underline{\theta}\right)}{2\left[(m+t)\left(8\theta_G^*-3\underline{\theta}\right)-2(n-t\rho)\right]}}_{<0}, \quad \text{(A7.1b)}$$

$$\frac{d\theta_B^*}{dt} = \frac{-s_t\left(\overline{\theta},\theta_B^*,t,\rho\right)}{s_B\left(\overline{\theta},\theta_B^*,t,\rho\right)}$$

$$= \underbrace{\frac{-\left[\overline{\theta}\theta_B^*\beta\left(\overline{\theta},\theta_B^*\right)+2\rho\alpha\left(\overline{\theta},\theta_B^*\right)\right]}{2\left[(m+t)\left(2\overline{\theta}-7\theta_B^*\right)\overline{\theta}+(n-t\rho)\left(3\overline{\theta}-4\theta_B^*\right)\right]}}_{<0}, \quad \text{(A7.1c)}$$

$$\frac{d\theta_B^*}{d\rho} = \frac{-s_\rho\left(\overline{\theta},\theta_B^*,t,\rho\right)}{s_L\left(\overline{\theta},\theta_B^*,t,\rho\right)}$$

$$= \frac{-t\alpha\left(\overline{\theta},\theta_B^*\right)}{\underbrace{\left[(m+t)\left(2\overline{\theta}-7\theta_B^*\right)\overline{\theta}+(n-t\rho)\left(3\overline{\theta}-4\theta_B^*\right)\right]}_{<0}} > 0. \quad \text{(A7.1d)}$$

Using these derivatives and observing $m+t<0 \Leftrightarrow \beta\left(\theta_G^*,\underline{\theta}\right)<0$ the entries in Table 7.1 follow.∎

Proof of Proposition 7.4
If the investment rate k is sufficiently low, then there exists an interval $\left\lfloor m_\rho,\overline{m}_\rho\right]$ such that $R_\rho>0 \Leftrightarrow m\in\left\lfloor m_\rho,\overline{m}_\rho\right]$. For all k, $\overline{m}_\rho<m_h'$ implying $R_\rho<0$ within an interior regime.

Substituting into (7.16) from (7.5a) and (7.13a), observing $r_\rho(\cdot)=\beta(\cdot)$ and rearranging terms we find $R_\rho>0 \Leftrightarrow N_\rho(m)=-m+\frac{(n-t\rho)\beta(\cdot)}{2\left(2\theta_G^*+\underline{\theta}\right)\underline{\theta}}>0$. Let $m_\rho := m|N_\rho(m)=0$. Note that $N_\rho(0)=\frac{(n-t\rho)\beta(\cdot)}{2\left(2\theta_G^*+\underline{\theta}\right)\underline{\theta}}<0$, where for $m=0$ it is true that $r(\cdot)=-(n-\rho)\beta(\cdot)>0 \Leftrightarrow \beta(\cdot)<0$ and $N_\rho(m)\big|_{m\geq m_h}<N_\rho(m_h)=-\left[4\alpha(\cdot)\left(2\theta_G^*+\underline{\theta}\right)-\beta(\cdot)^2\theta_G^*\right]\frac{(n-\rho)}{2\beta(\cdot)\left(2\theta_G^*+\underline{\theta}\right)\theta_G^*\underline{\theta}}<0$. The existence of an interval $\left\lfloor m_\rho,\overline{m}_\rho\right]$, where $N_\rho(m)$ and

$N_\rho(m) > 0 \Leftrightarrow m \in \lfloor \underline{m}_\rho, \overline{m}_\rho \rfloor$, can then be demonstrated numerically for low values of k. One parameter combination for which this interval can be shown to exist is given by $k = 0.01$, $n = \underline{\theta} = 1$. ∎

Proof of Proposition 7.5.1
Consider an increase in the transfer rate t from $t = 0$. For given levels of environmental performance, this (i) raises industry surplus if the transfer is a subsidy for both variants and the G firm dominates in market share, and (ii) lowers welfare if the transfer is a tax on both variants and the B firm dominates in market share. (iii) The net welfare increase is always greater for a subsidy (i.e. welfare decreases in ρ).

Parts (i) and (ii): Using (7.3a)–(7.4b), (7.5a) and (7.5b) in (7.18), we obtain

$$\frac{\partial W}{\partial t}\bigg|_{t=0} = \frac{\left(\theta_G^* - \theta_B^*\right)\left\{\begin{matrix} m\theta_G^*\theta_B^*\left(4\theta_G^* + \theta_B^* - 4\rho\right) \\ + n\left[4\theta_G^*\theta_B^* - \left(4\theta_G^* + \theta_B^*\right)\rho\right]\end{matrix}\right\}}{\left(4\theta_G^* - \theta_B^*\right)^2 \theta_B^*}. \tag{A7.2}$$

Observing the boundary value (7.10), the following can be easily checked.

$$m \geq m_q(0, \rho) \text{ and } \rho \leq \theta_B^* \Rightarrow \partial W/\partial t|_{t=0} \geq 0,$$
$$m \leq m_q(0, \rho) \text{ and } \rho \geq \theta_G^* \Rightarrow \partial W/\partial t|_{t=0} \leq 0.$$

Part (iii) follows from (7.21). ∎

Proof of Proposition 7.5.2
For given levels of environmental performance, a (weak) marginal tax on both variants, with $\rho = \theta_G^*$, enhances industry surplus if the environmental margin is sufficiently high relative to the baseline margin. This requires G market share dominance.

Evaluating (A7.2) at $\rho = \theta_G^*$ together with $n = 0$ proves a sufficient condition and $m = m_q(0, \rho)$ proves a necessary condition. ∎

Proof of Lemma 7.1
$m < m_l(0, \rho) \Rightarrow \kappa_G^t < 0$; $m > m_h(0, \rho) \Rightarrow \left\{\kappa_G^t, \kappa_B^t\right\} > 0$.

From (7.7) and (7.3a)–(7.3b) it is readily verified that $\varphi_i^* = p_i^*$, $i = G, B$, for $t = 0$, with p_i^* as given by (2.2a) and (2.2b). But then

$$\kappa_G^t\big|_{t=0} = \frac{\sigma_G(m)}{2\big(4\theta_G^* - \theta_B^*\big)^3}$$ (A7.3a),

$$\kappa_B^t\big|_{t=0} = \frac{\sigma_G^I(m)}{2\big(4\theta_G^* - \theta_B^*\big)^3 \theta_B^{*2}}$$ (A7.3b),

with $\sigma_G(m)$ and $\sigma_B^I(m)$ as defined in (A4.5b) and (A4.5c), respectively. It is then easily proved by analogy to the proof of Proposition 4.4 that $\sigma_G(m)\big|_{m \leq m_l(0,\rho)} < \sigma_G[m_l(0,\rho)] < 0$. Furthermore, we have shown as part of the proof of Proposition 4.4 that $\sigma_G(m)\big|_{m > m_h(0,\rho)} > \sigma_G[m_h(0,\rho)] > 0$ and $\sigma_B^I(m)\big|_{m > m_h(0,\rho)} > \sigma_B^I[m_h(0,\rho)] > 0$. ∎

Proof of Proposition 7.6.1:
Consider a marginal increase in the transfer rate from $t = 0$. This reduces (raises) industry surplus in the lower (upper) boundary regime.

Recall $d\theta_B^*/dt \neq 0 \Leftrightarrow m > m_h(0,\rho)$ and $d\theta_G^*/dt \neq 0 \Leftrightarrow m < m_l(0,\rho)$ from Corollary P7.2. Hence, for the lower boundary regime with $m < m_l(0,\rho)$, with $m_l(0,\rho)$ as in (7.14a),

$$\frac{dW}{dt}\bigg|_{t=0} = \frac{\partial W}{\partial t}\bigg|_{t=0} + \kappa_G^t\big|_{t=0}\frac{d\theta_G^*}{dt},$$

where $\partial W/\partial t\big|_{t=0}$ is given by (A7.2) and where $\kappa_G^t\big|_{t=0}$ and $d\theta_G^*/dt$ are given by (A7.3a) and (A7.1a), respectively. Using this together with the first-order condition $r\big(\theta_G^*, \underline{\theta}, 0, \rho\big) = 2m\alpha\big(\theta_G^*, \underline{\theta}\big) - n\beta\big(\theta_G^*, \underline{\theta}\big) = 0$, and observing that $\theta_G^* < \overline{\theta} < 13\underline{\theta}/4$, as by (2.13), one can verify by tedious but straightforward calculations that $m < m_l(0,\rho) \Rightarrow dW/dt\big|_{t=0} \leq 0$.

Using (7.14b), (A7.1c) and (A7.3b) we can prove in an analogous way that $m > m_h(0,\rho) \Rightarrow (dW/dt)\big|_{t=0} \geq 0$ is true. ∎

Proof of Proposition 7.6.2
For a transfer rate t sufficiently close to zero, subsidisation (taxation) is associated with a higher industry surplus in the lower (upper) boundary regime.

Using (7.3a)–(7.4b), (7.5a) and (7.5b) in (7.21), we obtain

$$\frac{\partial W}{\partial \rho}\Big|_{t\to 0} = \frac{-t\left(\theta_G^* - \theta_B^*\right)\left[4m\theta_G^*\theta_B^* + n\left(4\theta_G^* + \theta_B^*\right)\right]}{\left(4\theta_G^* - \theta_B^*\right)^2 \theta_B^*} < 0.$$

As in the previous proposition we find for $m < m_l(0, \rho)$,

$$\frac{dW}{d\rho}\Big|_{t\to 0} = \frac{\partial W}{\partial \rho}\Big|_{t\to 0} + \kappa_G^t\Big|_{t=0} \frac{d\theta_G^*}{d\rho},$$

where $\kappa_G^t\big|_{t=0}$ and $d\theta_G^*/dt$ are given by (A7.3a) and (A7.1b), respectively.[8] One can then verify in analogy to the proof of Proposition 7.6.1 that $m < m_l(0, \rho) \Rightarrow dW/d\rho\big|_{t\to 0} \leq 0$. Taxation being characterised by a greater ρ, this implies the statement in the proposition. The proof for the upper boundary regime with $m > m_h(0, \rho)$ is analogous.∎

Proof of Proposition 7.8
(i) The output-related effect of an increase in the transfer rate reduces industry emissions. (ii) A tax is always more efficient through the output effect. (iii) The transfer reduces overall emissions if G performance does not fall by too much.

Part (i): Consider

$$\frac{dE}{dt}\Big|_{e\left(\theta_G^*\right)=\bar{e}} = \frac{\partial E}{\partial t} + \frac{1}{\underline{\theta}}\frac{\partial E}{\partial \zeta}\frac{d\theta_G^*}{dt},$$

and, using (7.23a) and (7.24), rewrite this to

$$\left. \frac{dE}{dt} \right|_{e(\theta_G^*)=\bar{e}} = \frac{\left\langle \begin{array}{c} \left(4\zeta^* - 1\right)\left\{\left[2\bar{e} + e(\underline{\theta})\right]\zeta^* - \left[\bar{e} + 2e(\underline{\theta})\zeta^*\right]\frac{\rho}{\theta}\right\} \\ -\left[2\bar{e} + e(\underline{\theta})\right]\left[\left(\bar{v} - c + t\right) + 2\frac{(n-t\rho)}{\theta}\right]\frac{1}{\theta}\frac{d\theta_G^*}{dt} \end{array} \right\rangle}{\left(4\zeta^* - 1\right)^2}.$$

Observing $2\bar{e} + e(\underline{\theta}) \le \bar{e} + 2e(\underline{\theta})\zeta^*$, we obtain

$$\left. \frac{dE}{dt} \right|_{e(\theta_G^*)=\bar{e}} < \frac{\left[2\bar{e} + e(\underline{\theta})\right]\left\{\left(4\zeta^* - 1\right)\left(\zeta^* - \frac{\rho}{\theta}\right) - \left[(m+t) + 2\frac{(n-t\rho)}{\theta}\right]\frac{1}{\theta}\frac{d\theta_G^*}{dt}\right\}}{\left(4\zeta^* - 1\right)^2}.$$

Inserting $d\theta_G^*/dt = -\left[2\alpha(\zeta^*) + \rho\beta(\zeta^*)\right]\underline{\theta}^2/r_G$ as from (A7.1a), with $r_G = 2\left[(m+t)(8\zeta^* - 3) - 2\frac{(n-t\rho)}{\theta}\right]\underline{\theta} < 0$, $\alpha(\zeta^*) = 4\zeta^{*2} - 3\zeta^* + 2$ and $\beta(\zeta^*) = 4\zeta^* - 7$, and collecting terms we obtain

$$\left. \frac{dE}{dt} \right|_{e(\theta_G^*)=\bar{e}} < \frac{\left[2\bar{e} + e(\underline{\theta})\right]\chi}{\left(4\zeta^* - 1\right)^2 r_G} \qquad (A7.4)$$

$$\chi = \left\{ \begin{array}{c} 4(m+t)\left(16\zeta^{*3} - 8\zeta^{*2} + 1\right) - 8\frac{(n-t\rho)}{\theta}\left(\zeta^* - 1\right) \\ -\frac{\rho}{\theta}\left[(m+t)\left(64\zeta^{*2} - 44\zeta^* + 13\right) - 6\frac{(n-t\rho)}{\theta}\left(4\zeta^* - 3\right)\right] \end{array} \right\}.$$

From the first-order condition $r(\zeta^*, \underline{\theta}, t, \rho) = 0$, we have $(m+t) = \frac{(n-t\rho)}{\theta}\left[\beta(\zeta^*)/2\alpha(\zeta^*)\right]$. Inserting this and again collecting terms gives $\chi = (n - t\rho)\hat{\chi}(\rho)/\left[2\underline{\theta}\alpha(\zeta^*)\right]$ with

$$\hat{\chi} = \left[\begin{array}{c} 4\left(64\zeta^{*4} - 160\zeta^{*3} + 84\zeta^{*2} - 16\zeta^* + 1\right) \\ -\frac{\rho}{\theta}\left(64\zeta^{*3} - 336\zeta^{*2} + 156\zeta^* - 19\right) \end{array} \right].$$

Observing $\zeta^* \le \bar{\theta}/\underline{\theta} < 13/4$, as implied by condition (2.13), it is easily checked that $\partial\hat{\chi}/\partial\rho > 0$. It is now readily verified for any $\zeta^* = \bar{\zeta}$ that

$\chi\big|_{\zeta^*=\bar{\zeta};\rho>\underline{\theta}} > \chi\big|_{\zeta^*=\bar{\zeta};\rho=\underline{\theta}} > 0$. Observing this and $r_G < 0$ it follows from (A7.4) that $(dE/dt)\big|_{e(\theta_G^*)=\bar{e}} < 0$.

Part (ii): Using (7.25) and (7.23a) and observing $d\theta_G^*/d\rho = -t\beta(\zeta^*)\underline{\theta}/r_G$ it can be shown by an analogous proof that

$$\frac{dE}{d\rho}\bigg|_{e(\theta_G^*)=\bar{e}} = \frac{\partial E}{\partial \rho} + \frac{1}{\underline{\theta}}\frac{\partial E}{\partial \zeta}\frac{d\theta_G^*}{d\rho} < 0.$$

Part (iii) follows immediately from part (i) under observation of (7.27). ∎

Proof of Proposition 7.10
Suppose $n = 0$ and consider the introduction of a marginal transfer, where t is varied away from $t = 0$. (i) Suppose the spread between unit emissions is sufficiently narrow, i.e. $e(\theta_B^*)/e(\bar{\theta}) < 82$. Then, an increase in the transfer rate t lowers industry emissions by the output effect only if the transfer constitutes a tax on both variants, i.e. only if $\rho > \bar{\theta}$. (ii) A tax is more prone to decrease emissions by the output effect.

Consider the output-related impact of the transfer

$$\frac{dE}{dt}\bigg|_{e(\theta_B^*)=\underline{e};t=0} = \frac{\partial E}{\partial t} - \left(\frac{\zeta^*}{\theta_B^*}\frac{\partial E}{\partial \zeta} - \frac{\partial E}{\partial \theta_B}\bigg|_{\zeta^*=\bar{\zeta};e(\theta_B^*)=\underline{e}}\right)\frac{d\theta_B^*}{dt}.$$

From (7.23b), it follows that the second term in brackets is zero for $n = 0$. Then, using (7.24) and (7.23a), while still observing $n = 0$, rewrite the above expression to

$$\frac{dE}{dt}\bigg|_{e(\theta_B^*)=\bar{e};t=0} = \frac{\begin{pmatrix}(4\zeta^*-1)\{[2e(\bar{\theta})+\underline{e}]\zeta^* - [e(\bar{\theta})+2\underline{e}\zeta^*]\frac{\rho}{\theta_B^*}\} \\ + [2e(\bar{\theta})+\underline{e}]m\frac{\zeta^*}{\theta_B^*}\frac{d\theta_B^*}{dt}\end{pmatrix}}{(4\zeta^*-1)^2}.$$

Substituting $d\theta_B^*/dt\big|_{t=0}$ from (A7.1c) and collecting terms we obtain

$$\frac{dE}{dt}\bigg|_{e(\theta_B^*)=\underline{e};\ t=0} = \frac{\xi}{2(4\zeta^*-1)^2(2\zeta^*-7)}, \tag{A7.5}$$

$$\xi := \left\{\begin{array}{l} \left[2e(\overline{\theta})+\underline{e}\right]\zeta^*\left(16\zeta^{*2}-64\zeta^*+21\right) \\ -2\frac{\rho}{\theta_B^*}\left[e(\overline{\theta})\left(16\zeta^{*2}-36\zeta^*+11\right)+\underline{e}\left(16\zeta^{*3}-56\zeta^{*2}+11\zeta^*+2\right)\right]\end{array}\right\}.$$

From the first-order condition, $m(4\zeta^*-7)\zeta^*=0$ it follows that $\zeta^* = \overline{\theta}/\theta_B^* = 7/4$. Inserting this and rearranging yields

$$\xi = \frac{21}{4}\left\{\frac{\rho}{\theta}\left[2e(\overline{\theta})+43\underline{e}\right]-42\left[2e(\overline{\theta})+\underline{e}\right]\right\}.$$

Noting that $2\zeta^* = 7/2 < 7$, it follows from (A7.5) that $dE/dt\big|_{e(\theta_B^*)=\underline{e};\ t=0} \geq 0 \Leftrightarrow \xi \leq 0$. Obviously

$$\xi \leq 0 \Leftrightarrow \rho \leq \frac{42\left[2e(\overline{\theta})+\underline{e}\right]}{\left[2e(\overline{\theta})+43\underline{e}\right]}\overline{\theta},$$

where it is readily verified that the fraction is greater than one if $\underline{e}/e(\overline{\theta})<82$. In this case, only a sufficiently strong tax on both variants can guarantee $dE/dt\big|_{e(\theta_B^*)=\underline{e}} \leq 0$, as stated in part (i). Part (ii) of the Lemma follows by an analogous proof. ∎

NOTES

1. We have omitted from this list some notation which is used for auxiliary purposes in some of the proofs.
2. We write $R_i := \frac{\partial R(\cdot)}{\partial \theta_i}$; $i=G,B$, and similarly for the functions $T(\cdot)$, $r(\cdot)$, and $s(\cdot)$.
3. In contrast to much of the subsequent literature, Ronnen (1991: footnote 6) points out that the positive profit condition is not trivial.
4. For $\underline{\theta}=0$, this proof applies to a standard model of vertical differentiation with a quadratic investment cost such as the one in Motta (1993). Note the error in the proof in Appendix I

part (a) in Motta (1993), which erroneously simplifies his proof. For correctness, the present proof would have to be applied.

5. Obviously, in Nash equilibrium $b_G\left(\theta_B{}^*\right) = \theta_G{}^*$ and $b_B\left(\theta_G{}^*\right) = \theta_B{}^*$.

6. The first term in the bracelets is positive if $\theta_G > (7/4)b_B(\theta_G)$, which is satisfied in an interior equilibrium.

7. We find θ_B^* as a function $b_B(\zeta)$ of ζ alone.

8. Note that both $\partial W/\partial\rho$ and $d\theta_i{}^*/d\rho$, $i = G, B$ are linear functions of t. But then, $t \to 0$ has no implications for the sign of the derivative.

Bibliography

Aghion, P. and P. Bolton (1984), 'Contracts as a Barrier to Entry', *American Economic Review* **77**, 338–401.

Akerlof, G. (1970), 'The Market for Lemons: Qualitative Uncertainty and the Market Mechanism', *Quarterly Journal of Economics* **84**, 488–500.

Amacher, G.S., E. Koskela and M. Ollikainen (2004), 'Environmental Quality Competition and Eco-Labeling', *Journal of Environmental Economics and Management* **47**, 284–306.

Anderson, S.P., A. de Palma and J.-F. Thisse (1992), *Discrete Choice Theory of Product Differentiation*, Cambridge, Mass. and London: MIT Press.

Andreoni, J. (1990), 'Impure Altruism and Donations to Public Goods: A Theory of Warm-glow Giving', *Economic Journal* **100**, 464–77.

Anstine, J. (2000), 'Consumers' Willingness to Pay for Recycled Content in Plastic Kitchen Garbage Bags: a hedonic price approach', *Applied Economics Letters* **7**, 35–9.

Anton, W.R.Q., G. Deltas and M. Khanna (2004), 'Incentives for Environmental Self-regulation and Implications for Environmental Performance', *Journal of Environmental Economics and Management* **48**, 632–54.

Antweiler, W. and K. Harrison (2003), 'Toxic Release Inventories and Green Consumerism: Empirical Evidence from Canada', *Canadian Journal of Economics* **36**, 495–520.

Aoki, R. and T.J. Prusa (1996), 'Sequential versus Simultaneous Choice with Endogenous Quality', *International Journal of Industrial Organisation* **15**, 103–21.

Armstrong, M., S. Cowan and C. Doyle (1994), *Regulatory Reform – Economic Analysis and British Experience*, Cambridge, Mass.: MIT Press.

Arora, S. and T.C. Cason (1995), 'An Experiment in Voluntary Environmental Regulation: Participation in EPA's 33/50 Program', *Journal of Environmental Economics and Management* **28**, 271–86.

Arora, S. and S. Gangopadhyay (1995), 'Toward a Theoretical Model of Voluntary Overcompliance', *Journal of Economic Behaviour and Organization* **28**, 289–309.

Ayres, R.U. and A.V. Kneese (1969), 'Production, Consumption, and Externalities', *American Economic Review* **59**, 282–97.

Bansal, S. and S. Gangopadhyay (2003), 'Tax/subsidy Policies in the Presence of Environmentally Aware Consumers', *Journal of Environmental Economics and Management* **45**, 333–55.

Barnett, A.H. (1980), 'The Pigouvian Tax Rule under Monopoly', *American Economic Review* **70**, 1037–41.

Baron, D.P. (2001), 'Private Politics, Corporate Social Responsibility, and Integrated Strategy', *Journal of Economics and Management Strategy* **10**, 7–45.

Barrett, S. (1994), 'Strategic Environmental Policy and International Trade', *Journal of Public Economics* **54**, 325–38.

Bartik, T. (1987), 'The Estimation of Demand Parameters in Hedonic Price Models', *Journal of Political Economy* **95**, 81–8.

Baumol, W.J. and W.E. Oates (1988), *The Theory of Environmental Policy* (2nd edn.), Cambridge: Cambridge University Press.

Beath, J., Y. Katsoulacos and D. Ulph (1987) 'Sequential Product Innovation and Industry Evolution', *Economic Journal* (Supplement) **97**, 32–43.

Beath, J. and Y. Katsoulacos (1991), *The Economic Theory of Product Differentiation*, Cambridge: Cambridge University Press.

Becker, G.S. (1991), 'A Note on Restaurant Pricing and Other Examples of Social Influence on Price', *Journal of Political Economy* **99**, 1109–16.

Berry, S., J. Levinsohn, and A. Pakes (1995) 'Automobile Prices in Market Equilibrium', *Econometrica* **63**, 841–90, reprinted in L.M.B. Cabral (ed) (2000), *Readings in Industrial Organization*, Malden, Mass. and Oxford: Blackwell.

Besanko, D. (1987), 'Performance versus Design Standards in the Regulation of Pollution', *Journal of Public Economics* **34**, 19–44.

Besanko, D., S. Donnenfeld and L.J. White (1988), 'The Multiproduct firm, Quality Choice, and Regulation', *Journal of Industrial Economics* **36**, 411–29.

Biglaiser, G. and J.W. Friedman (1994), 'Middlemen as Guarantors of Quality', *International Journal of Industrial Organisation* **12**, 509–31.

Bjoerner, T.B., L.G. Hansen and C.S. Russell (2004), 'Environmental Labeling and Consumers' Choice – An Empirical Analysis of the Effect of the Nordic Swan, *Journal of Environmental Economics and Management* **47**, 411–34.

Blackman, A. and J. Boyd (1999), 'The Economics of Tailored Regulation: Will Site-specific Environmental Regulations Necessarily Improve Welfare?' Discussion Paper 00-03, Washington, DC: Resources for the Future.

Boerkey, P. and F. Levêque (1998), *Voluntary Approaches for Environmental Protection in the European Union*, Paris: OECD.

Bonanno, G. (1986), 'Vertical Differentiation with Cournot Competition', *Economic Notes* 2, 68–91.

Boom, A. (1995), 'Asymmetric International Minimum Quality Standards and Vertical Differentiation', *Journal of Industrial Economics* 43, 101–19.

Brockmann, K.L., J. Hemmelskamp and O. Hohmeyer (1996), *Certified Tropical Timber and Consumer Behaviour*, Heidelberg: Physica.

Buchanan, J.M. (1969), 'External Diseconomies, Corrective Taxes and Market Structure', *American Economic Review* 59, 174–7.

Cabral, L.M.B. (2000a), *Introduction to Industrial Organization*, Cambridge, Mass. and London, UK: The MIT Press.

Cabral, L.M.B. (2000b), *Readings in Industrial Organization*, Malden, Mass. and Oxford: Blackwell.

Caplin, A. and B. Nalebuff (1991), 'Aggregation and Imperfect Competition: On the Existence of Equilibrium', *Econometrica* 59, 26–61.

Carlsson, F. (2000), 'Environmental Taxation and Strategic Commitment in Duopoly Models', *Environmental and Resource Economics* 15, 243–56.

Carraro, C. and A. Soubeyran (1996a), 'Environmental Feedbacks and Optimal Taxation in Oligopoly', in A. Xepapadeas (ed), *Economic Policy for the Environment and Natural Resources*, Cheltenham, UK: Edward Elgar.

Carraro, C. and A. Soubeyran (1996b), 'Environmental Policy and the Choice of Production Technology', in C. Carraro, Y. Katsoulacos and A. Xepapadeas (eds.), *Environmental Policy and Market Structure*, Dordrecht: Kluwer.

Champsaur, P. and J.-C. Rochet (1989), 'Multiproduct Duopolists', *Econometrica* 57, 533–57.

Choi, C.J. and H.S. Shin (1992), 'A Comment on a Model of Vertical Product Differentiation', *Journal of Industrial Economics* 40, 229–31.

Conrad, K. (1993), 'Taxes and Subsidies for Pollution-Intensive Industries as Trade Policy', *Journal of Environmental Economics and Management* 25, 121–35.

Conrad, K. (1996), 'Energy Tax and Competition in Energy Efficiency. The Case of Consumer Durables', Paper presented at the European Association of Environmental and Resource Economists (EAERE) Conference, Lisboa.

Conrad, K. and J. Wang (1993), 'The Effect of Emission Taxes and Abatement Subsidies on Market Structure, '*International Journal of Industrial Organization* 11, 499–518.

Constantatos, C. and S. Perrakis (1998), 'Minimum Quality Standards, Entry, and the Timing of the Quality Decision', *Journal of Regulatory Economics* **13**, 47–58.

Constantatos, C. and E.S. Sartzetakis (1995), 'Environmental Taxation when Market Structure is Endogenous: the Case of Vertical Product Differentiation', Milano: ENI Nota di lavoro 76.95.

Couton, C., F. Gardes and Y. Thepaut (1996), 'Hedonic Prices for Environmental and Safety Characteristics and the Akerlof Effect in the French Car Market', *Applied Economic Letters* **3**, 435–40.

Crampes, C. and A. Hollander (1995), 'Duopoly and Quality Standards', *European Economic Review* **39**, 71–82.

Crampes, C. and L. Ibanez (1996), 'The Economics of Green Labels', Toulouse: University of Toulouse. G.R.E.M.A.Q. cahier 96.36.439.

Cremer, H. and J.-F. Thisse (1994a), 'On the Taxation of Polluting Products in a Differentiated Industry', Milan, Fondazione ENI Enrico Mattei: nota di lavoro 31.94.

Cremer, H. and J.-F. Thisse (1994b), 'Commodity Taxation in a Differentiated Oligopoly', *International Economic Review* **25**, 613–33.

Cremer, H. and J.-F. Thisse (1999), 'On the Taxation of Polluting Products in a Differentiated Industry', *European Economic Review* **43**, 575–94.

D'Aspremont, C., J. Gabsewicz, and J.-F. Thisse (1979), 'On Hotelling's Stability in Competition' *Econometrica* **17**, 1145–51.

Damania, D. (1996), 'Pollution Taxes and Pollution Abatement in an Oligopoly Supergame', *Journal of Environmental Economics and Management* **30**, 323–36.

Das, S.P. and S. Donnenfeld (1989) 'Oligopolistic Competition and International Trade. Quantity and Quality Restrictions', *Journal of International Economics* **27**, 299–318.

Dasgupta, S., H. Hettige and D. Wheeler (2000), 'What Improves Environmental Compliance? Evidence from Mexican Industry', *Journal of Environmental Economics and Management* **39**, 39–66.

De Fraja, G. (1996), 'Product Line Competition in Vertically Differentiated Markets', *International Journal of Industrial Organization* **14**, 389–414.

De Palma, A., V. Ginsburgh, Y.Y. Papageorgiou and J.-F. Thisse (1985), 'The Principle of Minimum Differentiation holds under Sufficient Heterogeneity', *Econometrica* **53**, 767–81.

Dixit, A. (1980), 'The Role of Investment in Entry-Deterrence', *Economic Journal* **90**, 95–106.

Dixit, A. and J. Stiglitz (1977), 'Monopolistic Competition and Optimum Product Diversity', *American Economic Review* **67**, 297–308.

Donnenfeld, S. and S. Weber (1992), 'Vertical Product Differentiation with Entry', *International Journal of Industrial Organization* **10**, 449–72.

Donnenfeld, S. and S. Weber (1995), 'Limit Qualities and Entry Deterrence', *RAND Journal of Economics* **40**, 229–32.

Donnenfeld, S. and L.J. White (1988), 'Product Variety and the Inefficiency of Monopoly', *Economica* **55**, 393–401.

Dorfman, R. and P.O. Steiner (1954), 'Optimal Advertising and Optimal Quality', *American Economic Review* **44**, 826–36.

Dos Santos Ferreira, R. and J.-F. Thisse (1996), 'Horizontal and Vertical Differentiation: The Launhardt Model', *International Journal of Industrial Organization* **14**, 485–506.

Dosi, C. and M. Moretto (1995), 'Pollution Accumulation and Firm Incentives to Promote Irreversible Technological Change Under Uncertain Private Benefits', Milano: ENI nota di lavoro 90.95.

Dosi, C. and M. Moretto (1996), 'Environmental Innovation and Public Subsidies under Asymmetry of Information and Nework Externalities', Milano: ENI nota di lavoro 84.96.

Dosi, C. and M. Moretto (2001), 'Is Eco-labelling a Reliable Environmental Policy Measure?', *Environmental and Resource Economics* **18**, 113–27.

Dowell, G., S. Hart and B. Yeung (2000), 'Do Corporate Global Environmental Standards Create or Destroy Market Value?', *Management Science* **46**, 1059–74.

Eaton, B.C. and R.G. Lipsey (1989), 'Product Differentiation', in R. Schmalensee and R.D. Willig (eds), *Handbook of Industrial Organization*, vol. I, Amsterdam and New York: Elsevier.

Ebert, U. (1991/92), 'Pigouvian Tax and Market Structure', *Finanz Archiv* **49**, 154–66.

Ecchia, G. and L. Lambertini (1997), 'Minimum Quality Standards and Collusion', *Journal of Industrial Economics* **45**, 101–13.

Economides, N. (1986), 'Minimal and Maximal Product Differentiation in Hotelling's Duopoly', *Economic Letters* **21**, 67–71.

Economides, N. (1989), 'Quality Variations and Maximal Variety Differentiation', *Regional Science and Urban Economics* **19**, 21–9.

EEA (European Environment Agency) (2000), 'Environmental taxes: recent developments in tools for integration', *Environmental Issues Series* 18, Copenhagen: EEA.

EEA (European Environment Agency) (2001), *Environmental signals 2001*, European Environment Agency regular indicator report, Copenhagen: EEA.

Ekins, P. (1999), 'European Environmental Taxes and Charges: Recent Experience, Issues and Trends', *Ecological Economics* **31**, 39–62.

European Commission (2003a), 'Reference Document on Best Available Techniques for Intensive Rearing of Poultry and Pigs', Sevilla, http://eippcb.jrc.es/cgi-bin/locatemr?ilf_final_0703.pdf.

European Commission (2003b), 'Reference Document on Best Available Techniques for the Textiles Industry', Sevilla, http://eippcb.jrc.es/cgi-bin/locatemr?txt_final_0703.pdf.

Feddersen, T.J. and T.W. Gilligan (2001), 'Saints and Markets: Activists and the Supply of Credence Goods', *Journal of Economics and Management Strategy* **10**, 149–71.

Feenstra, R.C. and J.A. Levinsohn (1995), 'Estimating Markups and Market Conduct with Multidimensional Product Attributes', *Review of Economic Studies* **62**, 19–52.

Frey, B.S. (1992), 'Tertium Datur. Pricing, Regulation and Intrinsic Motivation', *Kyklos* **45**, 161–84.

Fudenberg, D. and J. Tirole (1985), 'Preemption and Rent Equalization in the Adoption of New Technology', *Review of Economic Studies* **53**, 383–401.

Fullerton, D. and W. Wu (1998), 'Policies for Green Design', *Journal of Environmental Economics and Management* **36**, 131–48.

Gabel, H.L. and B. Sinclair-Desgagné (1993), 'Managerial Incentives and Environmental Compliance', *Journal of Environmental Economics and Management* **24**, 229–40.

Gabsewicz, J.J. and J.-F. Thisse (1979), 'Price Competition, Quality and Income Disparities', *Journal of Economic Theory* **20**, 340–59.

Gal-Or, E. (1983), 'Quality and Quantity Competition', *Bell Journal of Economics* **14**, 590–600.

Garella, P.G. and M. Peitz (2000), 'Intermediation can Replace Certification', *Journal of Economics and Management Strategy* **9**, 1–24.

Glachant, M. (1999), 'The cost efficiency of voluntary agreements for regulating industrial pollution: a Coasean approach', in C. Carraro and F. Lévêque (eds), *Voluntary Approaches in Environmental Policy*, Dordrecht: Kluwer.

Goldberg, P.K. (1998), 'The Effects of the Corporate Average Fuel Efficiency Standards in the US', *Journal of Industrial Economics* **46**, 1–33.

Golub, J. (1998), *New Instruments for Environmental Policy in the EU*, London and New York: Routledge.

Grilo, I., O. Shy and J.-F. Thisse (2001), 'Price Competition when Consumer Behavior is Characterized by Conformity or Vanity', *Journal of Public Economics* **80**, 385–408.

Haeckner, J. (1994), 'Collusive Pricing in Markets for Vertically Differentiated Products', *International Journal of Industrial Organization* **12**, 155–77.

Hamilton, J.T. (1995), 'Pollution as News. Media and Stock Market Reactions to the Toxics Release Inventory Data', *Journal of Environmental Economics and Management* **28**, 98–113.

Hanley, N., J.F. Shogren and B. White (1997), *Environmental Economics. In Theory and Practice*, Basingstoke and London: Macmillan.

Hansen, L.G. (1999), 'Environmental Regulation through Voluntary Agreements', in C. Carraro and F. Lévêque (eds), *Voluntary Approaches in Environmental Policy*, Dordrecht: Kluwer.

Harford, J.D. (1997), 'Firm Ownership Patterns and Motives for Voluntary Pollution Control', *Managerial and Decision Economics* **18**, 421–31.

Helfand, G.E. (1991), 'Standards versus Standards: The Effects of Different Pollution Restrictions', *American Economic Review* **81**, 622–34.

Henriques, I. and P. Sadorsky (1996), 'The Determinants of an Environmentally Responsive Firm: An Empirical Approach', *Journal of Environmental Economics and Management* **30**, 381–95.

Herguera, I. and S. Lutz (1996), 'Minimum Quality Standards as Facilitating Devices: An Example With Leapfrogging and Exit', London: CEPR Discussion Paper 1522.

Herguera, I. and S. Lutz (1997), 'International Leapfrogging and Subsidies', London: CEPR Discussion Paper 1606.

Hollander, H. (1990), 'A Social Exchange Approach to Voluntary Cooperation', *American Economic Review* **80**, 1157–67.

Holmstrom, B. and P. Milgrom (1991), 'Multi-task Principal Agent Analysis', *Journal of Theoretical and Institutional Economics* **147**, 24–52.

Hoppe, H.C. (2000), 'Second-mover Advantages in the Strategic Adoption of New Technology under Uncertainty', *International Journal of Industrial Organization* **18**, 315–38.

Hotelling, H. (1929), 'Stability in Competition' *Economic Journal* **39**, 41–57.

Hung, N.M. and N. Schmitt (1988), 'Quality Competition and Threat of Entry in Duopoly', *Economics Letters* **27**, 287–92.

Hung, N.M. and N. Schmitt (1992), 'Vertical Product Differentiation, Threat of Entry and Quality Changes', in J.M.A. Gee and G. Norman (eds), *Market Strategy and Structure*, New York: Harvester Wheatsheaf.

Jaffe, A.B., R.G. Newell and R.N. Stavins (2000), 'Technological Change and the Environment', Cambridge, Mass.: NBER Working Paper 7970.

Jaffe, A.B. and R.N. Stavins (1995), 'Dynamic Incentives of Environmental Regulations. The Effects of Alternative Policy Instruments on

Technology Diffusion', *Journal of Environmental Economics and Management* **29**, S43–63.

Katsoulacos, Y. and A. Xepapadeas (1995), 'Environmental Policy under Oligopoly with Endogenous Market Structure', *Scandinavian Journal of Economics* **97**, 411–20.

Katsoulacos, Y. and A. Xepapadeas (1996), 'Emission Taxes and Market Structure', in C. Carraro, Y. Katsoulacos and A. Xepapadeas (eds), *Environmental Policy and Market Structure*, Dordrecht: Kluwer.

Kemp, R. (1997), *Environmental Policy and Technical Change. A Comparison of the Technological Impact of Policy Instruments*, Cheltenham, UK and Brookfields, US: Edward Elgar.

Khanna, M. (2001), 'Non-mandatory Approaches to Environmental Protection', *Journal of Economic Surveys* **15**, 291–324.

Khanna, M. and W.R.Q. Anton (2002), 'Corporate Environmental Management: Regulatory and Market-based Pressures', *Land Economics* **78**, 539–558.

Khanna, M. and L. Damon (1999), 'EPA's Voluntary 33/50 Program: Impact on Toxic Releases and Economic Performance of Firms', *Journal of Environmental Economics and Management* **37**, 1–25.

Khanna, M., W.R.H. Quimio and D. Bojilova (1998), 'Toxic Release Information: a Policy Tool for Environmental Protection', *Journal of Environmental Economics and Management* **36**, 243–66.

Kirchhoff, S. (2000), 'Green Business and Blue Angels: a Model of Voluntary Overcompliance with Symmetric Information', *Environmental and Resource Economics* **15**, 403–20.

Klemperer, P. (1995), 'Competition when Consumers have Switching Costs. An Overview with Applications to Industrial Organization, Macroeconomics, and International Trade', *Review of Economic Studies* **62**, 515–39.

Kreps, D.M. and J.A. Scheinkman (1983), 'Quantity Precommitment and Bertrand Competition Yield Cournot Outcomes', *Bell Journal of Economics* **14**, 326–37.

Kreps, D.M., and R. Wilson (1982), 'Reputation and Imperfect Information', *Journal of Economic Theory* **27**, 253–79.

Krishna, K. (1990), 'Protection and the Product Line: Monopoly and Product Quality', *International Economic Review* **31**, 87–102.

Kuhn, M. (1998a) 'Environmental Policy, Firm Location and Green Consumption', in M. Accutt and P. Mason (eds), *Environmental Valuation, Economic Policy and Sustainability: Recent Advances in Environmental Economics*, Cheltenham UK and Northampton, Mass.: Edward Elgar.

Kuhn, M. (1998b) 'Going Green or Going Abroad? Environmental Policy, Firm Location and Green Consumerism', in N. Hanley and H. Folmer (eds), *Game Theory and the Environment*, Cheltenham UK and Northampton, Mass.: Edward Elgar.

Kuhn, M. (1999), 'Green Lemons. Environmental Labels and Entry into an Environmentally Differentiated Market under Asymmetric Information', University of Rostock: Thuenen-Series of Applied Economic Theory 20.

Kuhn, M. (2000a), 'Low Quality Leadership in Vertically Differentiated Duopoly', University of York: Discussion Papers in Economics 2000/38.

Kuhn, M. (2000b), 'Dominance and Market Coverage in a Model of Vertical Product Differentiation', unpublished mimeo.

Laffont, J.-J. and J. Tirole (1993), *A Theory of Incentives in Procurement and Regulation*, Cambridge, Mass. and London: The MIT Press.

Lancaster, K. (1966), 'A New Approach to Consumer Theory', *Journal of Political Economy* **74**, 132–57.

Lange, A. and T. Requate (1999), 'Emission Taxes for Price-setting Firms: Differentiated Commodities and Monopolistic Competition', in E. Petrakis, E.S. Sartzetakis and A. Xepapadeas (eds), *Environmental Regulation and Market Power: Competition, Time Consistency and International Trade*, Cheltenham, UK and Northampton, Mass.: Edward Elgar.

Lanoie, P., B. Laplante and M. Roy (1997), 'Can Capital Markets Create Incentives for Pollution Control?; Policy research working paper 1753, Environment, Infrastructure and Agriculture Division, Washington, DC: World Bank.

Lehmann-Grube, U. (1997), 'Strategic Choice of Quality when Quality is Costly: the Persistence of the High-quality Advantage', *RAND Journal of Economics* **28**, 372–84.

Leland, H. (1979), 'Quacks, Lemons, and Licensing: A Theory of Minimum Quality Standards', *Journal of Political Economy* **87**, 1328–46.

Lévêque, F. and A. Nadaï (1995), 'A Firm's Involvement in the Policy-Making Process', in H Folmer, H.L. Gabel and H. Opschoor (eds), *Principles of Environmental and Resource Economics*, Aldershot: Edward Elgar.

Lombardini-Riipinen, C. (2002), 'Essays on Environmental Quality Competition in a Vertically Differentiated Duopoly Model', PhD Thesis, University of Helsinki: Research Reports No. 92: 2002.

Lorek, S. and R. Lucas (2003), 'Towards Sustainable Market Strategies. A Case Study on Eco-textiles and Green Power', Wuppertal Institute for Environment and Energy: Wuppertal Papers No. 130.

Lutz, S. (1997), 'Vertical Product Differentiation and Entry Deterrence', *Journal of Economics* **65**, 79–102.

Lutz, S., T.P. Lyon and J.W. Maxwell (2000), 'Quality Leadership when Regulatory Standards are Forthcoming', *Journal of Industrial Economics* **48**, 331–48.

Maloney, M.T. and R.E. McCormick (1982), 'A Positive Theory of Environmental Quality Regulation', *Journal of Law and Economics* **25**, 99–123.

Mankiw, N.G. and M.D. Whinston (1986), 'Free Entry and Social Inefficiency', *RAND Journal of Economics* **17**, 48–58.

Mason, C.F. (2001), 'On the Economics of Eco-Labelling', Paper presented at the EAERE Conference 2001 Southampton.

Mattoo, A. and H.V. Singh (1994), 'Eco-Labelling: Policy Considerations', *Kyklos* **47**, 53–65.

Maxwell, J., T.P. Lyon and S.C. Hackett (2000), 'Self-regulation and Social Welfare: the Political Economy of Corporate Environmentalism', *Journal of Law and Economics* **43**, 583–618.

Milgrom, P. and J. Roberts (1986), 'Prices and Advertising Signals of Product Quality', *Journal of Political Economy* **94**, 796–821.

Millock, K. and F. Salanié (2000), 'Collective Environmental Agreements: An Analysis of the Problems of Free-Riding and Collusion', Milano: ENI nota di lavoro 108.2000.

Moorthy, K.S. (1988), 'Product and Price Competition in a Duopoly Market', *Marketing Science* **7**, 141–68.

Moraga-González, J.L. and N. Padrón-Fumero (1997), 'Pollution linked to Consumption: A Study of Policy Instruments in an Environmentally Differentiated Duopoly', Madrid: Universidad Carlos III working paper 97-06.

Moraga-González, J.L. and N. Padrón-Fumero (2002), 'Environmental Policy in a Green Market', *Environmental and Resource Economics* **22**, 419–47.

Motta, M. (1993), 'Endogenous Quality Choice: Price vs. Quantity Competition', *Journal of Industrial Economics* **41**, 113–31.

Motta, M. and J.-F. Thisse (1993), 'Minimum Quality Standards as an Environmental Policy: Domestic and International Effects', Milano: ENI nota di lavoro 20.93.

Motta, M. and J.-F. Thisse (1999), 'Minimum Quality Standards as an Environmental Policy: Domestic and International Effects', in E. Petrakis, E.S. Sartzetakis and A. Xepapadeas (eds), *Environmental Regulation and*

Market Power: Competition, Time Consistency and International Trade, Cheltenham, UK and Northampton, Mass.: Edward Elgar.

Mussa, M. and S. Rosen (1978), 'Monopoly and Product Quality', *Journal of Economic Theory* **18**, 301–17.

Myles, G.D. (1995), *Public Economics*, Cambridge: Cambridge University Press.

Myles, G.D. and A. Uyduranoglu (2002), 'Product Quality and Environmental Taxation', *Journal of Transport Economics and Policy* **36**, 233–66.

Naylor, R.A. (1990), 'A Social Custom Model of Collective Action', *European Journal of Political Economy* **6**, 201–16.

Neven, D. and J.-F. Thisse (1990), 'On Quality and Variety Competition' in J.J. Gabsewicz, J.F. Richard and L. Wolsey (eds), *Economic Decision Making: Games, Econometrics, and Optimization. Contributions in Honour of Jacques Dreze*, Amsterdam: North-Holland.

Newell, R.G., A.B. Jaffe and R.N. Stavins (1999), 'The Induced Innovation Hypothesis and Energy-Saving Technological Change', *Quarterly Journal of Economics* **114**, 941–75.

Nimon, W. and J. Beghin (1999), 'Are Eco-Labels Valuable? Evidence from the Apparel Industry', *American Journal of Agricultural Economics* **81**, 801–11.

Oates, W.E., P.R. Portney and A.M. McGartland (1989), 'The Net Benefits of Incentive Based Regulation: A Case Study of Environmental Standard Setting', *American Economic Review* **79**, 1233–42.

OECD (1991), *Environmental Labelling in OECD Countries*, Paris: OECD.

OECD (1997), *Eco-Labelling: Actual Effects of Selected Programmes*, Paris: OECD.

OECD (1999a), *Economic Instruments for Pollution Control and Natural Resource Management in OECD Countries. A Survey*, Paris: OECD.

OECD (1999b) *Trade Issues in the Greening of Public Purchasing*, Paris: OECD.

OECD (2000a), *Database on Environmentally Related Taxes*, Paris, OECD, http://www.oecd.org/env/policies/taxes/index.htm.

OECD (2000b), *Behavioural Responses to Environmentally Related Taxes*, Paris: OECD.

OECD (2000c), *Greening Tax Mixes in OECD Countries: A Preliminary Assessment*, Paris: OECD.

Opschoor, J.B. and H.B. Vos (1989), *Economic Instruments for Environmental Protection*, Paris: OECD.

Petrakis, E. (1999), 'Diffusion of Abatement Technologies in a Differentiated Industry', in E. Petrakis, E.S. Sartzetakis and A. Xepapadeas (eds), *Environmental Regulation and Market Power:*

Competition, Time Consistency and International Trade, Cheltenham, UK and Northampton, Mass.: Edward Elgar.

Petrakis, E. and A. Xepapadeas (1999), 'Does Government Precommitment Promote Environmental Innovation?' in E. Petrakis, E.S. Sartzetakis and A. Xepapadeas (eds), *Environmental Regulation and Market Power: Competition, Time Consistency and International Trade*, Cheltenham, UK and Northampton, Mass.: Edward Elgar.

Pigou, A.C. (1938), *The Economics of Welfare* (4th edn), London: Macmillan.

Poyago-Theotoky, J. and K. Teerasuwannajak (2002), 'The Timing of Environmental Policy: A Note on the Role of Product Differentiation', *Journal of Regulatory Economics* **21**, 305–16.

Prakash, A. (2000), *Greening the Firm. The Politics of Corporate Environmentalism*, Cambridge: Cambridge University Press.

Rauscher, M. (1995), *International Trade, Factor Movements, and the Environment*, Oxford: Clarendon Press

Rauscher, M. (1997), 'Voluntary Emission Reductions, Social Rewards, and Environmental Policy', University of Rostock: Thuenen-Series of Applied Economic Theory 10.

Rege, M. (2000), 'Strategic Policy and Environmental Quality: Helping the Domestic Industry to Provide Credible Information', *Environmental and Resource Economics* **15**, 279–96.

Requate, T. (1993), 'Pollution Control under Imperfect Competition: Asymmetric Bertrand Duopoly with Linear Technologies', *Journal of Institutional and Theoretical Economics* **149**, 415–42.

Requate, T. (1995), 'Incentives to Adopt New Technologies under Different Pollution-Control Policies', *International Tax and Public Finance* **2**, 295–317.

Ronnen, U. (1991), 'Minimum Quality Standards, Fixed costs, and Competition', *RAND Journal of Economics* **22**, 490–504.

Rosen, S. (1974), 'Hedonic Prices and Implicit Markets. Product Differentiation in Pure Competition', *Journal of Political Economy* **82**, 34–55.

Rothfels, J. (2000), 'Environmental Policy under Product Differentiation and Asymmetric Costs – Does Leapfrogging Occur and is it Worth it?' Paper presented at the EAERE Conference 2001, Southampton.

Salop, S.C. and D.T. Scheffmann (1983), 'Raising Rivals' Costs' *American Economic* Review, Papers and Proceedings **73**, 267–71.

Scarpa, C. (1998), 'Minimum Quality Standards with More than Two Firms', *International Journal of Industrial Organization* **16**, 665–76.

Schmelzer, D. (1999), 'Voluntary Agreements in Environmental Policy', in C. Carraro and F. Lévêque (eds), *Voluntary Approaches in Environmental Policy*, Dordrecht: Kluwer.

Segerson, K. and T.J. Miceli (1998), 'Voluntary Environmental Agreements: Good or Bad News for Environmental Protection?', *Journal of Environmental Economics and Management* **36**, 109–30.

Segerson, K. and T.J. Miceli (1999), 'Voluntary Approaches to Environmental Protection', in C. Carraro and F. Lévêque (eds), *Voluntary Approaches in Environmental Policy*, Dordrecht: Kluwer.

Shaked, A. and J. Sutton (1982), 'Relaxing Price Competition through Product Differentiation', *Review of Economic Studies* **49**, 3–13.

Shaked, A. and J. Sutton (1983), 'Natural Oligopolies', *Econometrica* **51**, 1469–83.

Shapiro, C. (1983), 'Premiums for High Quality Products as Returns to Reputations', *Quarterly Journal of Economics* **98**, 659–79.

Shapiro, C. (1986), 'Investment, Moral Hazard, and Occupational Licensing', *Review of Economic Studies* **53**, 843–62.

Sheshinski, E. (1976), 'Price, Quality and Quantity Regulation in Monopoly', *Econometrica* **43**, 127–37.

Simpson, R.D. (1995), 'Optimal Pollution Taxation in a Cournot Duopoly', *Environmental and Resource Economics* **6**, 359–69.

Simpson, R.D. and R.L. Bradford III (1996), 'Taxing Variable Cost: Environmental Regulation as Industrial Policy', *Journal of Environmental Economics and Management* **30**, 323–36.

Sinn, H.W. (1993), 'Pigou and Clarke Join Hands', *Public Choice* **75**, 79–91.

Spence, M. (1975), 'Monopoly, Quality and Regulation', *Bell Journal of Economics* **6**, 417–29.

Spence, M. (1976), 'Product Selection, Fixed Costs and Monopolistic Competition', *Review of Economics Studies* **43**, 217–35.

Spulber, D. (1999), *Market Microstructure: Intermediaries and the Theory of the Firm*, Cambridge, UK: Cambridge University Press.

Sterner, T. (2003) *Policy Instruments for Environmental and Natural Resource Management*, Washington, DC: Resources for the Future.

Swallow, S.K. and R.A. Sedjo (2000), 'Eco-labelling Consequences in General Equilibrium: a Graphical Assessment, *Land Economics* **76**, 28–36.

Teisl, M.F., B. Roe and R.L. Hicks (2002), 'Can Eco-labels Tune a Market? Evidence from Dolphin-Safe Labeling', *Journal of Environmental Economics and Management* **43**, 339–59.

Tirole, J. (1988), *The Theory of Industrial Organization*, Cambridge, Mass. and London: The MIT-Press.

Ulph, D. (1996), 'Environmental Policy Instruments and Imperfectly Competitive International Trade', *Environmental and Resource Economics* **7**, 333–55.

Van Long, N. and A. Soubeyran (1999), 'Pollution, Pigouvian Taxes and Asymmetric International Oligopoly', in E. Petrakis, E.S. Sartzetakis and A. Xepapadeas (eds), *Environmental Regulation and Market Power: Competition, Time Consistency and International Trade*, Cheltenham, UK and Northampton, Mass.: Edward Elgar.

Wauthy, X. (1996), 'Quality Choice in Models of Vertical Differentiation', *Journal of Industrial Economics* **44**, 345–53.

Willer, H. and T. Richter (2004), 'Europe', in H. Willer and M. Yussefi (eds), *The World of Organic Agriculture. Statistics and Emerging Trends*, Bonn: International Federation of Organic Agriculture Movements.

Willer, H. and M. Yussefi (2004), *The World of Organic Agriculture. Statistics and Emerging Trends*, Bonn: International Federation of Organic Agriculture Movements.

Xepapadeas, A. (1997), *Advanced Principles in Environmental Policy*, Cheltenham, UK and Northampton, Mass.: Edward Elgar.

Index